Experimentation and simulation in political science

Experimentation
and simulation in
political science

edited by
J.A. Laponce and Paul Smoker

University of Toronto Press

© University of Toronto Press 1972
University of Toronto Press, Toronto and Buffalo
Printed in Canada
ISBN 8020-1803-3
ISBN 8020-0118-1
LC 72-163827

Foreword

It is rare for the political scientist who handles data which he has not generated himself to cast his mind to that of an observer watching an experiment in progress or looking at the outcome of that experiment; it is equally rare for him to plan controlled experiments in which he creates his own data. We think that this lack of attention to the experimental aspect of political science hinders the development of the discipline, especially in relation to the building and testing of adequate theories. Hence a Round Table conference of the International Political Science Association was held in Vancouver in March 1970 to debate this problem around the themes of experimentation and simulation. The papers prepared for and presented at that meeting are included in this volume; that by Professor Riker has by agreement also been published in the *American Political Science Review*.

The Vancouver conference was held thanks to the assistance of the Canada Council, the Koerner Foundation, and the University of British Columbia. We very much appreciate their help. For their criticisms and suggestions we are indebted to Professors S. Clarkson, S.E. Finer, and J. Kyogoku.

We are particularly grateful to Diane Nelles for the editing, to Margaret Jensen for the artwork, and to Pamela Parker for her help in organizing the Round Table and supervising this publication.

June 1971

J.A. LAPONCE
PAUL SMOKER

Contributors

HAYWARD R. ALKER, JR, Department of Political Science, Massachusetts Institute of Technology

MICHAEL ARGYLE, Institute of Experimental Psychology, Oxford University

HECTOR M. CAPPELLO, Department of Social Psychology, College of Psychology, University of Mexico

CHERYL CHRISTENSEN, Department of Political Science, Makerere University, Kampala

PETER COLLETT, Institute of Experimental Psychology, Oxford University

OSCAR CORNBLIT, Instituto Torcuato Di Tella, Centro de Investigaciones Sociales, Buenos Aires

KARL W. DEUTSCH, Department of Government, Harvard University

HEINZ EULAU, Department of Political Science, Stanford University

ROBERT T. GOLEMBIEWSKI, Department of Political Science, University of Georgia

MICHAEL LANPHIER, Department of Sociology, York University, Toronto

J.A. LAPONCE, Department of Political Science, University of British Columbia

MICHAEL LEAVITT, Department of Political Science, University of Wisconsin, Madison

KINHIDE MUSHAKOJI, Institute of International Relations, Sophia University, Tokyo

ALLAN PELOWSKI, Department of Political Science, University of Washington

WILLIAM RIKER, Department of Political Science, University of Rochester
MARI HOLMBOE RUGE, International Peace Research Institute, Oslo
PAUL SMOKER, Department of Politics, University of Lancaster
ILAN VERTINSKY, Institute of Resource Ecology, University of British
    Columbia
JERZY WIATR, University of Warsaw, Institute of Philosophy and
    Sociology
WILLIAM JAMES ZAVOINA, Department of Political Science, Florida State
    University

Contents

Experimentation and simulation in political science

Experimenting:
a two-person game
between man and nature

In the endless series of experimentation in which they are caught, man and nature,[1] as in a two-person game, constantly lead, mislead, and surprise each other into revealing their possibilities and their limitations. Much has been said about man experimenting on nature (among many others by Piaget and Kelly), but surprisingly the species which has been referred to as sapiens, religiosus, economicus, and ludens has never yet to my knowledge been called experimenter. Such a name would show man to be an enormous consumer of variables, constantly driven by the desire to test and attracted by the process more than by the goal of his inventions; not so much a man who knows or a man who plays as a man moved by the ever unsatisfied temptation to test himself and his environment.

Of nature the experimenter I will have more to say later. Suffice it to note now that the acceptance of Darwinian theories has made the contemplation of the universe far more disturbing and discouraging than it ever was. When the world was thought to be an unchanging and balanced whole, where species would, without crossing boundaries, neatly duplicate themselves from generation to generation, swallowing back deviants and monsters, one might well have been awed by the great complexity of such a world, but the belief in the immutability of things was bound to be a comfort. Even if one failed to survey a universal matrix containing cells for all possible combinations of factors (physical as well as social, cultural as well as biological), one could at least be reassured by the thought that

---

1 I take nature to be the residual to the actor, which may be the whole species or a single individual, scientist or not.

such possibilities had already been fulfilled or would be, that the limits of
the possible were the limits of the factual. Imagining the same matrix
today one is more likely to be struck by its near emptiness and by the
likelihood of its remaining so. The modern social scientist, like the astro-
nomer, looks at a universe in constant expansion, a universe expanding
in what appears to be an endless series of non-realised possibilities.

DEFINING AN EXPERIMENT

Man never stops experimenting with nature, producing new combinations
of variables; nature never stops experimenting with man, producing new
types of individuals. The social scientist seeking to disengage himself from
this process, often by ignoring it, proposes ever new explanations. Any
man-made event, any interpretation of such an event is thus, in a sense,
the result of an experiment performed by nature on man as well as by man
on nature. It is not, therefore, surprising to find the definition of what
constitutes an experiment confronting loose constructionists such as
A. Kaplan and R.C. Snyder on one hand and strict constructionists such
as B.F. Skinner and B. Berelson on the other. To the first, experimenting
means producing data which would have otherwise remained dormant.
It means poking at nature, waking it up, and watching. By extension it
also implies considering as experiments the experiments which nature
performs on itself. Experimenting then becomes the state of mind with
which one looks at nature, when one discovers relationships, causal or not,
from the very controls which nature imposes on itself by its always being
new but never completely new. For the strict constructionist an experiment implies far more in that the experimenter should not only control the
stimulus which creates the data but should control also the existence and
intensity of at least one of the variables studied at the very time the data
are created.

According to the first definition, Durkheim's identification of factors
causing fluctuations in the rate of suicide and Weber's observations on
the effect of religion on capital accumulation could qualify as post-data
studies of natural experiments. If using the second definition, one
would, on the contrary, reserve the term to describe such research as
the Western Electric studies relating working conditions and level of
work and the Asch studies measuring the impact of group pressure on
individual perceptions.

The narrow definition, though more appealing because it is more
precise, is fraught with dangers. Adopting it could result in systematically
restricting the field of one's observations to situations where controls can

be best applied, just as it could focus research too exclusively on the laboratory. If one's research strategy is eclectic, if it calls for reasoning by anology, for testing the relationships between one's variables in the mind as well as in the field, in the laboratory as well as in history, one will prefer the loose constructionist's point of view if only for self-protection. This is my choice.

The narrow definition is ill adjusted to the variety of data and conditions to which the social scientist can apply experimental techniques. Take, for example, the contrast sometimes made – by Berelson in particular – between survey research and experimentation. If we bring subjects into a university laboratory, wire them to cardiographs and saliva counters, show them scenes of rioting in Montreal on St Jean Baptiste's day, and record their reactions in terms of secretion, heart beat, and spoken language, this undoubtedly would be considered an experiment. But if we send a middle-aged housewife to attempt to enter the house of a respondent selected at random from the electoral lists and if, after negotiating her way into the living room, she measures, on a seven-point scale, the subject's reactions to the saying that 'the wild life of the old Greeks and Romans was tame compared to some of the goings on in this country,' in what sense is this not also an experiment?

TYPES OF EXPERIMENTS

If we accept the all-embracing definition of the loose constructionists, the question worth considering is no longer whether or not political science is experimental but whether the latter makes adequate use of the various types of experimentation available to it. To map these various types, let us distinguish four major kinds of experiments according to whether the experimenter is man-the-researcher or nature, and according to whether the boundaries of the experimental situation are in the mind of the researcher or in the 'real' world (figure 1).

The 'researcher-mind' experiment, cell A, is the common, the ever present, the often forgotten experiment called by the many names of reasoning, intuition, inventiveness. In such an experiment the mind is treated as one would treat a laboratory; it is emptied of unwanted ideas, of unwanted variables, it is made to relate only the factors under study which are either left free to play and interact among themselves as subjects in a Moreno therapeutic session or on the contrary have to interact according to specific rules. These experiments in the mind, these 'anticipatory' experiments which, in a writer, produce plays and novels, in a social scientist, result in theories, formulae and computer simulations.

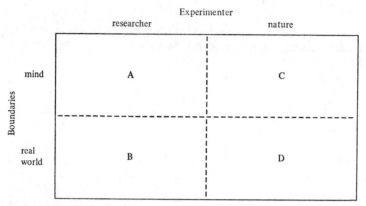

Figure 1 Types of experiments.

The experiment described by cell B, that initiated by the researcher in the real world, like the experiment of cell A qualifies as 'pre-data' since it gives to the experimenter the initiative in the selection of his variables and the initiative in relating these variables among themselves before the creation of the data to be analysed; but this time the props and the subjects are real.

The 'nature-mind' experiment of cell C describes one of the processes through which nature diversifies its options by linking different variables in the minds of different individuals. Since we cannot close our mind to the environment, either social or physical, it deposits in the mind ideas which perform there their own stimulations and simulations. This type of experiment has a broken-mirror quality, each mind catching only a few fragments of nature's play. It produces, or at least contributes to producing, what one values as most typical of oneself: ideals, tastes, emotions, memories, and, to the scientist, his preferred tools and experiments. Typically the data falling in cell C are recovered through introspection.

The 'nature-real world' experiment of cell D is that segment of nature's play which we call either data or history. In the hands of social scientists it lends itself to post-data experimental manipulations.

An essential characteristic of this fourfold typology, when we look at it from the point of view of the experimental scientist, is that each cell, at the same time as it defines a kind of experiment, is also a microcosm, though distorted, of the whole matrix.[2] Should we seek to free our mind

2   As suggested by Karl Deutsch this fourfold matrix can be profitably unfolded into fourteen ideal types corresponding to the possible combinations of A, B, C, and D. This more refined typology would facilitate the comparative study

completely of all unwanted variables before performing the experiment described by cell A, we would never start such anticipatory simulation since we cannot possibly disengage ourselves from the experiments which nature performs on us; we can gain some but not all the space in the laboratory of the mind. Furthermore, we cannot entirely reduce the field of the experiment to the mind, for the outside world is bound to interfere; the mind cannot but be in an environment which is also a laboratory of sorts. Inversely, the scientist who performs an experiment in the real world cannot prevent both nature and his own mind from smuggling their own experiments inside the boundaries of his observations. In any experimental situation the experimenter is among the naive subjects.

The difficulty of separating these various experiments from one another, the difficulty of preventing one from contaminating the others, has led the social scientist to worry, as he should, about the boundaries of his observations, to try to limit the number of variables at play within his experiments, and to put those he could not control – the metaphor is revealing – into a black box. This legitimate concern for boundaries and controls seems, however, to have had the frequent effect of restricting the field of one's experimentations to those settings with which one has become familiar, of specializing and grouping social scientists not primarily according to the variables they observe but rather according to the settings where such variables are studied, and of making such social scientists obsessed gatekeepers who would have locked themselves in, as it were, refusing to take evidence from other types of settings. Notwithstanding the calls and examples of Fourastié, Schelling, and Vernon Smith, economics has made only minimal use of real-world pre-data experiments; judging by the evolution of the *American Economic Review*, and the *Journal of Political Economy*, that discipline is well anchored in cells A and D. Judging by such journals as the *Psychological Review*, the *Journal of Experimental Social Psychology*, and *Sociometry*, psychologists and social-psychologists hardly ever move out of cell B. History fits cell D; political science and sociology cover B and D. Of course, for each researcher and for each branch of a discipline, one would get different mappings of the spread of experiments over the ideal types. The combination of A and D describes econometrics better than economics in general, the combination of B and C some types of social psychology and

of experiments. One could also give a time dimension to the matrix by stretching it into a self-replicating column where one could chart the specific path of specific experiments and determine whether the order in which research proceeds from one to another (A → D → B → A, or A → B → A → D, etc.) has any relevance to the outcome and in particular to the kind of theory generated. See p. 32.

group dynamics as well as sociology, but on the whole the dominant impression is one of concentration rather than of spread of each of the social science disciplines among the possible types of experimental settings. This impression is reinforced when we note the selective use made by political scientists of the various kinds of experiments covered by cell B and when we note that, unlike psychologists, the political scientist, in a B experiment, usually limits his intervention to supplying the stimulus which creates the data, without attempting to control and vary the intensity of the variables studied. Furthermore, he uses this stimulus to tap attitudes through questioning rather than to manipulate the social or physical environment and determine the latter's effect on behaviour.

THE USE OF PRE-DATA EXPERIMENTS IN POLITICAL SCIENCE

I purposely grouped under the single name of real world experiments those made in a 'natural' as well as those made in a 'laboratory' setting,[3] if only to emphasize that if they take place outside the mind experiments have, of necessity, to take place in the real world; to emphasize that the zoo is as real as the jungle; to emphasize that, if there are differences between a zoo setting and a jungle setting which would make it difficult to extrapolate from the one to the other, the difficulty is of the same order as extrapolating from one type of jungle to another type of jungle; to emphasize in short that there are serious dangers in paying too much attention to the boundaries of an experiment if this detracts from the attention one should pay to other and more important variables, namely the variables related within the experiment. What makes an animal comparable to another animal is not the net with which it was caught. Yet, reading the footnotes and bibliographies of psychology, sociology, and political science journals reveals a marked tendency for each discipline to restrict supporting evidence to data obtained within the same type of experimental settings: laboratory findings are compared to other such findings, surveys are compared to surveys, field experiments to field experiments. One could measure this tendency to segregation by plotting the use made of specific findings in subsequent studies. To take an example at random, one could trace the impact of a recent finding by Tedeschi and his colleagues who, using the prisoner's dilemma and put-

3 I use 'laboratory' in the narrow sense of the term, meaning a more or less permanent and specialized setting perceived as artificial by the subjects. The term is sometimes used, especially by social psychologists, to describe any experimental setting whether in a university small-group laboratory or in the field.

ting their subjects alternatively in weak and strong positions, observed that the subjects who were submissive in the face of power were more likely to use power in a benevolent fashion when they had it. Judging by the pattern of the past decade one would expect that this laboratory finding will be compared to other laboratory findings, that it will be used mostly by social psychologists, somewhat by sociologists, and hardly by political scientists. If judged by the more immediate past, the future is only slightly more encouraging. Of the forty-three articles published in the 1957 *APSR*, only one referred in its footnotes to an experiment in which the experimenter manipulated and controlled, at the time the data were created, the effect of at least one of the variables studied (a pre-data experiment); in 1967 the proportion was ten out of thirty-eight; in 1969, seven out of forty-seven.

Though many political scientists, as advisers to governments, have been in a favourable position to perform realistic simulations, they have either refrained from doing so, because they were not able to convince the politicians with whom they had to collaborate or, more likely, had not thought of it. The examples of Gosnell, Hartmann, and Eldersveld, who studied experimentally the effects of propaganda on voter turnout and election results by controlling the amount and types of canvass, have hardly been followed. Considering the importance given by political science to the electoral process one cannot but share Dean Jaros' and Donald Campbell's surprise at the small number of studies in which the researcher himself controlled the electoral process in order to observe electoral behaviour. Notwithstanding the recent interest in games and simulations, pre-data experiments with pre-data manipulation of the variables studied remain the exception. In the *APSR* of 1969, I counted thirty-one articles which could qualify as empirical and quantitative. Of those, only one (3.2 per cent[4]) fell into the category of pre-data experimental manipulations, the remainder relying typically on surveys and censuses and on post-data controls (table 1).

Judging still by the articles published in the *APSR* of 1969, the favourite technique for gathering data is the questionnaire survey of individuals: 45 per cent of the articles listed in table 1 (and 93 per cent of those in the category of 'data created by the original researcher') relied primarily on that technique. Has not this heavy reliance on a given tool narrowed the range of questions which political science has sought to answer in the past two decades? More specifically, has not this reliance on the questionnaire survey of individuals led to the study of attitudes

4 The same year none appeared in the *Canadian Journal of Political Science,* *Political Studies,* or *Revue française de science politique.*

TABLE 1

Source of the data used in the empirical and quantitative studies*
of the *APSR* of 1969
(N = number of articles)

I	DATA PRODUCED BY THE RESEARCHER	N	Per cent
a	with pre-data control over the stimulus producing the data and over one at least of the independent and intervening variables studied	1	3.2
b	with pre-data control over the stimulus but only post-data control over the variables studied	14	45.1
II	DATA NOT PRODUCED BY THE RESEARCHER		
a	roll calls, election statistics, census	13	41.8
b	newspapers, bibliographies, party publications	3	9.6
	TOTAL	31	100

* Defined as the articles containing at least one table, figure, or chart relating variables quantitatively, thus excluding the theoretical or descriptive studies using quantitative data incidentally.
If an article used data pertaining to both I and II it was counted in I only; if it contained data
pertaining to Ia and Ib, it was classified in Ia. In other words, the articles were sifted from Ia to
IIb as on a series of grids.

more than of behaviour? Has it not concentrated our attention on cultural and social variables to the exclusion of biological and physical-
environmental factors? Has it not also contributed to shifting the discipline from the study of power conflicts to the simple identification of the
social and cutural groupings, of the patterns resulting from the interplay
of the forces of attraction/avoidance among the individuals studied, an
identification which falls short of explaining the power relationship between these aggregates? My reading of the thirty-one studies of table 1
is that only two gave attention to biological factors, only three to the
physical ecology, and that only five were more than incidentally interested
in stratification and power relationships. The latter is curious, to say the
least, in a discipline which seeks to build a theory of power.

For political science to regain its earlier interest in power and influence and yet to remain empirical there is more than one prescription.
The growing interest in the study of international conflicts, the regained
interest in the use of aggregate statistics, will facilitate this reorientation.
So would, I think, the more frequent use of pre-data experiments since,
whether in the form of simulations, games, or other types of controlled
interaction, they lend themselves very well to the study of conflict, influence, and social control as demonstrated by the experiments of Asch,
Lewin, Milgram, and Snyder. However, for such pre-data experiments to

increase significantly in number and reach the critical mass necessary for them to influence the discipline, some ideological obstacles must be removed.

THE OBSTACLES TO EXPERIMENTATION

Should we seek to draw a world map of the political scientist's freedom to experiment, we could assign to selected academics at selected universities the task of overcoming the administrative and ideological obstacles to the duplication of studies chosen as typical: the Flacks questionnaire study of student activists, the Rapoport prisoner's dilemmas games, the Guetzkow internation simulation, the Milgram study of reactions to the suffering of others when the suffering is ordered by a legitimate authority, the German study of 1932, to which I found only vague references (see Harding), testing whether the sons of alcoholics were as fast in the hundred yard dash as those of non-alcoholics, etc. Assuming cost to be no problem we could measure the ease of access of the experimenter to both the subjects and the tools he needs. Can he ask his students to fill a questionnaire? Any kind of questionnaire not related to their course work? How much time and energy need he spend to obtain the necessary authorizations? Does he have access to a laboratory? We might find that, occasionally, Eastern European scholars have better opportunities for conducting realistic simulations and *in vivo* experiments, but on the whole we would almost certainly find North America to be the least restrictive of experimentation.

Within a given country the obstacles to experimentation in the social sciences vary from discipline to discipline, from department to department. In my own case, experimenting with social science students in the field, that is, in their classroom, is rarely a problem; access to high school students is a little more difficult but still easy; setting an experiment in a small group laboratory instead of the regular classroom is easy. This situation is probably typical. If political scientists have relied mostly on post-data experimentation, if they do not try to manipulate their variables in pre-data experiments any more than they do, it is not, in North America at least, because of administrative obstacles; the reason is ideological.

The restraints built into one's professional ideology are of two kinds: moral and scientific. The moral restraints are in the form of a still unformulated code of ethics based on the ideal that no experiment should be carried out without the consent of the subjects, an ideal not any more strictly adhered to by social scientists than by biologists and physicians, but one which is nevertheless an effective and welcome restraint. For lack of more precise guidance, the experimenter asks himself whether he would have felt seriously slighted or hurt had he been in the position of the subject. These moral restraints – which should be codified and strengthened – do not, because of their present laxity, explain the minimal use of pre-data experiments in political science; the explanation is in the political scientist's scientific ideology.

One of the most obvious and critical restraints to experimenting built into that ideology shows in the boundaries which the political scientist sets for his experiments and observations, boundaries which define his real world and which are by and large made to fit or approximate the political boundaries of what has traditionally been considered a political unit of government (alliances, states, committees, electoral districts, etc.).

The behaviouralist like the institutionalist usually defines his research by the boundaries of his observations (electoral study, small group research, etc.) rather than by the variables he handles. This seems to have restricted him to only certain types of experimentation. If one thinks of oneself as a student of elections and if the term means a specific setting with real candidates for specific offices such as the presidency or a seat in parliament, the amount of experimenting one can do is limited to surveys, panel studies, and to what the Michigan School has done in the past twenty years; if, on the contrary, one thinks of oneself as an election specialist but where election means 'delegation of authority through coalition formation' one may then, taking one's variables along, travel from history to laboratory to field to mind, no longer hindered by boundaries which, though still there, have been lowered to the point where, ceasing to be obstacles, they are merely intellectual guides.

That the political scientist considers his real world to be that which resembles best the world of politics as defined by the layman and that it is not usual for him to impose boundaries of his creation explains why the discipline has relied mostly on post-data experiments and why, when creating data through contrived situations such as interviews, it gave more attention to control over the stimulus producing the data than to control and manipulation over the independent variables. The political scientist's narrow conception of the real world has turned him away from settings such as the laboratory. Though psychologists now expand out of the latter, the time has come for political scientists to enter it. That they have hardly begun to do so is indicated by the fact that in 1969 as in 1967 only 3 per cent of articles in the *APSR* were either laboratory or realistic simulation studies, and that out of a sample of 130 social science titles taken at random from American journals indexed by *ABS* between 1957 and 1968, none of those having laboratory settings and none of those characterized by the manipulation of one at least of the independent variables at the time of the creation of the data was made by political scientists (altogether 10 per cent of the articles met this criteria; 70 per cent of the latter by psychologists).

Of course, freer access to the laboratory and the creation of journals specialized in reporting pre-data experiments, such as the recent *Simulation and Games* and *Experimental Study of Politics*, would invite political scientists to seek greater control than they now have over their variables, but it remains that the great obstacle to the wide use of such pre-data experiments is ideological, lying in the political scientist's conception of what constitutes the real world.

The prejudices often encountered against experiments with high visibility of the experimenter and high control over the subject, usually in laboratory settings, remind one of the criticisms made of Koelreuter's findings. Anticipating Mendel by more than a century, Koelreuter (1733–1806) had, against accepted opinion, been able not only to obtain hybrids – this had been done before by Linnaeus and Buffon among others – but he had obtained hybrids which would reproduce. Such an achievement, which contradicted the universally accepted belief in the immutability of nature, was dismissed by his contemporaries for a number of reasons worth listing because of their similarity to contemporary arguments in the social sciences. According to one of Koelreuter's biographers (see Olby 1966), the findings were ignored because, first, as I have said, they violated the dominant scientific-religious belief of the time. Secondly, Koelreuter's research techniques were not in style; instead of travelling to far away lands, he used the data near at hand, working with the plants provided by his environment. And third because, instead of breeding his plants in natural ground, he had put them in pots. The pot culture (culture in the gardener's language, but I like the analogy the word suggests) was thought sufficiently aberrant and unnatural for his findings to be dismissed as not proving anything.

Having just argued for more laboratory experiments I should now introduce an essential qualifier. If the discipline is to benefit most from the diversification of the types of experiments it performs; if to do so it must enter the laboratory much more often than it has done, this should not be at the expense of losing interest in the experiments made by nature (those we assigned to cell D) or the mind experiments (those assigned to cells A and C). The suggestion is for diversification of the techniques of experimentation, not for the concentration, as occurred at one time in psychology, on certain types of experiments; the suggestion is for expansion, not for migration; for moving to the laboratory not for locking one-self in it.

REFERENCES

ASCH, S.E. 'Studies of Independence and Comformity: A Minority of One Against a Unanimous Majority,' *Psychology Monographs*, 20, 9 (1956).
BERELSON, B. and G.A. STEINER *Human Behaviour*. New York: Harcourt Brace, 1964.
CAMPBELL, DONALD T. 'Prospective: Artifact and Control' in R. Rosenthal and R.L. Rosnow, eds. *Artifact in Behavioural Research*, New York: Academic Press, 1969.
ELDERSVELD, S.J. 'Experimental Propaganda Techniques and Voting Behaviour,' *American Political Science Review*, 50 (1956), pp. 154–65.
FLACKS, R. 'The Liberated Generation: An Exploration of the Roots of Student Protest,' *Journal of Social Issues*, 23 (1967), pp. 52–75
FOURASTIÉ, JEAN *L'Evolution des prix à long terme*. Paris: Presses universitaires de France, 1969.
GOSNELL, H.F. *Getting Out the Vote*. Chicago: University of Chicago Press, 1927.
GUETZKOW, H. *et al. Simulation in International Relations*. Englewood Cliffs: Prentice-Hall, 1963.
HARDING, T.S. 'Are We Breeding Weaklings?' *American Journal of Sociology*, 47 (1937), pp. 672–81.
HARTMANN, G.W. 'A Field Experiment on the Comparative Effectiveness of "Emotional" and "rational" Political Leaflets in Determining Election Results,' *Journal of Abnormal and Social Psychology*, 31 (1936), pp. 99–114.
JAROS, D and G. MASON 'Party Choices and Support for Demagogues: An Experimental Examination,' *American Political Science Review*, 63 (1969), pp. 100–10.
KAPLAN, A. *The Conduct of Inquiry*. San Francisco: Chandler, 1964.
KELLY, G.A. *A Theory of Personality*, New York: Norton, 1955.
LEWIN, K. and R. LIPPITT 'An Experimental Approach to the Study of Autocracy and Democracy: A Preliminary Note,' *Sociometry*, 1 (1938), pp. 292–300.
MILGRAM, S. 'Behavioural Study of Obedience,' *Journal of Abnormal and Social Psychology*, 67 (1963), pp. 371–8.
OLBY, R.C. *Origins of Mendelism*. London: Constable, 1966.
RAPOPORT, A. *Two-Person Game Theory: The Essential Ideas*. Ann Arbor: University of Michigan Press, 1966.
SCHELLING, T. *The Strategy of Conflict*. Cambridge: Harvard University Press, 1960.

SMITH, VERNON L. 'Experimental Auction Markets and the Walrasian Hypothesis,' *Journal of Political Economy*, 73 (1965), pp. 387–93.

SKINNER, B.F. 'The Flight from the Laboratory,' *Current Trends in Psychological Theory*. Pittsburgh: University of Pittsburgh Press, 1958.

SNYDER, R.C. 'Some Perspectives on the Use of Experimental Techniques in the Study of International Relations,' in H. Guetzkow *et al.*, eds. *Simulation in International Relations*. Englewood Cliffs: Prentice-Hall, 1963.

TEDESCHI, J. *et al.* 'Social Desirability, Manifest Anxiety, and Social Power,' *Journal of Social Psychology*, 77 (1969), pp. 231–9.

Experiments
and political theory

The contribution of experiments within the framework of political theory

Before discussing the significance of experimentation within the context of political theory, let me summarize my notions on theory.

1   Theory is, first of all, a *coding* scheme for the storage and retrieval of information. Theory organizes what people think, know, or think they know about political behaviour by arranging information in such a way that it is not completely chaotic, can be easily stored, and, what is more important, easily retrieved.[1]

2   Theory's second function is heuristic. The way we order our theoretical information has something to do with the associations we are likely to make and the questions we are likely to ask. To that extent theory becomes a *search* instrument – an instrument for sensitizing our research course and our information intake. We use theory to take information from the universe, or from what Professor Laponce would call nature, which includes all the outside world and human society as well.[2] It follows that theories can, in quite a real sense, be more intelligent than the theorists who create them, for a theory is an engine for getting information out of a universe which contains as far as we know, an unlimited amount of possible information, while there is only a limited amount of such information in the mind of a theorist. A theory can thus generate more information and sometimes more highly relevant or creative infor-

1   Karl W. Deutsch, 'On Theories, Taxonomies, and Models as Communication Codes for Organizing Information,' *Behavioral Science*, 11, 1 (January 1966), pp. 1–17.
2   See p. 3.

mation, than the theorist who thought it up. This point is made with some precision in the famous article by W. Ross Ashby, 'Can an Automatic Chess Player Outwit its Designer?' Ashby's answer on these grounds, of course, is yes, indeed it can.[3]

3   Theory is also a *closure* device which tends to conserve human attention.[4] A good theory conserves or saves receptor and decision time, as well as channels and resources for decision making. The consistency and closure aspects of theory lead to ideology, while the information search aspects of theory are non-ideological The more ideological a theory becomes the more its closure functions prevail, and when the theory eventually becomes nearly impermeable to new and incongruent information, we speak of an extreme ideology. In this sense, there is an operational distinction between nationalism and extreme nationalism, liberalism and extreme liberalism, Marxism and extreme Marxism.[5]

4   The fourth aspect of theory is that of an *image*, in which various information is organized for simultaneous confrontation and inspection. When you draw yourself a map or an image you can see at one glance, many of the main features – in Susanne Langer's term, 'presentationally.'[6] In the image aspect of theory the information stored is grossly oversimplified. If we had all the details, then we could not inspect them simultaneously, but by having gross abbreviations of the information right there, presented in a pictorial, image-like form for simultaneous inspection, we can scan it immediately for consistency and for implications, so that deductions or inferences can be made. In this respect, theory is analogous to, or serves the function of, consciousness both in the individual and in the work of groups.[7]

5   Theory is a potential instrument for dissociating and *recombining* information. It may either facilitate these operations or make them more difficult. Usually, a good theory facilitates a wider range of acts of dissociation. Some information is found in nature in one bundle, or what Bertrand Russell calls 'bundles of events.'[8] In our minds, these bundles

3   W. Ross Ashby, 'Can a Mechanical Chess-player Outplay Its Designer?' *British Journal for the Philosophy of Science*, 3, 44 (1952).
4   Herbert A. Simon, 'Designing Organizations for an Information Rich World' in Martin Greenberger, ed. *Computers, Communications and the Public Interest* (Baltimore: Johns Hopkins University Press, 1971), pp. 37–72.
5   Karl W. Deutsch, *'Politics and Government: How People Decide Their Fate* (Boston: Houghton Mifflin, 1970), p. 9.
6   Suzanne K. Langer, *Philosophy in a New Key* (Cambridge, Mass.: Harvard University Press, 1942).
7   Karl W. Deutsch, *The Nerves of Government* (New York: Free Press, 1966).
8   Bertrand Russell, *A History of Western Philosophy* (New York: Simon and Shuster, 1945), pp. 832–3.

can be dissociated in various ways. Certain of their aspects can be thought of quite separately and can be processed in information processing systems apart from their original associations in nature. Thus they are turned into a larger number of separate elements available for selection and recombination. This means, in turn, that the resources for recombination go up by a very considerable order of magnitude. Theory, as an instrument for dissociation and recombination, becomes, therefore, a creative device. It also serves as a basis for prediction. Predictions are often made by extracting certain parts of information from the past and then extrapolating second-order symbols from this time series of past events.

6   Every theory is a link in a sequence of coding schemes. In addition theory is *self-transcendent*. If a theory is good, it will lead to the acquisition of so much information and the creation of so many dissociations and new recombinations that information incompatible with the original scheme will eventually be produced. Rather than being exploded and the remnants put into the museum, the original theory will, as it were, transform itself – actually, it will be transformed by thinking persons who are acting under the impact of the inner logic and contradictions of the old theory and with the knowledge which it helped to produce. It may be possible with this transformed theory, to accommodate the new way of looking at things.

The properties of self-transcendence and self-transformation are thus important aspects of theories. If a theory works in this way, it can continue to assist in the accumulation of knowledge. In the long run, all cumulative knowledge is self-transcending knowledge, organized around a sequence of coding schemes, each with these properties of self-transcendence and self-transformation.

Such cumulative knowledge is likely to consist of a sequence of theories which contains an accumulation of existential statements.[9] Sir Karl Popper has made the point that theories can only be refuted, not confirmed, and I have both read him and heard him making the point that existential statements – statements of the form 'there is' – are not really important in science. I find, to my pleasure, that in the latest paperback edition of his well-known book, *The Logic of Scientific Discovery*, he no longer makes this point.[9] Indeed, one of the most important things about theories is that they lead to statements of the form 'there is', such as 'there is a continent west of Europe and east of Asia,' or 'there could be',

9   Karl W. Deutsch, 'On Methodological Problems of Quantitative Research,' in Mattei Dogan and Stein Rokkan, eds. *Quantitative Ecological Analysis in the Social Sciences* (Cambridge, Mass.: MIT Press, 1969), pp. 19–39.

such as 'there could be a machine heavier than air and capable of flight.' When particular theories of geography, such as the earth is a perfect sphere, turn out to be untenable and have to be overthrown in favour of a new theory, such as the earth is a flattened rotational ellipsoid, the successor theory is not arbitrarily chosen. It must accommodate the existential statements contained in its predecessor, or at least most of them.

7   This need to *accommodate* the confirmed existential statements of its predecessor theories is the seventh major aspect of theory. The sequence from predecessor to successor theories is not arbitrary but is to a considerable extent determined by the requirements of accommodating the existential statements of the predecessors, insofar as these existential statements have been verified. This is the meaning of cumulative knowledge. This is what explains why, at one and the same time, theories can be overthrown again and again in physics and biology and other fields (politics and economics are no exceptions), and why nevertheless we report from the past whether there has indeed been accumulative knowledge and to what extent.

A STATISTICAL VIEWPOINT: ACTUAL EVENTS VERSUS THE DISTRIBUTION OF POSSIBLE OUTCOMES

What can experiments contribute in the context of cumulative knowledge? My general viewpoint is that proposed by Norbert Wiener that anything that actually happens and is observed is most usefully interpreted in the context of the ensemble of what could have happened: every actual outcome should be interpreted in the ensemble of possible outcomes.[10] For example, the fall of a pair of dice is interpreted in terms of the fall of all possible pairs of dice. An outcome of seven for a roll of two dice is then six times as likely to occur as an outcome of two, if the dice are fair. If we find out eventually that the dice are loaded, then the same fall of the dice may now have to be interpreted differently. (By freakish circumstances, however, this pair of dice, so loaded, may sometimes give an outcome close to what honest dice would have given.) In any case, we always want to ask the question, 'what else could have happened?' This is the opposite of the style of question of the professional politician or the professional soldier, who resent greatly 'iffy' questions, and 'wisdom after the event.' In fact in his professional role, the soldier will replay

10   Norbert Wiener, *The Human Use of Human Beings* (Boston: Houghton Mifflin, 1954), 'Preface: The Idea of a Contingent Universe.'

battle after battle time and again in order to train the next generation of officers.

Interpreting actual outcomes in the context of all possible outcomes is essential for ethical and moral judgments, and for judgments of good practice. When a bridge collapses, the engineer who designed it is not asked whether he could have foreseen all accidents and contingencies; rather, he is asked: 'If you build a thousand bridges just like this one, on this kind of soil, where there are these conditions of wind and water, how many of them would have collapsed?' If it turns out that the collapse of this bridge was wildly improbable, he is acquitted and is said to have followed good practice. If it turns out that ordinarily most bridges so built would have collapsed, we would consider this bridge miserably built. Similarly, this is true for the difference between the physician and the quack. A physician who has followed good practice, even though his patient died, is one who has done the best he could in the sense that, if he had applied this particular therapy to a large number of patients in closely similar circumstances, most of them would have survived or improved. On the other hand, the quack whose victim somehow survives by a near miracle is still a quack and the difference is one of probability. It turns out, therefore, that we need probabilistic viewpoints and that we must engage in what the medical people call postmortems, and what many politicians resent as Monday morning quarterbacking.

Testing of probabilities – of the frequency distribution of alternative outcomes – can to a large extent be done by simulation experiments. After a crisis occurs, such as the Cuba crisis of 1962, it might be perfectly sensible to simulate its course as closely as possible, both by human role-playing and by computer models, to find out how often the participants would have been blown up. From this we can then estimate whether the performance of the statesmen was, on the whole, an admirable example of prudent statesmanship or an exercise in bilateral folly on the brink of disaster. Such a judgment will involve our values which also may lead us to destruction. If we value our national prestige very highly and the avoidance of nuclear disaster not very much, we would obviously accept a closer approach to the brink than if our scheme of preferences were reversed. But apart from our values, we can find out what the probabilities are in each situation, and this will make our value judgments a great deal more informed.

Political simulation experiments have very fundamental, ethical and normative, as well as cognitive, implications. The ethical imperative to Kant's famous 'pure good will' implies the will to get the very best knowledge available at the time and place at which one acts. A good will, or a desire for a good outcome, that is not linked to the desire for the best relevant knowledge obtainable is itself a deception of others or oneself.

THE USE OF NULL MODELS

The statistical view leads to a type of experimentation which consists of the construction of statistical time sequence null models. That is, given certain simple assumptions, what, under given conditions of probability, is likely to happen? Here again theory and experiment come together.

Consider the familiar concept of the 'wise man' in an organization who has made the right decision at the critical moment. For instance, it could be a general who won one battle then later on won a second. Supposing you have now a general who has won eight battles in succession, although in each case the contending forces were evenly matched. Was it a really superior ability in generalship that led to victory? Is he now indeed a military genius? A probability model will tell you that you must note the number of generals in the entire armed forces of the victorious side. If there are four hundred generals in the army, such as the Austrian-Hungarian army had in 1918, it turns out that there ought to be at least eight 'military geniuses' of this type among them, even if none of them are brighter than a true coin or a blind chicken, picking one of two alternatives at random. This is so because eight binary choices made at random equal 2 to the eighth power which gives 256, and there ought to be at least one sequence of 8 successful chance outcomes among our 400 cases of generals here.[11]

The experiment can be of value if applied not only to wise bureaucrats who make eight right decisions but also to countries where party lines change and to party officials who eight times in succession made exactly the right adjustments at the necessary time. In each case we can see that if the particular system produces markedly more of the right decisions or the right decision sequences then fewer accidents or breakdowns will occur. Then and then only can we say that the system as such has a higher propensity to produce the right decisions.

Another null model is, of course, the device of computing the probable transactions in a sociogram among school children or the probable choice of coalition partners among politicians, trade partners, or allies

11   Karl W. Deutsch and William G. Madow, 'A Note on the Appearance of Wisdom in Large Bureaucratic Organizations,' *Behavioral Science*, 6, 1 (January 1961), pp. 72–8.

in international politics. To find out which countries have a high propensity to make alliances or to engage in international transactions, we need to construct a null model which says how much the high transactors ought to do for one another if they have no particular preferences or propensities, and then note the deviation of the actual interaction for each pair of actors from the probabilistic null model value.[12] This is also a statistical device for analysis which can be used for real-world experiments (which are in box D of Professor Laponce's scheme) or for laboratory controlled experiments (which would be in his box B).[13]

Finally, the null model approach could be used for analysing other phenomena. If we define an automobile accident as an interaction between two automobiles, it would follow that, if the skill of drivers should remain constant, and the road system would not change relative to the cars (so that we should have just as many square miles of road per car as before), then the number of automobile accidents should go up in proportion to the square of the number of automobiles on the road. If we define a murder or a crime of violence as an interaction between two human beings, and if we furthermore take note of the fact that most crimes of violence are committed by people between the ages of fifteen and twenty-five in spatial proximity to each other, then the number of murders in a country ought to go up in proportion to the square of the number of young men between the ages of fifteen and twenty-five years in metropolitan areas. We may then put second-order parameters or coefficients into the equation for the propensity to violence associated with the particular culture, or cultures, prevailing or frequent among the metropolitan population during the time period which we study. (Civilization has been defined as the progress from crimes of force to crimes of fraud: rural folk more often commit murders and urban people more often forge cheques.) And if it turns out that many young men from low cheque forging but high violence rural backgrounds go to towns, and that there are many first-generation urban children of parents coming from rural backgrounds, we may have to put an extra coefficient into the formula for expected murders. But unless we make such calculations, we cannot evaluate the statistics of 'rising crimes,' because we cannot know how much of the increase is pure probabilistic product of a Gibbsian

12 I. Richard Savage and Karl W. Deutsch, 'A Statistical Model of the Gross Analysis of Transaction Flows,' *Econometric*, 28, 3 (July 1960), pp. 551–72; Richard W. Chadwick and Karl W. Deutsch, 'International Trade and Economic Integration: Further Developments in Matrix Analysis to Estimate the Effect of Background Conditions *versus* Political Controls,' forthcoming.
13 See p. 6.

universe, and how much is a particular outcome for which we may now discover some specific reasons for the deviation from what was most expected.

SELF-CHANGING PROBABILITIES

Of particular interest to us as social scientists are those outcomes and patterns which are improbable in their origin but which, once they have occurred, are probable in their persistence. Many of the more frequent and enduring political institutions are of this character, resulting from patterns of human interaction, or patterns of interlocking roles, which came into existence with a moderate or low probability but which had a high probability of persisting once they were found and established. In this respect, we may have to modify, at least in part, the old notion of evolution as a process of incremental tiny changes which are then selected by experience. The philosophical approach I am proposing here would consider this view as either false or, at the least, one-sided. The improbable but persistent patterns, the winning solutions, often are not easily approximated or reached by incremental steps. Bold steps away from the preceding state of affairs – or even several nearly simultaneous and mutually reinforcing major changes – may be needed in order to achieve a combination that will persist. In this way, we may think of political evolution, like all other evolution, as a self-changing probability process, that is, a process in which patterns are selected which change the probability for the occurrence of subsequent patterns.

EXTREME VALUES AND CUMULATIVE RISKS

We are interested in this kind of statistical thinking and analysis not only for the central tendency, or averages, of the statistics of the frequency of behaviour which we have but also for the extreme values at the tail ends of the curve as well. We want to know the whole range of distribution and take it fully into account.

For instance, we want to know something about cumulative risks. Supposing we take as an example Professor Riker's data about the average frequency of error about the decisions of a partner.[14] He puts before us 25 errors out of 300 decisions, or 8.3 per cent error. But if we deal with cumulative risks, it may turn out that if the actor has to go through a long sequence of such acts 8 per cent might be an ab-

14   See p. 146.

solutely fatal error, whereas in some certain other contingencies this could be easily coped with by the individual and by the system. And some of our most important questions, both experimental and theoretical, are: When do dangerously high error margins occur in critical situations of cumulative risk? Where do the errors, risks, and failures cumulate in sequence? And when do they occur in parallel, so that they can be more easily dissipated or dealt with?

A related point is the probability of extreme values.[15] If a certain distribution usually gives a moderate value, and if an extreme value occurs only once in a thousand times, then it follows that if doctors and drug firms give five million mothers sleeping pills containing thalidomide, they are likely to produce several thousand badly damaged babies. And in the 1960s a catastrophe on this scale actually happened. The key question was not whether the single-pill risk had been much higher than one in a thousand; the crucial problem was that there were so many pills given to so many mothers. When the United States army defines as non-poisonous a gas that kills no more than 2 per cent of the people exposed to it, then dropping such a gas on settlements with a total population of, say, 100,000 people will probably slaughter 2,000 persons, which is exactly what we would consider a 'weapon of mass destruction.' In other words, in cases of low probability values and extremely unlikely outcomes we must look into the frequency of the process to see whether we can afford not to take these extreme values into account. A great deal of nineteenth-century conventional theorizing was limited largely to thinking about the central tendency of the statistics of political and social behaviour. It then treated these as predictable and reserved all the extreme values to intuition and to vague notions of chance or genius. We must do better than that.

We also need to pay more attention to the improbable combination of several circumstances. The central tendency of tides on the coast of Massachusetts is that they are not very high. Furthermore, it is fairly unlikely that the moon, the earth, and the sun all will be lined up in one line and that there will have been a storm twenty-four hours earlier 1500 miles offshore just in time for the big waves to arrive at the shore. When these improbable things all coincide, a riptide occurs, and if you neglect the probability of riptides you ought not to have a cottage too close by the seashore. We have not studied the riptide phenomena in politics, and we have not often used experiments to discover the likelihood of several improbable but relevant things occurring together.

15   Emil J. Gumbel, *Statistics of Extremes* (New York: Columbia University Press, 1958).

Where do experiments help us in these matters? They often can help us in measuring or estimating some crucial parameters of political or social processes in cases where our theories have told us that a particular magnitude is important. Let us consider, for instance, a deterrence or threat situation between two actors, such as two individuals, two groups, two organizations, or two nations. If we follow the pure theory of Thomas Schelling, the actor who precommits himself and makes it clear that he can no longer change his behaviour has a markedly better chance of getting his way. Hence, says Schelling, if you wish to cross an intersection ahead of other cars, speed up. If you do so, it will become obvious that you cannot slow down, and all rational drivers will give you the right of way. There is some truth in this argument, as far as it goes, but what is the probability of some slight error occurring on the part of some participant, and what is the cumulative probability of what will happen to you if you cross a hundred intersections in this manner? As the number of encounters rises, the cumulative probabilities become overwhelming. The larger the probability of error or disaster in each individual encounter, however, the sooner this will happen. For this reason, we also must measure the individual error probabilities.

ASSUMPTIONS OF RATIONALITY VERSUS
MEASUREMENT OF ERROR RATES

In political theory there has long been a debate between those who say that people are most often irrational, that they vote in order to reaffirm their group affiliations, as Paul Lazarsfeld has said, and those who say that they most often vote in order to get a calculated rational advantage in terms of some value salient to them. (This could be a respect or attitude value; it does not have to be a monetary value.) We need to know how often people try to act rationally and exactly what their average, median, mode, and rates of error are.

Consider a complicated political system. A systems analyst might tell us that this system can survive with a 4 per cent error rate; he might add that its fate will be doubtful if the error rate is between 4 and 9 or 10 per cent, and that if the error rate should go above 10 per cent, the ruin of the system would be likely. This is much the same as to say that when an automobile driver wobbles on a freeway about four inches to the right and left from his lane in heavy traffic, the system is still manageable, but if he should wobble ten inches to the right and left, there would be accidents. There are also margins of tolerance of performance in political systems. We can identify them by observing and analysing the system. But we may have to go to the laboratory or a group experiment to find out what the expectable error rates are.

In general, we need to know both the rates of compliance (how often people do something which they have been told to do – obey a government, follow a law, follow certain rules) and the rates of error. What are the rates of each kind observable in society, to what extent can we parallel these rates in the laboratory setting, and what measurements do we get?

The next question is the sequential depth of the major operations. If the sequence of the set of operations in society, administration, or politics is shallow in the sense that only very few operations occur one after the other, then high error rates are more nearly tolerable and more often tolerable than if the 'logical depth' (i.e., the sequential depth) is high.[16] Here again, we may have to go back to the laboratory for data.

We can use a mathematical measure for a first approach to this problem. If we define the rate of error as a frequency on a percentage base, we may call E this frequency of error; and if we assume that error will lead to failure (for it is serious errors we are concerned with), then we can compute the half-life of an operation. By half-life we mean either that we have a large number of actors, one-half of whom will be eliminated, or that we have a single actor whose chance of survival will be less than 0.5. If we call this half-life H, then H nearly equals 70 divided by E. It follows from this formula that if the tough bargainers of the Riker experiment were in a situation where it would be fatal to fail to guess the outcome of the coalition, their error rate of 8 per cent would give them on the average a less than even chance of surviving 9 encounters.[17] If they had far fewer than 9 encounters, this might be good enough. If they had many more than 9 encounters, a half-life of 9 encounters means that for 18 encounters they would have only one chance in 4 of surviving; for 27 encounters, one chance in 8; for 36 encounters, one chance in 16; and for 90 encounters, only one chance in 1024. Some cumulative effect of this type holds for any error rate, and even very moderate error rates can do a great deal of damage to people in situations of great logical depth.

16   John Von Neumann, *The Computer and the Brain* (New Haven: Yale University Press, 1958).
17   The formulas are $H = 70/E$; and for the probability of survival, S, after n encounters,

$$s = 2^{-n/H} = 2^{-nE/70}.$$

These relationships are based on a property of the natural logarithm e which is involved in the formula for the more detailed calculation. See Richard W. Chadwick and K.W. Deutsch, 'Doubling Time and Half Life,' *Comparative Political Studies*, 1, 1 (April 1968), pp. 139–45.

Let me add an empirical datum from the real world and ask for comparison with data from experiments. In the real world we find that 20 per cent of all wars initiated between 1815 and 1910 were lost by the governments initiating them. Since nineteenth century wars did not end in draws, we can say who won and who lost, and we find that governments in those days had a 4 to 1 chance of winning a war they had started. Thus, on the whole the nineteenth-century politician was rather smart – an average somewhat pulled up by Bismarck and Cavour and somewhat pulled down by Napoleon III. Making war in those days was a fairly safe operation. But then something changed. From 1911 to 1965 60 per cent of all wars ended in the defeat of the governments initiating them. Perhaps statesmen have become three times as stupid as they were in the nineteenth century; or this world has become three times as unpredictable; or, thanks to mass participation in politics, statesmen have become too busy to be concerned with war; or because domestic factors have a greater effect on policy decisions now than they had in the days of Metternich and Bismarck, let alone Castlereach or Palmerston. In any case, we now find these remarkably high error rates.

But what error rates would seem realistic? How accurate and reliable is twentieth-century human nature in deciding about war and peace? Now that we have hundreds of simulation games we can ask: What is the frequency with which players misjudge what other players are doing or intending to do? At a training exercise at the Industrial College of the Armed Forces (ICAF), where I happened to be an observer, one team of US officers trying to play the role of Communist Chinese political and military strategists was planning a move for Communist China; they were also starting guerrilla warfare actions in the Himalayas against India. When asked what they expected to accomplish, they replied: 'We expect to focus attention on China, and to force India to sponsor our way into the United Nations; we want to become United Nations members.' Across the corridor the American team had just been notified of this growing unrest in the Himalayas and now were planning counter-moves. They were asked what they thought the Chinese were up to and answered: 'Oh, they are trying to test our will. They are trying to overrun India and conquer it, and to test whether the United States will stop them.' It seemed clear that there was mutual gross misperception. The Chinese team misperceived how its own actions would be viewed by the Americans; the Americans misperceived what the Chinese were trying to do. In actual fact, the players on both sides came from the same culture – they were mid-level United States officers. If they had been real Communist Chinese and real Americans, the probabilities of mutual misunderstanding would have been even higher. Experiments of this type ought to give us error rates and failure rates for many aspects of the simulated political system or at least of the type of personnel involved in the simulation.[18] The same would be true about probabilities of orders being executed, probabilities of things simply not being done, or of policies being modified by bias or corruption. We ought to get probability margins on many major variables in our political theories and systems, and we ought to get many of these previously unobtained data from experimental work.

THE CONTRIBUTION OF EXPERIMENTS TO THE MULTIPLICITY OF EVIDENCE

This leads me to stress the point made by Professor Laponce of the importance of insisting on a multiplicity of evidence from very many different sources.[19] The truth is not in any one kind of evidence but in the relation of many kinds. This search for multiple evidence may require laboratory experiments, survey research, content analysis, general observations and case studies, individual and aggregative data, and therefore five or six kinds of evidence for every serious effort to understand what is going on. This requirement for multiple corroboration will increase research budgets, as well as pressures on time and manpower, but in serious matters, where lives or vast expenditures are at stake, nothing less will really do.

This leads also to a philosophic concept of reality. Reality is conceived in this approach as the relationship among different series of tests. 'If you doubt whether this brick is real, Sir,' said Dr Johnson, 'try kicking it.' That is to say, the testimony of our eyes and the testimony of our toe has to agree. If we can get five or six different tests, we have a better reason to think that the relation is real. In operational terms, the statement 'X is real' is a prediction which says that an unlimited number of tests from t_1 to t_n, all different and mutually independent, will always give results compatible with the statement that 'X exists.' A statement about reality is a statement of a prediction about future tests of different kinds, including possible tests not yet invented. If a brick is real, it will show up on an x-ray picture, and Dr Johnson should have expected it to do so, even though he didn't know about x-rays.[20]

This line of thought suggests more experiments with subsystems, but

18 Karl W. Deutsch and Dieter Senghaas, 'Simulation in International Politics: How to Get Your Money's Worth,' *Perspectives in Defense Management* (March 1970), pp. 37–40.
19 See p. 13.
20 See note 1 above.

I think that Professor Laponce's scheme separates too sharply the experiment in the mind from the experiment in nature, and the author-initiated and the nature-initiated.[21] Instead of the fourfold table, one where the middle rows and columns would be labelled 'combined' or 'joined' would be preferable. We often combine experiments and sequences of thoughts. Typically, we use a series of data from the outside world, and then we quite deliberately perform more or less sophisticated mathematical operations on it. Or we have a survey, which is largely something which happens in the world out there, but we deliberately have half of the interviewers white and half of them black, or we formulate the same question in two different ways and find out how many percentages of the respondents change their answers. About 12 per cent, in some cases, will change; interviewer effects similarly are 15 to 20 per cent. We combine the observational work and the experimental work, or self-selected subsystems or individuals with things which we have selected.

We also can treat the fifty states of the United States as fifty experiments on the effect of the death penalty. A study of correlations in different states between murder rates and the introduction or abolition of the death penalty, or its persistence over long or short periods, gives a fairly rich experimental design. Such analyses have been made, and they show the death penalty has no significant effect on the frequency of murders.

We can also apply probabilistic and experimental methods on a more general basis. Much of our thinking on law is based on the thinking of the lawyer and not the social scientist. As a result we either make a law for everybody or we do not make it at all. A private business firm pretested nylon stockings in six selected cities to find out whether, in what qualities, and at what prices ladies liked them, and only then went on to a nationwide sales campaign. It is quite rare for a government to make a law for six cities; one example is the Nowy Sacz experiment, which Professor Wiatr reported,[22] and another example is the experiment of providing a guaranteed annual minimum income to poor families in a few cities in the United States, which showed that their motivation to work did not decline but, if anything, grew stronger.[23] Such experimental pretests of potential legislation could be used more widely. If we could run each such experiment for several towns, varying the size, location, and other relevant conditions, we would get an experimental design for six or eight places, so as to pretest laws much the way we can pretest industrial commodities or other institu-

21 See p. 6.
22 See p. 94.
23 Fred J. Cook, 'When You Just Give Money to the Poor,' *New York Times Magazine*, 3 May 1970, pp. 23, 109–12.

tions. It might then be possible to make the final decision through the appropriate legislative body or administrative agency in the light of much more accurate information than is available now.

There is one set of experiments which has not been made thus far but which has now become feasible. We have many books and writings which say that a particular aspect of human affairs would be quite different if only the social system were different. For many years Marxist writers have asserted that robbery, theft, and prostitution would disappear if capitalist business enterprise would disappear. We now have fourteen communist countries in the world and we ought to try to use them as a cognitive resource. Social scientists living outside of them can take a reasonably detached view, and our colleagues on the other side might actually think that capitalist countries have their uses as a cognitive resource for them. One might then begin to experiment with new practices and institutions and to observe specific phenomena under both social systems: how many thefts occur, how much juvenile delinquency there is, how many accidents per million cars or passenger miles there are, how many failures of maintenance occur in a certain type of industry. If we could find out what the frequencies are under different political systems – bearing in mind that there is capitalism and capitalism, such as in Switzerland and Haiti, and that there are Communist and Communist states, such as East Germany and Outer Mongolia – we might find considerable differences both across and within these social systems. Through the international collaboration of scholars a chance exists to set down observations where the big parameters which social scientists always thought they could not vary, such as Western versus non-Western culture, or private enterprise versus collectivist centrally planned economies, are varied. We could then also try to see how people from each of these large cultures or social systems behave in laboratory experiments. Take Rapoport's prisoners' dilemma experiments or, better still, his threat games, which measure for each group of players the frequency with which they submit to power when they are at a disadvantage and the frequency with which they exploit power ruthlessly when they have got it, against their tendency to revolt when put at a disadvantage and their tendency of being reasonably accommodating or permissive or generous when they have an advantage which they themselves may suspect as unfair.[24]

24 Anatol Rapoport, Melvin Guyer, and David Gordon, 'A Comparison of Performances of Danish and American Students in a "Threat Game," ' International Political Science Association, Eighth World Congress of Political Science, Munich, 31 August–5 September 1970; Anatol Rapoport and Albert M. Chammah, *Prisoner's Dilemma: A Study in Conflict and Cooperation* (Ann Arbor: University of Michigan Press, 1965).

34   Karl W. Deutsch

Can we systematically rerun the Riker experiment,[25] and some of
the Rapoport experiments, east and west of the assorted cultural ideological dividing lines and see how much of human behaviour really corresponds to a response to these divisions? The answers, I suspect, to all these
questions will rarely be 'yes' or 'no'; usually they will be 'how much.' But if
observation and experiment can help us to know or estimate how much,
how many, and how fast, we will find that in many of our models of society
these simple inconspicuous numbers could make a difference.

REFERENCES

ASHBY, W. ROSS 'Can a Mechanical Chess-Player Outplay Its Designer?'
British Journal for the Philosophy of Science, 3, 44 (1952).
CHADWICK, RICHARD W. and KARL W. DEUTSCH 'Doubling Time and Half Life,'
Comparative Political Studies, 1, 1 (April 1968), pp. 139–45.
CHADWICK, RICHARD W. and KARL W. DEUTSCH 'International Trade and
Economic Integration: Further Developments in Matrix Analysis to
Estimate the Effect of Background Conditions versus Political Controls,'
forthcoming.
COOK, FRED J. 'When You Just Give Money to the Poor,' New York Times
Magazine, 3 May 1970.
DEUTSCH, KARL W. 'On Theories, Taxonomies, and Models as Communication
Codes for Organizing Information,' Behavioral Science, 11, 1 (January
1966), pp. 1–17.
DEUTSCH, KARL W. Politics and Government: How People Decide Their Fate.
Boston: Houghton Mifflin, 1970.
DEUTSCH, KARL W. The Nerves of Government. New York: Free Press, 1966.
DEUTSCH, KARL W. 'On Methodological Problems of Quantitative Research,'
in Mattei Dogan and Stein Rokkan, eds. Quantitative Ecological Analysis
in the Social Sciences. Cambridge, Mass.: MIT Press, 1969.
DEUTSCH, KARL W. and WILLIAM G. MADOW 'A Note on the Appearance of
Wisdom in Large Bureaucratic Organization,' Behavioral Science, 6,
1 (January 1961), pp. 72–8.
DEUTSCH, KARL W. and DIETER SENGHAAS 'Simulation in International Politics:
How to Get Your Money's Worth,' Perspectives in Defense Manage-
ment (March 1970), pp. 37–40.
GUMBEL, EMIL J. Statistics of Extremes. New York: Columbia University
Press, 1958.
LANGER, SUZANNE K. Philosophy in a New Key. Cambridge, Mass.: Harvard
University Press, 1942.

25   See p. 132, and W.H. Riker 'Bargaining in a Three-person Game,'
American Political Science Review, 61 (1967), pp. 642–56.

LAZARSFELD, PAUL F., B. BERELSON, and H. GAUDET *The People's Choice.* New York: Columbia Press, 1944.

POPPER, KARL *The Logic of Scientific Discovery.* New York: Harper Torch-books, 1968.

RAPOPORT, ANATOL, MELVIN GUYER, and DAVID GORDON 'A Comparison of Performances of Danish and American Students in a "Threat Game," ' International Political Science Association, Eighth World Congress of Political Science, Munich, 31 August–5 September 1970.

RAPOPORT, ANATOL and ALBERT M. CHAMMAH *Prisoner's Dilemma: A Study in Conflict and Cooperation.* Ann Arbor: University of Michigan Press, 1965.

RIKER, WILLIAM H. 'Bargaining in a Three-person Game,' *American Political Science Review,* 61 (1967), pp. 642–56.

RUSSELL, BERTRAND *A History of Western Philosophy.* New York: Simon and Shuster, 1945.

SAVAGE, I. RICHARD and KARL W. DEUTSCH 'A Statistical Model of the Gross Analysis of Transaction Flows,' *Econometric,* 28, 3 (July 1960), pp. 551–72.

SCHELLING, THOMAS *The Strategy of Conflict.* Cambridge, Mass.: Harvard University Press, 1960.

SIMON, HERBERT A. 'Designing Organizations for an Information Rich World,' in Martin Greenberger, ed. *Computers, Communications and the Public Interest.* Baltimore: Johns Hopkins University Press, 1971.

VON NEUMANN, JOHN *The Computer and the Brain.* New Haven: Yale University Press, 1958.

WIENER, NORBERT *The Human Use of Human Beings.* Boston: Houghton Mifflin, 1954. 'Preface: The Idea of a Contingent Universe.'

PART TWO

Pre-data and
post-data experiments

International tension
as a function of
reduced communication

In their application of the InterNation Simulation model (INS) to Mexico, W.J. Crow and John Raser found that during negotiations Mexican subjects exchanged more messages than did Americans, were more likely to maintain a formal style of communication characterized by its respect for grammar, formality, and diplomatic phrasing, and were markedly less aggressive. The authors (Crow and Raser 1964) explained these differences by assuming that when confronted by stress situations Mexicans were more passive than Americans. An alternative explanation substantiated by the experiment reported in this paper is that the greater stress and aggressiveness of the American subjects was the very consequence of the lesser number of messages they could exchange.

Indeed, the literature leads us to expect that the reduction of tension is positively related to the amount of communication. Studying patterns of communication in an international group, Alger (1965) noted that the multiplication of ways of communicating between nations produces, in cases of conflict, continual adjustments in national policies, thus tending to substitute a host of small adjustments for extraordinary confrontations that would have required adjustments of great magnitude. Robinson (1962) found that a high level of group communication reduces the danger that decisions will be made solely on the basis of personal values. In an attractive study, Deutsch (1958) revealed that among pairs of college students motivated to maximize their own rewards, an increase in the possibility of communicating results in an increase of co-operative as opposed to competitive action. Loomis (1959) suggested that an increase in the level of communication raises not only the level of co-operation but also the level of trust. Lawson (1961), Cohen and Bennis (1961), and Cohen (1961, 1962) have shown that the structure of communication affects many of a group's output variables and that this effect is not merely the result of physical communication constraints but on the contrary is largely the consequence of the quality and amount of interaction.

HYPOTHESES

We expect that communication structure has a very specific effect on group behaviour, an effect related to the kind of communication the group is able to develop. The Crow and Raser experiment with Mexican subjects included a key variable which may explain why Mexicans tended to be more co-operative and less competitive than Americans. The former, unlike the latter, could use as many messages as they wished. We should thus expect, if our hypothesis is correct, that changing the communication structure of the INS would produce changes in groups' outputs.[1] More specifically we expect that the group playing the INS game under restricted communications (fewer messages available) would produce more conflicts. This should happen because the subjects, confronted by the lack of information, will exaggerate the importance of their opponents' actions, especially those actions that can be considered threatening and harmful. Lack of information is expected to generate negative attitudes, to increase the perception of tension, and consequently to increase the level of actual threats. In short, when the level of communications is reduced we expect a higher level of tension than when the exchange of messages is not restricted.

EXPERIMENTAL DESIGN

In order to test these hypotheses we designed the following experiment.

We took sixty-four subjects in their first year of psychology and assigned them at random to either of two different experimental conditions: in the first the INS was played with total freedom to write as many messages as desired; in the second the number of messages was restricted. Instead of the average of one hundred messages per person per simulation,

---

1 Reducing or increasing experimentally communication flow in a group has of course the unavoidable disadvantage of creating an artificial system. The group is not free to develop naturally. Our observations should thus be read with this situation in mind.

the restriction called for only forty.[2] Both groups played nine periods. At the end of every period each participant had to answer a questionnaire which contained four scales (seven-point scales) intended to test:

SCALE 1 the information level from very low to very high,
SCALE 2 the perception of tension-co-operation from high co-operation to high tension,
SCALE 3 the hostility of other nations towards one's own nation (from low to high), and
SCALE 4 the hostile intention of one's own nation towards other nations (from low to high).

In all four scales the lower scores are given to the negative side of the scale. For example, a low score on scale three means a high level of perceived hostility from other nations.

INITIAL CONDITIONS AT THE START OF THE INS

The simulated world consisted of seven nations called Erga, Ingo, Omne, Utro, Rena, Soro, and Algo. The nation Algo was divided into two parts as a result of an international agreement made between the two parts of Algo and the two big nations of that time: Omne and Utro. This agreement made it possible to stop an intestine war from which Algo suffered for a long time. However, even though the agreement put a stop to the war it was unable to solve all conflicts between the two parts of Algo. One part was helped by Utro (Upper Algo) and the other was helped by Omne (Lower Algo). Upper Algo entertained the idea of being the authentic government for the whole of Algo and at all times it acted inside Lower Algo, provoking continuous struggles, guerrilla warfare and student riots.

The international situation was worsened by the appearance of Rena in the international arena. Rena was a third big nation which supported the claims of Upper Algo without having any formal relations with Upper Algo. Utro was very suspicious of Rena's interest in Upper Algo, specially because both big nations differed deeply in their interpretation of a similar ideology. Rena made persistent attacks against Omne's ideology and engaged in propaganda against Omne in the other countries. Omne argued against and strongly opposed the ideology as well as the so-called unavowed purposes of both Rena and Utro.

The world was shaped into three alliances: a / Utro, Ingo, and Upper Algo; b / Omne, Erga, and Lower Algo; and c / Rena and Soro.

2 The hundred message average was observed in previous INS games.

Rena and Soro had no formal relations with Omne, Erga, or Lower Algo; Utro and Ingo had formal relations with all the countries except Lower Algo; Lower Algo had relations with Omne and Erga. Rena and Soro were not members of the International Organization (IO).

INSTRUCTIONS

Both groups were instructed in the rules of the game for two days. These rules follow very closely those of the Guetzkow INS model (1963), except for minor changes which simplified the computations. The subjects were asked to practise in order to become familiar with the procedures of the game. After they understood the rules and how to go along with the instructions of the game they were assigned to the two experimental conditions.

Control of the messages in the communications-restricted condition was introduced as follows: each one of the simulated nations was, in each period, given either seventeen or eighteen message forms (altogether 160 for the nine periods). We told the subjects that this amount (seventeen to eighteen) would hold for every period; the reason given was that we were short of message forms.

LOCALE OF THE EXPERIMENT

The locale used for the experiment was a very spacious room. Each of the participants was placed in an enclosed cabinet. The only way he could communicate with others was through the use of the message forms. In each period participants could attend cabinet meetings for three minutes in the experimental group and for ten minutes in the control group. Obviously the time spent by the experimental group at cabinet meetings was not enough to cover all the topics they had to discuss, the more so as the game progressed. We were very strict in eliminating the possibility of the participants communicating with each other than through the specified channels. There were two IO meetings which only the EDM (exterior decision-maker) could attend.

Each nation was represented by four persons playing the following roles: a central decision-maker, an exterior decision-maker, a military decision-maker, an aspiring central decision-maker. A newspaper, called the *International Times*, had its office outside the simulation room. It only appeared twice, in the second and in the eighth periods, and its information was very superficial, ignoring any topic specifically related to developments in the INS

THE RESULTS

Our hypotheses are tested on two kinds of data: a / those obtained from the questionnaire, and b / the observed outcomes of the INS game, such as the frequency of military attacks and the number of hostile messages sent from one nation to another. To analyse the questionnaire data we used the average score obtained by each group on the four scales for all nine periods of the game. Military attacks were not quantified but treated qualitatively; the number of hostile messages was measured in relation to the total production of messages for the nine periods.

The group under communications restriction (table 1 scale 1) felt that they did not have enough information. Their perceptions on this point were significantly different from those of the control group ($t = 2.5$; $p < 0.02$; $df = 17$). In their perception of tension-co-operation, the two

TABLE 1

Comparison of control and experimental groups on selected scales

	Control group		Experimental group			Level of significance
	$\bar{x}$	s^2	$\bar{x}$	s^2	t value	
Scale 1 Information level	5.00	0.60	3.50	2.60	2.50	0.02
Scale 2 Tension co-operation perception	3.02	0.10	2.70	1.20	1.00	0.10
Scale 3 Other nations hostility perception	3.27	0.80	2.55	0.80	1.76	0.05
Scale 4 Hostile intention towards other nations	3.55	0.90	2.90	0.50	1.80	0.05

groups do not show strong statistical differences (t is significant only at the 0.10 level). But the perception of other nations' hostility towards one's own nation revealed a statistically significant difference between the two groups (table 1 scale 3). With regard to the perception of hostile intentions of one's own nation towards other nations both groups show a statistically significant difference (table 1 scale 4). Thus the scale scores indicate that the group under communications restriction manifests more hostility, perceives more hostility, and perceives a little more tension than the group not hindered by any communications restriction.

Table 2 confirms what table 1 led one to expect: the proportion of hostile messages is much larger in the experimental than in the control group. Thus, communication reduction raised the level of hostility.

During the game there were three military attacks, all of them

TABLE 2

Messages originating from the control and experimental groups

	Per cent hostile	Per cent non-hostile	Number of messages
Control group	52	48	3201
Experimental group	73	27	1280

NOTE $X^2 = 169.95$; level of significance $= 0.001$; DF $= 1$.

TABLE 3

Average score of the control and experimental groups obtained in each one of the four scales in every period

	Scale 1		Scale 2		Scale 3		Scale 4	
Periods	CG	EG	CG	EG	CG	EG	CG	EG
1	5.3	6.2	3.4	4.3	3.6	3.8	3.6	3.8
2	5.0	5.4	3.1	4.5	4.1	3.6	4.2	4.0
3	5.5	5.2	2.3	4.0	3.9	3.8	4.3	3.6
4	5.0	3.3	2.5	2.6	3.9	2.1	4.0	2.0
5	4.8	3.1	3.0	2.5	4.2	2.4	4.5	3.1
6	5.8	3.0	3.6	2.2	1.3	2.0	1.4	2.8
7	5.5	2.2	2.6	2.0	2.4	2.1	3.1	2.4
8	4.2	2.0	3.5	2.1	3.1	2.0	3.1	2.4
9	4.5	1.4	3.2	1.1	3.1	1.2	3.8	2.0

coming from the experimental group: during period 3 Lower Ingo attacked Soro; in period 7, Soro attacked Lower Algo; and in period 8, Ingo was attacked by Rena. In these conflicts, Utro acted as a mediator between Soro and Lower Algo, between Soro and Ingo, and between Rena and Ingo. During the conflict between Soro and Lower Algo, Omne played an important role by putting all her pressure resources on Utro and Rena to solve the conflict. The experimental group was more tense, produced more stress, and was more aggressive than the control group (table 3).

CONCLUSION

On the basis of the experiment it appears that the structural features of the INS model have a considerable effect on the behaviour of the subjects who play the game. The communications structure appears at least partly responsible for the kind of tension which arises among simulated nations.[3] But before concluding, a caveat is in order. Regrettably, our INS experiment in some ways is not truly an experiment. Despite our efforts we

3 Note that although the game greatly reduces the complexity of the real world, its outcomes have striking similarities to what one would expect from real-world situations.

could not exert as much control over our subjects and over the situation as would have been desirable in a laboratory experiment. The setting was at best quasi-experimental, a cross between a laboratory and a field experiment. However, notwithstanding its limitations, the technique we used appears suitable not only as a heuristic tool but also as a test of theories of international behaviour. To such theories we contribute the following findings:

1   Under restricted communications, the experimental group produced more conflicts than the control group.
2   Under restricted communications the experimental group manifested a higher level of perceived hostility than the control group.
3   Under restricted communications the experimental group was more hostile than the control group.

Thus, it appears that what Crow and Raser attributed to passivity and the avoidance of threatening situations can be explained more simply by the level of communications and the number of messages exchanged.

REFERENCES

ALGER, F. 'Personal Contact in Intergovernmental Organizations,' in H.C. Kelman, *International Behaviour*. New York: Holt, Rinehart and Winston, 1965.
COHEN, ARTHUR M. 'Changing Small-Group Communication Networks,' *Journal of Communication*, II (1962), pp. 116–28.
COHEN, ARTHUR M. and WARREN G. BENNIS 'Continuity of Leadership in Communication Networks,' *Human Relations*, 14, 4 (November 1961), pp. 351–69.
CROW, WAYMAN J. and R.J. RASER *A Cross-cultural Simulation Study*, La Jolla, California: Western Behavioural Institute, 1964.
DEUTSCH, MORTON 'The Effect of Motivational Orientation upon Trust and Suspicion,' *Human Relations*, 13, 2 (May 1960), pp. 123–40.
DEUTSCH, MORTON 'Trust and Suspicion,' *Journal of Conflict Resolution*, 2, 4 (December 1958), pp. 265–79.
GUETZKOW, H., F.C. ALGER, A.R. BRODY, C.R. NOEL, and C.R. SNYDER *Simulation in International Relations*. Englewood Cliffs, NJ: Prentice-Hall, 1963.
LAWSON, E.D. 'Change in Communication Nets and Performance,' paper read at the Eastern Psychological Association Convention (1961).
LOOMIS, JAMES L 'Communication: The Development of Trust and Co-operative Behaviour,' *Human Relations*, 12, 4 (1959), pp. 305–15.
ROBINSON, J.A. *Congress and Foreign Policy-making*. Homewood, Illinois: Dorsey Press, 1962.

J.A.LAPONCE

The use of visual space to measure ideology

I INTRODUCTION

Although the method presented in this paper is not, in its applications, restricted to the substantive interests which led to its formulation, knowing these interests will help the reader to follow and check this apologia for the use of visual space to measure political ideology.

II RESEARCH INTERESTS UNDERLYING THE METHOD PRESENTED

Generally, my purpose is to study the effects of biological and physical constraints on political perceptions; specifically, to link the way man relates spatially to his physical environment and the way he 'sees' society. I assume a relationship between the pull of gravity and man's perception of hierarchies, between the concentration of his sensory organs at the front of his face and his conception of history, between the dominant imbalance in his body, which makes all societies dextrous, and the way he orders his political landscape.

The sequence in which the child acquires his notions of space, the fact that his perception of up-down precedes that of front-behind which precedes that of left-right, the fact that biological and physical factors beyond our control make us value up more than down (if the major sensory organs were concentrated in the foot or the knee, we might not value up as much), the fact that we do not control what occurs behind us as well as what occurs in front of us, the fact that – whether because of the better blood irrigation of the left side of the brain or for some other cause – man has specialized his hands and created a hierarchy between the two,[1] influence significantly, may well determine entirely, the categories, the metaphors, the theories by which we explain the world around us. Such is, at least, the theory guiding my enquiries.

Within this overall theoretical framework, my research thus far has been exclusively at the perceptual rather than at the biological end of the problem; it has sought to identify the spatial translations of political perceptions in terms of left and right and to a lesser extent in terms of up and down. To do so I used a modified version of the semantic differential (Osgood 1957), which consists of mapping spatially the distance between concepts (such as self, father, country, God, etc.) as one maps the distance between atoms or molecules in a multidimensional model.

III   FROM NOMINAL TO VISUAL SCALES

Ordering of nominal categories in what constitutes in fact a visual scale is commonly done, though sometimes unwittingly. Take the following problem:

Indicate your personal preference on the following left to right scale.
1 Extreme left   5 Centre right
2 Left   6 Right
3 Centre left   7 Extreme right
4 Centre

Such a display of nominal alternatives translates, though in a rough and broken way, a logical into a visual continuum. Little is required to refine this ordering into a more immediately comprehensible visual scale; indeed one needs only to list the alternatives in single file either horizontally or vertically. Recognition of the advantages of such a display led to the wide use of the Likert type of scale (Likert 1932) where the visual takes precedence over the written, such as:

Locate yourself in the following left to right scale.

Left   Right

1   The theory that right-handed dominance is the result of inherited character-
     istics has come under the increasingly well-documented challenge of child

A vertical adaptation of the Likert scale is the thermometer sometimes used in surveys of attitudes to measure intensity of support or belief:

How much to the left (politically) would you say you are? (Give your
answer by drawing a line which will fill up the thermometer at the level
of your choice.)

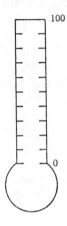

IV   VARIATIONS ON THE LIKERT SCALE

For the study of left and right it was logical and tempting that I use a
horizontal uncluttered Likert measure. Pretests with second and third
year social science students at the University of British Columbia showed,
for my purpose at least, the need for some changes in that classical scale.
It appeared first of all that the centre position on the seven-point scale
was used much too often for my liking, especially in the location of concepts such as God; I could not tell whether a centre answer meant absten-
tion or a specific location. Secondly, the subject asked to make a large
number of visual locations in a succession of Likert scales does not always
start measuring distance from the same starting point; the cross or check
by which he marks his answer is sometimes related to one extreme, sometimes to the other, sometimes to the centre, sometimes to preceding
classifications.

In order to overcome these two major difficulties, at least partially,
the concepts my subjects had to locate between left or right were boxed
and listed under one another in the middle of the page of the question-

psychologists, who support the theory that it is exclusively culture bound (see
surveys in Hildreth 1949, Palmer 1963). My reading of the literature leads
me nevertheless to favour, on balance, the first explanation.

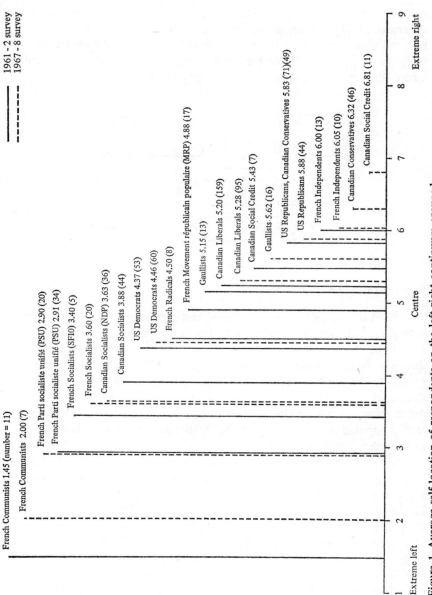

1961 - 2 survey
1967 - 8 survey

French Communists 1.45 (number = 11)
French Communists 2.00 (7)

French Parti socialiste unifié (PSU) 2.90 (20)
French Parti socialiste unifié (PSU) 2.91 (34)
French Socialists (SFIO) 3.40 (5)
French Socialists 3.60 (20)
Canadian Socialists (NDP) 3.63 (36)
Canadian Socialists 3.88 (44)
US Democrats 4.37 (53)
US Democrats 4.46 (60)
French Radicals 4.50 (8)
French Movement républicain populaire (MRP) 4.88 (17)
Gaullists 5.15 (13)
Canadian Liberals 5.20 (159)
Canadian Liberals 5.28 (95)
Canadian Social Credit 5.43 (7)
Gaullists 5.62 (16)
US Republicans, Canadian Conservatives 5.83 (71)(49)
US Republicans 5.88 (44)
French Independents 6.00 (13)
French Independents 6.05 (10)
Canadian Conservatives 6.32 (46)
Canadian Social Credit 6.81 (11)

1   2   3   4   5   6   7   8   9
Extreme left   Centre   Extreme right

Figure 1 Average self-location of respondents on the left-right continuum grouped
by nationality and by party preference.

naire; the respondent had to indicate the distance from the centre to either extreme by drawing an arrow as short or as long as he wished. The temptation to give central answers was reduced, and the respondent was obliged to bring his hand and eyes back to the centre whenever he started a new classification. A typical answer is given in figure 2.

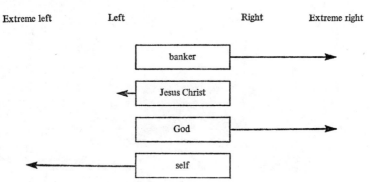

Figure 2 Types of experiments.

That such drawing of arrows is a good and simple way of obtaining an individual's ideological position is shown in a report (Laponce January 1970) the findings of which are confirmed by a subsequent replication shown in figure 1 which compares the earlier (1961–2) and the latter (1967–8) data by locating the average position of French, American, and Canadian student respondents grouped by party preference on the extreme left to extreme right continuum (to measure this position I arbitrarily imposed a nine-point scale of equal intervals on the visual scale used by the respondents).

Six years apart and for two different sets of individuals the only major difference is in the location of the Social Credit, a group in many ways akin to the French Poujadists and, like them, difficult to locate ideologically between right and centre (Smiley 1962). The stability of the group means is all the more remarkable because, with the exception of French Communists, the variance is relatively high (figure 3). This conjunction of stable means and high variance is explained by the fact that self-location between left and right defines not only the position of one's own party but also one's ideological leanings within that party. This was shown by relating spatial self-location to ideological position measured on a Guttman scale of leftism drawn from policy questions (Laponce, January 1970).

I find it remarkable and fascinating that subjects brought up in dif-

1961 - 2

	French Communists	Parti socialiste unifié (PSU)	French Socialists	Canadian Socialists	US Democrats	French Radicals	French MRP	Gaullists	Canadian Liberals	Canadian Social Credit	US Republicans	Canadian Conservatives	French Independents
French Communists													
Parti socialiste unifié (PSU)	X												
French Socialists	X												
Canadian Socialists			X										
US Democrats			X										
French Radicals			X	X	X								
French MRP			X	X	X								
Gaullists					X	X							
Canadian Liberals			X	X	X	X	X						
Canadian Social Credit				X		X	X	X	X				
US Republicans					X	X	X	X	X	X			
Canadian Conservatives							X	X	X	X	X		
French Independents				X			X	X	X	X	X	X	

1967 - 8

	French Communists	Parti socialiste unifié (PSU)	French Socialists	Canadian Socialists	US Democrats	Canadian Liberals	Gaullists	US Republicans	French Conservatives	Canadian Conservatives	Canadian Social Credit
French Communists											
Parti socialiste unifié (PSU)											
French Socialists				X							
Canadian Socialists					X						
US Democrats											
Canadian Liberals							X				
Gaullists								X	X	X	X
US Republicans									X	X	X
French Conservatives										X	X
Canadian Conservatives											X
Canadian Social Credit											

Standard deviations (1961)(1968): French Communists (0.52)(0.57); Parti socialiste unifié PSU (0.83)(1.02); French Socialists (0.54)(1.14); Canadian Socialists (0.68)(1.26); US Democrats (1.30)(1.79); French Radicals (1.05); French MRP (1.61); Gaullists (1.21)(1.62); Canadian Liberals (1.34)(1.69); US Republicans (1.43)(1.60); Canadian Conservatives (1.00)(1.60); French Independents (1.52)(1.17); Canadian Social Credit (1.13)(1.66).

Figure 3 Tests of the difference of mean (x = pairs for which the difference of means is not significant at the 0.05 level on two-tailed t).

ferent cultures, answering at different times on different continents, when asked to locate themselves politically between the two margins of a piece of paper produced the ordering of figure 1. Their answers justify treating the visual left-right continuum as an interval scale.

V   SOME FINDINGS ON THE CONTENT OF THE
     LEFT-RIGHT LANDSCAPE: A DIGRESSION

Prior to the nineteenth century, in all Indo-European languages the terms left and right had acquired a rich symbolic meaning, but a meaning which was either social or religious, not political (Wile 1934, Fritsch 1967). A few examples taken from languages, customs, and rituals will be sufficient: Jesus Christ sits on the right of his father; in mediaeval paintings and sculptures, the devil is often left-handed; in the Masonic temple the two columns signify, on the right the luminous masculine principle, on the left the feminine destructive one; in the symbolism of the Greek classical chorus a turn to the right measures agreement with the vital forces; in Indo-European languages right signifies either directly, or through derivatives, goodness, quickness of execution, exactitude, and often, as in French and German, law, lawful; left means awkward, stupid, underhanded. Meillet (1906) noted in his study of euphemisms that the words signifying the right side are more stable than those assigned to the left, a fact which according to the laws of linguistics (Salomon 1966, Bloomfield 1933) indicates a higher positive content in the right than in the left words. The first usage of the terms left and right in a strictly political sense can be dated to the French revolution of 1789 and the seating arrangement in the national assembly (the right being the king's side).

    Has this extension of the usage of a symbolic spatial classification affected its very meaning and content? Has the perceptual landscape of left-right been modified? What kind of symbolic dissociation, if any, have occurred as a result of this translation of what used to be a general social and religious categorization into a specifically political one?

    From the answers given by my student respondents I note that, now as before the nineteenth century, strength and religion are the stable elements of the right side of the perceptual landscape, whereas the anti-religious and weak are the stable elements of the left (Laponce, January 1970; June 1970). Contrary to expectation the terms describing past and present and old and young were not stable, but there was a clear tendency for the terms describing youth and future to be attracted towards the left more than towards the right. This cultural pull, drawing young to the left, appears in the fact that the distance between the concept self and the concept young increases as the location of self is more to the right.

These findings led me to hypothesize that if the application of left and right to the field of politics had not affected the association of strong and religion with the right side, it had resulted in the left no longer being the systematically negative pole it used to be. The latter now attracts symbols such as young and future which are positively valued in the cultures studied. My data indicates however, that such a revolution in the balance of positive and negative charges associated with the left or the right side can only be partial; if right can be totally positive, left can only be partially such. If correct, this interpretation suggests a similarity between the realm of perception and that of physics; left could never be a perfect inverted mirror image of right.

VI   FROM THE CLASSIFICATION OF CONCEPTS TO THE CLASSIFICATION OF FIELDS

Useful as it is in reaching and locating ideology, the method described in section IV shares with all such semantic differential techniques the disadvantage of creating a rigid field of perception which influences subsequent answers made by the respondent. The concepts classified first influence the location of those classified afterwards but not vice versa, or at least not to the same extent. In order to make it possible that every concept studied be classified as a function of all the others, one can ask the respondent to read and reflect upon the list of concepts subjected to his choice before he classifies them. Better still, one can make the concepts physically mobile in order to enable the respondent to move them and locate them spatially as he would move books on a shelf or pictures on a wall.

To obtain such mobility, I asked the respondents to locate on the left-right dimension words printed on loose pieces of paper. Using a single dimension for such classification was found too constraining;[2] the respondents, even when instructed not to do so, often tended to use two-

2   I asked subjects (students at the University of British Columbia) to locate the movable concepts of figure 5 along a left-right dimension represented by a line drawn in the middle and across the length of an otherwise empty letter sized page. The subjects were repeatedly told in the instructions that they were to order the concepts in the political left-right dimension. Notwithstanding these instructions, 72 per cent (N = 11) of those to whom the line had been presented horizontally used distance from the line as well as order on the line to locate the concepts. When the line was presented vertically 38 per cent of a different set of respondents (N = 13) still used a two-dimensional system of classification.

Up

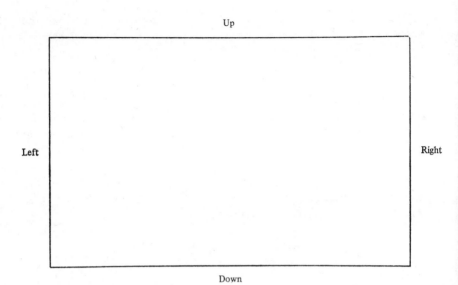

Left   Right

Down

Figure 4 Rectangle, half the original size, within which the respondent was asked
to classify selected concepts.

dimensional space. Removing this constraint, I asked that the concepts
be located within the boundaries of an empty rectangle such as that of
figure 4.

A serious limitation of this technique of classifications is in the relatively small number of concepts which can be handled at any given time
by the subject. The largest number I have tried is twelve; smaller numbers were found preferable. Using terms describing religion, social class,
and the flow of time and asking the respondent to classify these terms in
a rectangle, the sides of which were identified as up, down, and left, and
right, I found confirmation, among the English-Canadian subjects studied,
that when the respondent's mind was oriented to politics, words such as
religion and banker belonged to the right and atheism and worker to the
left, even when controlling for the subject's own position in the left-right
scale. Conversely the terms describing future and youth, though attracted
to the left, were subject to considerable variations related to the self-
location of the subject.

VII COMBINING FIELD CLASSIFICATION
     AND MIND SIMULATION

Our remarkable ability to treat our mind as a laboratory, to focus in
quick succession on different fields of perception, to be a spectator of

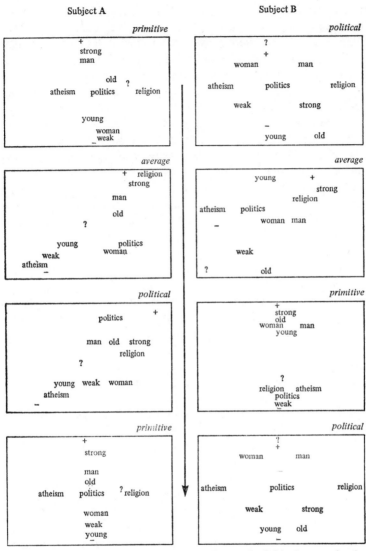

Figure 5 Examples of changes in classification as the field of perception is varied.

our own plays, and our ability to simulate suggested that I ask the subjects to shift their minds to different fields of perception and repeat their field classification after each shift.

A first example of changes in the ordering of a group of words as one varies the respondent's perceptional field is given by figure 5 for two subjects taken at random from 118 who were tested, both English-Cana-

dian students politically left of centre. The first, subject A, was asked at
the beginning of the experiment to orient his mind to that of a simple-
minded individual (the instructions were 'try to orient your mind so that
it is that of a very simple man, a primitive if you wish, somebody who
has a very simple, an all purpose, an unchanging way of seeing things'),
and he was given five minutes to locate within an empty rectangle, the
sides of which were identified as left, right, up, and down, twelve concepts printed on separate pieces of paper. He was then asked to shift his
mind to that of an average man and was again given five minutes to
classify the same concepts without reference to his previous ordering.
A third classification required him to turn his mind to politics ('shift
your mind to politics, not politics as you would like it to be but as it is').
Finally, in a fourth and final classification, always without reference to
those preceding it, he was instructed to shift his mind back to the primitive field from which he started. For subject B the order of presentation
of the field was inverted – political, average, primitive, political.

These two subjects are typical of those tested in that their first
and last answers are almost similar, thus showing the measuring technique not to be unduly sensitive to random variations. They are typical
also in that they distinguish clearly the primitive from the political system
of classification (note the tendency to use up-down primarily in the
primitive field) thus showing the test to be sensitive enough to record
the variations expected. Subject A verifies also our expectation that,
whether in the primitive or in the political system of thought, religion is
on the right and atheism on the left. Subject B, on the contrary, deviates
from the norm, at least in his classification of religion in the primitive
field. Measures of this norm are given by figures 6 and 7. Figure 6 records
the changes in the location of the concept religion in two different groups
of subjects asked to shift from the primitive to the political or vice versa.
Figure 7 records the same type of change when, instead of plotting individual variations, we locate group means in nine groups tested separately.
In accordance with our expectations religion is more to the right in the
political than in the primitive field and higher in the primitive than in the
political. That this change is far from universal among our respondents is
evidenced by the fact that, on the concept religion, only 54 per cent
($N = 118$) verified the expected left-right movement, and only 65 per
cent the movement expected between up and down. But that the hypothesis is, at the group level, verified nine times out of nine on the up down
movement and seven times out of nine on the left-right movement is
indicative of a clear pattern, unlikely to be a result of randomness. The
magnitude of the difference between the individual and the group statis-

Group A: primitive to political   Group B: political to primitive

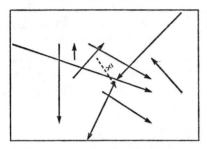
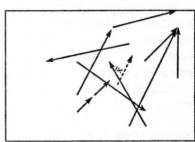

Figure 6 Example of changes in the location of the concept religion as the field of perception is shifted from primitive to political or vice versa, in two different groups of respondents, using one arrow per subject.

Primitive to political   Political to primitive

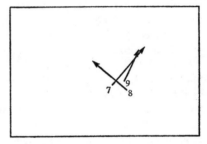

Number of subjects per group: Group 1 (12); Group 2 (15); Group 3 (13); Group 4 (12); Group 5 (9); Group 6 (12); Group 7 (16); Group 8 (19); Group 9 (10).

Figure 7 Examples of changes in the mean group location of the concept religion as the respondents' field of perception is shifted from primitive to political or vice versa (one arrow per group) N of subjects per group: group 1 (12), group 2 (15), group 3 (13), group 4 (12), group 5 (9), group 6 (12), group 7 (16), group 8 (19), group 9 (10).

tics shows, in this case, the advantage of using group means to reduce the effect of random and compensatory idiosincratic classifications.

VIII CONCLUSION

Wanting to free the respondent from the rigidities of the original semantic differential technique used for the location of concepts in dichotomous scales, combined with my interest in the specifically spatial dimensions of left-right and up-down, led me to ask the subjects tested to classify a mobile field of words in a two-dimensional space. By itself or in conjunction with mind simulation this modified semantic differential technique, tested on student respondents, appeared to be sensitive enough to produce meaningful classificatory patterns but not so sensitive as to pick up too much unwanted noise or many random variations. Beyond those presented in this paper the technique offers possibilities of more refined recording. One could, for example, follow cinematographically or photographically the moving of the concepts within the box before the subject settles on his final choice.

REFERENCES

BLOOMFIELD, L. *Language.* New York 1933.
FRITSCH, V. *La Gauche et la droite : vérités et illusions du miroir.* Paris: Flammarion, 1967.
HILDRETH, G. 'The Development and Training of Hand Dominance,' *Journal of Genetic Psychology,* 75 (1949), pp. 197–254.
LAPONCE, J.A. 'Note on the Use of the Left-Right Dimension,' *Comparative Political Studies* (January 1970).
–   'Dieu à droite ou à gauche,' *Canadian Journal of Political Science,* III, 2 (June 1970), pp. 257–74.
LIKERT, R. 'A Technique for the Measurement of Attitudes,' *Archives of Psychology* (1932), N 140.
MEILLET, A. 'Comment les mots changent de sens,' *Année sociologique,* 9, (1906).
OSGOOD, C.E. *et al. The Measurement of Meaning.* Urbana: Illinois University Press, 1957.
PALMER, R.D. 'Hand Differentiation and Psychological Functioning,' *Journal of Personality,* 31 (1963), pp. 445–61.
SALOMON, L.B. *Semantics and Common Sense.* New York: Holt, Rinehart and Winston, 1966.
SMILEY, D. 'Canada's Poujadists: A New Look at Social Credit,' *Canadian Forum* 42 (62), pp. 121–3.
WILE, I. *Handedness: Right and Left.* Boston 1934.

HEINZ EULAU

Policy-making in American cities: comparisons in a quasi-longitudinal, quasi-experimental design*

In recent years several efforts have been made to explain public policies by the use of a study design which treats the outputs of policy as dependent variables, usually by relating them to such independent variables as a polity's socio-economic or political-structural characteristics. One of the weaknesses of this research has been that it does not include data on the political attitudes and orientations of policy-makers themselves, for one might expect that their positions on public issues make a difference in policy outputs. Hence conclusions reached about the importance of 'politics' in the formation of policies are incomplete at best.

But this weakness, partly remedied in the research reported here, is not my major concern. Rather, what interests me is the attempt to explain public policy by way of causal models, for this strikes me as something of an anomaly. At issue, therefore, is the question of whether the design of research involved in causal modelling of public policy is sufficiently isomorphic with policy as a behavioural process in the real world to warrant confidence in the inferences that are made about the emergence of policy.

The plausibility of causal modelling being an appropriate technique for explaining public policy is largely predicated on acceptance of the familiar conception of the political system that deals in inputs and outputs. This conception is congenial to causal modelling because it permits a quick and easy step from treating inputs as 'causes' to treating outputs

* The larger project of which this study is part, the City Council Research Project is sponsored by the Institute of Political Studies, Stanford University, and is supported by the National Science Foundation.

as 'effects.' In other words, policy outcomes are assumed to be the ultimate dependent variable to be accounted for,[1] and the research question is whether exogenous variables (environmental, economic, social, etc.) or endogenous variables (political structures and processes) account for variance in policy. The prior question – whether the input-output system model corresponds to what goes on in the real world of policy – is largely ignored. Also ignored is Easton's caveat that this 'approach to the analysis of political systems will not help us to understand why any specific policies are adopted by the politically relevant members in a system.'[2]

The problem of whether causal modelling is the proper technique for explaining public policy is exacerbated by the perplexing and discomforting findings that political variables seem to account for little or none of the variance in policy outputs.[3] 'This, I submit,' comments Salisbury after reviewing the relevant research, 'is a devastating set of findings and cannot be dismissed as not meaning what it plainly says – that analysis of political systems will not explain policy decisions made by those systems.'[4]

In spite of Easton's own caveat and Salisbury's blunt conclusion, policy research continues causal modelling. Instead of raising questions about the conception of policy implicit in causal modelling, the failure to find relationships between political variables and policy outputs is attributed to the inadequacy of input or output indicators or to errors in measurement. Much effort, perhaps misspent, is devoted to the search for more valid indicators of both independent political and dependent policy variables, and to the correction of measurement errors.

If modelling is to be used in the analysis of public policy, it should follow rather than precede an empirically viable conception of policy.

1   See, for instance, Thomas R. Dye, *Politics, Economics and the Public: Policy Outcomes in the American States* (Chicago: Rand McNally, 1966), pp. 3–4. The nomenclature of policy research is ambiguous. Output and outcome are sometimes treated as synonyms, sometimes as antonyms, as when outcome is conceived of as a consequence of output. Our own use of policy-related concepts will be explained below.
2   David Easton, *A Framework for Political Analysis* (Englewood Cliffs, NJ: Prentice-Hall, 1965), p. 89.
3   The output of relevant studies is considerable. See especially the work of Thomas R. Dye, Richard I. Hofferbert, Ira Sharkansky, Richard E. Dawson and James A. Robinson, and others. For a critical evaluation, see Herbert Jacob and Michael Lipsky, 'Outputs, Structure, and Power: An Assessment of Changes in the Study of State and Local Politics,' in Marian D. Irish, ed., *Political Science: Advance of the Discipline* (Englewood Cliffs, NJ: Prentice-Hall, 1968, pp. 220–48, esp. pp. 221–9.
4   Robert H. Salisbury, 'The Analysis of Public Policy: A Search for Theories and Roles,' in Austin Ranney, ed., *Political Science and Public Policy* (Chicago: Markham, 1968), p. 164.

Such a conception is not likely to emerge, in *deus ex machine* fashion, from causal modelling all kinds of indicators of presumed inputs and outputs that may or may not be germane. Of critical importance are not the indicators but the designs for their analysis. An analytical design is a way to produce the readings of the empirical indicators. Like a definition, it may be wilful, but it must not be arbitrary. Thoughtlessly imposing a causal model on the policy process is not likely to yield valid knowledge.

This paper describes alternate ways of exploring, if not explaining, public policy. Following Stouffer's injunction that 'exploratory research is of necessity fumbling, but ... the waste motion can be reduced by the self-denying ordinance of deliberately limiting ourselves to a few variables at a time,' it initially presents a rather simplistic causal model of policy that employs only five variables.[5] It also presents a rather intricate post facto quasi-longitudinal design for observing variations in components of the causal model. This design seeks to make the best of empirical data which are basically static, but it is inspired by another Stouffer comment that we need 'many more descriptive studies involving random ratlike movements on the part of the researcher before we can even begin to state our problems so that they are in decent shape for fitting into an ideal design.'[6] Before proceeding, it is necessary to explain the conception of policy that is employed and introduce the variables that are being manipulated in the analyses.

A CONCEPTION OF POLICY

Policy is a strictly theoretical construct that is inferred from the patterns of choice behaviour by political actors and the consequences of choice behaviour. Choice behaviour is manifest in actual decisions such as the vote counts in legislative bodies, budgetary allocations, or the assignment of personnel to specified tasks. The consequences of choice behaviour are manifest in the behaviour that follows upon choice, especially compliance or non-compliance. If the behavioural patterns are consistent and regular, the existence of policy is inferred and identified. But behavioural patterns themselves, whether intended or not, are not policy but manifestations from which the nature or direction of policy is inferred.

So defined, policy is distinguished from the intentions, goals, or preferences that political actors may entertain in making choices. Although intentions, goals, or preferences may influence choice, policy

5 Samuel A. Stouffer, 'Some Observations on Study Design,' in *Social Research to Test Ideas* (New York: Free Press, 1962), p. 297.
6 *Ibid.*

cannot be inferred from them. Policy may be consonant with intentions, goals, or preferences, but this can only mean that they have been realized in practice. This conception of policy differs from the conventional usage, when we say, for instance, that it is the policy of government to end discrimination in housing. It may be the intention of the government to end discrimination, but behaviour in pursuit of this intention may or may not occur. Because something is intended, it does not follow that it is in fact the policy.

As a process, policy is the collectivity's response to conditions of the physical and social environment. A policy is operative as long as it is successful, that is, as long as the response that it represents proves rewarding. In fact, it is the rewarding of the response that makes policy what it is – a set of consistent and regular behavioural patterns through which governing units cope with environmental conditions. Changes in policy, that is, changes in response, presumably occur when there are changes in environmental conditions. If there is no appropriate response, and if the old response pattern or policy continues, no reward is likely to be forthcoming. As the policy no longer proffers rewards, it may actually become dysfunctional, if insisted upon, or it may simply be obsolete. In responding to environmental conditions, the characteristics of the governing unit may affect the form of response – its political structure, its human and physical resources, the degree of mass or elite involvement in governance, the vitality of private interests making public demands, and, last but not least, the perceptions, orientations, and preferences of policy-makers themselves.

The problems of policy-making arise out of the relationship between changes in the environment that call for some response, the ways in which these changes are experienced as problems requiring solutions, and the values that policy-makers may seek in responding to changes. Policy, then, functions as a response to environmental conditions, both physical and social, that has built into it an anticipation of a future state of affairs. If this is the case, a change in policy is both causal and purposive: it is 'caused' by environmental stimuli, but it is also directed towards a goal and shaped by a purpose. The tension arising out of the simultaneity of causal and purposive 'forcings' is a basic property of policy.

The problem of causal modelling policy is congruent with the nature of policy in the real world. Policy as a response to environmental challenges inferred from behavioural patterns manifest in outputs or outcomes of choice processes is truly 'caused.' However, as the response is also in pursuit of a goal, value, or end-in-view, it is purposive. But behaviour in pursuit of a goal, or purposive behaviour, is 'caused' in a sense quite different from that we have in mind when we say that a change in environmental conditions brings about or causes policy as a response. When we say, therefore, that a purpose 'informs' or 'orients' a response, we do not mean that the response is 'caused' by a purpose in the same sense that it is caused by an environmental stimulus. If this is so, grave doubts may be raised about the applicability of causal assumptions to policy analysis. For causal modelling does not and probably cannot discriminate between genuinely causal and what are, in effect teleological assumptions about policy.

The problem is confounded by the fact that the relationship between environment and policy is probably symmetrical. In the sense that policy is a response, it is caused by environmental conditions; but as policy is itself a sequence of behavioural patterns through time, it has a reactive effect on the environment. Put differently, it is best to assume that policy and environment are interdetermined. As policies cumulate through time they come to constitute an environment of their own that persists because, insofar as policy proves rewarding, the behavioural patterns involved in responding to environmental challenges have proved rewarding and therefore are continued. But it is just for this reason that the values or goals that policy-makers pursue in responding to the environment are not independent of the interdetermined relationship between environment and policy. If this is so, it goes a long way in explaining what has been called 'incremental decision-making,' though this formulation places the explanatory accent elsewhere.[7] Empirically, it means that current policies do not deviate widely from the goals implicit in policy as a response to the environment. Hence the finding that past expenditure patterns are the best predictors of future expenditures, apparently leaving little room for other variables to affect policy.[8] Psychologically, it means that policy is inert, unless environmental challenges are so overwhelming that innovative behavioural responses are called out. Given the fact that goals are implied in ongoing policy, it is simply 'easier' or 'cheaper' to behave incrementally than to act otherwise.

The model of the policy process that emerges from these considerations consist of three major variables – the physical-natural environment, the policy environment (i.e., the configuration of relevant policies that emerges through time), and what may be called the 'policy map'

---

7 On incrementalism as an approach in choice behaviour, see Charles E. Lindblom, *The Intelligence of Democracy* (New York: Free Press, 1965); and Aaron Wildavsky, *The Politics of the Budgetary Process* (Boston: Little, Brown, 1964).

8 Ira Sharkansky, *The Politics of Taxing and Spending* (Indianapolis: Bobbs-Merrill, 1969), pp. 113–25.

of policy-makers. The policy map, in turn, consists of three components: first, policy-makers' perceptions of the environmental challenges
or problems which they are called to act upon; second, the goals or images
of the future which they have in mind as they respond or fail to respond
to the environment; and third, the positions they take in making choices
in regard to the problems confronting them. The operational definitions
of these variables and the measures used will be introduced in the next
section.

The propositions that can be derived from our conception of policy
and that constitute a theoretical model of the policy process are as follows:
1   The physical-social environment and the policy environment are
interdetermined. For instance, there is a reciprocal relationship between
urbanization as an environmental stimulus and policy as a response. But
policy can also influence the course of urbanization as when land is set
aside for industrial or commercial growth or when taxing policies favour
urbanization. As an interdeterminate relationship, it is subject to the
conditions of a moving equilibrium: a change in environmental stimuli
engenders a change in policy, and a change in policy alters the environment.
2   An environmental challenge calling for a policy response has the
expected effect only if it is perceived by policy-makers as constituting a
problem situation. Unless environmental challenges are experienced as
problems, policy responses are not likely to be forthcoming.
3   Environmental challenges may be, but need not be, directly related
to policy-makers' images of the future. They need not be related because
goals or images refer to the future and can be independent of past or
present conditions. But images may be related indirectly to environmental
conditions if the latter are perceived as problems and suggest a reformulation of images.
4   Environmental challenges are not directly related to policy positions,
for positions need only be taken if the challenges are seen as problems and
become issues to be settled.
5   The policy environment, i.e., the set of ongoing policies that has
emerged through time, may be, but need not be, related to the perception
of challenges from the environment as problems. Policy environment will
not be related to problem perceptions if the relationship between it and
the environmental challenge is in equilibrium; it will be related if the latter
relationship is disturbed. Put differently, if ongoing policies successfully
cope with environmental challenges, the latter are unlikely to be perceived as problems.
6   The policy environment is related to policy-makers' images of or

goals for the future. The policy environment is, by definition, rewarding. And if the policy environment is rewarding, images and goals are not likely to deviate widely from the goals or images that are implicit in ongoing policies and, in fact, are likely to be congruent with them.

7   The policy environment is not directly related to policy positions. For positions are at best intentions that may or may not be consonant with ongoing policies.

8   The relationship between the perception of problems and policy images is highly problematic. On the one hand, one can assume that images as views of the future are totally independent of perceptions of current problems. On the other hand, one can also assume that the perception of strong challenges from the environment lead to a reformulation of images or that the perception of problems, even if rooted in the reality of environmental challenges, is 'coloured' by preferences or expectations inherent in images. Put differently, what policy-makers perceive as problems and what they envisage for the future may be at loggerheads; but perceptions of problems may reshape images, or images may shape the perception of problems. As a result, the relationship between problem perceptions and policy images as such is indeterminate and depends largely on antecedent conditions.

9   Policy images are directly related to policy positions. Because positions are policy-makers' declarations of how they intend to cope with environmental challenges, they are likely to be tutored by their images or ends-in-view.

10   Perceptions of problems, stimulated by environmental challenges, are directly related to policy positions. For if no problems stemming from environmental conditions are perceived, there is no need to adopt policy positions.

DATA AND MEASURES

The data for the two analyses that follow were collected by the City Council Research Project in 1966–7. Interviews were conducted with 435 city councilmen in 87 cities of the San Francisco Bay region. The interviews covered a wide range of questions of political interest.[9] For the

9   Of the publications of the project issued so far that are especially germane here, the following might be cited: Heinz Eulau and Robert Eyestone, 'Policy Maps of City Councils and Policy Outcomes: A Developmental Analysis,' *American Political Science Review*, 62 (March 1968), pp. 124–43; and Kenneth Prewitt and Heinz Eulau, 'Political Matrix and Political Representation: Prolegomenon to a New Departure from an Old Problem,' *American Political Science Review*, 63 (June 1969), pp. 427–41.

purposes of this paper, individual responses were aggregated at the council level so that the council rather than the councilman serves as the empirical unit of analysis. The method of coding and aggregation will be described in connection with the measures used. In addition to the interview data, ecological, demographic, and budget data were collected.

In the following analyses, not all of the 87 city councils in which interviews were conducted could be used. The reduction in numbers is due to a variety of reasons, as follows:

Number of councils in which not enough individual councilmen were interviewed to warrant aggregation at council level   5
Number of councils for which census or budget data are missing (recently incorporated cities)   3
Number of councils with code categories on one or another of the three policy map components too small to permit meaningful analysis   16
Number of councils with environmental characteristics of no interest in the quasi-longitudinal analysis   6

As a result the number of councils available for analysis was reduced to 65 in the first analysis and further reduced to 59 in the second analysis.

Variable 1   City size as an indicator of urbanization

We assume that city size is an appropriate indicator of the level of urbanization that represents the intensity of environmental challenges. There is overwhelming evidence that city size correlates highly not only with other indicators of urbanization such as population density, industrialization, and commercialization but also with the community's 'social pluralism.'[10] The larger the city, the more demanding and more complex is not only its physical environment but also its social environment. City size data come from the 1965 Census of Population. The set of 82 cities included in the main study was dichotomized at the median. As a result 41 cities with a population of over 17,000 were characterized as 'more urbanized,' and 41 cities below the median with a population of under 17,000 were characterized as 'less urbanized.'

10   See, for instance, Jeffrey K. Hadden and Edgar F. Borgatta, *American Cities: Their Social Characteristics* (Chicago: Rand McNally, 1965), for evidence of the correlative power of size as an indicator of a city's demographic and ecological diversity and pluralism.

Variable 2 State of policy development as indicator of policy environment

This variable derives from a complex analysis of city expenditure ratios for development planning and amenities over a period of eight years, 1958–65. Space limitations here do not permit a full explanation of the measures.[11] In general, cities with limited expenditures in planning and amenities, judged by the grand median for all cities, which remained in the same expenditure category over the period of eight years were categorized as 'retarded.' At the opposite end, cities above the grand median in planning and amenities expenditures for the whole period were categorized as 'advanced.' Cities moving across the grand medians on either planning or amenities expenditures were variously categorized as 'emergent,' 'progressed,' or 'maturing.' For the purpose of analysis here the five categories were collapsed into two: cities whose policy environment, defined by the cumulative effect of planning and amenities expenditures, is 'more developed' (maturing and advanced), and those whose policy environment is 'less developed' (retarded, emergent, and progressed).

Variable 3 Perception of policy problems

The data stem from an interview question that reads: 'Mr. Councilman, before talking about your work as a councilman and the work of the Council itself, we would like to ask you about some of the problems facing this community. In your opinion, what are the two most pressing problems here in [city]?' Once individual responses had been coded, they were categorized into four major types: problems relating to services and utilities, urban growth, social and remedial matters, and governmental or intergovernmental affairs. For the purpose of aggregation, the type receiving most individual responses was recorded, provided it received at least 30 per cent of all responses. As a result of this aggregation, only problems related to services and utilities, on the one hand, and growth, on the other hand, appeared frequently enough to warrant analysis. A council was characterized, then, as stressing either one of the other type of these two problem perceptions in its policy map. 49 councils saw growth as problematic, 23 councils perceived services or utilities as problems, and 10 councils fell into the other two categories which were

11 For a detailed discussion of how the policy development typology was constructed and cities assigned to a stage or phase of policy development, see Robert Eyestone and Heinz Eulau, 'City Councils and Policy Outcomes: Developmental Profiles,' in James Q. Wilson, ed., *City Politics and Public Policy* (New York: John Wiley and Sons, 1968), pp. 37–65.

omitted. For convenience of expression, we shall speak only of growth problems and service problems.

Variable 4 Policy images

The data come from an interview question which reads: 'Now, taking the broadest view possible, how do you see [city] in the future? I mean, what kind of a city would you personally like [city] to be in the next twenty-five years or so?' Once individual responses had been coded, it appeared that there were, for all practical purposes, only three types of response into which the individual responses could be aggregated: councils with a residential image or goal for the future, councils with a balanced residential-industrial image, and councils which were split. A council was categorized as having a residential image if 51 per cent or more of the individual councilmen favoured this image and as having a balanced image if 51 per cent or more favoured it. Of the councils, 32 held a residential image and 37 a balanced image. Thirteen of the councils could not be so categorized and were omitted from the analysis.

Variable 5 Policy positions

The data come from an interview question which reads: 'Now, looking toward the future, what one community-wide improvement, in your opinion, does the city 'need most' to be attractive to its citizens?' Once individual responses had been coded, they were categorized into five major types: positions relating to services and utilities, amenities, promotion and development, social and remedial matters, and governmental or inter-governmental affairs. A council was characterized as stressing one or another position on the basis of the highest proportion of responses in one or another of the five categories. As a result of this aggregation, only positions relating to amenities and development appeared often enough to be included in the analysis; 43 of the councils favoured amenities as position, 30 favoured development, and 9 fell into other categories omitted from the analysis.

ALTERNATE DESIGNS FOR POLICY RESEARCH

The task at hand is to ascertain just what kind of analytic design represents the 'best fit' with the theoretical model of the policy process. Moreover, the design should be appropriate for the data that are available. The causal designs implicit in most policy research have in fact been dictated by available data, and to admit this is the better part of wisdom (but a wisdom rarely articulated in policy studies). However, even if data collection precedes rather than follows the formulation of the design, it should specify its criteria of proof in advance.

Causal modelling recommends itself as an analytic design in manipulating non-experimental data, and the more explicit the assumptions associated with different causal models, the more trustworthy are the inferences that can be drawn. On the other hand, this should not lead to a situation where alternate designs making use of the same data are ruled out. There has been a strong tendency to do this, largely because of failure to recognize that the design implicit in causal modelling is, at best, just one truncated design derivative of the classical experimental design. In fact, causal models are only one alternative in adaptations of the classical experimental design to real-world policy analysis. A few examples can demonstrate this.

Research on public policy is severely hampered by obstacles to genuine experimentation that inhere in real-world conditions. If public policy is a political unit's response to challenges from the environment, and if it is to be proved that policy is due to the intervention of policy-makers, research in terms of the classical design would have to deal with at least two political units whose behaviour is to be compared – an experimental unit in which policy-makers intervene much like an experimental stimulus is introduced in the laboratory experiment, and a control unit in which the stimulus is absent. The design would look as shown in figure 1.

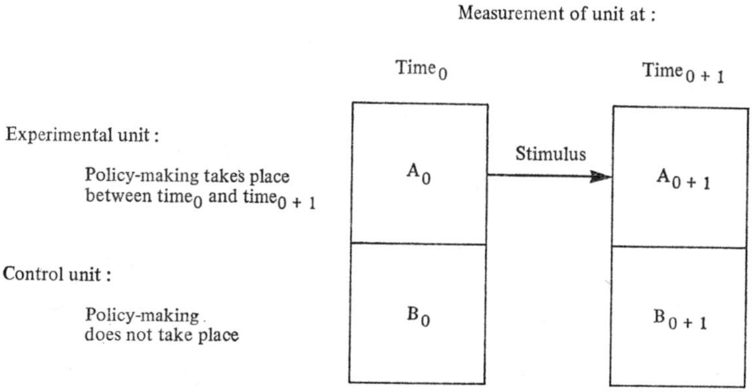

Measurement of unit at :

	Time$_0$	Time$_{0+1}$
Experimental unit : Policy-making takes place between time$_0$ and time$_{0+1}$	A_0	Stimulus → A_{0+1}
Control unit : Policy-making does not take place	B_0	B_{0+1}

Figure 1 The classical experimental design.

If, on measurement, $A_{0+1} - A_0$ is significantly different from $B_{0+1} - B_0$, the result may be taken as proof that the difference in outcomes is due to the intervention of policy-makers.

An experimental design of this kind is extraordinarily difficult to execute in the real world of politics. There is no need to dwell at length on the many obstacles involved in meeting the requirements of this design, such as the random assignment of the experimental stimulus so that any change in the experimental unit's conditions at $time_{0+1}$ can be attributed with confidence to the intervention of policy-makers,[12] or the problem of obtaining a sufficient number of units through time so that the intervention of policy-makers in the experimental units can be observed and measured.

The purpose of reviewing the classical experimental design is not to set up an unduly perfectionist criterion of proof. Rather, it is to show that any research design, no matter how simple, is a derivative of the classical design. This is true even of the design which, in practice, is no design at all and which has only minimal truth value. For instance, the proposition is advanced that there is today a 'generation gap' that is greater than it was yesterday, and an attempt is made to explain the gap in terms of some cause. The design implicit in this proposition is represented in figure 2.

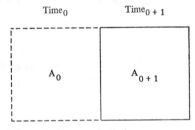

Figure 2 Case study design.

In stating the proposition, the observer 'fills in' the 'before situation' with imagined data (represented by the cell with the broken lines). The design is highly truncated, for there is no control group to make sure that the hypothesized cause is in fact operative and the presumed difference between yesterday and today is not due to extraneous factors.

Suspicious as we rightly are of the highly truncated case study design, it may come as a shock to learn that the design most commonly used in contemporary policy research, though considerably more sophisticated and creditable, is also truncated in that it lacks a 'before situation.' In this design, let us call it the after-correlational design, two units or sets of unit

12   See Ronald A. Fisher, *The Design of Experiments* (Edinburgh: Oliver and Boyd, 1937), pp. 20–4.

are compared by way of cross-tabulation or correlation, and statistical controls are used in order to hold any number of variables constant so that the effect of a test variable can be identified and measured. As figure 3 shows, the two units are compared in terms of a test variable at $time_{0+1}$, but nothing is known about the state of the units at $time_0$. Causal modelling is only a special case of the after-correlational design.

Time$_0$ Time$_{0+1}$

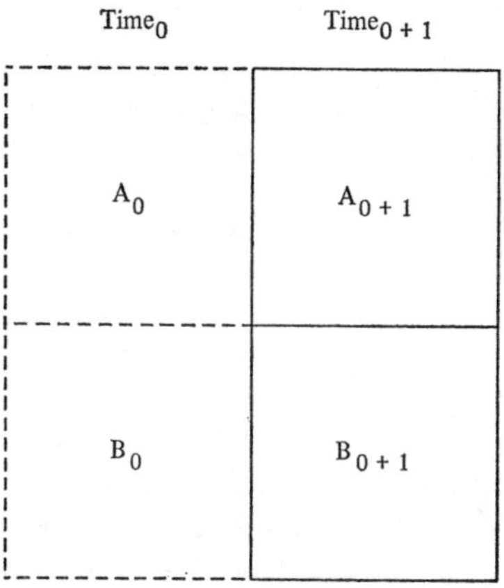

Figure 3 After-correlational design.

There are several other truncated designs, but only one other will be reviewed here because it is relevant to the design to be employed later in this paper. In this design, let us call it the random-panel design (as distinct from the longitudinal-panel design in which the same unit is observed at two points in time),[13] two different units or sets of unit are compared at different times. As shown in figure 4, the assumption is made that if the unit observed at $time_0$ had also been observed at $time_{0+1}$, it would have the characteristics of the second unit actually observed at that time. Vice versa, the assumption is made, of course, that if the unit actually observed at $time_{0+1}$ had been observed 'before' at $time_0$, it would have been identical in properties with the unit actually observed at that time.

13   This is the design usually employed by the University of Michigan's Survey Research Center in its famous election studies. A national random sample of respondents is interviewed prior to the election, and the same sample is interviewed after the election. Changes in response to the same question are assumed to be due to events, including the election itself, in the intervening period. See Angus Campbell, Philip E. Converse, Warren E. Miller, and Donald E. Stokes, *The American Voter* (New York: John Wiley & Sons, 1960), pp. 16–17.

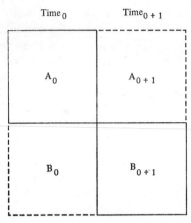

Figure 4 Random panel design.

The juxtaposition of a number of truncated or quasi-experimental designs and the classical experimental design serves to sensitize the analyst to the truth value of the proof involved in his design. None of the quasi-experimental designs satisfy the theoretical assumptions and technical requirements of the classical design. However, because they are not satisfactory from the perfectionist's perspective, it does not follow that they are not creditable; it only follows that the proof of any hypothesis tested by the design is at best partial.

The validity of the propositions advanced earlier cannot, therefore, be proved in any strict sense. The best proof can be harnessed by subjecting the propositions to alternate designs in order to determine whether they predict observations. There are two designs possible with the kind of data that are available. Both designs are predicated on the initial empirical observation of a close and strong relationship between urbanization as the environmental challenge and policy environment as the response. Table 1 presents the data. The strength of the relationship alerts us to two observa-

TABLE 1

Policy development and urbanization (size) in percentages

City size	Retarded N = 10	Emergent N = 15	Progressed N = 27	Mature N = 15	Advanced N = 15
< 10,000	90	80	37	7	0
10 – 50,000	10	20	52	53	47
> 50,000	0	0	11	40	53
$g = 0.82$	100	100	100	100	100

tions. First, it is important to keep in mind that the data used to measure level of urbanization and degree of policy development refer to a time period clearly prior to the time period in which the data for the policy map components were collected. In other words, the possibility that any one of the policy components has an antecedent effect on either urbanization or policy development, or both, can be ruled out, and the relationship between urbanization and policy development need not be subjected to 'control' in order to determine whether it is spurious. And second, the strength of the relationship suggests that there may be a strong 'interaction effect' on observed relationships between each of the two variables and the components of the policy map and among the latter themselves.

Because so much current policy research is cast in the after-correlational design, we shall first examine the fit between the theoretical model derived from our conception of policy and the empirical causal model that can be constructed from the data. We shall then present an alternate design which, by introducing further assumptions about the nature of quasi-experimental designs, may represent a stronger test for the propositions of the theoretical model.

THE CAUSAL MODEL

For the purpose of modelling the relationships among the variables of the theoretical model, we shall treat level of urbanization and state of policy environment as independent variables, problem perceptions and policy images as intervening variables, and policy positions as the dependent variable.

Our first task is to determine the independence of the relationships between the two independent variables and the dependent variable (propositions 4 and 7), for only if these relationships are zero, as hypothesized, can it be assumed that problem perceptions and policy images are truly intervening variables. To test the null hypothesis, we control the relationships by both problem perceptions and policy images. The resulting second-order partial correlation coefficients are 0.07 for the urbanization-position relationship, and −0.03 for the policy environment-position relationship. Clearly, we cannot reject the null hypothesis of no direct relationship between the two independent variables and the dependent variable. Problem perceptions and policy images can be assumed to function as intervening variables.

We shall deal next with the bothersome question of the relationship between the two intervening variables (proposition 8). It will be recalled that the relationship was characterized as indeterminate. Because this relationship has important implications for all the model's linkages, we shall present it as a zero-order relationship, and as a partial relationship controlling successively for the other three variables individually and jointly.

It appears from table 2 that, if uncontrolled, the relationship between problem perception and policy image is quite weak. In other words, there is only a very slight tendency for policy-makers with a balanced (rather than residential) image to perceive growth problems (rather than service-related matters). When the possible reactive effect of policy position on the relationship is partialled out, the relationship becomes somewhat stronger. However, it declines when controlled for the possible effect of policy environment, and it altogether vanishes when controlled for level of urbanization. To explore the relationship further, it was controlled for the possible simultaneous effect of urbanization and policy environment. The result, as table 2 shows, is highly instructive. The relationship continues to remain weak, but significantly changes in direction. It now appears that it is policy-makers with a residential (rather than balanced) image who perceive problems of growth confronting them, while those with a balanced image now perceive service-connected matters as problems. However, the weakness of the relationship confirms our initial proposition that the direction of the relationship is quite indeterminate.

The implications of this indeterminacy require elaboration. One way of doing this is to examine the relationship between problem perception and policy position. If this relationship is controlled for the possible effect of policy image, it appears to be quite strong ($g = -0.61$) as expected (proposition 10). But its direction is confounding. One might have expected that policy-makers perceiving growth problems would advocate further development. This is clearly not the case. Instead, those perceiving growth as a problem take an amenities position, and those perceiving service problems favour further development (hence the negative sign of the coefficient).

We can also shed at least some light on the indeterminate relationship between problem perception and policy image by examining the relationship between policy image and policy position. The relationship is moderately strong ($g = 0.54$) and reveals that those with a residential image take a position favouring amenities, while those with a balanced image favour further development.

If we juxtapose the findings concerning the relationship between problem perception and policy position, on the one hand, and between policy image and policy position, on the other hand, the indeterminacy of the problem perception-image relationship becomes explicable. It

TABLE 2

Zero-order and partial relationships among components of policy map

$g_{PI,PP} = 0.24$	$g_{PP,PoP} = -0.43$	$g_{PI,PoP} = 0.54$
$g_{PI,PP}/PoP = 0.50$	$g_{PP,PoP}/PI = -0.61$	$g_{PI,PoP}/PP = 0.54$
$g_{PI,PP}/PoEn = 0.32$	$g_{PP,PoP}/PoEn = -0.35$	$g_{PI,PoP}/PoEn = 0.54$
$g_{PI,PP}/Urb = 0.04$	$g_{PP,PoP}/Urb = -0.51$	$g_{PI,PoP}/Urb = 0.52$
$g_{PI,PP}/PoEn, Urb = -0.32$	$g_{PP,PoP}/PoEn, Urb = -0.62$	$g_{PI,PoP}/PoEn, Urb = 0.57$
$g_{PI,PP}/PoP, PoEn, Urb = -0.26$	$g_{PP,PoP}/PI, PoEn, Urb = -0.90$	$g_{PI,PoP}/PP, PoEn, Urb = 0.66$

NOTE PI = Policy image; PP = Problem perception; PoP = Policy position; $PoEn$ = Policy environment; Urb = Urbanization.

appears that policy-makers with a residential image perceive problems of growth because these problems probably jeopardize the residential image of the future that they prefer. They therefore take an amenities position that is congenial to their image of the future. Vice versa, those seeing or preferring a balanced city do not perceive problems of growth as threatening and, seeing service problems, favour further development as their position, presumably because further development will maximize the city's resources needed for the effective provision of services. It would seem, therefore, that policy positions are 'doubled-caused' by problem perceptions and policy images. This seems to be a true double-causation relationship and explains, therefore, the weak relationship between problem perceptions and policy images, for this relationship does not need to exist in a model of this kind at all.

However, it would be unduly hasty to accept this interpretation. As both policy images and problem perceptions were assumed to be related to policy environment (propositions 5 and 6), a third-order partial test controlling for policy environment, level of urbanization, and successively for each component of the policy map seemed indicated. Table 2 shows the outcome. Not only is the relationship between policy image and problem perceptions further weakened ($g = -0.26$), but the relationships among the policy map's other components are strengthened ($g = -0.90$ and 0.66, respectively). We infer that the major pathway of environmental conditions and ongoing policies moves, in fact, through the cognitive screen of problem perceptions, although the effect of policy images on policy positions is also strong. The relationship between policy image and problem perceptions is not a crucial link in the chain of causation.

We shall turn now to the independent variables of the model. We have noted already that levels of urbanization and policy environment are not directly related to policy positions. However, both independent variables, being highly related to each other and interdeterminate (proposition 1), are likely to be stimuli for problem perceptions (propositions 3 and 6). The question of causal ordering the effect of the independent on the intervening variables is hardly at issue because the time order of the variables is unambiguous.

Of interest, therefore, is largely the question of which of the two independent variables contributes more to the variance in problem perceptions and policy images. Table 3 presents the zero-order correlation coefficients, the first-order partials (controlling for one of the independent and one of the intervening variables). Some of the consequences of the sequentially introduced controls are noteworthy. In the first place (see table 3, A) a fairly strong positive relationship links level of urbanization

TABLE 3

Zero-order and partial relationships between urbanization, policy environment, and components of policy map

A $g_{Urb,PP} = 0.57$ $g_{Urb,PP}/PoEn = 0.73$ $g_{Urb,PP}/PoEn, PI = 0.64$	C $g_{PoEn,PP} = 0.08$ $g_{PoEn,PP}/Urb = -0.32$ $g_{PoEn,PP}/Urb, PI = -0.53$
B $g_{Urb,PI} = 0.58$ $g_{Urb,PI}/PoEn = 0.30$ $g_{Urb,PI}/PoEn, PP = 0.10$	D $g_{PoEn,PI} = 0.81$ $g_{PoEn,PI}/Urb = 0.75$ $g_{PoEn,PI}/Urb, PP = 0.80$

and problem perceptions and withstands all controls (in support of proposition 2). The more urbanized the environment, i.e., the more intense environmental challenges, the more likely will policy-makers perceive problems connected with growth. Second, (see table 3, B), the relationship between urbanization and policy image, weak in the first place, almost vanishes when it is controlled (in support of part of proposition 3). Third, (see table 3, D) the state of the policy environment has a strong effect on the formulation of policy images and withstands successive controls(in support of proposition 6). In other words, the more mature or advanced the policy environment, the more do policy-makers hold a balanced image of the city's future. In entertaining policy goals, it seems, policy-makers do not entertain 'far-out' views. Finally (see table 3, C), and this is perhaps the most interesting finding, the relationship between policy environment and problem perceptions, evidently non-existent when uncontrolled, grows increasingly stronger as it is controlled by urbanization and policy image. As suggested in proposition 7, this relationship is likely to vary with the degree of equilibrium in the relationship between environmental challenges and policy environment. The negative coefficients show that the less mature or the less advanced the policy environment, the more are policy-makers likely to perceive problems related to growth.

This result, however, pinpoints a problem that the causal model cannot successfully tackle. We can best state the problem in the form of a syllogism that reflects the data, as follows:

The more urbanized the environment, the more developed is the policy environment ($g = 0.80$).

The more urbanized the environment, the more are problems related to growth perceived ($g = 0.64$).

The more developed the policy environment, the more are problems related to growth perceived.

The data, however, show that the logical conclusion derived from the premises is not empirically viable. In fact, the opposite is true: the less developed the policy environment, the more are problems of growth at policy-makers' focus of attention ($g = -0.53$). It would seem, therefore, that there is a condition present in the relationship between urbanization and policy environment that eludes the causal model. Proposition 7 suggested that this condition may be the degree of equilibrium in the relationship. The equilibrium condition is concealed in the causal model and can only be ascertained by a design that manipulates the data in a different way. As we shall see in the next section, there are a number of cities which are, in fact, in disequilibrium – those that are highly urbanized but whose policy environment is less developed than one should expect from an equilibrium point of view.

Figure 5 summarizes all the relationships obtained by partial correlation analysis. It is of the utmost importance to emphasize the tentative nature of the results because 'all other things' are probably not equal, and relevant error terms are probaly not uncorrelated. Determining causal directions under these conditions is likely to be controversial. While in the present model there is no doubt as to the true independence and priority of the urbanization and policy environment variables, and while direct relationships between them and the dependent variable – policy position – probably would not exist even if additional variables were introduced, the flow of causation through the two intervening variables is not self-evident. For instance, are the effects of urbanization or policy environment on the taking of policy positions mediated more through policy images or problem perceptions? To answer this question, we can compare the predictions that are possible with the actual results that were obtained for the intermediate links of the causal sequence.

If problem perceptions or policy images are truly intervening between the independent and the dependent variables, we should predict that the relationship between the independent variable x and the dependent variable y equals the product of the correlations between each and the intervening variable z. In other words, we predict that $r_{xy} = (r_{xz})$. (r_{zy}). Table 4 presents the calculations.

Comparison of the predicted and actual outcomes shows that, while far from perfect, the fit is excellent for the chain in which urbanization and policy positions are linked by problem perceptions and good for the chain that runs through policy images. The fit is fair for the chain that links policy environment to policy positions through policy images so that we need not reject it. But it is poor for the chain from policy environment to policy positions through problem perceptions. We con-

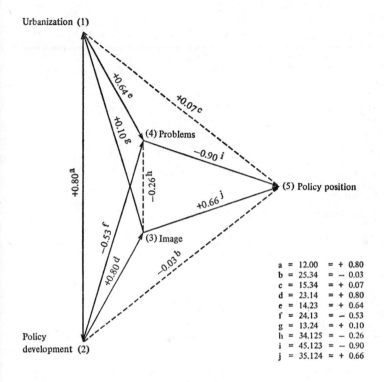

a = 12.00 = + 0.80
b = 25.34 = − 0.03
c = 15.34 = + 0.07
d = 23.14 = + 0.80
e = 14.23 = + 0.64
f = 24.13 = − 0.53
g = 13.24 = + 0.10
h = 34.125 = − 0.26
i = 45.123 = − 0.90
j = 35.124 = + 0.66

Code for interpreting direction of coefficients:

Image − problem perception:
(+) = Balance-growth or residential-service
(−) = Balance-service or residential-growth

Image − policy position:
(+) = Balance-development or residential-amenities
(−) = Balance-amenities or residential-development

Problem perception − policy position:
(+) = Growth-development or service-amenities
(−) = Growth-amenities or service-development

Figure 5 Causal model of policy process.

clude, therefore, that policy positions are primarily taken in response to the perceptions of problems that stem from environmental challenges, and are secondarily influenced by policy images weakly related to the nature of environmental challenges (urbanization), but strongly to on-going policies (policy environment). We can reject the assumption that

TABLE 4

Test of models of policy process

		Predicted	Actual	Fit
1	Urbanization x $\downarrow$0.57 Problem perception z $\downarrow$0.42 Policy position y	$r_{xy} = 0.24$	$=0.25$	Excellent
2	Urbanization x $\downarrow$0.58 Policy image z $\downarrow$0.54 Policy position y	$r_{xy} = 0.31$	$=0.25$	Good
3	Policy environment x $\downarrow$0.08 Problem perception z $\downarrow$0.42 Policy position y	$r_{xy} = 0.03$	$=0.29$	Poor
4	Policy environment x $\downarrow$0.81 Policy image z $\downarrow$0.54 Policy position y	$r_{xy} = 0.44$	$=0.29$	Fair

NOTE: Predictions are based on uncontrolled correlations between variables.

ongoing policies have an effect on policy position through the intervention of problem perceptions.

A HYPOTHETICAL-LONGITUDINAL DESIGN

Although the causal model, if cautiously interpreted, fits the theoretical
model of the policy process quite well and may be accepted as constituting
some explanation, it lacks longitudinal depth. Assumptions were made
about the time ordering of the relationships between each of the two independent variables and the two intervening variables, but not about any
time ordering between the two independent variables alone. They were
treated as synchronic, although it was suggested that the reciprocal relationship between them could alternately be one of equilibrium and disequilibrium. But if this assumption is made, it follows that the relationship
at any one point in time is only a special case of 'alternating asymmetries'
at different points in time.[14] Is there a design, then, appropriate to treating
the data in such a way that inferences can be made from the observed

14   See Morris Rosenberg, *The Logic of Survey Research* (New York: Basic
     Books, 1968), pp. 8–9.

relationship between the independent variables that is synchronic to hypothetical relationships that are diachronic?

One of the drawbacks of the causal model cast in the after-correlational design is that it disguises original relationships in the data among
the variables of the model. For instance, as shown in table 1, the relationship between level of urbanization (measured by city size) and the state
of the policy environment is so strong from the correlational perspective
that we are prone to ignore the cases that deviate from the regression line.
In order to pinpoint these deviant cases more sharply, table 5 presents the

TABLE 5

Policy environment and urbanization (size), variables dichotomized

		Size dichotomized:	
		Less urban < 17,000 N = 41	More urban > 17,000 N = 41
Development dichotomized:			
Retarded, emergent, progressed	Less (N = 52)	A 35	B 17
Mature, advanced	More (N = 30)	C 6	D 24

cross-tabulation of the data in bivariate form. It shows that we are dealing
with two kinds of deviant situations. First, in cell c we note six cases of
cities which are 'more developed' in spite of limited environmental challenges. These cases are 'truly deviant.' They cannot be accounted for by
the contingent relationship between urbanization and policy environment.
In other words, the observed outcome can be attributed simply to policy-
makers' purposes, preferences, and efforts.

But this is not possible with the seventeen cases in cell b. Although
they are statistically deviant, they could be considered truly deviant only
if one were to assume that the relationship between urbanization and
policy environment is invariably in equilibrium. But this is a quite unrealistic assumption. If we conceive of a reciprocal relationship as a succession
of 'alternating asymmetries,' it is much more realistic to assume that there
is likely to be a lag between stimulus and response, that as urbanization

proceeds and challenges the policy-maker, an appropriate response is not immediately forthcoming. This reasonable assumption allows us to construct a dynamic model of the policy process. 1 / As long as environmental challenges are weak (the city is small, les urbanized), the policy environment is 'less developed' – challenge and response are, indeed, in equilibrium. 2 / As the city grows and environmental challenges become urgent (the city is now large, more urbanized), there is an initial lag in policy response – the policy environment remains 'less developed' so that challenge and response are in disequilibrium. 3 / As the challenges from the environment are not likely to abate, and as ongoing policies are not appropriate, policy-makers as purposive actors will, sooner or later, adopt positions that re-establish the equilibrium between urbanization and policy environment.

This transformation of the static into a dynamic model of the relationship between environmental conditions and the policy environment suggests that the seventeen cases in cell B cannot be considered truly deviant. They represent situations that can be expected to occur 'normally' in the sequence of events that link past and future. In searching for a design appropriate to the analysis of data that are synchronic but which, nonetheless, should be interpreted diachronically, it is clearly advantageous to make a number of assumptions that combine familiar assumptions made for the after-correlational design with assumptions made for the random-panel design, as follows:

1   As in the panel design, the less urbanized, less developed cities are assumed to be 'control groups.' Having not been exposed to the stimulus of urbanization, they have no opportunity to respond. The two sets of cities that are more urbanized (whether less or more developed) are assumed to be experimental groups. Both have been exposed to the stimulus of urbanization.

2   As in the panel design, it is assumed that if both experimental group cities had been observed at an earlier time, they would have looked like the control group cities; or the second experimental group of cities (more urbanized, more developed) would have looked like the first experimental group (more urbanized, less developed) at an earlier time. A corollary assumption is that if it were possible to observe the control group cities at a later time, after more urbanization has taken place, they would in sequence look like the two experimental group cities.

3   As in the after-correlational design, it is assumed that the two experimental group cities are similar in all respects except for the differences in policy environment; the control group and the first experimental group cities are assumed to be similar in all respects except for the difference in level of urbanization.

4   As in the after-correlational design, the difference in outcome (policy environment) between the two experimental group cities is assumed to be due to a third factor (or several other factors) which is the test variable – in our case the components of the policy map, and especially the relationships among these components themselves.

Although the set of assumptions made in constructing the design is complex, it merely combines a number of assumptions now routinely made in quasi-experimental designs for the analysis of real-world data. What the design shows is that once latent assumptions are made explicit, comparison of evidently static situations can be used to test hypotheses about change in the real world for which direct data are not available. Although the three sets of cities being compared are actually observed at the same point in historical time, longitudinal assumptions derived from adaptations of the classical experimental design serve to infuse an element of dynamic interpretation into comparative analysis – a recognition of the fact that comparative statics is, indeed, a special case of dynamics.

As figure 6 shows, the design permits three kinds of comparison by way of test variables. 1 / comparison of A_0 and B_{0+1}; 2 / comparison of A_0 and C_{0+2}; and 3 / comparison of B_{0+1} and C_{0+2}. As we postulate that urbanization is a necessary but not sufficient condition for policy change, the comparison between A_0 and C_{0+2} is not enlightening for, while the two situations can be expected to differ significantly on test variables, we cannot say whether the difference in the policy environment is due to the test factors or change in urbanization. Moreover, both situations are in equilibrium. Of the other two comparisons that are possible, that between

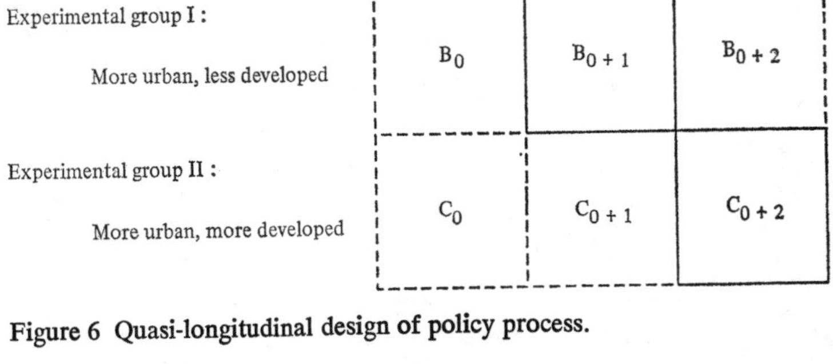

	Time $_0$	Time $_{0+1}$	Time $_{0+2}$
Control group: Less urban, less developed	A_0	A_{0+1}	A_{0+2}
Experimental group I: More urban, less developed	B_0	B_{0+1}	B_{0+2}
Experimental group II: More urban, more developed	C_0	C_{0+1}	C_{0+2}

Figure 6 Quasi-longitudinal design of policy process.

84 Heinz Eulau

A_0 and B_{0+1} serves as a control test. As no change in policy environment is observed, yet there is a change in urbanization, it follows that increased urbanization is not sufficient to bring about a change in policies. The comparison between B_{0+1} and C_{0+2} is the most relevant because it is the appropriate test for rejecting the null hypothesis that a change in the policy environment is not due to purposive action.

The research question asked is why it is that in situation B_{0+1} the policy environment has not changed in spite of a change in the necessary condition for such change, i.e., increased urbanization. Our hypothesis is, of course, that policy change has not taken place because of policy positions taken by policy-makers that impede it.

QUASI-LONGITUDINAL ANALYSIS

The data will be analysed within the constraints of the quasi-longitudinal design in three ways: first, as marginal distributions; second, as conjunctive patterns; and third, as correlations.

1   *Marginal analysis*

Table 6 shows the marginal distributions of the councils on the three components of the policy map. They will be treated as if the data were genuinely longitudinal. From this perspective, table 6 is highly informative.

First, growth is experienced as a problem by majorities of the councils in all three periods, but it is most felt in $time_{0+1}$ when the 'eco-policy system' (as we shall call the relationship between urbanization and policy environment) is in disequilibrium. In the third period, when there has been an appropriate policy response to restore the equilibrium, the urgency

TABLE 6

Distribution of councils on policy map components by states of eco-policy system in percentages

Components of policy map	$Time_0$ Less urban, less developed N = 27	$Time_{0+1}$ More urban, less developed N = 14	$Time_{0+2}$ More urban, more developed N = 18
Growth is problem	56	93	78
Development is position	37	36	56
Balance is image	33	50	89
Problem-position differential	19	57	22

of problems connected with growth is somewhat reduced, but these problems continue to concern policy-makers.

Second, in view of the prominence of growth problems at $time_{0+1}$, it is revealing that so few councils (36 per cent) at that time take policy positions in favour of development. In fact, they do not differ at all from $time_0$. Only in the third period, when the eco-policy system is again in equilibrium, do a majority of councils take positions that are presumably capable of coping with the problems of growth. It may be noted that a discrepancy between perceiving growth as a problem and taking pro-development positions also occurs in the equilibrium situations at $time_0$ and $time_{0+2}$, but it is considerably less than in the disequilibrium state at $time_{0+1}$ (19 and 22 per cent, respectively, versus 57 per cent). The need for services and not growth-related problems, the earlier causal analysis has shown, makes for policy positions favouring development. But as service problems are not seen as critical at $time_{0+1}$, it becomes understandable why positions preferring amenities are more widely held in this period by comparison with the third period.

Third, as table 6 shows, policy images change dramatically and systematically through time. While at $time_0$ only 33 per cent of the councils envisage a balanced future for their cities, 39 per cent do so at $time_{0+2}$. Of particular interest, however, is the fact that at $time_{0+1}$, when the eco-policy system is in disequilibrium, the councils are exactly split, with half holding an image of a balanced, and another half holding an image of a residential, future. In the disequilibrium situation, councils tend to behave quite randomly. For instance, councils do not unequivocally adopt policy positions in favour of development, in spite of the fact that they are keenly aware of problems connected with growth. These problems, it would seem, are looked upon as nuisances that can be wished away by pursuing amenities policies, and if problems connected with service are not perceived, further development is an option that does not enter the policy map.

Although we cannot prove, with the data at hand, that the policy environment as a response to the challenge of urbanization is facilitated or impeded by the policy map, we can look at the data as if they could be used as tests, provided we read them cautiously. In treating the same data in this hypothetical manner (as if the policy map components were the independent variables and the eco-policy system the dependent variable), we should read table 7 as follows. For instance, while of the councils with a residential image 67 per cent are 'found' at $time_0$ (in the less urbanized, less developed state of the eco-policy system), of those holding a balanced image 50 per cent are 'found' at $time_{0+2}$ (when the system

TABLE 7

Distribution of councils on states of eco-policy system by policy map components
in percentages

	Policy map components					
	Image		Problem		Position	
Eco-policy system	Balanced $N = 32$	Residential $N = 27$	Growth $N = 42$	Services $N = 17$	Developed $N = 25$	Amenities $N = 34$
$Time_0$	28	67	36	71	40	50
$Time_{0+1}$	22	26	31	5	20	26
$Time_{0+2}$	50	7	33	24	40	24
	100	100	100	100	100	100
	$g = -0.69$		$g = -0.45$		$g = -0.24$	

is more urban, more developed); and so on. If we read the data in this
way, it is evident that the image component of the policy map discriminates most strongly among the three states or periods of the eco-policy
system ($g = -0.69$), that problem perceptions discriminate moderately
($g = -0.45$), and that policy positions discriminate very little ($g =
-0.24$). This is not surprising; as we noted in the causal model (figure 5),
neither urbanization nor policy environment as separate variables have a
direct effect on policy positions. As the causal model demonstrated, the
perception of problems and policy images are critical intervening variables that link reality to policy positions. But the marginal distributions
also suggest that the topography of the policy map may be quite different
at different periods or in different states of the eco-policy system. We shall
pursue this theme further by looking next at the conjunctive patterns in
the policy map that can be observed at different time periods.

2   Conjunctive patterns

The data can be looked at in terms of the particular combinations formed
by the components of the policy map. These conjunctive patterns probably constitute the most 'realistic' representations of the policy maps as
'wholes.' Eight such patterns are possible, and our interest is in the
frequency of particular patterns at different points in time or in different
states of the eco-policy system. Table 8 presents the data.

It appears from table 8, that some conjunctive patterns occur only
at $time_0$, that some occur mainly at $time_0$ and time $_{0+1}$, and that some
occur in all three periods, although dominantly at $time_{0+2}$. One pattern
(BSA) does not occur at all. Councils with a residential image which

TABLE 8

Distribution of councils by conjunctive patterns of policy map components in three states of eco-policy system in percentages

Conjunctive patterns	$Time_0$	$Time_{0+1}$	$Time_{0+2}$	Total
RSD (N = 3)	100	0	0	100
RSA (N = 7)	100	0	0	100
RGD (N = 4)	50	25	25	100
RGA (N = 13)	46	46	8	100
BGD (N = 11)	27	27	46	100
BGA (N = 14)	29	21	50	100
BSD (N = 7)	14	29	57	100
BSA (N = 0)	0	0	0	100

NOTE R = Residential image; S = Service problems; A = Amenities position; B = Balanced image; G = Growth problems; D = Development position.

perceive service problems are exclusively found at $time_0$, regardless of their positions on policy. However, when councils with a residential image experience growth problems, they are not only found at $time_0$ but also at $time_{0+1}$ when the eco-policy system is in disequilibrium. Again, policy positions seem to make little difference. As a balanced image is adopted but problems of growth continue to be experienced, councils are now more often found at $time_{0+1}$ and time $_{0+2}$, but especially in the later period. When a balanced image is combined with a recognition of service as a problem and a pro-development position is taken, the majority of councils has reached the state of the eco-policy system that is characteristic of the last time period, although some remain in the earlier states as well. While the configuration of patterns is by no means monotonic, it is far from random (yielding a gamma coefficient of 0.56). Above all it gives more detailed insight than do the marginal distributions into why it is that some councils experience disequilibrium in their eco-policy system, i.e., why it is that the policy environment is not in step with the challenges of the urbanizing environment and all that urbanization implies. These are evidently councils in which, because residential images prevail, growth is experienced not as a problem to be handled by appropriate policies, but as a problem that is unwelcome. However, when a balanced image comes to be accepted, policies to cope with growth problems are adopted and, in due time, the eco-policy system regains equilibrium.

3 Correlation analysis

It remains to look at the transformation through time of the relationships among the components of the policy map. It is likely that at different times

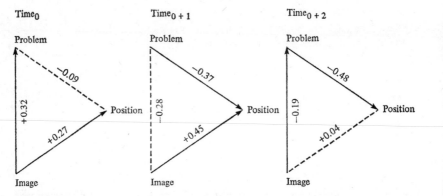

Figure 7 Structure of policy map in three states of eco-policy system.

one or the other component is more relevant to the adoption of a particular policy position. Moreover, as the relationships among policy map
components are more or less interdependent, it is desirable to observe
the flow of the effects of one component on the other. Figure 7 presents
the models using the phi coefficient.[15]

The diagrams suggest that the relationships among map components
not only assume different values at different times, but that the map itself
seems to undergo structural change. At $time_0$, when the challenges of
urbanization are weak and the policy environment is relatively little
developed, councils perceiving growth as a problem tend to entertain a
balanced image of their city's future and favour development, while
councils perceiving service-connected problems tend to hold a residential
image and favour amenities as their policy positions (phi = 0.32). The
perception of problems is unrelated to policy positions (phi= −0.09). In
fact, of course, and whatever the internal structure of the policy map, we
know that the policy environment is little developed – ongoing policies,
compared with those at later periods, do not particularly stress either
development or amenities. Available resources are invested in meeting the
minimal service needs of these communities. The policy environment is
static and in equilibrium with the urban condition.

At $time_{0+1}$, as the challenges of urbanization come to be felt, the

15   We opt here for the phi measure because it is not subject to a difficulty arising
     in gamma for a 2-by-2 tables, also known as Yule's Q. For, in the case of the
     latter, if one of the cells vanishes, the measure appears as unity (+1 or −1) in
     spite of an imperfect relationship between the variables. Phi, like Q, is a
     symmetric measure and may be interpreted as the Pearson r. Its values are
     likely to be less than those of Q. Hence the phi and gamma values are not
     directly comparable.

structure of the map changes drastically. Councils perceiving problems of growth now tend to hold a residential image (phi = −0.28), a rather anomalous behaviour, and they tend to favour amenities policies. This is, of course, the *RGA* pattern observed in table 8 that seems to be so characteristic of this period. The anomaly may be due to the effect that policy images seem to have in $time_{0+1}$. Although problems are seen quite realistically, policy images tend to have a fairly strong effect on the policy positions that are taken (phi = 0.45). On the other hand, councils perceiving service problems now have a balanced image. But, more significantly, there is now a linkage between problem perceptions and policy positions. Councils seeing growth problems still favour amenities positions, while councils perceiving service problems advocate further development (phi = −0.37).

An anomalous situation is unlikely to persist. Sooner or later the policy map will be restructured to fit the exigencies of urbanization. Our quasi-longitudinal design permits us to observe how the policy map is restructured. Most notable at $time_{0+2}$ is the fact that the relationship between policy images and policy positions vanishes (phi = 0.04), while the relationship between problem perceptions and policy positions becomes stronger (phi = −0.48). Moreover, the relationship between problem perceptions and images is also almost vanishing (phi = −0.19). The fact that two of the relationships among map components more or less disappear is due, of course, to the emergence of balanced images in council policy maps in this state of the eco-policy system. As we saw in table 6, sixteen of the eighteen councils (89 per cent) entertain an image of balance at $time_{0+2}$. As a result, there is little room for images to discriminate among policy positions or problem perceptions. And, as a further result, it is the perception of problems that now almost alone influences the policy positions that are taken. Councils seeing service-connected problems favour development policies, presumably to mobilize the resources needed to pay for swelling demands for such services in the wake of increased urbanization; while councils experiencing the pangs of growth tend to favour amenities, presumably to offset the unpleasantness of growing urbanization. The policy environment at this time is, not unexpectedly, in congruence with the policy map. By operational definition, it is in an environment in which ongoing policies are geared to both development and amenities policies. In any case, the policy map no longer blocks, as it did at $time_{0+1}$, the taking of positions congenial to the emergence of a policy environment that is in equilibrium with the challenges stemming from heightened urbanization.

If we say that not only the values in the relationships among policy map components change but that the structure of the map itself changes, we mean, of course, that different models define the linkages between the map's points. To determine the adequacy of alternate models, table 9 presents predicted and actual results for the following three models of three-variable relationships (figure 8).

Table 9 shows that the dual effect model best characterizes the policy-map structure at $time_0$. Policy images, it seems, have a pervasive effect on the structure of the map, influencing both the perception of problems and the positions that are taken. The fit of prediction and result is only fair, but it is adequate enough to retain the model. At $time_{0+1}$, the effect of the

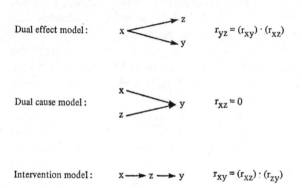

Dual effect model: x z $r_{yz} = (r_{xy}) \cdot (r_{xz})$
                               y

Dual cause model: x y $r_{xz} = 0$
                               z

Intervention model: $x \longrightarrow z \longrightarrow y$ $r_{xy} = (r_{xz}) : (r_{zy})$

Figure 8 Three models of three variable relationships.

TABLE 9

Predicted and actual relationships between policy map components in alternate models during three states of eco-policy system

	Predicted	Actual	Fit
DUAL EFFECT MODEL AT TIME			
0	0.08	−0.09	Fair
0 + 1	−0.13	−0.37	Poor
0 + 2	−0.00	−0.48	Poor
DUAL CAUSE MODEL AT TIME			
0	−0.02	0.32	Poor
0 + 1	−0.17	−0.28	Good
0 + 2	−0.02	−0.19	Fair
INTERVENTION MODEL AT TIME			
0	−0.03	0.27	Poor
0 + 1	−0.10	0.45	Poor
0 + 2	0.09	0.04	Very good

TABLE 10

Predictive model of policy development

	Observations on policy map at		
	$Time_0$	$Time_{0+1}$	$Time_{0+2}$
Policy image	Residential	Ambivalent	Balanced
Problem perception	Services	Growth	Services and growth
Policy position	Amenities	Amenities	Development and amenities
Predicted eco-policy state	Less urban, less developed	More urban less developed	More urban, more developed

policy image on policy positions is complemented by a relatively independent effect of problem perceptions, as predicted in the dual cause
model. In the last period, insofar as policy images are still relevant, their
effect is totally mediated through the intervention of problem perceptions.
They have no independent effect on policy positions which are strongly
determined by problem perceptions. The fit of the intervention model at
$time_{0+2}$ is very good.

Although it has been repeatedly pointed out that the data cannot be
used to test the validity of the inferences made about the course of policy
through historical time, it appears that comparative cross-sectional data
can be analysed by way of a post-facto, quasi-longitudinal design, and
that this analysis yields a model of policy which is not only plausible, but
which is in principle testable in a genuine natural-state experiment if
appropriate data are collected at the proper time. We can summarize the
model as in table 10.

CONCLUSION

Policy as a response to challenges from the physical and social environment is an emergent property of politics contingent on political behaviour
that is, in part, purposive but that, in part, is not unrelated to changing
environmental conditions. Because political behaviour is imbued with
purposes that are its goals or ends-in-view, policy inferred from behavioural patterns may, at times, be at odds with environmental requirements for appropriate responses. The resultant disequilibrium in the relationship between environment and policy is resolved as the configuration
of relevant orientations – what we have termed the policy map – under-
goes structural change. This change, it appears, is largely due to cognitive

adjustments to environmental pressures. It serves to ease behavioural rigidities in the relationship between policy and environment so that a satisfactory equilibrium can be re-established. Put differently, 'what is' and 'what ought to be' are dimensions of political behaviour which constitute an interlocking series of events through time. In this moving manifold of events, policy emerges as a resultant of causal and purposive forcings which are themselves interrelated in ways that seem commensurate with ongoing policies – what we have termed the policy environment.

REFERENCES

CAMPBELL, ANGUS, PHILIP E. CONVERSE, WARREN E. MILLER, and DONALD E. STOKES *The American Voter*. New York: John Wiley & Sons, 1960.
DYE, THOMAS R. *Politics, Economics, and the Public*: *Policy Outcomes in the American States*. Chicago: Rand McNally, 1966.
EASTON, DAVID *A Framework for Political Analysis*. Englewood Cliffs, NJ: Prentice-Hall, 1965.
EULAU, HEINZ and ROBERT EYESTONE 'Policy Maps of City Councils and Policy Outcomes: A Developmental Analysis,' *American Political Science Review*, 62, 1 (March 1968), pp. 124–43.
EYESTONE, ROBERT and HEINZ EULAU 'City Councils and Policy Outcomes: Developmental Profiles,' in James Q. Wilson, ed. *City Politics and Public Policy*. New York: John Wiley & Sons, 1968.
FISHER, RONALD A. *The Design of Experiments*. Edinburgh: Oliver and Boyd, 1937.
JACOB, HERBERT and MICHAEL LIPSKY 'Outputs, Structure, and Power: An Assessment of Changes in the Study of State and Local Politics,' in Marion D. Irish, *Political Science: Advance of the Discipline*. Englewood Cliffs, NJ: Prentice-Hall, 1968. Also published in *Journal of Politics*, 30, 2 (May 1968), pp. 510–38.
HADDEN, JEFFREY and EDGAR F. BORGATTA *American Cities*: *Their Social Characteristics*. Chicago: Rand McNally, 1965.
LINDBLOM, CHARLES E. *The Intelligence of Democracy*. New York: Free Press, 1965.
PREWITT, KENNETH and HEINZ EULAU 'Political Matrix and Political Representation: Prolegomenon to a New Departure from an Old Problem,' *American Political Science Review*, 63, 2 (June 1969), pp. 427–41.
ROSENBERG, MORRIS *The Logic of Survey Research*. New York: Basic Books, 1968.
SALISBURY, ROBERT H. 'The Analysis of Public Policy: A Search for Theories and Roles,' in Austin Ranney, ed. *Political Science and Public Policy*. Chicago: Markham, 1968.

SHARKANSKY, IRA *The Politics of Taxing and Spending*, Indianapolis: Bobbs-Merrill Company, 1969.
STOUFFER, SAMUEL A. 'Some Observations on Study Design,' in Samuel A. Stouffer, ed. *Social Research to Test Ideas*. New York: Free Press, 1962.
WILDAVSKY, AARON *The Politics of the Budgetary Process*. Boston: Little, Brown, 1964.

JERZY J.WIATR

Experiments in self-government: the Polish case

The main object of this essay is to examine the implications – both for the theory of political science and for the strategy of economic and political development – of some so-called 'experiments,' which have been conducted in Poland since the late 1950s.

1   IN VIVO EXPERIMENTS IN POLITICAL SCIENCE

In the pursuit of objectivity in political research we turn to experimentation with the hope that it will enable us to narrow the gap between the natural and the social sciences. The study of personality characteristics and small-group dynamics profits considerably from the systematic application of controlled experiments, but beyond individual and social psychology 'the controlled or laboratory experiment ... serves as a model with which other techniques can be compared and as a goal toward which development of these techniques should strive.'[1]

   An application of laboratory experiments to the study of politics consists of introducing 'political variables,' such as, for example, political information, and studying the impact of such variables on small group behaviour. It can contribute to our knowledge of small groups in politics but cannot provide information on the functioning of larger political units. This inevitable limitation of laboratory experiments makes in vivo

1   Hanan G. Selvin, *The Effects of Leadership* (Glencoe. 1960), p. 52

experiments particularly important. In practice, however, experiments in vivo confront an experimenter with several difficulties, which – if not resolved – result in considerable departures from the accepted standards of experimentation.

The aim of experimentation is to create different conditions for at least two similar units of observation by introducing in some of them a variable whose impact we want to analyse. In natural political situations (experiments in vivo) this means that we purposefully create less favourable conditions in some units of observation, which necessarily are also units of practical political action. Hartmann's experiment in which he compared the effect of a 'logical' appeal for socialism with that of an 'emotional' appeal, is a good example. The experimenter was himself a Socialist candidate in a constituency where Socialists never won. Therefore, the purely political risks were minimized by the fact that even the 'stronger' electoral approach (using emotional approach in all wards, rather than in only four of them) hardly could bring about a Socialistic victory. Murphy noted that it is not news, of course, that an emotional appeal is more effective than a rational one, but it is a scientific event of significance when such a common assumption is put to the test of a deliberately devised experiment having to do with realistic behaviour of run-of-the-mill adults in a complex social situation.[2] It is not news that emotional appeal is more effective, but it would be news if a candidate with reasonably good chances of victory undertook a similar experiment to test the effectiveness of both techniques.

If an experimenter does not know which technique is best, he should test each of them, preferably in vivo and preferably in a systematically controlled experiment. It is a pity that the latter has been used so rarely by either political scientists or practical politicians. Because of this failure we must be satisfied, as in the case reported here, with quasi-experiments.

II   THE NOWY SACZ 'EXPERIMENT': A CASE STUDY

In 1957 local authorities in one of the 321 Polish counties were given permission to start an experimental policy of regional economic development. Their prerogatives were extended and financial resources increased.

2   Murphy, G., L.B. Murphy, and T.M. Newcomb, *Experimental Social Psychology: An Interpretation of Research upon Socialization of the Individual* (New York 1937). The technique and results of the experiment are reported in G.W. Hartmann, 'A Field experiment on the Comparative Effectiveness of "Emotional" and "Rational" Political Leaflets in Determining Election Results,' *Journal of Abnormal and Social Psychology*, 31, 1 (April-June

After the experiment had brought positive results, the national parliament passed a law by which it increased the prerogatives of all local county authorities, more or less after the pattern of the 'experimental' county. It was the first case of a field experiment being conducted in Poland before a law was amended by parliament. From the point of view of economic development and regional planning the experiment amounted to a testing of the alternative politics of economic growth. Before discussing its theoretical and methodological implications let us concern ourselves with the background, history, and aftermath of the Nowy Sacz experiment.

The political background of the Nowy Sacz experiment lies in the political changes of 1956 which resulted in considerable democratization of the state apparatus. Public discussion in the press indicated that greater local autonomy would be considered one of the practical avenues to democratization. Since the prerogatives of the local councils had been defined in the Parliamentary Act of 1954, public discussion indicated the need of parliamentary revision of the act, and proposals to that effect were made in the mass media. However, the local authorities of Nowy Sacz were the first, and for the time being the only ones, who were ready to put these proposals to a test before they became part of the new law. On 3 November 1957 the main newspaper of the Polish United Workers' party, *Trybuna Ludu*, published the 'Manifesto' of the Economic Council of Nowy Sacz in which the county called for experimental revision of the centralist system of planning and economic policy. Why Nowy Sacz? To answer this question tentatively, one has to inquire into the conditions prevailing in Nowy Sacz county on the eve of the experiment.[3]

Nowy Sacz is an underdeveloped county in the southern part of Poland in Kraków province. In 1957 its population was 170,000, 80 per cent of whom lived in villages: Local industry such as the Railway Repair Works and some smaller factories employed 5,000 workers. Craft industries, which before the second world war employed almost 20 per cent of the labour of the county, were in the depths of a depression. Reserves

1936), 99–114; see also John Madge, *The Tools of Social Science* (Garden City 1965), pp. 302–3 for a short summary.

3   The present discussion is based on an unpublished paper by my collaborators, Zygmunt Kacpura and Jacek Tarkowski, 'Experiment Sadecki' (1969, in Polish) as well as on documents and other information on the Nowy Sacz experiment collected by them during a case study in Nowy Sacz county. I gratefully acknowledge their help in collecting information on the Nowy Sacz experiment as well as their contribution to the discussion of its implications. Zygmunt Kacpura's working paper on 'Socio-economic experiments in sociological literature' (unpublished, in Polish, 1970) served also as a valuable source of bibliographic references and data inventory .

of the labour force in the countryside were estimated at 20,000, with 7,500 in the towns. Agriculture was poorly developed, partly because of the low quality of the soil and partly because of a rigid policy of agricultural development which did not take into consideration that Nowy Sacz county had been traditionally an area of pomiculture. One of the results of this was that the local fruit manufacturers could use only a quarter of the total fruit production of the county. Cattle-raising was below the possible level mostly because governmental policy favoured pig-raising. In general, one could say that in spite of progress from 1945 to 1956 Nowy Sacz was an underdeveloped county which had profited less from the years of rapid industrialization than most of the other Polish counties.

Nowy Sacz, however, was not only an underdeveloped county, but it was also a county with a strong tradition of independent local initiative. One of the first rural counties to have its own artistic theatre before first world war, it was also a homeland of a culturally sophisticated and politically active local elite. Two high schools of the Nowy Sacz town, one of them one hundred and fifty years old, helped to create a nucleus of locally educated modernizers. Among them the feeling of togetherness was stronger than in most of the other counties; people who came from Nowy Sacz and were educated there continued to maintain close contacts with the life of the county even after living and working in the other parts of Poland for many years. There was also a workers' milieu with strong traditions of trade union and party activity. These factors explain why the dissatisfaction with the old status quo resulted in initiatives for change, and why these initiatives took the sophisticated form of a local experiment.

During the period from 1953 to 1956 several analyses, undertaken either on the request of local authorities or on the initiative of provincial authorities, showed the need of restructuring Nowy Sacz's economy. Practical suggestions based on these analyses emphasized the development of pomiculture and the expansion of tourist facilities. During these years, the nucleus of a modernizing elite was formed and became known, at least locally. However, prior to 1956 local initiatives were handicapped by the existence of a rigid centralized system and the concentration of resources at a higher level of economic management.

During the political changes of 1956 a group of local leaders from Nowy Sacz county and town initiated the formation of the Economic Council at the County Committee of the Polish United Workers' party. The council itself was an experiment, patterned, as a matter of fact, on the newly established Economic Council of the national government.

Among the leaders who were instrumental in the formation of the Economic Council, particularly active were the first secretary of the PUWP County Committee, the presidents of the county and town local councils, and two managers of the local economy. The initiative emerged from within the established system of local government, and this makes even more important the fact that it was directed towards a new 'model' of local administration and local economy. After almost a year, in the fall of 1957, the Economic Council published its program. This program proposed a radical departure from the centralized system of government and economic management and amounted to the application of principles of territorial autonomy.

The Nowy Sacz 'Manifesto' of November 1957 emphasized, first of all, that: a / local authorities should have stronger influence on industrial enterprises under the 'central plan,' including control over investments and a share in the profit of these enterprises; b / local industry should be developed; c / pomiculture, cattle-raising, and vegetable-growing, as well as corresponding industry, should be given more attention; d / local authorities should take possession of and expand tourist facilities and health resorts; e / a special Fund of Development for the Nowy Sacz region should be created, financed partly by taxing the enterprises which belonged to the 'central plan' and partly from local resources (extra tax on alcohol, on cinemas, etc.); f / a special agency for expansion and exploitation of tourism and folklore should be established and given prerogatives to develop these branches of local economy. Generally speaking, the manifesto called for extended local autonomy and fuller use of economic calculations in deciding priorities for the future development of the county.

Under the existing law most of the proposals of the Economic Council had to be directed to higher, that is, provincial or central, state authorities. Then they were referred to the Planning Commission of the government which began analysing the situation of the county and the perspectives of the experiment. In the meantime, the local initiators made attempts to build support for their program. They presented it to the prime minister and to the first secretary of the Central Committee of the Polish United Workers' Party from whom they received general approval of their initiatives. Moreover, at the end of 1957 a 'Club of the Nowy Sacz Region' was established with local branches in Nowy Sacz, Warsaw, and Kraków. The club recruited influential people who were born and/or educated in Nowy Sacz and used the positions and contacts of its members in lobbying for the experiment. Finally, on 3 May 1958, the

Council of Ministers passed its 'resolution 151/158' under which Nowy Sacz was allowed to start the experiment.

The architects of the Nowy Sacz experiment, when interviewed recently on its history, recalled that considerable difficulties were created by various central departments and described the resolution 151/158 as only a '40 per cent fulfillment of local demands.' This may be a fair evaluation. However, one aspect of the policy decision should not be forgotten. While the Nowy Sacz Economic Council demanded certain rights for this particular county as an exception from the general rule of centralization, the government's resolution gave some new prerogatives to Nowy Sacz authorities on an experimental basis. Rather than being an exception to the rule, Nowy Sacz was to become a testing field for a revision of the rule itself.

On the other hand, the overlapping of Nowy Sacz experiment with other changes in the system of local government make it difficult to evaluate net results of the experiment. Resolution 151/58 went further than the changes in the system of local government introduced by the new law on 'local councils,' which had been passed by the parliament in January 1958. However, the Nowy Sacz experiment reflected the same spirit of limited decentralization which was manifested in the new law. In the 1960s the amendments to the law on local councils gave them the same prerogatives which in 1958 had been given to the Nowy Sacz councils on an experimental basis. In a sense one may see in this a confirmation of the positive results of the experiment. However, the general tendency towards greater local initiative and autonomy make it impossible to compare the experimental Nowy Sacz with a typical 'conservative' county. Changes occurred everywhere. The difference between Nowy Sacz and the other counties was that here the changes came earlier, were introduced more radically, and were better prepared. The Nowy Sacz experiment, if analysed from the point of view of the local community, was a compromise between more radical initiatives originating among the local leadership and among the local public and the restrictions imposed upon them by the centralized system of economic management. From the point of view of the central authorities, it was an attempt to assess empirically the possibilities of extending prerogatives of local government in the whole country.

This dual character of the experiment explains some of the departures from the pure principles of the experimental method. The central authorities did not choose the experimental unit; on the contrary, the choice itself was imposed on them by the uniqueness of the unit under observation. The fact that the local plans were put to a test created a special atmosphere in Nowy Sacz. Both the leaders and the public mobilized all available resources to show that after all they were right in their plans for local economic expansion. Such an attitude – being a special result of the experiment – introduced a non-comparable element which would not have been present had similar changes been introduced everywhere by decisions from above.

The experiment consisted of granting to the local county and town councils of Nowy Sacz prerogatives which at the end of the 1950s did not belong to the local councils generally. They were given power to control industrial enterprises, which belonged to the central plan, and to draft their own plans for local economic development. This was done with special emphases on tourism, pomiculture, exploitation of the resources of mineral water, rehabilitation of craft industries, etc. Local planning of economic development on the county level was then a novelty; in the 1960s, however, the principle of county economic planning was generally applied throughout Poland. The economic results of the experiment are difficult to assess. Nowy Sacz developed during the decade 1958–68, but so did the other regions of the country. Economically it is still one of the less developed counties, but the distance between it and the more developed counties narrowed a little.

The results of the experiment cannot, however, be evaluated purely in terms of the economic position of the county after ten years of its new economic policy. Even if adequate to meet local needs, it was too limited in scope and resources to change dramatically the economic position of the county. On the other hand, since it has been followed by similar changes in the other counties, the net economic result of the experiment cannot be assessed with precision.

The experiment was, I think, clearly successful in two ways: 1 / it helped to mobilize local initiatives and to create an atmosphere of local 'patriotism' which became an important element of economic and social development of the region; 2 / it contributed to further revisions of the system of local government in Poland in the direction of greater autonomy and initiative of the lower levels of the administrative system.

III   EXPERIMENTS WITH WORKERS' TRIBUNALS

The first workers' tribunals were created as a result of local initiatives.[4] They operated temporarily outside the legal system of the country, hav-

4   Experiments with workers' tribunals began in 1960 in Wrocław voivoship; empirical research, conducted by the Central Institute of Labour Protection,

ing been accepted only as experimental novelties. 'For the first years, following 1960, there was no legislation that would give legal status to the activity of workers' tribunals; at that time they operated according to their own regulations. The relations with the police and other law enforcement agencies as well as the relations with factory management were arranged merely on a temporary basis.'[5] The results of the experiments, positively evaluated by researchers, public opinion, and legislators, created a firm basis for the Workers' Tribunal Act, passed by the Sejm (parliament) in March 1965.

The idea of workers' tribunals was based on Karl Marx's prediction of the 'withering away' of the state, which had been identified with the institutionalized organs of legalized violence. The voluntary tribunals were supposed to substitute moral sanctions for the legal sanctions in cases of minor offences and malfeasance. It was also hypothetically predicted that moral pressure exercised by one's fellows could be more effective than pressure exercised by law enforcement and that the tribunals would have educational effects both on the offenders and the others. After the experimental period of 1960–65, the parliamentary act gave strong support to the development of workers' tribunals and formed a legal basis for their future activities. The act itself resulted from the experiences of the tribunals as collected and evaluated by systematic sociological and legal research. Taking into consideration the differences in the extent to which the workers' tribunals had proved to be effective, the act supported a selective strategy of developing the tribunals; they should be created only where the majority of workers' communities could guarantee their proper operation. Scientific control over the results of the experiment was provided mainly by two opinion surveys in 1961 and 1963 in which opinions of workers, their leaders, and offenders were

started in 1961 with the aim of evaluating the results of the experiments. A voivoship is an administrative unit, which is the equivalent of a region. The best short study in English of the workers' tribunal reform is: Jan Górski, 'Workers' Tribunals in Poland, 1960–1965: Past Experiences and Future Prospects,' *Polish Round Table – Yearbook 1968* (Wroclaw: Polish Association of Political Sciences, 1969, pp. 69–74. In Polish see Adam Podgórecki, 'Eksperyment w socjologii prawa' (An experiment in the sociology of law). *Państwo i Prawo*, 17, 1 (1962); Eugeniusz Modliński 'O społecznych sądach robotniczych' (On workers' social courts), *ibid.*, 1, (1962); Jan Górski, 'Sądy robotnicze w opinii ich przewodniczących' (Workers' tribunals in the opinion of their chairmen), *ibid.*, 20, 2 (1965); Jan Górski, 'Prawo, moralność i opinia w sądzie robotniczym' (Law, morality and opinion in the workers' tribunals), *ibid.*, 22, 7 (1967); Jan Górski, *Doświadczenie i perspektywy sądów robotniczych w Polsce, 1960–1965* (Experiences and perspectives of workers' tribunals in Poland) (Warsaw 1967).

5 See Górski, 1969, *op cit*, p. 59

studied, as well as on the case studies of workers' tribunals in selected enterprises. The surveys and the case studies showed both the irregular territorial distribution of the tribunals and wide differences in the efficiency of the tribunals among voivodships. They also tended to indicate that the activity of the tribunals depended largely on the degree of involvement of the local organs of the Polish Workers' party and, to some extent, on the degree of involvement of the trade unions, lawyers' organizations, etc. Finally, the studies showed that the tribunals enjoyed a considerable moral authority among the workers and could influence their behaviour and moral opinion.

It seems to me that the most significant aspect of the experiment with workers' tribunals was that the scientific control over the experiment in vivo resulted not only in approval and extension of the experiment itself, but also in correcting overoptimistic predictions which accompanied the creation of the first tribunals. The experiment saved the country the consequences of hasty reform which potentially could have been a failure without, however, sacrificing the search for new solutions. In this sense, the experiment became an important instrument of locally originated but centrally sanctioned reform.

IV EXPERIMENTS IN ECONOMIC MANAGEMENT

These experiments originated in economic reform of the late 1950s and early 1960s. They included such changes as the introduction in the years 1956–8 of the first workers' self-governments in selected enterprises, as well as experimental changes in the system of management and planning at the enterprise level. Unfortunately, only very few of these changes have been studied during and/or immediately after the experiments.

The tendency towards greater autonomy of industrial management on the one hand and towards greater workers' participation on the other constituted the common background of various economic experiments at the enterprise level. Since the economic system of the country as a whole remained unchanged, at least as far as the centralized system of planning and management was concerned, the changes were accepted initially only on a limited, experimental scale. In the case of workers' self government, the experimental changes of 1956–8 resulted in the creation in 1959 of the uniform system of the Conference of Workers' Self government, composed of elected workers' councils, party organizations, and trade unions. In the case of selective experiments in management and planning, which included experimental changes in the system of economic incentives within enterprises, the results were also used for programming a general economic reform. Burhard's analysis indicated another essential function of these experiments.[6] In the case he studied, the experiment resulted in growing discrepancies of income between management and the workers, as well as in dissatisfaction of the latter. The economic reforms undertaken by the Polish government in 1968–9 takes into consideration the social factors of economic changes, profiting thus by the previous experiences.[7]

V CONCLUSION

These economic and social experiments cannot be considered as strictly scientific experiments. With few exceptions they lacked systematic scientific controls as well as fully comparable units of observation. In a sense they were examples of initiatives, both local and central, which aimed at a step-by-step reform of selected economic or legal rules. The step-by-step strategy included, however, practical, experimental testing of new proposals on a limited scale. In a system which is centralized, the experimental approach to social change is a potentially useful instrument for proving the efficacy of new solutions before they become elements of the system itself. It also widens opportunities for local initiatives, which in their initial stage can be presented as purely experimental.

The role of social and particularly political science in this type of experiment is of critical importance. The Polish experiences to date do not provide us with examples of a full use of the scientific control required by experiments in vivo. It can perhaps be said that one of the limitations of the Polish experiments was a gap between practical initiatives and scientific control over their execution. Most Polish studies remain based on ex post facto analyses, they also lack systematic comparisons between experimental and control groups.

Nevertheless, even with all these limitations it is important that political scientists played a role in conducting some of these experiments and in providing scientific tools for their evaluation. Specifically, the case of the workers' tribunals can serve as an example of the potential use of

6 The most comprehensive study of one of the economic 'experiments' has been presented by Stanisław Burhard in his PH D thesis on 'Social relations in a state industrial enterprise against a background of experimental changes in planning and management' (Warsaw 1970, unpublished, in Polish). The author, however, relied mostly on a post facto analysis of the results and effects of the experiment.

7 The point is now frequently made by leading economists of Poland. Cf. Kazimierz Secomski, *Czynniki społeczne we współczesnym rozwoju gospodarczym* (Social factors in contemporary economic development). Warsaw 1970.

social science research for controlling the experimental stages of social change. For the future three observations can be offered.

1 / Centrally planned reform of economic, social, and political institutions can profit by the use of systematic experiments if and when they are based on preceding policy discussions and executed with the proper use of the methodological tools of social science. Experiments can in this case optimize the effects of reform by maximizing gains and reducing risks of an overall change. Rather than learning through tests and errors – what seems to be a common but too expensive practice – the reformers can learn by conducting well-planned and carefully executed research.

2 / The experiments can also serve as a way of educating the public. In a new structure created by a reform, one of the most important factors is the discrepancy between new rules and old traditions. The public does not adjust itself to a new set of rules as rapidly as the reformers change the rules. Therefore, the experiments can serve as instruments to educate the general public and to prepare them for eventual change.

3 / Experiments in vivo confront the political scientist with methodological problems of – at least partly – a different nature than those created by the laboratory experiments. While the sophistication of experiments often has to be sacrificed for reasons of expediency, it is important to try to narrow the gap between the two types of experiments. In a sense laboratory experiments can serve as ideal models for the experiments in vivo, which should be conducted in a way as close to that of the laboratory experiments as the nature of the problem and the character of the environment permit.

REFERENCES

BURHARD, STANISŁAW 'Social relations in a state industrial enterprise against a background of experimental changes in planning and management.' University of Warsaw, PH.D dissertation, 1970. (In Polish.)
GÓRSKI, JAN Doświadczenia i perspektywy sadów robotniczych w Polsce, 1960–1965 (Experiences and perspectives of workers tribunals in Poland, 1960–1965). Warsaw: Ksiażka i Wiedza, 1967.
–   'Prawo, moralność, i opinia w sądzie robotniczym' (Law, morality and opinion in the workers tribunals), Państwo i prawo, 22 (July 1967), pp. 97–106.
–   'Sądy robotnicze w opinii ich przewodniczacych' (Workers tribunals in the opinion of their chairmen), Państwo i prawo 20 (February 1965), pp. 264–72.
–   'Workers' Tribunals in Poland, 1960–1965: Past Experiences and Future Prospects,' Polish Round Table Yearbook, 2 (1968), pp. 69–74.

HARTMANN, GEORGE W. 'A Field Experiment on the Comparative Effectiveness of 'Emotional' and 'Rational' Political Leaflets in Determining Election Results,' *Journal of Abnormal and Social Psychology*, 31, 1 (April-June 1936), pp. 99–114.

MADGE, JOHN *The Tools of Social Science*. Garden City, NY: Doubleday, 1965.

MODLIŃSKI, EUGENIUSZ 'O społecznych sądach robotniczych' (On workers' social courts), *Państwo i prawo*, 17, 1 (January 1962), pp. 36–45.

MURPHY, GARNER, LOIS B. MURPHY and THEODORE M. NEWCOMB *Experimental Social Psychology: An Interpretation of Research upon the Socialization of the Individual*. New York: Harper, 1937.

PODGÓRECKI, ADAM 'Eksperymenty w socjologii prawa: Badania nad sądami robotniczymi' (An experiment in the sociology of law: research on workers' courts), *Państwo i prawo*, 17, 1 (January 1962), pp. 46–57.

SECOMSKI, KAZIMIERZ '*Czynniki społeczne we współczesnym rozwoju gospodarczym*' (Social factors in contemporary economic development), Warsaw 1970.

SELVIN, HANAN C. *The Effects of Leadership*. Glencoe, Ill.: Free Press, 1960.

PART THREE

Social and paper games

KINHIDE MUSHAKOJI

The strategies of negotiation:
an American-Japanese comparison

INTRODUCTION

This paper summarizes the results of a new game, the ABC (accommodate, boycott, or confront) game, played by Japanese and American students in Tokyo.[1] The Japanese-American comparison contained in this paper is but a first step in an endeavour which aims to include many countries in the various regions of the world.

There have been a variety of games studying the negotiation process in connection with game theory.[2] Replications of these games designed in the United States have been conducted in Japan and elsewhere. Although they provide interesting information about the subjects in different countries, they do not tap a basic dimension along which we may reasonably expect cultural differences to exist, a dimension relating to the pattern of strategic choices in negotiation. Does mini-max rationality apply to negotiators of all cultures in the world?[3] As a Japanese, I cannot help being interested by the cultural dimension of the Japanese 'irrational decision' to attack Pearl Harbor. Contrary to the game-theoretical assumption of mini-max rationality, the Japanese preferred a non-mini-max

1 For another cross-cultural negotiation game, 'NEMO,' see Mushakoji (1968).
2 See references, especially Contiti (1967), Deutsch (1962), Dresher (1961), Ikle and Leites (1962), Rapoport and Chammah (1965), Rapoport and Orwant (1962), Shubik (1964), Stone (1958), Suzuki (1970).
3 About mini-max rationality see Luce and Raiffa (1957), pp. 278–84; Suzuki (1959), pp. 37–43.

standard, a risk-taking one, in their decision to terminate negotiations.[4] A similar non-mini-max situation seems to exist in the prolonged Paris talks on Vietnam. Indeed, cultural factors may play a certain role in many other negotiations.

I must hasten to say that I am not pretending that culture is the most significant factor determining negotiation behaviour; rather I am merely bothered by the lack of attention addressed to this factor. Needless to say, the cross-cultural comparison discussed in this paper must be improved by bringing into the game design independent variables other than culture so as to determine the contribution of the cultural factors in explaining variance in negotiation behaviour. However, before refining the design of this experiment, it would be well to analyse the results obtained in an experimental negotiation using cross-cultural variables.

THE MODEL

Negotiation can be defined in various ways.[5] In view of our research interest here, we use three basic concepts to define a particular type of negotiation, *redistribution negotiations*. The negotiations we are interested in involve a *message exchange process* between (two) parties with *conflicting goals* which they can reach only by increasing their share in the *control* of an *uncertainty-laden arena*.

The first concept introduced, the message exchange process, implies that negotiations involve a series of consecutive partial decisions; the second, conflicting targets, that the negotiation being analysed is basically a zero-sum situation in terms of the ultimate goals of the negotiating parties, although there may be non-zero-sum temporary situations during the negotiation process. The third implies two things: first, that each negotiator must draw relatively closer to his own target than his opponent in order to control the arena; second, that the arena is uncertainty-laden, that is, a certain amount of risk-taking is unavoidable.

A typical example of redistribution negotiations is a peace conference in which 1 / the negotiation process involves successive decisions about the diverse conditions of ceasefire. 2 / both opponents have fundamentally opposed targets, and 3 / the arena, including the battlefield, is in a highly uncertain situation.[6] More constructive negotiations, in which the

4 Risk-taking is a social-psychological concept. See for example Scodel, Ratoosh, and Minas (1960).
5 For a taxonomy of negotiation see Ikle (1964), pp. 26–42.
6 Ikle (1964) would define a peace conference as a negotiation for normalization. However, making abstraction of the fact that a peace talk often takes the form of a search for a return to the status quo ante, we use this example

parties share a common target and in which their control of the environment is possible only by co-operation (as in the case of negotiations to build a new organization), are excluded from the following analysis.

In negotiations of the above type, three kinds of negotiation strategies, i.e., principles guiding the choice of the negotiators, can be distinguished:[7] 1 / The possible-gain maximizing strategy which aims at maximizing the gain the subject (S) may obtain if lucky. This is a risky strategy, gambling with the uncertainty-laden arena. 2 / The mini-max strategy which aims at minimizing the possible loss as measured by S's increased distance from his target. 3 / The self-sacrificing relative-gain maximizing strategy which consists of imposing an important loss on the opponent, by acepting a (smaller) loss for himself. This strategy, which is 'irrational' in a one-shot decision situation, is fully justifiable in a process where future choices may enable S to recover his previous loss.

This threefold classification is logically derived from the above definition of negotiation. To acquire more control over the uncertain arena may mean one of two things, either to increase one's own control or to decrease the opponent's. The latter approach leads to the third type of strategy. To increase control one may choose either to minimize the possible loss or to maximize the possible gain; the first alternative is the mini-max strategy, while the second is the possible-gain strategy.

In a sense, the three strategies are different in terms of how they deal with uncertainty. The mini-max strategy has a pessimistic outlook on uncertainty: it avoids taking a chance. The possible-gain maximizing strategy has an optimistic view of the future: it tries to get the best out of what the future allows one to hope for. The relative-gain maximizing strategy has a manipulative approach towards uncertainty. Instead of

to illustrate the fact that negotiations are accompanied by an ever changing power relationship between the negotiating parties of which the battlefield is a typical example.

7 We distinguish three types here because among the four possible types mentioned below one is trivial and can be discarded. Negotiators determine their strategies either actively or in a passive way. In the former case, they build their estimate on their own chance of success, in the latter they first estimate their opponent's chance and compare theirs to it. In both cases the negotiators can be either optimistic or pessimistic, i.e., they can either try to maximize their possible gain or minimize their possible loss. Therefore we can distinguish four types of negotiating strategies: 1 / active and optimistic – the possible-gain maximizing strategy; 2 / active and pessimistic – the possible-loss minimizing strategy; 3 / passive, pessimistic about opponent but optimistic about self – trivial since identical to the active optimistic case; 4 / passive, optimistic about opponent but pessimistic about self – relative-gain maximizing strategy where the negotiator seeks to maximize the difference between the opponent's possible gain and his own possible loss.

trying to reduce uncertainty by drawing closer to one's target, it accepts uncertainty by simply decreasing the opponent's chance of success (i.e., by forcing his opponent relatively further from the target). The third approach which, to my knowledge, has not yet been studied in the literature, plays an important role in conflicts and negotiations between opponents of unequal power. It was represented during the war in the Pacific by the Japanese emphasis on 'letting the enemy cut your flesh in order to cut his bones.' It is now one of the basic principles of guerrilla strategy (Castro-style) and the people's war doctrines (Mao-style).

Roughly speaking, we expect the mini-max rational approach to be preferred in Western cultures and the relativistic approach in Eastern cultures. Risk-taking is present in all cultures, since without it no positive action can be taken in an uncertain environment. But, such a crude approach does not tell us about actual negotiation behaviour, in which different combinations of the three types of strategies are necessarily used. It is, indeed, highly improbable that during a prolonged negotiation process the negotiators would persist in using just one strategy. The ABC game has been designed to obtain a sequence of choices in a setting where the above-mentioned characteristics of negotiations are present.

THE RULES OF THE GAME

The ABC game uses the movement of a *negotiation point* to represent the players' ever-changing distance from their targets, which are located on the northwest and the southeast extremities of the board (figure 1). The game starts at point 0, and the movement of the negotiation point is determined by the combination of the two players' strategy and, at times, a chance factor in favour of either one of the players. Chance is introduced to represent arena uncertainty and to emphasize the risk involved in the second alternative.

The game is played according to the rules represented in table 1. (The first number indicates horizontal movement; + to the right, and − to the left. The second number indicates vertical movement; + upward, and − downward. Where chance is introduced A indicates Algo dominates, and B shows the case where Bingo is favoured.) The above rules are designed in such a way that:

i   When both sides are possible-gain maximizers, chance intervenes and the favoured party maximizes his gain.
ii   When one party is possible-gain maximizer and the other is possible-loss minimizer, a moderate gain is attributed to the side favoured by chance.

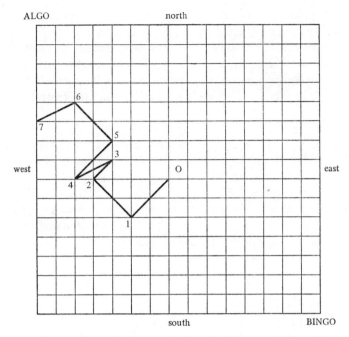

Figure 1 Example showing a typical path of the negotiation point in the *ABC* game.

TABLE 1

Matrix of strategies and pay offs in the ABC game
Algo

		a	b	c
	a	+1, +1	0, −1	*A:* 0, +1 *B:* +1, 0
Bingo	*b*	−1, 0	−2, −2	−2, −1
	c	*A:* 0, +1 *B:* +1, 0	−1, −2	*A:* −2, +2 *B:* +2, −2

NOTE On this and the following tables *a* = accommodation, *b* = boycott, *c* = confrontation.

iii When both sides are possible-loss minimizers, the negotiating point moves but without advantage to either side. If both persist in using this strategy, the negotiation point will move towards the northeast end of the board, which is equally far from both targets.

iv When one side chooses the possible-gain maximizing strategy (maxi-max) and the other chooses a relative-gain maximizing strategy, the relative-gain maximizer loses moderately, while the possible-gain maximizer loses more.

v   When one side plays the mini-max strategy and the other the relative-
     gain maximizing strategy, the former loses moderately.
vi   When both sides play the relative-gain maximizing strategy, the nego-
     tiating point moves, but without advantage to either side. If they
     persist in this combination the negotiation point will approach the
     southwest side of the board which is equally far from the targets of
     A and B.[8]

The interest of the rules of ABC lies in the fact that chance plays an
important role, and the strategic choice consists of the way the Ss cope
with the uncertainty built into the game. Since the parties have to move
the negotiation point to either the upper left (Algo) or the lower right
(Bingo), it is most helpful to take the maxi-max strategy which is the
only one to allow motion in both the horizontal and the vertical directions
at the same time. But it becomes helpful to mix with this strategy either of
the other two so as to avoid too much risk.

THE GAME

ABC was administered as a paper game in which the Ss were told to play
Algo against a Bingo whose strategies were revealed to them by means of
a table giving the Bingo responses to each one of Algo's choices together
with information as to who prevailed in the arena. (Another way to administer ABC is to play it in the usual laboratory situation.) We decided to
use the paper game approach for two reasons. From the point of view of
methodology, it enabled us to give a standardized opponent to all the Ss; in
practical terms it enabled the collection of more cases. We had forty-five
Japanese Ss (hereinafter referred to as Js) and thirty-six American Ss
(hereinafter As).

The instructions given to them defined the setting, the objective, and
the strategies of the game in the following way:
i   GAME SETTING You represent Algo in peace talks with Bingo
(whose actions are described in the attached Bingo response list). Various
issues are discussed by the negotiators one by one, and you and your
opponent state your respective positions alternately.
ii   OBJECTIVE Whether you are more successful than Bingo during the
process of negotiation is determined by the position of a point (the negotiation point) on the negotiation board. The game starts at point 0. Your

8   On table 1 and on the following tables and figures, confrontation is the maxi-
     max strategy, accommodation the minimax strategy, and boycott the relative-
     gain maximizing strategy.

choice of a strategy and Bingo's response to it, plus a chance factor, determine the movement of the negotiation point. Your objective is to bring it as close as possible to the point on the upper left-hand corner of the negotiation board, whereas Bingo wants to pull it towards the point on the lower right-hand corner of the board. Both you and your opponent have influence units (in some games we used ten, in others twenty units) which represent military potential, diplomatic efforts, or propaganda campaign costs which are available in order to support your negotiations on the battlefield or in the international environment. The game terminates either when you have spent all your influence units or when the negotiation point goes off the board.

iii STRATEGIES You have three alternatives: accommodation, boycott, and confrontation (henceforth referred to as *a, b, c*). You need two influence units to play *c*, and one each for *a* or *b*. Bingo will also choose either strategy *a, b*, or *c*. When strategy *c* is chosen by yourself or Bingo, the movement of the negotiation point is determined by chance. This is meant to represent the risk you have to take in your negotiations because of the uncertain state of the battle field. If chance favours you, you will gain more by playing strategy *c*, but if it favours your enemy, you will lose more. Strategy *a* is the safest, but you will gain less when you choose it than when you play *c* and chance works in your favour. Strategy *b* does not help you to bring the negotiation point closer to your target, but it does take the point further away from Bingo's target. You must also realize that if, in this case, Bingo chooses *c*, the point moves one position down and two positions to the left, so that you will have to accept a slight loss in order to impose on your opponent a bigger disadvantage.

The same instructions were given to all the *S*s, except for one point, the number of influence units. To 22 *J*s and 19 *A*s, 10 influence units were given; and to 23 *J*s and 17 *A*s, 20 influence units. The former, hereafter referred to as *J-I*s and *A-I*s, were put in a weaker position under high time pressure; whereas the latter, hereafter referred to as *J-II*s, and *A-II*s, were in a more favourable position with more time to bring the negotiation point close to their respective targets.

HYPOTHESES AND PREDICTIONS

The following hypotheses about the cultural difference in the Japanese and American negotiation style can be tested by means of ABC.[9]

9 By 'testing' we mean a procedure of analogical inference as described in Polya (1964), pp. 27–8.

HYPOTHESIS 1 The Japanese negotiation culture, more than other cultures, favours the relative-gain strategy. This hypothesis is based on previously mentioned folk knowledge and historical examples.[10]

HYPOTHESIS 2 The American negotiation culture is more possible-loss minimizing than non-Western cultures. The assumption of Western rationality versus Oriental irrationality can be summarized in this hypothesis.

HYPOTHESIS 3 The Japanese negotiation culture favours accommodation more than other cultures.[11] Accommodation is risk avoidance through co-operation. The Japanese tend to avoid a clash of interests when they are uncertain about winning the contest. This constitutes the Japanese version of possible-loss minimization.

It must be noted that hypotheses 2 and 3 lead to opposite predictions, although they are not logically mutually exclusive. As to the predictability of response strategies, the following hypotheses can be formulated.

HYPOTHESIS 4 The Japanese negotiation culture tends to tolerate more ambiguity than Western cultures. Tolerance of ambiguity includes the idea that Japanese tend to formulate the issues to be negotiated in a vaguer way than their opponent. Also, they tend to be more flexible in their position, which changes according to the environmental conditions.

HYPOTHESIS 5 Therefore, the way successive strategies are chosen during a negotiation process is less predictable for Japanese negotiators than for Western negotiators.

HYPOTHESIS 6 It is also often pointed out that the Japanese negotiation culture favours more response-consistency, whereas the Western cultures favour more self-consistency. In other words, the Japanese try to maximize the efficiency of their environment-adaptivity by defining their choice in accordance with their opponent's action, while the Western negotiators tend to maximize the power of their position by building a self-consistent set of arguments.

The above hypotheses are not, of course, exhaustive. They are just meant to provide a basis for the formulation of predictions about the ABC game results. The following predictions are derived from the above hypotheses.

10   See Mushakoji (1968).
11   About the characteristics of the Japanese negotiation culture see Mushakoji (1967), pp. 155–72.

PREDICTION 1 *A*s will tend to prefer strategy *b* less than the *J*s.

PREDICTION 2 The *A*s will rely on strategy *a* more heavily than the *J*s.

PREDICTION 3 The difference in the pattern of strategy selection of the two categories of *J*s will be greater than that of the two categories of *A*s.

PREDICTION 4 The redundancy of the successive choices of the *A*s will be higher than that of the *J*s.

PREDICTION 5 The *J*s pattern of response will be more redundant than their pattern of successive choices, whereas the contrary will be true for the *A*s.

ANALYSES AND FINDINGS

Various analyses were used to test these predictions, to refine them, and to formulate more valid hypotheses. After tabulation of the choice sequence of each *S*, dyads composed of all pairs of successive choices, and triads of all three-member substrings of the choice sequences were tabulated. In addition, response matrices showing for each Bingo choice the frequency of *S*s following strategy were also composed. Predictor analysis, multi-variate analysis using the type III Hayashi quantification theory model, and information theoretical analysis were applied to the above data.[12] Without entering into technical details, it may be useful to discuss very briefly the nature of the three methods before each discussion on the results obtained with them.

Predictor analysis is a simple model which helps to visualize the relative predictive power of the various substrings of a sequence of events according to the probability of their joint-occurrence. Among all substrings represented on figure 2, those closer to the northwest corner are better predictors that the *S* choosing the given combination of strategies is an *A*. Those closer to the southeast corner indicate that the *S* making such a choice sequence is a *J*. The points closer to the southwest corner indicate that such a string is rare in both *A*s and *J*s, while points towards the northeast corner correspond to strings common in both *A* and *J* choice sequences so that prediction is difficult because of ambiguity.

The points representing one-step predictors such as *c*, two-step predictors such as *cc*, or three-step predictors such as *ccc* have more or less predictive power. First, in terms of how frequently they can be used as predictor, the further to the upper right the more frequent is their occur-

12 About predictor analysis see Mushakoji (1970), pp. 55–60, and Mushakoji (1969). About the Hayashi quantification theory model see Yasuda (1969), pp. 201–10, and Alker (1969). About information theoretical measures see for example Staniland (1966), pp. 19–27.

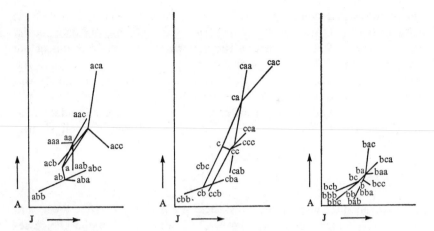

Figure 2 Predictor analysis of various strategy sequences. On this and on the following figures a = accommodation, b = boycott, c = confrontation.

rence. Secondly, predictive power is related to how safe it is to predict on the basis of their occurrence that the S who uses the string is either an A or a J. The further to the upper left, the safer is the prediction that he is an A, whereas the further to the lower right the safer one can predict that he is a J.

The lines in the diagram indicate the connections between the one-step, two-step, and three-step substrings. They help to determine the change in the predictive power brought about by the additional information contained in the additional step. A line connecting a given predictor, say c, to the related two-step predictors such as cc, ca, cb indicates, when it extends towards the upper left that the addition of the second step has shifted the direction of the prediction towards A. If the line is oriented towards the lower right it indicates that the additional information provided by the second step has weighed on the side of J. A predictor is stable when the next step does not shift the prediction too far away from it, i.e., when the lines connecting it to the next step predictors do not extend too much in the upper left or the lower right directions. In brief, predictor analysis visualizes not only the relative predictive power of the predictors, but also the shift in the direction of the prediction which occurs when the new steps are added.

Applying this analysis to the ABC game results, we find (figure 2) that

i   All one-step predictors are inconclusive, but a slight hint of prediction exists with b in Js direction and c and a in As direction.

ii   Among the three one-step predictors, *b* is the rarest. It can seldom serve as a predictor. However, when *b* occurs, it is a good predictor for *J*. In other words, if an *S* ever uses *b*, there is a good chance that he is a *J*.

iii   *c* is the best predictor in terms of the high frequency of its occurrence.

iv   Among two-step predictors, *ca* has the strongest discriminating power. It is a predictor for *A*. In other words, there is a fairly good probability of *ca* occurring, and it allows the prediction that the *S* who uses it is an *A*.

      It is, however, also true that:

v   Among the two-step predictors *ca* together with *ac* are the most unstable, i.e., the additional step makes the greatest difference. In both cases, when *a* comes next, *caa* or *aca* tends strongly towards *A*.

vi   Among the three-step predictors, *aca* for *A* and *cab* for *J* have the strongest predictive power.

vii   All three-step predictors with a *b* as their first step do not occur very often; but they are all predictors for *J*, with the exception of *bac*.

viii Comparing *A-I*s and *A-II*s, *aca* and *ccc* are the best predictors for the former and the latter respectively.

ix   Comparing *J-I*s and *J-II*s, *cab* and *cbb* are the best predictors for the former and the latter respectively.

The above findings seem to corroborate several of our hypotheses. Findings i and ii support hypotheses 1 and 2, since they indicate that when a relative-gain strategy is used it is safer to predict that the *S* using it is a *J*; whereas, with a possible-loss minimizing strategy, the safe bet is on the *A* side. Finding iv confirms prediction 2. In terms of the three-step predictors, however, it must be noted that the third step which discriminates *A*s and *J*s best is not *a* versus *b* or possible-loss minimization versus relative-gain maximization, but rather *a* versus *c*. This raises an interesting question about the different ways *c*s and *a*s are mixed in the strategies of *A*s and *J*s. To take v into account, a new hypothesis must be formulated, pointing out that the Japanese tend to prefer choice sequences where gain-maximizing is more often used than loss-minimizing, whereas the Americans prefer the sequences in which loss-minimizing is used more often than gain-maximizing.

Finding vii shows that the relative-gain strategy plays an important role in the Japanese negotiation culture. However, it indicates also that this does not mean that this strategy is most preferred by the Japanese, since all the predictors, including an original *b*, occur very rarely as is indicated by the fact that they are all located in the lower left-hand side of figure 2.

Let us turn next to multi-variate analysis. The predictor analysis gave us a very rough idea about the choice sequence of the Ss, but it was mainly concerned with how to predict who chose a particular combination of strategies rather than with the problem of how the various combinations of dyads and triads were used by the Ss. We need, therefore, another approach to find the patterns of preference of the Ss. For example, the predictor analysis did not make clear whether a given J would use *cac* and *bca* together more often than *acc* and *aab*. We will use the quantitification theory model to find the preference pattern of the Ss as to the combined use of the various three-step strategy strings.

The Hayashi type III quantification theory model is a kind of *canonical correlation analysis* with dummy variables. It is most appropriate to use it for our analysis since, without any assumption as to the distribution of the data, it attributes weights to both the Ss and the dyads (or triads) so as to maximize the correlation between the two kinds of weights. The Ss and the dyads (or triads) are thus represented as vectors in a multi-dimensional space. The distances among the Ss, among the dyads (or triads), and between the Ss and the dyads (or triads) indicate their similarity or dissimilarity. A major contrast with factor analysis is that the model is not built to identify different factors but rather to determine the distribution of the Ss and their attributes (dyads or triads) in a multi-dimensional space where the correlation between the weights assigned to the Ss and the attributes is maximized.

A comparison of the J's and A's response matrices analysed separately shows that when the length of each dyad vector in the space is compared (figure 3):

i   *cc* is the shortest for the Js. Therefore, for the Js, response to a *c* by a *c* is the most common, whereas response to a *b* by an *a* is most uncommon.

ii   In the case of the As, the most commonly adopted strategy is to respond to a *c* by an *a*, and the one with rarest support is the response to a *b* by a *b*.

iii In general, *b* responses are more familiar to the Js than to the As.

iv   All the *a* responses are more familiar to the As than to the Js.

In terms of the distribution of the dyads in the plane composed by the two principal factors, we can find that (figure 4):

i   The A's dyads are less dispersed than the J's dyads, which means that the former are better structured than the latter.

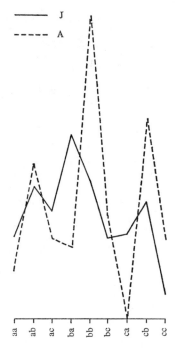

Figure 3 Canonical correlation comparing the strategy sequences (dyads) of American and Japanese subjects.

ii In *J*'s case, *bb* is closer to *aa* and *cc*. We may assume the existence of a tit-for-tat strategy, whereas in *A*'s case, *bb* is located on the far end of the space with a high loading on the first factor, with *ab* in a less striking but similar position. In *A*'s case, a *b* response to either *a* or *b* is particularly uncommon.

The distribution of the *S*s around the nine dyads indicates the pattern of clustering of the *S*s in terms of the response they use most often. This analysis – entirely different from the usually used cluster analysis procedures – consists of choosing for all *S*s the closest dyad in the two-dimensional space. Thus we obtain for *J*s and *A*s, as well as for their subcategories *J-I*, *J-II*, *A-I*, and *A-II*, the number of *S*s in the neighbourhood of each dyad (see table 2).

iii The most striking difference when we compare the clusters of *J*s and *A*s is found in *ab* and *aa*. In the former case, the *J*s constitute a more

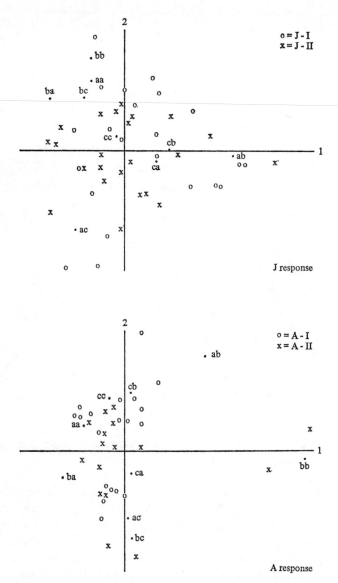

Figure 4 Pattern of strategy sequences (dyads) of Japanese and American students.

TABLE 2

Subjects clustered by group characteristics and preferred sequence of responses

	J – I	*J – II*	*A – I*	*A – II*	*J*	*A*
aa	1 (5.0)	0 (0.0)	3(15.8)	3(17.6)	1 (2.3)	6(16.7)
ab	4(20.0)	2 (8.7)	1 (5.3)	0 (0.0)	6(14.0)	1 (2.8)
ac	3(15.0)	2 (8.7)	3(15.8)	2(11.8)	5(11.6)	5(13.9)
ba	0 (0.0)	3(13.1)	0 (0.0)	1 (5.9)	3 (7.0)	1 (2.8)
bb	1 (5.0)	0 (0.0)	0 (0.0)	2(11.8)	1 (2.3)	2 (5.4)
bc	1 (5.0)	1 (4.3)	0 (0.0)	2(11.8)	2 (4.7)	2 (5.4)
ca	1 (5.0)	5(21.7)	3(15.8)	4(23.5)	6(14.0)	7(19.4)
cb	4(20.0)	2 (8.7)	5(26.3)	0 (0.0)	6(14.0)	5(13.9)
cc	5(25.0)	8(34.8)	4(21.0)	3(17.6)	13(30.2)	7(19.4)
N	20	23	19	17	43	36

NOTE The percentages, in parentheses, do not always add up to 100 because of rounding.

important cluster than the *A*s, while in the latter the *A*s are more numerous.

iv Comparing *J-I*s and *J-II*s, as well as the *A-I*s and *A-II*s, the responses to *c* show an interesting contrast: the *J-I*s and *A-I*s prefer *cb*, and the *J-II*s and *A-II*s opt for *ca*. This contrast is greater in the *J*'s case.

v Although the number of cases is too small to be really significant, the *bb* cluster contains one *J-I*, two *A-II*s, and neither *J-II* nor *A-I*.

The results of analysing figure 4 indicate that finding i related to prediction 4, which says that the *J*s are flexible and non-redundant in their choice. Findings ii and iii are related to the *J*'s preference for a relative-gain strategy as stated in prediction 1. Finding iv is not covered by any previous prediction; it seems to indicate, however, that when an *S* has fewer units of influence (less favoured and under higher-time pressure) he tends to prefer relative-gain strategy. This tendency is stronger among *J*s who use this strategy more often than do the *A*s. Finding v may corroborate this hypothesis in terms of the fact that for *A-I*s the *bb* cluster is vacant, whereas two *J-II*s are included in it. We must note in passing that for an *S* to be contained in a cluster means that *S* has a special familiarity with the response pattern, but does not necessarily mean that he uses this response most frequently.

The internal structure of the choice sequences used by the *S*s has to be more carefully analysed by means of the Hayashi quantification model. To make the analysis more subtle, we will use triads composed of three successive choices of the *S*s. Since there are three strategies, twenty-seven triads can be distinguished. These triads are distributed quite differently in the *J*'s and the *A*'s cases (figures 5 and 6). It can be observed that:

i The *A*s are more tightly clustered than the *J*s. This is a tendency also found in the case of the response dyads.

ii The first factor represents for both *J* and *A* the contrast between the triads with *c*s or *a*s and those with *b*s.

iii In *J*, the triads with *c*s and *a*s tend to be located in the lower part of figure 6, whereas those with three different strategies are in the centre east.

iv In the *A*'s case, it is difficult to find any clear pattern outside of the cluster of triads with *c*s and *a*s.

The above findings indicate that it is profitable to compare triads in terms of how they mix the three strategies. When an analysis of each triad's distance from point 0 is made, the results are:

v In all triads composed only of *c*s and/or *a*s, with the exceptions of *acc* and *cca*, the distance from point 0 to the triads is shorter for *A* than for *J*. In other words, *ccc, cac, caa, aca, aac,* and *aaa* are more commonly chosen by *A*s than *J*s.

vi In contrast, *aab, aba, abb,* and other triads composed of *a*s and *b*s, with the exceptions of *baa* and *bba*, are more common for *J*s than for *A*s.

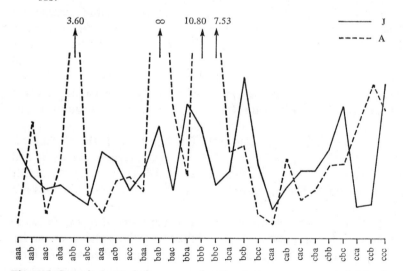

Figure 5 Canonical correlation comparing the strategy sequences (triads) of American and Japanese subjects.

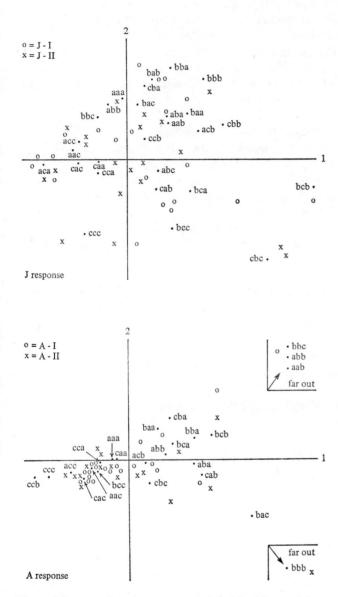

Figure 6 Pattern of strategy sequences (triads) of Japanese and American subjects.

Finding v supports prediction 2, which is based on the hypothesis that the *A*s prefer loss-minimizing strategies. Finding vi is in accordance with prediction 1 about the *c* preference of the *J*s.

To make the comparison more detailed it is necessary to use the cluster analysis approach again. There are twenty-seven triads which will be classified into five groups to make the comparison easier. The grouping will be made according to the following classification:

1   Triads with a single strategy: *aaa, bbb*, and *ccc*.
2   Triads with *a*s and *b*s: *aab, aba, baa, abb, bab, bba*.
3   Triads with *a*s and *c*s: *aac, aca, caa, cca, cac, acc*.
4   Triads with *b*s and *c*s: *bbc, bcb, cbb, bcc, cbc, ccb*.
5   Triads with three different strategies: *abc, acb, bac, bca, cab, cba*.

The percentages for each category are indicated in table 3 as for the dyads, in terms not only of *J*s and *A*s but also of their subcategories: *J-I, J-II, A-I*, and *A-II*. The following points deserve attention:

vii   The use of the same strategy three successive times is preferred only by *J-II*s.
viii   The *ac* triads contain more than half of the *A*s, while only one-third of the *J*s.
ix   The *bc* triads contain many more *J*s than *A*s.
x   The *bc* triads are preferred among the *J*s by *J-I*s, and among the *A*s by *A-II*s.
xi   *A-II*s do not cluster around the *ab* triads.

TABLE 3

Frequency of use of various strategy sequences in percentage

	J – I	*J – II*	*A – I*	*A – II*	*J*	*A*
1	0.0	18.2	0.0	0.0	8.8	0.0
2	25.9	13.8	23.7	0.0	19.9	11.2
3	34.7	32.0	52.6	68.4	33.3	61.1
4	21.6	13.8	5.9	10.6	17.7	8.4
5	17.3	22.2	17.7	21.1	19.9	19.5

Finding vii seems to contradict hypotheses 4, 5, and 6, which, if valid, would point towards an opposite trend. However, it must be remembered that the cluster analysis does not reveal the frequency with which a given triad is used, but rather whether a particular *S* has a special preference for the strategy mix represented by the triad. Therefore, the above hypotheses, which are corroborated by other findings – especially those which will be discussed later – are not disproved by finding vii which points out, rather, that a particular group of *J*s is especially persistent in their reiterated choice. It may well happen that the Japanese culture contains such a subculture. This is a point which deserves further investigation.

The interpretation of findings viii and ix is not difficult. They just corroborate predictions 1 and 2. Finding x seems to indicate that a combination of risk-taking gain-maximization with a self-sacrificing relative-gain maximization is an approach used by the *J*s when they feel themselves to be in an unfavourable position. In the *A*'s case, *A-I*s may be deterred from using this strategy because the weaker they feel themselves to be, and the stronger the time pressure, the stronger is their tendency to take fewer chances and avoid their own loss. This interpretation is, naturally, subject to further testing. As to finding xi, I suggest an explanation requiring further inquiry. When *A*s feel strong enough to take a risk, they do not favour a strategy mix of a conservative strategy *a* and a loss-incurring strategy *b*.

Let us now turn to the redundancy analysis results. This analysis is especially useful when one wants to compare the degree of orderliness and structure of given choice sequence patterns. When all the alternatives arc chosen with the same frequency, the pattern is most orderly and best structured. In the present experiment, two matrices were built, one the response matrix already discussed, and the other a one-step transition matrix giving the frequency of a transition from one strategy to another. We called the latter a sequence matrix. Total redundancy was computed for each *S*; conditional redundancy for the two *J* groups, as well as for the two *A* groups, was measured.

To test prediction 5, we compared the redundancy revealed in the two matrices. Response redundancy is represented by H_r, and sequence redundancy by H_s. Prediction 5 was interpreted to mean

$$H_{sj} < H_{rj} \text{ and } H_{sa} > H_{ra},$$

where the second subscript *j* means 'for *J*s' and *a* means 'for *A*s.' The figures in table 4 indicate:

i   The difference between *J*s and *A*s is significant only when we compare *J-II*s and *A-II*s. In this case, a χ^2 test shows significance at the 0.05 level. For the total groups of *J*s and *A*s, the significance level is 0.10.

TABLE 4

Comparison of response redundancy (H_r) and sequence redundancy (H_s) among American and Japanese subjects

	J – I	J – II	A – I	A – II	J	A
$H_s < H_r$	10	12	6	3	22	9
$H_s = H_r$	6	2	4	5	8	9
$H_s > H_r$	6	9	9	9	15	18

TABLE 5

Comparison of the predictive power of the subject's and of the opponent's previous choice of strategy for Americans and Japanese

		J – I	J – II	A – I	A – II
Sequence	a	0.0063	0.0984	0.1705	0.1942
redundancy	b	0.2113	0.0921	0.1191	0.0895
	c	0.1143	0.1320	0.4580	0.1972
Response	a	0.0109	0.1251	0.1572	0.2536
redundancy	b	0.0284	0.1071	0.9341	0.2056
	c	0.1230	0.0801	0.1431	0.1684
Difference	a	− 0.0046	− 0.0267	+ 0.0133	− 0.0595
	b	+ 0.1829	− 0.0150	− 0.8150	− 0.1161
	c	− 0.0087	+ 0.0519	+ 0.3139	+ 0.0288

Turning to the analysis of the conditional redundancy of the sequence and response matrices, we compared the sequence and response redundancies, i.e., the ease of predicting the S's choice on the basis of his previous a, b, or c choice with the facility of predicting it when the opponent's previous choice is known to be a, b, or c. Table 5 shows the results. We can read in the above tables the following tendencies:

i   As to the sequence redundancy, the A's choices are more easily predicted than the J's when they have cs and as as predictors. When the predictor is b, the Js are more redundant.

ii   The above holds with response redundancy.

iii With the exception of b for J-Is and of c for J-IIs, the response redundancy of the Js is higher than their sequence redundancy.

iv   In the A's case, response redundancy is smaller for c and a in the case of A-Is and for c for the A-IIs.

Therefore our hypotheses have to be revised to take account of 1 / the uncertainty associated with the relative-gain maximizing strategy in the choice pattern of the As; 2 / the self-consistency of J's choice sequences (using strategy *b*) when *J* is in the weak-position, high-time-pressure situations; and (using strategy *c*), in the stronger-position, more-time situations, 3 / the *A-II* tendency to have a high predictability in the response pattern to an opponent's choice of *a*, and 4 / *A-I*'s tendency to have a highly redundant response pattern towards an opponent's *b*. These revisions may lead to the following hypotheses.

HYPOTHESIS 7 The American negotiation culture has not yet institutionalized the rules associated wtih the use of the differential gain approach, except in terms of how to respond to it when one is in an unfavourable situation.

HYPOTHESIS 8 The Japanese negotiation culture has institutionalized the self-consistent use of relative-gain strategy in disadvantageous situations and the gain-maximizing approach in advantageous situations.

CONCLUSION

The present paper summarizes the results of a paper game, the ABC, which was administered to Japanese and American *S*s to test several hypotheses about the differences between the Japanese and the American – as examples of the East and West – negotiation cultures. Most of the hypotheses were corroborated by the findings obtained; however, several findings indicated the necessity of further experimentation based on a more refined set of hypotheses. To this effect, the same game is now being conducted in a laboratory situation where maximum research efficiency is sought through a combination of laboratory and paper games. I plan also to expand the number of countries being compared so as to obtain more universal results.

REFERENCES

ALKER, HAYWARD R. JR. 'Statistics and Politics: The Need for Causal Data Analysis', in Seymour Martin Lipset, ed. *Politics and the Social Sciences*. New York: Oxford University Press, 1969.

ATTNEAVE, FRED *Application of Information Theory to Psychology: A Summary of Basic Concepts, Methods and Results*. New York: H. Holt, 1959.

BOULDING, KENNETH E. *Conflict and Defense: A General Theory*. New York: Harper, 1962.

BUCHANAN, JAMES and G. TULLOCK *The Calculus of Consent: Logical Foundations of Constitutional Democracy*. Ann Arbor, Mich.: University of Michigan Press, 1962.

BUCHLER, IRA R. and HUGO G. NUTINI *Game Theory in the Behavioral Sciences*. Pittsburgh: University of Pittsburgh Press, 1968.

CONTITI, B. *The Value of Time in Bargaining Negotiations*, Part I: 'A Dynamic Model of Bargaining'; Part II: 'Experimental Evidence.' University of California, Center for Research in Management Science Working Paper, 207 and 208, Berkeley, 1967.

CROSS, J.G. 'A Theory of Bargaining Process,' *American Economic Review*, 55 (1965), pp. 67–94.

DEUTSCH, MORTON 'A Theory of Cooperation and Competition,' *Human Relations*, 2 (1949), pp. 129–52.

DEUTSCH, MORTON and ROBERT M. KRAUSS 'Studies of Interpersonal Bargaining,' *Journal of Conflict Resolution*, VI (1962), pp. 52–76.

DRESHER, MELVIN *Games of Strategy: Theory and Application*. Englewood Cliffs, NJ: Prentice-Hall, 1961.

IKLE, CHARLES F. *How Nations Negotiate*. New York: Harper & Row, 1964.

IKLE, CHARLES F. and NATHAN LEITES 'Political Negotiation as a Process of Modifying Utilities,' *Journal of Conflict Resolution*, VI (1962), pp. 19–28.

KUHN, HAROLD W. 'Game Theory and Models of Negotiation,' *Journal of Conflict Resolution*, VI (1962), pp. 1–4.

LALL, ANAND *Modern International Negotiation: Principles and Practice*. New York: Columbia University Press, 1966.

LUCE, ROBERT DUNCAN and HOWARD RAIFFA *Games and Decision: Introduction and Critical Survey*. A study of the Behavioral Models Project, Bureau of Applied Social Research, Columbia University. New York: Wiley, 1957.

MUSHAKOJI, KINHIDE *Kokusai Seiji to Nippon (International Politics and Japan)*. Tokyo 1967.

– 'Seiji-teki Hatsugen no Riron (A Theory of Political Discourse),' in Mitsuo Suzuki, *Kyoso-Shakai no Game no Riron*. Tokyo 1970.

– 'Kozo to Kakunin – "Rashisa" no Shakudo ni tsuite' (Structure and Discrimination: A Scale of 'likelihood') in *Jochi Daigaku Gaikokugo Gakubu Kiyo*, no 4 (1969).

– 'Negotiation between the West and the Non-West,' in *Proceedings of the International Peace Research Association Second Conference*. I Assen: Van Forcum, 1968.

NASH, J.F. 'The Bargaining Problem,' *Econometrica*, 2 (1953), pp. 128–40.

POLYA, GEORGE *Mathematics and Plausible Reasoning*, II. *Pattern of Plausible Inference*. Princeton, NJ: Princeton University Press, 1964.

PRUITT, DEAR G. 'An Analysis of Responsiveness between Nations,' *Journal of Conflict Resolution*, VI (1962), pp. 5–18.

RAPOPORT, ANATOL *Fights, Games, and Debates*. Ann Arbor, Mich: University of Michigan Press, 1960.

RAPOPORT, ANATOL and ALBERT M. CHAMMAH *Prisoner's Dilemma: A Study in Conflict and Cooperation*. Ann Arbor, Mich: University of Michigan Press, 1965.

RAPOPORT, ANATOL and CAROL ORWANT 'Experimental Games: A Review,' *Behavioral Science*, 7 (1962), pp. 1–37.
RUSSETT, BRUCE M. ed. *Economic Theories of International Politics*. Chicago: Markham, 1968.
SCHELLING, THOMAS C. *The Strategy of Conflict*. Cambridge, Mass: Harvard University Press, 1960.
– 'What is Game Theory,' in James Clyde Charlesworth, ed. *Contemporary Political Analysis*. New York: Free Press, 1967.
SCHRODER, HAROLD M., MICHAEL J. DRIVER, and SIEGFRIED STREUFERT *Human Information Processing: Individuals and Groups Functioning in Complex Social Situations*. New York: Holt, Rinehart & Winston, 1967.
SCODEL, ALVIN, P. RATOOSH, and J.S. MINAS 'Some Personality Correlates of Decision-Making Under Conditions of Risk,' in Dorothy Willner, ed. *Decision, Values and Groups*. I. Oxford: Pergamon Press, 1960.
SHUBIK, MARTIN, ed. *Game Theory and Related Approaches to Social Behavior: Selections*. New York: Wiley, 1964.
STANILAND, ALAN CHARLES *Patterns of Redundancy: A Psychological Study*. Cambridge: Cambridge University Press, 1966.
STONE, J.J. 'An Experiment in Bargaining Games,' *Econometrica*, 26 (1958), pp. 286–96.
SUZUKI, MITSUO *Game no Riron (The Theory of Game)*. Tokyo 1959.
– *Kyoso-Shakai no Game no Riron (The Theory of Game in Competitive Societies)*. Tokyo 1970.
TANAKA, YOSHIHISA *Shinrigaku-teki Sokuteiho (Psychological Measurement)*. Tokyo 1961.
TANAKA, YASUMASA *Kigo-Kodo-Ron (Sign Behaviour)*. Tokyo 1968.
WATANABE, SATOSHI *Knowing and Guessing*. New York 1969.
WILLNER, DOROTHY, ed. *Decision, Values and Groups*. I. Oxford: Pergamon Press, 1960.
WILDE, D.J. *Optimum Seeking Methods*. Englewood Cliffs, NJ: Prentice-Hall, 1964.
WILSON, KELLOG V. and V. EDWIN BIXENSTINE 'Forms of Social Control in Two-Person Two-Choice Games,' *Behavioral Science*, 7 (1962), pp. 92–102.
YASUDA, SABURO *Shakai Tokei-Gaku (Social Statistics)*. Tokyo 1969.
YOUNG, KENNETH TODD *Negotiating with the Chinese Communists: the United States Experience, 1953–1967*. New York: Published for the Council on Foreign Relations by McGraw-Hill, 1968.

WILLIAM H. RIKER & WILLIAM JAMES ZAVOINA

Rational behaviour in politics: evidence from a three-person game*

I

A fundamental controversy in political theory from ancient times until the present has centred around the rationality of political actors, what it is, if it exists at all, and whether or not humans display it in politics. Many political scientists have become impatient with this controversy because it remains open after so much (apparently futile) discussion. They should not be. The problem of rationality is necessarily embedded in even the simplest kinds of political research, where, if overlooked, misinterpretation and even outright error may result.

Suppose, for example, in an investigation of legislators, one uses the notion of party loyalty as an independent variable to explain behaviour. This seems simple and straightforward enough and not, therefore, likely to involve one in philosophical controversy. But in fact party loyalty can be interpreted in a variety of ways and the choice among them necessarily involves a choice on one side of the controversy over rationality. Loyalty can be thought of, for example, as a truly independent variable, as a product of political socialization, as an expression of affect, and hence as an essentially irrational motive. On the other hand, it may be thought of as itself dependent on bargains rationally satisfying the preferences of legislators. Such bargains may be either short term or long

* The work on this essay was undertaken with the support of a grant from the National Science Foundation. We thank the Foundation very much.

term so that a legislator's manifest party loyalty may result from a series of advantageous bargains with party leaders on particular bills or from an implied bargain with them on career advantage. But in either case if party loyalty is the product of bargains, it is something quite different from loyalty based on affect. And this variation in turn makes a profound difference in the interpretation of the behaviour of legislators, for a loyalty based on bargains is subject to strains and stresses not found in a loyalty based on affect. Which kind of loyalty exists influences the prediction of behaviour and, thus, the quality of prediction depends on a decision in the philosophical controversy.

This controversy is pervasive in political science. The controversy implicit in the notion of party loyalty as applied to legislators is equally implicit in the notion as applied to voters and, beyond that, is implicit in such concepts as class interest, national interest, alliance membership, etc., when used as variables to explain the behaviour of men or nations. It is not possible, therefore, to avoid the controversy in serious political research.

Pervasive as this controversy is, political science has made remarkably little effort to resolve it for its own concerns. Although the present form of the question is 'Are men rational in making decisions?' the greater portion of the philosophizing about political rationality has been in terms of the issue as it was raised by Plato, the Stoics, and the philosophers (e.g., Hobbes and Rousseau) and lawyers (e.g., Grotius and Blackstone) of early modern times. These writers saw no issue in whether or not men are rational; all assumed they are. Rather they debated the nature of this rationality. Do men, in behaving rationally, seek to maximize self-interest or to maximize some external goal as set forth for them in divine law, natural law, or the general will? An illustration of the regressive quality of much of current political philosophy is the recent volume on rationality in which almost all the discussion is in these anachronistic terms.[1]

But while political philosophers keep on debating the issues raised by Hobbes and Rousseau, the controversy has changed. Now, as a result of philosophical and scientific inquiry in the two intervening centuries, the question has become: 'When faced with the necessity of decision among several alternatives, do men order their preferences among them and choose that alternative which maximizes their utility?' Of course, utility is understood as a measure on ordered preferences. Or, assuming

1 Carl J. Friedrich, ed., *Nomos VII: Rational Decision* (New York: Atherton Press, 1964). There is, however, one work which blends the old and the new very nicely: Paul Diesing, *Reason in Society* (Urbana: University of Illinois Press, 1962).

a general affirmative to that question: 'On the basis of what goals do men order their preferences?'[2] Around these questions today there are a variety of philosophical positions, among the most important of which are:
1   Those which assert that choosers maximize utility. Although the contemporary intellectual world is often described as antirationalist, the science of economics, which is the most practically successful and intellectually elegant of the social studies, is built entirely on the premise of rational behaviour. In an antirationalist world, it has kept alive one side of the older rationalism (i.e., the radical individualism and nominalism of Hobbes and Bentham), but it has so refined the problem that its genetic resemblance to its ancestor is only barely visible. Its picture of the rational calculus is that men order preferences according to their tastes, although they impose on the ordering some elementary logical requirements of coherence and consistency. Once ordered, men then behave in situations involving risky choice as if they were maximizing expected utility, where utility is a numerical measure on preference orders. If one assumes that tastes are given and inscrutable, then the will appears as arbiter of taste, and reason appears as the efficient servant of the will. In such a view of rationality, which we call procedural, men are invariably rational. The only way an observer can discover the inscrutable goals is by observing choices among alternatives. From the choice, and from the assumption that the chooser maximized his utility, the observer infers the subject's goals. Although this theory is tautological it does assert something testable – namely, that men behave as if they are rational calculators. In many economic and political applications, however, one assumes further that a particular goal is appropriate for all men in the particular circumstances of the choice. In this view of rationality, which we call substantive, men as producers are said to maximize profit, men as consumers are said to minimize cost, etc. This theory, since it is not tautological, allows tests of assertions about calculation, but unfortunately it also involves the scientist in attributing goals and necessarily, therefore, includes the chance of error from this source. Both versions of rationality, regardless of whether or not a goal is postulated do, however, assume that men are rational calculators, which is what other, subsequently listed, theories do not assume.
2   Those which assert that choosers choose by habit and discovery rather than by analysis of preference. Learning theory, which derives from that great nineteenth-century realization that man is part of the animal kingdom and from the great twentieth-century realization that laboratory animals (and thence man) could be taught to respond posi-

2   This question, while superficially resembling the old one, differs in the expectation that goals are empirically investigated rather than attributed.

tively to stimuli associated with rewards, offers a totally different picture of choice from that implied in the question as we have stated it. In learning theory, choices are said to occur as a result of rewards and punishments administered for previous behaviour. If a subject – man or rat – chooses in random exploration an alternative that results in a reward, then on subsequent presentation with the same alternatives he chooses that which led to the reward. The chooser, of course, has preferences, even ordered preferences, and in this sense learning theory is like the theory of rationality in that men are said to choose what is preferred over what is not preferred. But the theories differ because in learning theory the choice results not from a calculus but from the recall of previous consequences. Naturally, there is no maximization of utility here, merely the satisfaction of some desires, which are not necessarily the most pressing ones.

3   Those which assert that choosers do not maximize utility. Here the most well-known position is the psychoanalytic, which ultimately derives from the exaltation of will against reason in such writers as Schopenhauer and Nietzsche. Against the rationalistic view that reason is the servant of the will, here will and reason are at war. Not unexpectedly, therefore, the very notion of ordering preferences is rejected as an unrealistic description of behaviour. Instead, choice is interpreted as the product of sexual forces modified by rationalizing and socializing counter-forces in an essentially disordered way. To the psychoanalyst, therefore, the answer to the question of whether or not men choose so as to maximize utility is not simply 'no' but rather that men are likely to choose exactly oppositely. Somewhat similar to the psychoanalytic position in this respect is the theory of cognitive dissonance. According to this notion, the relation of choice to preference as we stated it in our initial question is a reversal of nature. Instead of choosing so as to maximize utility (a measure of preference), men are said to construct preferences in order to rationalize choice. What comes first is choice based on some wholly unrationalized affect such as identification or Oedipal urges or what not. If this choice is challenged, then preferences are ordered to rationalize it. Hence choice is first and preference second, an outright reversal from the theory of rational behaviour. Naturally, the theory of cognitive dissonance, like psychoanalysis, has no place for choice that maximizes utility.

Such is the confrontation of rationalism and antirationalism as it appears today in social science. A remarkable feature of the dispute is that each of the viewpoints, while supposedly universal, is actually quite closely linked to the behaviour studied. Thus the main contemporary exponents of the model of calculating man are economists, who study behaviour in the market. The main exponents of the model of choice by habit and discovery are learning theorists, who study behaviour in the rat maze and the classroom. The main exponents of the model of choice by reason of sexual drives are psychoanalysts, who study behaviour in dreams and fantasy-making. And the notion of cognitive dissonance with its emphasis on choice as against preference was first applied in a study of religious behaviour. Each theory, however, seems to work fairly well when applied to behaviour for which it was created and to appear insufficient when applied to behaviour generally.

This fact creates a difficult problem for political theory. If, as we have argued, the quality of political research depends in part on the position the researcher takes on the question of rationality, he must choose among the theories in this spectrum. But to do so he needs to make some decision about the kind of behaviour he is studying. Is political behaviour closer to behaviour in the market or to behaviour in fantasy? If we could answer this question with assurance, we could adopt wholesale a theory from another discipline. But assuming politics is, in Easton's words, the authoritative allocation of values, it is uncertain whether utility theory or something quite different applies. So far as politics is allocation, it seems analogous to economics, which is often defined as the allocation of scarce resources. So far as politics is authoritative, however, it seems analogous to the world where learning theory applies, with its emphasis on rewards and punishments, or even to the dark and vicious world of fantasy where power is thinly veiled sadism and authority is power with yet another veil.

Given this ambiguous nature of politics, it seems desirable, therefore, to investigate action in a political setting in order to determine in some preliminary way, at least, what kind of behaviour is political behaviour and hence what kind of theory about rationality is appropriate for political science. That is, we need to look at characteristically political behaviour with a view towards determining what kind of theory of rationality fits it best.

To a small degree, such work has been done. A generation ago Harold Lasswell studied several politicians psychoanalytically, though the relation between their behaviour on the couch and their behaviour in political office was never made clear.[3] Furthermore, Lasswell wrote as a proponent of a particular theory rather than as an evaluator of competing theories. More recently Robert Lane has studied by depth interviews the thought processes on political issues of a few ordinary citizens, although again the relation of their attitudes to their political actions was not in-

3   Harold Lasswell, *Psychopathology and Politics* (Chicago: University of Chicago Press, 1930).

vestigated.[4] Much of the early survey research on voting by Paul Lazarsfeld and especially Bernard Berelson was interpreted by its authors in antirationalist terms, thereby setting something of a style for subsequent writers, but V.O. Key responded in *The Responsible Electorate* with what reads very much like an interpretation in terms of utility theory of the whole range of data from survey research about voting.[5] Recently Peter Ordeshook and Riker attempted to interpret data on the decision to vote so that behaviour followed directly from the assumptions of utility theory, although one term of the equation looks very much as if it originated in learning theory.[6] Herbert Simon is responsible for introducing political scientists to learning theory (through his notion of 'satisficing' as contrasted with 'maximizing'), but he never really used it to investigate political behaviour. Others, however, have, especially Charles Lindblom, whose notion of incrementalism is derived from Simon's 'satisficing' and is offered as a general rule of political decision.[7] And Richard Fenno and Davis, Dempster, and Wildavsky have applied something of this notion to explain appropriation decisions.[8] Unfortunately this short survey mentions most of the important work that has been done. And except for the work by Key none of it has been undertaken in a mood of evaluation and for the purpose of offering an answer to the question of what kind of theory about rationality is appropriate for political science. Clearly more diverse investigations than these are desirable in order to clarify this question. In this essay, therefore, we offer a report on one such investigation which suggests that political behaviour is the kind of behaviour for which utility theory is appropriate.

II

It would be fortunate if we could study rationality in politics directly, and sometimes we can as when we investigate whether or not people vote in accordance with previously expressed preferences. But most political

4 Robert Lane, *Political Ideology* (Glencoe: Free Press, 1962).
5 Paul Lazarsfeld, Bernard Berelson, and Hazel Gaudet, *The People's Choice* (New York: Duell, Sloan and Pearce, 1944). Bernard Berelson, Paul Lazarsfeld, and William McPhee, *Voting* (Chicago: University of Chicago Press, 1954). V.O. Key, *The Responsible Electorate* (Cambridge: Belknap Press of Harvard University Press, 1966).
6 William H. Riker and Peter Ordeshook, 'A Theory of the Calculus of Voting,' *American Political Science Review*, 62, 1 (1968), pp. 25–42.
7 David Braybrooke and Charles Lindblom, *Strategy of Decision* (Glencoe: Free Press, 1963).
8 Richard Fenno, *The Power of the Purse* (Boston: Little Brown, 1966). Otto Davis, M.A.H. Dempster, and Aaron Hildavsky, 'A Theory of the Budgetary Process,' *American Political Science Review*, 60 (1964), pp. 529–47.

activity, especially that most interesting kind involving the work of professional makers of majorities and public policy, is not readily open to
direct investigation. Consequently, we have used surrogate political subjects in a surrogate political setting and we offer evidence about their
behaviour as indirect evidence about political behaviour in a wider world.

This study is based on the assumption that what happens in n-person
games is closely analogous to what happens in politics. The main activity
in an n-person game is making coalitions (that is, making policies that
satisfy a majority), which is what political leaders spend most of their
time doing. Political followers, when they act politically (as in voting)
are mainly engaged in joining coalitions. Hence the game activity of
making coalitions is very much like the essential activity of politics.

Games are not, of course, perfect analogies for unabstracted natural
events – nor indeed are any other laboratory experiments in any social
or natural science – but they are closer analogies for politics than any
others yet offered. Surely they are closer to the characteristic action of
politics than fantacizing on a psychoanalyst's couch. At least games involve those interpersonal transactions which are essential to politics,
while behaviour in confession does not involve even that. Games, furthermore, seem to us to be better analogies than learning experiments, which
typically involve only problem-solving and the avoidance of error. Politics,
doubtless, involves this, but it includes much more, especially the manipulation of relationships with others, creativity in organization, and the
like. And these are precisely the kind of activities that are captured in
the n person game.

Conversely, behaviour in games is probably more closely analogous
to politics than is behaviour in the market. Transactions in the market are
by definition harmonious, for every sale is a purchase and both buyer and
seller invariably leave the market better off in utility. Even if no trades
occur, no one is worse off. It is not so with politics. Some political situations such as elections are zero-sum, such that the winner wins what the
loser loses. And this guarantees the existence of losers – people who are
worse off because they entered the political arena. Even if politics is not
zero-sum, typically there are losers. Consider a civil war, say the American Civil War, which may have been zero-sum with respect to the governments but was surely not so with respect to the participants. The losers of
that war precipitated it to protect (and extend) slavery; what they got for
their trouble was the Thirteenth Amendment. The war was not zero-sum
because the winners did not get the slaves the losers lost. But the losers
surely lost something and from hindsight we know they would have been
wiser not to have fought at all. So it is with much of politics. Entry into the

political arena necessarily involves the risk of loss which is not fully captured by market analogies. Game analogies, however, catch this feature of the real world.

There are, of course, many points at which the game analogy fails. One can try in the laboratory to introduce some of the features of the political world, but the game remains an analogy, not the real stuff of politics. In this experiment we have tried to compensate in a few ways not likely to occur to psychologists for the fact that the laboratory is not the wider world. For example, our subjects were self-selected (that is, they answered advertisements) and were allowed to drop out if they didn't like the game (usually because they lost), just as politicians are self-selected and remain or drop out by a kind of natural selection of winners. In some of the experiments the subjects played against each other several times and knew from the beginning that this would be so, just as politicians know and are constrained by the fact that they expect to meet again. (From the protocols, we know our subjects were conscious of the repetition, but we suspect that they were not nearly so preoccupied with it as politicians are said to be.) Again, our subjects, while initially unacquainted, saw each other in the laboratory often enough in intense situations to develop strong feelings of friendship and enmity, which we interpreted as the laboratory equivalent of loyalty, hostility, and even ideology in the political world. But we know, of course, that these putative equivalents are pale imitations of these forces in political life. So, although we have tried to fit the laboratory circumstance to the political circumstance, we know we have not been wholly successful and the game remains only an analogy of politics, not politics itself. But until we can get real politicians to answer questions they would surely regard as silly, we think games in the laboratory are about the best we can do to study political behaviour in exhaustive detail.

III

Although Riker has elsewhere described this game in some detail, we repeat a brief description of its major features:[9]
1   There are three players. In most groups of subjects these have been college undergraduates, although one group consisted of businessmen. All were from middle-class backgrounds. Subjects were assigned to all three positions so that each subject played each position in about one-third of the matches he played.

9   William H. Riker, 'Bargaining in a Three-person Game,' *American Political Science Review*, 61, 3 (1967), pp. 642–56.

2   The players negotiate in pairs about coalitions, usually thus: (1,2) for five minutes, while 3 is in another room; (1,3) for five minutes, while 2 is in another room; (2,3) for five minutes, while 1 is in another room; This order is then repeated for three (or in some cases, three to six) more conversations. With two groups the order of conversations was varied.
3   At the end of negotiations, players are asked privately and individually what coalition they have formed. If two agree, they are paid, otherwise not.
4   Payments are according to the following schedule: if (1,2) forms, it receives \$4.00; if (1,3) forms, it receives \$5.00; if (2,3) forms, it receives \$6.00; if (1), (2), (3), or (1,2,3) form they receive nothing.
5   The Von Neumann-Morgenstern solution to this game is that one of the following divisions of the stakes occur (the 'principal points'):

Player 1	Player 2	Player 3
\$1.50	\$2.50	0
\$1.50	0	\$3.50
0	\$2.50	\$3.50

or that any one of an infinity of divisions occur, having the properties either

1    $1.50 \leqslant x_1 < 3.50, 2.50 \leqslant x_2 < 4.50, 0 < x_3 < 2.00$,
and $\sum_{i=1}^{3} x_i = \$6.00$, or

2    $1.50 \leqslant x_1 < 2.50, 0 < x_2 < 1.00, 3.50 < x_3 < 4.50$,
and $\sum_{i=1}^{3} x_i = \$5.00$,

where x_i is the payment to the ith player.[10] The informal rules of this game were such that a division of the latter two sorts were hard to arrive at, although a few of our ingenious subjects found ways to get to them.

IV

As we interpreted the behaviour of the initial group of subjects, it became apparent that they were behaving rationally in some profound and not

10   John Von Neumann and Oskar Morgenstern, *The Theory of Games and Economic Behavior* (Princeton: Princeton University Press, 1953, 3rd edition), pp. 403–18. A simple exposition of the derivation of this solution from the notions of utility theory can be found in R.D. Luce and Howard Raiffa, *Games and Decisions* (New York: Wiley, 1957), pp. 200–3, and William H. Riker, 'Bargaining in a Three-person Game.'

immediately obvious sense. Experimentation was started with a game which had a solution of [(0,2.00,0), (0,0,4.00), (0,2.00,4.00)] but then was changed to the present game because the subjects found the original game boring. It was not until this first group had nearly completed its matches with the present game that we realized that they were averaging something quite close to the Von Neumann-Morgenstern solution, which is derived directly from utility theory and some elementary standards of rational behaviour. That these subjects in these circumstances should, fairly consistently, come close to a socially rational solution seemed to us compelling evidence that utility theory was an appropriate description of their behaviour. Even more compelling was the fact that both the subjects and the experimenters were in effect unsophisticated about the solution.

Subsequent groups of subjects further and strongly confirmed our belief by coming as close or closer to the solution, although in some groups some of the subjects were initially sophisticated (either because they had solved the game immediately upon learning the rules or because they had learned the solution from subjects in previous groups) and communicated their knowledge among the other subjects as the matches progressed for several weeks. Of the seven groups reported on here, the first, fourth, and seventh were initially unsophisticated and the first and seventh remained so to the end. Since sophisticated and unsophisticated subjects behaved about the same way in arriving at outcomes and since we know from observation and protocols that sophisticated subjects seldom let their knowledge hinder them from pressing a bargaining advantage or sadly recognizing a disadvantage, the degree of sophistication appears to be irrelevant. On the other hand, in their consistent propensity, sophisticated or not, to come close to the solution, each group of subjects further confirmed the belief that they were in sum and on the whole behaving rationally. Even in the five matches in groups of six where three-person coalitions were formed, the divisions were within the solution and hence quite rational.

In table 1 is recorded a summary of the results of 206 matches in seven groups. The actual outcomes of each match are reported elsewhere.[11] For each two-person coalition, table 1 records in the first row the number of times this coalition occurred. (Matches in which only single-member coalitions occurred – 16 in all – are omitted as are the 5 matches where three-person coalitions were formed.) In the second row

11 For groups one to three, see Riker, 'Bargaining in a Three-person Game.'
    For groups four to seven, see Riker, 'An Experimental Interpretation of Formal and Informal Rules of a Three Person Game,' in Bernhardt Lieberman, *Social Choice* (forthcoming).

TABLE 1

Summary of outcomes of matches by groups*

	Coalition (1,2)		Coalition (1,3)		Coalition (2,3)	
	1	2	1	3	2	3
GROUP 1						
n	9		10		13	
$\hat{\mu}$	1.69	2.31	1.42	3.58	2.52	3.48
$\hat{\sigma}$	0.349	0.349	0.307	0.307	0.360	0.360
t	0.54		0.25		0.05	
$Pr[t]$	$P[\lvert t \rvert > 0.54] \simeq 0.60$		$P[\lvert t \rvert > 0.25] \simeq 0.80$		$P[\lvert t \rvert > 0.05] \simeq 0.96$	
GROUP 2						
n	4		3		12	
$\hat{\mu}$	1.56	2.44	1.62	3.38	2.47	3.53
$\hat{\sigma}$	0.658	0.658	0.262	0.262	0.589	0.589
t	0.09		0.46		0.05	
$Pr[t]$	$P[\lvert t \rvert > 0.09] \simeq 0.90$		$P[\lvert t \rvert > 0.46] \simeq 0.60$		$P[\lvert t \rvert > 0.05] \simeq 0.95$	
GROUP 3						
n	5		15		18	
$\hat{\mu}$	1.46	2.54	1.41	3.59	2.47	3.53
$\hat{\sigma}$	0.055	0.055	0.222	0.222	0.214	0.214
t	0.73		0.41		0.14	
$Pr[t]$	$P[\lvert t \rvert > 0.73] \simeq 0.50$		$P[\lvert t \rvert > 0.41] \simeq 0.60$		$P[\lvert t \rvert > 0.14] \simeq 0.85$	
GROUP 4						
n	9		5		14	
$\hat{\mu}$	1.44	2.56	1.77	3.23	2.88	3.12
$\hat{\sigma}$	0.556	0.556	0.365	0.365	0.187	0.187
t	0.10		0.74		2.03	
$Pr[t]$	$P[\lvert t \rvert > 0.10] \simeq 0.90$		$P[\lvert t \rvert > 0.74] \simeq 0.50$		$P[\lvert t \rvert > 2.03] \simeq 0.05$	
GROUP 5						
n	8		11		16	
$\hat{\mu}$	1.39	2.61	1.48	3.52	2.55	3.45
$\hat{\sigma}$	0.306	0.306	0.265	0.265	0.295	0.295
t	0.35		0.07		0.17	
$Pr[t]$	$P[\lvert t \rvert > 0.35] \simeq 0.75$		$P[\lvert t \rvert > 0.07] \simeq 0.95$		$P[\lvert t \rvert > 0.17] \simeq 0.80$	
GROUP 6†						
n	11		7		15	
$\hat{\mu}$	1.55	2.45	1.66	3.34	2.53	3.47
$\hat{\sigma}$	0.151	0.151	0.374	0.374	0.142	0.142
t	0.33		0.43		0.21	
$Pr[t]$	$P[\lvert t \rvert > 0.33] \simeq 0.75$		$P[\lvert t \rvert > 0.43] \simeq 0.65$		$P[\lvert t \rvert > 0.21] \simeq 0.80$	
GROUP 7						
n	4		10		6	
$\hat{\mu}$	1.41	2.59	1.50	3.50	2.52	3.48
$\hat{\sigma}$	0.086	0.086	0.161	0.161	0.249	0.249
t	1.05		0.00		0.08	
$Pr[t]$	$P[\lvert t \rvert > 1.05] \simeq 0.35$		$P[\lvert t \rvert > 0.00] \simeq 1.00$		$P[\lvert t \rvert > 0.08] \simeq 0.90$	

*   Matches resulting in single member coalitions omitted.
†   Matches resulting in grand coalitions omitted.

is the mean amount $\hat{\mu}$ earned by the player in the designated position, while the third row contains the standard deviation $\hat{\sigma}$ around the mean. (Since we have treated these as samples out of a population of possible matches, we have put hats over μ and σ to indicate they are sample estimates, in the case of σ an unbiased estimate.) In the fourth row is the t statistic and in the fifth row is the probability that a t statistic of that absolute value might be achieved by chance.

The information in table 1 permits us to observe how close the subjects often came to the Von Neumann-Morgenstern solution. The null hypothesis is that the mean payoff to the players is, for 1, $1.50, for 2, $2.50, and for 3, $3.50. The probabilities of the occurrence of ts of the particular absolute value (since this is a two-tailed test) indicate whether or not the null hypothesis can be rejected. From these probabilities, it is clearly apparent that the null hypothesis cannot be rejected, except possibly in the case of coalition (2,3) for group 4.[12] All other ts are well within the range of chance occurrence. The inference then is that in all but, perhaps, this one case, the variations around $1.50, $2,50, and $3.50 are insignificant random variations showing no particular direction or amount of deviations. Furthermore, one also infers that, whether the subjects knew it or not, they were coming close to the solution and hence were acting as if to secure the predicted dollar rewards.

Nevertheless, while the net results of transactions as expressed in the divisions appeared clearly to result from rational behaviour, paradoxically the individual behaviour did not in itself appear to be rational in the sense of maximizing utility. Often subjects voted (and usually thereby chose between two alternative coalitions) in such a way as to reject the coalition that offered them the largest absolute value. For example, player 3 might be offered $3.80 out of $5.00 by player 1 and $3.45 out of $6.00 by player 2, and yet might choose (2,3) and $3.45 instead of (1,3) and

12 By reason of another consideration this one case in which rejection of the null hypothesis is feasible does not invalidate the inference because the exception has a special explanation. See Riker, 'Experimental Interpretation.' In groups 1–3, 5, and 6, the order of negotiations was [(1,2), (1,3), (2,3)] so that player 1 was omitted from the last certain conversation. For Group 7, the order was [(2,3), (1,2), (1,3)], so that 2 was omitted, while for group 4, it was [(2,3), (1,3), (1,2)], so that 3 was omitted. The effects of omission were, for 1 and 2, that they simply did not win as frequently as might be expected, although they won the expected amounts in each match. Player 3, however, won just about as frequently when omitted, but won significantly less money. Recognizing that this variation in outcome was thus occasioned by the informal rule that brought the mathematical game into temporal reality, we can then understand that this one deviation in the outcomes reflects not a failure to achieve the rational solution but rather a rational adjustment of the solution in response to a special rule.

$3.80. On a simple interpretation of maximization, clearly such a player was not maximizing. Still his behaviour on the average turned out to be very close to what an abstract maximizer is calculated to bring about. Clearly, there is something wrong with an explanation in which individual irrationalities add up to group rationalities.

It seemed likely on the basis of unsystematic questioning, however, that the subjects were not really behaving irrationally in their individual choice. Instead of maximizing dollar amounts, they initially seemed to be maximizing expected values of the prizes, that is, they seemed to be discounting their anticipated share of the payoff to a coalition by the probability that the coalition would actually occur. Hence, the choice of a smaller amount over a larger might indicate simply a greater confidence that the coalition with the smaller individual payoff would actually form.

Logical analysis, however, revealed that the expected utility calculus ignored the dynamic aspects of the bargaining process and, hence, was not an appropriate model. The weighting process on each alternative, which is central to this calculus, assumes that the utility payoff on an alternative is independent of the probability associated with its occurrence. The nature of the bargaining process forces recognition that a functional relationship exists between the probabilities and utilities in coalition formation. A player proposes a given division of the payoffs because he feels that a coalition could form around this division and alters this proposed payoff structure in an attempt to increase the likelihood of forming a winning coalition. A player who wished to win would not make proposals that he felt had little chance of acceptance.

One rational choice model, however, recognizes the importance of both dynamics of the bargaining process and the functional relationship between the utility payoffs and probabilities associated with them. The probability maximization model assumes that players approach coalition formation with a different perspective than either the utility maximization or expected utility maximization models. Coalitions are seen as being either winning coalitions or losing coalitions. Consequently, a player would attempt to form that coalition which he perceives as having the highest probability of winning, that is, he would vote for the player he felt is most likely to vote for him.

In order to test for this possibility, subjects in groups 5, 6, and 7 were asked (after each set of three conversations) to estimate the probability that each of the others would vote for them, as well as probabilities for their own vote and for the formation of the several coalitions. To ensure that these probabilities were not thoughtlessly estimated, the questions were constructed so that the subject was forced to add them up to 1.00.

The data from those questionnaires filled out just before the voting provide the basis for a test of the probability maximization interpretation.

Assume that the subject ordered his preferences so that, if P_1 and P_2 are the perceived probabilities of winning such that $0 < P_1 < P_2$, then the subject preferred P_2 to P_1 and P_1 to 0 and P_2 to 0. Note that this is an assumption of substantive rationality, that is, we have imposed a goal for the subjects to maximize towards and assumed that this goal is appropriate to the situation they are in. We know that his goal may not be wholly appropriate for at least two subjects, both of whom were fairly consistent losers. One subject in group five who, out of ten matches, won only the first, third, and ninth, became especially sulky after his eighth match. After a long dry spell, he had confidently expected to win because of a long-term agreement made in his first match. But he lost and felt betrayed and announced he would play no more. He subsequently agreed to play the two further matches for which he was scheduled, but his heart was not in it. Although he actually won one of them, he behaved as if it were beneath his dignity to win and it is possible – though not certain – he preferred to lose. Another subject in group six, who out of nine matches won only the fourth and eighth, adopted a stance in bargaining that made him an almost certain loser. Midway in this series subjects invented a method of enforcing trust by exchanging objects of value (such as books, meal tickets, etc.) to be re-exchanged after a bargain to vote for each other was carried out. But the losing subject rejected all such bargains proffered on the ground, invented by himself, that they were not in harmony with the game. It seemed to these observers that his policy served the purpose only of providing himself beforehand with an excuse for anticipated failure. He could say to himself: 'I may be losing, but at least I am more ethical than these other fellows.' So he too may actually have preferred to lose, for by guaranteeing himself a loss ahead of time he avoided thus the shame of losing when he was trying to win. But these are only two subjects out of thirty-four in the three groups and their possible preference for losing might have occurred in only six of their nineteen matches. Using these two as contrasts, all other subjects appeared to the observers to want to win. We feel safe, therefore, in attributing to all subjects the preference order of P_2 to P_1, P_1 to 0, and P_2 to 0.

To determine whether or not subjects were maximizing subjective probability of winning, let $\hat{P}(ij)$ be the ith player's estimate of the probability that the jth player will vote for i, and let $\hat{P}(ik)$ be the ith player's estimate of the probability that the kth player will vote for i. If subjects were maximizing probabilities, then their decision rule must be the following:

If $\hat{P}(ij) > \hat{P}(ik)$, then i votes for j;

If $\hat{P}(ik) > \hat{P}(ij)$, then i votes for k;

If $\hat{P}(ij) = \hat{P}(ik)$, then i votes for either j or k.

On the basis of this analysis, we find that the subjects' voting behaviour overwhelmingly supports the probability maximization model. A detailed test for each case is contained in the appendix. Almost 92 per cent of the voting decisions studied (275 out of 300) can be explained by the probability maximization criterion. Considering that we were careful never to discuss their probability estimates with the subjects in order not to encourage them to rationalize their choices, 92 per cent seems a remarkably high proportion of maximizations.

Yet not all of the twenty-five who failed to maximize can be consigned to the dark world of the irrational. For example, two subjects recognizing that they could more likely win by voting differently, nevertheless chose not to maximize in the current match in order to maximize in a future one. Thus in group 7, match 18, player 1 estimated his chances: from 3, $1.65 at odds of 0.8 or $1.24; from 2, $1.45 at odds of 1.0 or $1.45. He voted for 3 and won, explaining his choice on the questionnaire thus: 'I have 2, but am thinking of the future.' (Since there were only six subjects in the group, each of whom was matched with each of the other four times, he knew for certain that he would meet 3, but not 2, in the one match remaining for him to play. In the conversation after the match, he indicated that this consideration had been the controlling one for him throughout the entire match and indeed he had used it as an argument to secure the adherence of 3.)

Thus of the twenty-five non-maximizers, eleven appear to have been attempting to maximize in the conventional sense. So it can be said that 286 out of 300 or about 95 per cent behaved as if they were maximizing.

The remaining 5 per cent, however, appear not to have maximized. Some failed to do so quite deliberately for they expressed (in remarks on the questionnaire) opinions that indicated other goals were greater for them than maximization of probability of winning. For some the sanctity of a promise was of greater value. Thus in group 6, match 16, player 3 (who lost) explained: 'My word to player 1 is inviolable, although I don't think he considers it such. I'm probably throwing money away, but my vote is 1.' (Player 3 was the one, previously mentioned, who almost always lost and refused to bargain in the accepted way because he – iconoclastically – believed this way to be out of harmony with the rules.) For others, it was more important than money to avoid hurting another. Thus in group 6, match 38, player 1, who by reason of a row between 2 and 3 (of which he had taken advantage) knew that both would vote for him, wrote somewhat shamedly on his questionnaire: 'I really feel rotten about the whole thing. I don't want to screw anyone, so I flipped a coin to determine which player to vote for.' For still others, gambling itself was of greater value than a sure prize. Thus in the last match in group 7, player 1, who was sure of $1.50 from 2 and less sure of $1.55 from 3, still chose 3, explaining: 'I'll try for 3 'cause I'm a gambling man – can't lose that much – even though joining with 2 seems a surer victory.'

Of the fourteen instances of apparent non-maximization, most seem to be based on a sense of honour or the impulse to gamble. Were we using a procedural criterion of rationality, these would also be considered rational since they clearly preferred honour and some money to dishonour and more money. But since we are using a substantive criterion (higher probability of winning rather than less), we must count them as irrational. The remaining instances seem to be that kind of conventional irrationality best summarized by the subject (group 6, match 7, player 1) who wrote on his questionnaire: 'Total confusion, total insecurity, complete distrust.' In these instances, subjects probably behaved irrationally because they were confused (or in some cases, stupid) and distressed by losing.

v

On the basis of the evidence just offered that from 92 to 95 per cent of the choosers tried to maximize the probability of winning and the majority of others were apparently trying to maximize where some alternative other than winning stood higher in their order of preferences, it seems to us clearly the case that the probability maximization theory describes this surrogate political behaviour very well. One can confidently expect, however, that proponents of other viewpoints will try to explain this fairly strong evidence away. Anticipating such reaction, therefore, we offer further evidence that not only is probability maximization a good explanation, but also that it is a better explanation than the alternatives.

Those who assert that choosers do not employ a rational calculus but make up their preferences to fit some previously determined and affective choice are usually hard to answer because one has no way to get inside the choosers' psyches. So if it is said, for example, that player *i* voted for *j* because *i* felt an intense homosexual attraction for *j*, it is usually not possible to prove or refute such an assertion. No evidence pro or con exists. And in the absence of evidence, the psychoanalytic and the probability maximization theories seem equally good (though equally unverifiable) explanations.

For this experiment, however, there is a way to get inside the psyches, at least a little bit, and thus to make a judgment on the adequacy of the alternative explanations. In this case, the choices made depend not only on the preference structure of the chooser but also on his estimate of the state of nature. One can, therefore, look at these estimates: Are they accurate or inaccurate? Do they apparently reflect an intent to make a careful estimate or do they reflect simply indifference?

We offer the following theory. If the subjects make accurate estimates of the actions of the others (the state of nature), then it can be supposed that, when they choose as if maximizing the probability of winning, they are in fact doing so. If, on the other hand, subjects make inaccurate estimates, then it can be supposed that the state of nature is irrelevant to their choice and that the apparent maximization is simply window dressing to cover up to themselves (i.e., reduce the cognitive dissonance occasioned by their Oedipal urges, etc.).

Suppose the subjects are found to make accurate estimates of the external world. Then the plausibility of the probability maximization theory is strengthened because it appears that subjects are making a careful estimate of their chances to win – the crucial feature of the probability maximization calculus. It appears also that in expending energy on careful estimates, subjects want to maximize. Suppose, however, subjects are inaccurate. Then the plausibility of the probability maximization theory is weakened for it appears to be based on a half-fictional calculation.

Conversely, for the antirational theories, inaccuracy about the external world renders calculation meaningless and suggests therefore that the subjects were not calculating to begin with – which is precisely what the notions of cognitive dissonance and psychoanalysis assert. Thus inaccuracy strengthens their plausibility as explanations. But accuracy weakens it, for if subjects expend enough energy to be accurate, it appears that subjects believe knowledge of the state of nature is important in their choice, indeed in their calculation. Hence the probability estimates are more than window dressing and the plausibility of a theory that restricts them to this role is weakened.

In these experiments, subjects were on the average surprisingly accurate in their estimates of the state of nature (i.e., their judgments of how the other players were going to vote). The data are set forth in table 2, where the estimates of a player are compared to what the other players actually did. Since the subjects estimated a probability between 0 and 1 for receiving the votes of each of the others, while the voting itself was dichotomous, one cannot measure individual accuracy except in a gross way. But the accuracy of the entire group of judgments can be measured thus: For all those who estimated that another player would vote for them

TABLE 2

Accuracy of subjects' estimates of other players' votes

Probability of receiving others' vote	Estimates of others' votes										
	0.01 – 0.20		0.21 – 0.40		0.41 – 0.60		0.61 – 0.80		0.81 – 1.00		
Others' actual vote	For	Against	For	Against	For	Against	For	Against	For	Against	
GROUP 5 less victims of conspiracy*	1	31 (−2)	10	11 (−1)	30	31 (−4)	40	33 (−8)	38	15 (−3)	240 (−18)
GROUP 6 less victims of conspiracy*	4 (−1)	32 (−1)	9	19	34 (−1)	45	29	20	43	5 (−1)	240 (−4)
GROUP 7	4	4	3	16	5	16	17	16	31	8	120
TOTAL VOTES	8	64	22	45	68	88	86	61	112	24	588
Per cent received	11		33		44		60		83		

* In eleven matches, two of the players formed a conspiracy against the third. Thus i and j agreed on a satisfactory imputation and on a plan of conversations of i with k and j with k. This plan typically provided that both would falsely report to k an (i,j) agreement highly advantageous to j and that i would then seek a better agreement with k, though still not as good for i as the real (i,j) agreement, while j would seek an agreement with k (also not as good for j as the real agreement) on the ground that he (j) distrusted i's extravagant offer. Functionally, this served to guarantee to both i and j that they were better off with each other and that they could trust each other. Of course, it also meant that k's judgment of the external world had no relevance to what that world was really like. Since his judgment concerns a fictional world created for him by the conspirators, we have omitted k's judgments from this table.

with a chance between 0 and 0.2, it should be the case, if the group is perfectly accurate, that 10 per cent of those so estimated (i.e., the midpoint of the interval between 0 and 0.2) actually do so. For estimates in the interval 0.21 to 0.4, 30 per cent of those so estimated should actually do so. Thus we have a definition of accuracy for the entire group. Inaccuracy, on the other hand, would occur if, for all those who estimate that another player would vote for them within a given interval of probability (say, again, 0 to 0.2), it is actually the case that 50 per cent of the others actually do so. Thus inaccuracy is discovered by the fact that voting by the others is random with respect to the subjects' estimates.

The results stated in table 2 are depicted in figure 1, where the per cent voting for the estimater (on the vertical axis) is plotted against the estimates in intervals of 0.2 (on the horizontal axis). The background lines in the figure represent perfect accuracy and perfect inaccuracy, while the bold face indicates the actual degree of the subjects' accuracy about the other players' behaviour.

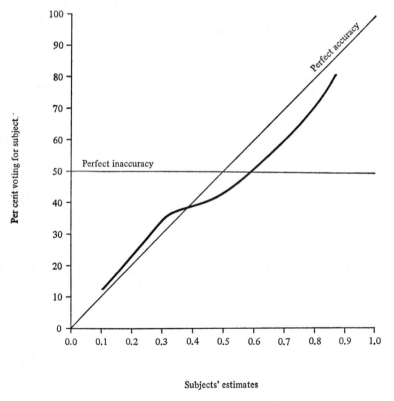

Figure 1 Accuracy of subjects' estimates of the state of the external world.

It is apparent from the figure that subjects were on the average quite accurate with respect to the behaviour of their partners. The line connecting the per cent voting for, in each of the five categories, is close to and has about the same slope throughout as the line indicating perfect accuracy. Moreover, it has been demonstrated elsewhere that these discrepancies from perfect accuracy can be attributed to sampling error.[13]

It is not so easy to reject learning theory. For the events of these experiments, an explanation in terms of learning theory would emphasize that subjects determined their partners not by a calculus but by more or less random experimentation which, if successful, would be repeated and, if not, not. Indeed, something of this appears to have happened. One can reject learning theory, therefore, not because it fails to explain behaviour, but simply because it does not explain it as well as the utility maximization theory.

In the 100 matches studied here, there were, of course, 300 pairs of subjects. Of these 160 pairs were inexperienced with each other in the sense that they had not met previously in a match – and in most cases had never met consciously at all. There were, however, 140 pairs in which subjects were experienced with each other in the sense that the members of the pair had played with each other in a previous match, in some cases in two or even three previous matches. While learning theory could hardly say much about behaviour of subjects in the 160 inexperienced pairs, it can say something about the behaviour in the 140 experienced ones.

In general, learning theory suggests that, for these 140 pairs, if previous experience had led to success (i.e., voting for or against and winning), then the members of these pairs would repeat the previous choice. If previous experience had led to failure (i.e., voting for or against and losing), then the prediction is not so clear. However, if on a previous experience in a pair, a player voted for and lost, it would seem to be a good indication to vote against on the second match, if only because he knows that voting for is not successful. On the other hand, if a player voted against another and lost on the first meeting, there is almost no guide to action. He knows only that voting against the other did not work, but he is quite inexperienced about the results of voting for. In such a case, there is no really good prediction inasmuch as it is reasonable either to vote for as an experiment or to vote against on the basis of experience. The data to validate these predictions are set forth in table 3, where the individual experience on the just-previous match – earlier matches, when they occurred, are ignored – is compared with the action taken by the individuals in the current match.

13 William James Zavoina, 'The Rational Calculus of Coalition Formation' (unpublished PH D thesis, University of Rochester 1969).

TABLE 3

Voting in experienced pairs

Action of subject in current match	Experience of subject in just previous match involving other player in pair			
	Voted for		Voted against	
	Won	Lost	Won	Lost
Votes for	63	22	36	27
Votes against	31	26	50	25
Total	94	48	86	52

Theory	Truth value	Binomial probability
cell (1,1) > cell (2,1)	True	*Pr[63 for] < 0.00063
cell (1,2) < cell (2,2)	True	Pr[22 for] < 0.33
cell (1,3) < cell (2,3)	True	Pr[36 for] < 0.08
cell (1,4) $\simeq$ cell (2,4)	Approximately true	†

*   That is, assuming independent choices with a 0.5 probability of choosing for, the probability of obtaining by chance 63 or better fors out of 94 tries is less than 0.00063.

†   Since there is no standard of randomness here, a probability of deviation from it cannot be calculated.

As is apparent from table 3, the tests of the predictions from learning theory are in part beyond chance. Still, the explanation is not very good compared with the explanation from utility theory. In the first place, learning theory says nothing about the majority of the cases, for the subjects had to act in an environment that denied them a previous experience. (Some will say this is not a fair test of a theory, but then the world is full of new conditions and the rat has to go through the maze a first time.) Even when a previous experience was provided, however, the explanation from learning theory is weak. Only 53 per cent of the relevant behaviour is explained (i.e., that recorded in the first three columns of table 3), while in the probability maximization theory from 92 to 95 per cent of the relevant behaviour is explained. Furthermore, only the behaviour summarized in column 1 of table 3 is explained well because the favourable results of the test in columns 2 and 3 may easily have occurred by chance. On the other hand, the possibility that chance may have produced the result in the test of probability maximization is almost zero; the probability that one might obtain by chance 275 'yes' out of 300 tries (as set forth in the appendix) is less than 0.000001. This value is considerably smaller than that associated with the best prediction under learning theory. Thus, comparing the two viewpoints, learning theory only weakly explains behaviour in the limited range of behaviour to which it applies, while the theory of probability maximization explains behaviour most of the time. Certainly, for this surrogate political behaviour, probability maximization appears to be the more plausible theory.

VI

In the introduction we observed that each of the viewpoints towards rational behaviour was supported by good evidence in the area of behaviour to which the viewpoints were originally applied. Furthermore, we pointed out that, owing to the neglect by political theorists, we had no idea of which area of behaviour was the one where political behaviour typically belonged and hence we had no idea of what viewpoint of rationality was appropriate for political science. Finally, we indicated that, whether we wanted to or not, our ignorance on this point had to be repaired if we wished to do sophisticated political studies.

This essay is an effort to repair this ignorance. Unfortunately it deals with surrogate politicians in a surrogate political setting. Since this is probably the best we can get, however, the conclusion that the theory of probability maximization is a more plausible explanation than its alternatives, for the behaviour studied suggests that in the interpretation of real political phenomena it is safest to assume that politicians are calculating maximizers.

Doubtless, however, some will resist the analogy from the game saying that the behaviour studied was 'really' economic rather than political since it involves a monetary reward. But, at least since Marx, most students of politics have been willing to admit that all of politics involves monetary rewards, and certainly the calculating behaviour in this game involves something more than the economic process of maximizing a monetary reward inasmuch as the subjects had to maximize in the face of a highly political kind of uncertainty about how others would vote.

Doubtless, also, some will resist the analogy saying that the behaviour studied was simple compared to the complex world of real politics. But it is hard to be sure about degrees of complexity. Surely our subjects often faced a world fully as uncertain as the world of politicians. And while they had but two alternatives to choose from, it is also true of the political world that politicians constantly seek to narrow their range of choice, not only in personal decision, but also in our institutions. Thus, we vote on two candidates, we vote yea and nay on motions, and we are offered two parties (or, failing that, government and opposition). In short, in the world outside the laboratory, we seek constantly to make the problem of decision no more complex than the decisions facing our subjects. So far as we succeed, there is not much difference in complexity between the two worlds.

Nevertheless, others will resist the analogy saying that, even if politicians succeed in simplifying their decision problems, still the laboratory scene and the people in it lack all that lush growth of ideology and organization found in the real political world. This, of course, we admit; but it still is true that our subjects, while simply students, were drawn from the class of people who grow up to be politicians and that the laboratory scene did have those features of coalition-formation, winning and losing, manipulation of others by both rhetoric and contrivance, etc., all of which are fundamental to politics and are the building blocks of ideology and organization.

It is possible that one kind of real political situation exists for which the game analogy is quite inappropriate and this is the situation where participants are not conscious of having a choice. One can hardly compare alternatives where there are none to compare. And it may be that much of the time people have no choice, though one strong theological and philosophical tradition insists that choice is always present. But where choice is possible, the message in the evidence from this experiment, though indirect, is crystal clear: probability maximization is the theory that fits political behaviour best.

APPENDIX

Subjects' calculations of voting decision

Match	Subject i	Others j	k	$\hat{P}(ij)$	$\hat{P}(ik)$	Predicted vote	Actual vote	Is prediction accurate?
GROUP 5								
1	1	2	3	.66	.25	2	2	Yes
	2	1	3	.30	.60	3	1	No
	3	1	2	.66	.66	1 or 2	2	Yes
2	1	2	3	.50	.50	2 or 3	3	Yes
	2	1	3	.20	.60	3	3	Yes
	3	1	2	.70	.60	1	1	Yes
3	1	2	3	.40	.70	3	3	Yes
	2	1	3	.50	.99	3	3	Yes
	3	1	2	.25	1.00	2	2	Yes
4	1	2	3	.00	.20	3	3	Yes
	2	1	3	1.00	1.00	1 or 3	3	Yes
	3	1	2	.50	.70	2	2	Yes
5	1	2	3	.50	.60	2 or 3	2	Yes
	2	1	3	1.00	.55	1	1	Yes
	3	1	2	.80	1.00	2	1	No
6	1	2	3	.75	.75	2 or 3	3	Yes
	2	1	3	.75	.80	3	3	Yes
	3	1	2	.25	.75	2	2	Yes
7	1	2	3	1.00	.00	2	2	Yes
	2	1	3	.50	.66	3	3	Yes
	3	1	2	.05	.95	2	2	Yes
8	1	2	3	.40	.30	2	3	No
	2	1	3	.00	.75	3	3	Yes
	3	1	2	.80	1.00	2	2	Yes
9	1	2	3	.40	.75	3	3	Yes
	2	1	3	.75	.00	1	1	Yes
	3	1	2	1.00	.00	1	1	Yes
10	1	2	3	.99	.99	2 or 3	3	Yes
	2	1	3	.00	1.00	3	3	Yes
	3	1	2	.75	.75	1 or 2	2	Yes
11	1	2	3	.50	.10	2	2	Yes
	2	1	3	.50	.80	3	3	Yes
	3	1	2	.60	.60	1 or 2	2	Yes
12	1	2	3	.50	.75	3	3	Yes
	2	1	3	.10	.75	3	3	Yes
	3	1	2	.50	.90	2	2	Yes
13	1	2	3	.80	.30	2	3	No
	2	1	3	.25	.75	3	3	Yes
	3	1	2	.10	.75	2	2	Yes
14	1	2	3	.50	.80	3	3	Yes
	2	1	3	.75	.75	1 or 3	1	Yes
	3	1	2	.50	.60	2	2	Yes
15	1	2	3	.30	.50	3	3	Yes
	2	1	3	.50	.50	1 or 3	3	Yes
	3	1	2	1.00	1.00	1 or 2	2	Yes

Match	Subject i	Others j	k	$\hat{P}(ij)$	$\hat{P}(ik)$	Predicted vote	Actual vote	Is prediction accurate?
16	1	2	3	.50	.85	3	3	Yes
	2	1	3	1.00	1.00	1 or 3	1	Yes
	3	1	2	.99	.99	1 or 2	1	Yes
17	1	2	3	.10	.90	3	3	Yes
	2	1	3	.20	.60	3	3	Yes
	3	1	2	.90	.80	1	1	Yes
18	1	2	3	.75	.75	2 or 3	3	Yes
	2	1	3	.20	.60	3	1	No
	3	1	2	1.00	.80	1	2	No
19	1	2	3	.75	.75	2 or 3	2	Yes
	2	1	3	1.00	1.00	1 or 3	3	Yes
	3	1	2	.50	.70	2	2	Yes
20	1	2	3	.70	.50	2	2	Yes
	2	1	3	.75	.75	1 or 3	1	Yes
	3	1	2	.60	.50	1	1	Yes
21	1	2	3	.40	.30	2	2	Yes
	2	1	3	.80	.00	1	1	Yes
	3	1	2	1.00	.00	1	1	Yes
22	1	2	3	.50	.80	3	3	Yes
	2	1	3	.20	.80	3	3	Yes
	3	1	2	.80	.75	1	1	Yes
23	1	2	3	.60	.90	3	3	Yes
	2	1	3	.50	.75	1	1	Yes
	3	1	2	1.00	1.00	1 or 2	2	Yes
24	1	2	3	.90	.50	2	2	Yes
	2	1	3	.95	.00	1	1	Yes
	3	1	2	.00	.00	1 or 2	1	Yes
25	1	2	3	1.00	.90	2	2	Yes
	2	1	3	.90	.10	1	1	Yes
	3	1	2	.80	.20	1	1	Yes
26	1	2	3	.70	.60	1	2	Yes
	2	1	3	.70	.60	1	3	No
	3	1	2	.50	.75	2	1	No
27	1	2	3	.50	.50	2 or 3	2	Yes
	2	1	3	.65	.65	1 or 3	1	Yes
	3	1	2	.65	.50	1	1	Yes
28	1	2	3	.70	.80	3	3	Yes
	2	1	3	.65	.00	1	1	Yes
	3	1	2	.75	.00	1	1	Yes
29	1	2	3	.60	.60	2 or 3	3	Yes
	2	1	3	.75	.90	3	1	No
	3	1	2	.75	.50	1	1	Yes
30	1	2	3	.60	.60	2 or 3	3	Yes
	2	1	3	.75	.00	1	1	Yes
	3	1	2	.50	.00	1	1	Yes
31	1	2	3	.63	.50	2	2	Yes
	2	1	3	1.00	.00	1	1	Yes
	3	1	2	.30	.00	1	1	Yes
32	1	2	3	.50	.50	2 or 3	3	Yes
	2	1	3	.25	1.00	3	3	Yes
	3	1	2	.95	.99	2	2	Yes
33	1	2	3	.50	.50	2 or 3	3	Yes
	2	1	3	1.00	1.00	1 or 3	1	Yes
	3	1	2	.50	.75	2	2	Yes

Match	Subject i	Others j	k	$\hat{P}(ij)$	$\hat{P}(ik)$	Predicted vote	Actual vote	Is prediction accurate?
34	1	2	3	.70	.50	2	2	Yes
	2	1	3	.60	.60	1 or 3	3	Yes
	3	1	2	1.00	1.00	1 or 2	2	Yes
35	1	2	3	.40	.99	3	3	Yes
	2	1	3	1.00	1.00	1 or 3	1	Yes
	3	1	2	.75	.50	1	1	Yes
36	1	2	3	.70	1.00	3	3	Yes
	2	1	3	.75	.70	1	1	Yes
	3	1	2	.99	.10	1	1	Yes
37	1	2	3	.75	.25	2	2	Yes
	2	1	3	.25	.65	3	3	Yes
	3	1	2	.80	.80	1 or 2	2	Yes
38	1	2	3	.60	.30	2	2	Yes
	2	1	3	1.00	1.00	1 or 3	3	Yes
	3	1	2	.75	.75	1 or 2	1	Yes
39	1	2	3	.50	.25	2	2	Yes
	2	1	3	1.00	1.00	1 or 3	3	Yes
	3	1	2	.10	.40	2	2	Yes
40	1	2	3	.50	.50	2 or 3	2	Yes
	2	1	3	.75	.75	1 or 3	3	Yes
	3	1	2	.00	.50	2	2	Yes

GROUP 6

Match	Subject i	Others j	k	$\hat{P}(ij)$	$\hat{P}(ik)$	Predicted vote	Actual vote	Is prediction accurate?
1	1	2	3	.90	.50	2	2	Yes
	2	1	3	.80	.50	1	1	Yes
	3	1	2	.50	.40	1	1	Yes
2	1	2	3	.50	.25	2	2	Yes
	2	1	3	.60	.60	1 or 3	1	Yes
	3	1	2	.70	.70	1 or 2	2	Yes
3	1	2	3	.60	.50	2	3	No
	2	1	3	.40	.60	3	1	No
	3	1	2	.70	.60	1	1	Yes
4	1	2	3	.10	.40	3	3	Yes
	2	1	3	.50	1.00	3	3	Yes
	3	1	2	.75	.55	1	2	No
5	1	2	3	.95	.40	2	2	Yes
	2	1	3	.65	.45	1	1	Yes
	3	1	2	.60	.40	1	1	Yes
6	1	2	3	.60	.60	2 or 3	3	Yes
	2	1	3	.80	.80	1 or 3	3	Yes
	3	1	2	.60	.55	1	2	No
7	1	2	3	.50	.50	2 or 3	3	Yes
	2	1	3	.80	.80	1 or 3	3	Yes
	3	1	2	.50	.70	2	2	Yes
8	1	2	3	.50	.30	2	2	Yes
	2	1	3	.30	.70	3	3	Yes
	3	1	2	.80	.80	1 or 2	1	Yes
9	1	2	3	.75	.90	3	3	Yes
	2	1	3	.75	.75	1 or 3	3	Yes
	3	1	2	.55	.55	1 or 2	1	Yes
10	1	2	3	.50	.65	3	3	Yes
	2	1	3	.80	.60	1	1	Yes
	3	1	2	.70	.70	1 or 2	1	Yes

Match	Subject i	Others j	k	$\hat{P}(ij)$	$\hat{P}(ik)$	Predicted vote	Actual vote	Is prediction accurate?
11	1	2	3	.55	.00	2	2	Yes
	2	1	3	.50	.70	3	3	Yes
	3	1	2	.00	.70	2	2	Yes
12	1	2	3	.30	.20	2	2	Yes
	2	1	3	.80	.90	3	3	Yes
	3	1	2	.40	.60	2	2	Yes
13	1	2	3	.50	1.00	3	3	Yes
	2	1	3	.70	.60	1	3	No
	3	1	2	.80	.50	1	1	Yes
14	1	2	3	.50	.60	3	2	No
	2	1	3	.30	.40	3	3	Yes
	3	1	2	.50	.50	1 or 2	2	Yes
15	1	2	3	.70	.50	2	2	Yes
	2	1	3	.10	.05	1	1	Yes
	3	1	2	1.00	1.00	1 or 2	2	Yes
16	1	2	3	.75	.50	2	2	Yes
	2	1	3	.90	.50	1	1	Yes
	3	1	2	.20	.20	1 or 2	1	Yes
17	1	2	3	.60	.30	2	2	Yes
	2	1	3	.50	.60	3	3	Yes
	3	1	2	.50	.75	2	2	Yes
18	1	2	3	.70	.50	2	2	Yes
	2	1	3	.50	.50	1 or 3	1	Yes
	3	1	2	.50	.40	1	1	Yes
19	1	2	3	1.00	.50	2	2	Yes
	2	1	3	.70	.30	1	1	Yes
	3	1	2	.60	.60	1 or 2	2	Yes
20	1	2	3	1.00	.50	2	2	Yes
	2	1	3	1.00	1.00	1 or 3	3	Yes
	3	1	2	.00	.60	2	2	Yes
21	1	2	3	.50	.50	2 or 3	2	Yes
	2	1	3	.40	.60	3	3	Yes
	3	1	2	.40	.40	1 or 2	2	Yes
22	1	2	3	.80	.50	2	2	Yes
	2	1	3	.60	.60	1 or 3	1	Yes
	3	1	2	.70	.70	1 or 2	2	Yes
23	1	2	3	1.00	.50	2	2	Yes
	2	1	3	.90	.50	1	1	Yes
	3	1	2	.00	.30	2	2	Yes
24	1	2	3	.50	.51	3	3	Yes
	2	1	3	.50	.90	3	3	Yes
	3	1	2	1.00	1.00	1 or 2	2	Yes
25	1	2	3	.40	.10	2	2	Yes
	2	1	3	.90	1.00	3	3	Yes
	3	1	2	.00	.75	2	2	Yes
26	1	2	3	.90	.70	2	2	Yes
	2	1	3	.90	.70	1	1	Yes
	3	1	2	.40	.40	1 or 2	2	Yes
27	1	2	3	1.00	.40	2	2	Yes
	2	1	3	1.00	.75	1	1	Yes
	3	1	2	.50	.60	2	1	No

Match	Subject i	Others j	k	$\hat{P}(ij)$	$\hat{P}(ik)$	Predicted vote	Actual vote	Is prediction accurate?
28	1	2	3	.20	.20	2 or 3	3	Yes
	2	1	3	.50	.50	1 or 3	1	Yes
	3	1	2	.95	.50	1	1	Yes
29	1	2	3	.00	1.00	3	3	Yes
	2	1	3	.00	.50	3	3	Yes
	3	1	2	.00	.50	2	2	Yes
30	1	2	3	1.00	.10	2	2	Yes
	2	1	3	.50	1.00	3	3	Yes
	3	1	2	.00	.75	2	2	Yes
31	1	2	3	.60	.50	2	2	Yes
	2	1	3	.90	.90	1 or 3	3	Yes
	3	1	2	.25	.75	2	2	Yes
32	1	2	3	.40	.40	2 or 3	2	Yes
	2	1	3	.50	.80	3	3	Yes
	3	1	2	.20	.90	2	2	Yes
33	1	2	3	.05	.00	2	2	Yes
	2	1	3	1.00	1.00	1 or 3	3	Yes
	3	1	2	.00	1.00	2	2	Yes
34	1	2	3	.90	.90	2 or 3	3	Yes
	2	1	3	.50	.25	1	1	Yes
	3	1	2	.50	.00	1	1	Yes
35	1	2	3	.10	.20	3	3	Yes
	2	1	3	.00	1.00	3	3	Yes
	3	1	2	.40	.50	2	2	Yes
36	1	2	3	.00	.50	3	3	Yes
	2	1	3	.00	.75	3	3	Yes
	3	1	2	1.00	1.00	1 or 2	2	Yes
37	1	2	3	.20	.00	2	2	Yes
	2	1	3	1.00	.90	1	3	No
	3	1	2	.00	.90	2	2	Yes
38	1	2	3	1.00	1.00	2 or 3	3	Yes
	2	1	3	.10	.00	1	1	Yes
	3	1	2	.90	.00	1	1	Yes
39	1	2	3	.60	.40	2	2	Yes
	2	1	3	.60	.70	3	3	Yes
	3	1	2	.70	1.00	2	2	Yes
40	1	2	3	.75	.10	2	2	Yes
	2	1	3	.80	.80	1 or 3	3	Yes
	3	1	2	.50	.75	2	2	Yes
GROUP 7								
1	1	2	3	.30	.00	2	2	Yes
	2	1	3	.00	.95	3	3	Yes
	3	1	2	.30	.95	2	2	Yes
2	1	2	3	.35	.55	3	3	Yes
	2	1	3	.65	.80	3	1	No
	3	1	2	.90	.40	1	1	Yes
3	1	2	3	.95	.90	2	2	Yes
	2	1	3	1.00	.85	1	1	Yes
	3	1	2	.80	.90	2	2	Yes
4	1	2	3	1.00	1.00	2 or 3	3	Yes
	2	1	3	.50	.60	3	1	No
	3	1	2	.90	.70	1	1	Yes

Match	Subject i	Others j	k	$\hat{P}(ij)$	$\hat{P}(ik)$	Predicted vote	Actual vote	Is prediction accurate?
5	1	2	3	.50	.60	3	3	Yes
	2	1	3	.25	.95	3	3	Yes
	3	1	2	.95	.95	1 or 2	2	Yes
6	1	2	3	.40	1.00	3	3	Yes
	2	1	3	.70	.70	1 or 3	3	Yes
	3	1	2	.65	.90	2	2	Yes
7	1	2	3	.40	.80	3	3	Yes
	2	1	3	.50	.50	1 or 3	3	Yes
	3	1	2	.99	.99	1 or 2	1	Yes
8	1	2	3	.65	.40	2	2	Yes
	2	1	3	.55	.50	1	3	No
	3	1	2	.70	.80	2	2	Yes
9	1	2	3	.60	.60	2 or 3	3	Yes
	2	1	3	.30	.80	3	3	Yes
	3	1	2	.65	.70	2	2	Yes
10	1	2	3	.80	.45	2	2	Yes
	2	1	3	1.00	1.00	1 or 3	3	Yes
	3	1	2	.30	.80	2	2	Yes
11	1	2	3	.40	.90	3	3	Yes
	2	1	3	.10	.90	3	3	Yes
	3	1	2	.90	1.00	2	1	Yes
12	1	2	3	.00	.70	3	3	Yes
	2	1	3	.10	.80	3	3	Yes
	3	1	2	.95	.80	1	1	Yes
13	1	2	3	.90	.10	2	2	Yes
	2	1	3	.95	.95	1 or 3	1	Yes
	3	1	2	.60	.40	1	1	Yes
14	1	2	3	.80	.00	2	2	Yes
	2	1	3	.70	.70	1 or 3	1	Yes
	3	1	2	.50	.45	1	1	Yes
15	1	2	3	.70	.70	2 or 3	3	Yes
	2	1	3	1.00	1.00	1 or 3	3	Yes
	3	1	2	.90	.90	1 or 2	1	Yes
16	1	2	3	.80	.85	3	3	Yes
	2	1	3	.70	.70	1 or 3	1	Yes
	3	1	2	.30	.50	2	1	No
17	1	2	3	.90	.00	2	2	Yes
	2	1	3	.60	.40	1 or 3	1	Yes
	3	1	2	.70	.50	1	1	Yes
18	1	2	3	1.00	.80	2	3	No
	2	1	3	.80	.30	1	1	Yes
	3	1	2	.90	.40	1	1	Yes
19	1	2	3	.40	.70	3	3	Yes
	2	1	3	.50	.70	3	3	Yes
	3	1	2	.60	.65	2	1	No
20	1	2	3	.90	.70	2	3	No
	2	1	3	.50	.60	3	3	Yes
	3	1	2	.85	.25	1	1	Yes
TOTAL	Yes—275
	No— 25

REFERENCES

BERELSON, BERNARD, PAUL LAZARSFELD, and WILLIAM MCPHEE *Voting.* Chicago: University of Chicago Press, 1954.
BRAYBROOKE, DAVID and CHARLES LINDBLOM *Strategy of Decision.* Glencoe: Free Press, 1963.
DAVIS, OTTO A., M.A.H. DEMPSTER, and AARON WILDAVSKY 'A Theory of the Budgetary Process,' *American Political Science Review*, 60, 3 (September 1966), pp. 529–47.
DIESING, PAUL *Reason in Society.* Urbana: University of Illinois Press, 1962.
FENNO, RICHARD *The Power of the Purse.* Boston: Little, Brown, 1966.
FRIEDRICH, CARL J., ed. *Nomos VII: Rational Decision.* New York: Atherton Press, 1964.
KEY, V.O. *The Responsible Electorate.* Cambridge: Harvard University Press, 1966.
LANE, ROBERT *Political Ideology.* Glencoe: Free Press, 1962.
LASSWELL, HAROLD *Psychopathology and Politics.* Chicago: University of Chicago Press, 1930.
LAZARSFELD, PAUL, BERNARD BARELSON, and HAZEL GAUDET *The People's Choice.* New York: Duell, Sloan, and Pearce, 1944.
LUCE, ROBERT DUNCAN, ROBERT R. BUSH, and EUGENE GALANTER, eds. *Handbook of Mathematical Psychology*, 3 vols. New York: Wiley, 1963–5.
LUCE, ROBERT DUNCAN and HOWARD RAIFFA *Games and Decisions: Introduction and Critical Survey.* New York: Wiley, 1957.
RIKER, WILLIAM H. and PETER C. ORDESHOOK 'A Theory of the Calculus of Voting,' *American Political Science Review*, 62, 1 (March 1968), pp. 25–42.
RIKER, WILLIAM H. 'Bargaining in a Three-person Game,' *American Political Science Review*, 61, 3 (September 1967), pp. 642–56.
– 'An Experimental Interpretation of Formal and Informal Rules of a Three Person Game' in Bernhardt Lieberman, *Social Choice* (forthcoming).
VON NEUMANN, JOHN and OSKAR MORGENSTERN *The Theory of Games and Economic Behavior.* 3rd ed. Princeton: Princeton University Press, 1953.
ZAVOINA, WILLIAM JAMES 'The Rational Calculus of Coalition Formation: Evidence from a Three Person Game.' Unpublished PH D thesis, University of Rochester, 1970. *Dissertation Abstracts International*, 31 A (October 1970), p. 1865.

MICHAEL ARGYLE AND PETER COLLETT

Social skills and intercultural communication in politics

I INTRODUCTION: RESEARCH METHODS

The intention of this paper is to introduce a dimension to the study of politics that is not normally considered – the process of communication and interaction, face-to-face or otherwise, between the various participants in political activities.[1]

Some social scientists have approached the political problem of bargaining, or negotiation, by doing laboratory experiments inspired by the theory of games. In these experiments subjects play competitive or co-operative games with other subjects, the aim usually being to win as much money as possible. We believe that most implementations of this approach are misguided, simply because they leave out some of the most important features of social situations and are therefore unable to provide findings which relate to most forms of human interaction. In many areas of psychology it has been found that the results obtained in very 'stripped down' experiments failed to apply in real situations; we would now say that such experiments lack 'external validity.'

In research which is designed to investigate face-to-face social behaviour, the following elements should appear and be studied: 1 / verbal interaction between participants, 2 / non-verbal communication, 3 / a social structure defining the relations between people, 4 / a social situation and cultural background with known rules and conventions. It will

---

1   For an account of social interaction, see among others M. Argyle, *Social Interaction* (London: Methuen; New York: Atherton, 1969).

be noticed that the game-playing experiments usually fail to take all four aspects into consideration and sometimes omit them all.[2]

We want to say something about two main topics: 1 / the process of establishing a relationship with another person and methods of training people in social skills, and 2 / the difficulties of interacting with people from a different cultural background, and how they may be overcome.

II SOCIAL SKILLS: SOCIAL INTERACTION

Dyadic relationships

We shall deal here only with two-person relationships, but similar principles operate for groups of three, four, or more. There are also a number of further processes which occur in groups but which there is not space to discuss here.

The relation between two participants in the political process depends partly on the official relations between the groups they represent; it also depends on their personalities and the pattern of interaction that develops between them. Some pairs of people simply cannot form a relationship at all, others can form a relation only on the assumption that A is superior to B, or that B is dependent on A. We will describe some examples of research with dyadic behaviour.

It is possible to communicate one's attitude to another person in two ways – in words or by non-verbal behaviour. We have recently completed a series of experiments in which equated verbal and non-verbal signals for *friendly, hostile, superior, equal,* and *inferior* were combined. The actual method was for a performer to speak a number of verbal messages in different non-verbal styles; these performances were then put on videotape and subjects were asked to rate their impression of them. The verbal and non-verbal components were standardized beforehand to be of equivalent strength.

It was found that where conflicting verbal and non-verbal messages were combined the non-verbal ones accounted for about twelve times as much variance as verbal ones and produced shifts on rating scales about four-and-one-half times as great as those produced by verbal cues (Argyle *et al.* 1970). The non-verbal cues which appear to be important in

2 Some kinds of political negotiation, which are not carried out in face-to-face situations, have some resemblance to game-playing experiments. It is better to study them by field studies or by laboratory experiments involving similar kinds of negotiation and incorporate as many of the background features as possible, such as conventions and social structure. (See Morley and Stevenson 1970.)

studies like this are facial expression, tone of voice, head position and movements, gestures and posture, direction of gaze, bodily orientation, and proximity. It seems likely that in political encounters, too, the way a communication is received will depend on non-verbal signals, as well as on the context of the message and the relationship between those concerned.

Many aspects of the process of interaction in dyads have been studied. When two people meet it is unlikely that their spontaneous styles of behaviour will synchronize immediately. They have to work out a temporal sequence where it is agreed how long each will speak, how to minimize long pauses and interruptions, and how to ensure a smooth flow of conversation. We have found that this is achieved by a supportive system of non-verbal signalling − head nods, shifts of gaze, and grunts (Kendon 1967) − and that when another's eyes are concealed by dark glasses there are more pauses and interruptions than there are during unhindered face-to-face communications (Argyle, Lalljee, and Cook 1968).

Each member of a dyad has plans or preferences for how the other will behave. If A behaves as B would like, B will reinforce him by smiling, nodding his head, looking A in the eye, leaning forward, or making encouraging noises. The effect of this is for A to change his behaviour in the way that has been reinforced − talking more or about particular topics or indeed modifying any aspect of his behaviour. It seems that the sender is normally unaware he is giving such reinforcements and the receiver is affected by them without his being aware either. Such reinforcements may affect a person's status in the group, his conformity, or any aspect of his verbal or nonverbal behaviour (Argyle 1969, p. 176ff).

Implicit situational rules

Erving Goffman (1963) and others have drawn attention to the way in which our social behaviour is regulated by an elaborate set of rules governing behaviour in particular situations. Few people, apart from a few social scientists and writers of books on etiquette, could state what these rules are, but we nevertheless succeed in keeping to them most of the time. The rules include not only regulations about what clothes shall be worn and how to reply to invitations, but also how close one should stand, where one should look, what bodily movements should be used to enter and leave a social situation, and so on.

There are a large number of different 'behaviour situations' in any society − Barker and Wright (1955) found hundreds of them in a small town in Kansas – each of which has its rules, for example, going to church, drinking coke in the drug store, etc. These rules are based on the patterns of behaviour worked out by previous generations of participants. Some of us would disagree with Goffman and his followers in that we think that some of these rules are universal laws of social behaviour. The universal features of all social situations, and the differences between them, can be accounted for by including in the laws the dimensions of the situation, such as formal and informal. When the situational rules are broken, public order is disrupted, embarrassment may result, and efforts are made to restore regular patterns of behaviour. This may include defining the offender as a mental patient and putting him inside a place where normal rules are largely suspended (Goffman 1961).

Social skills

Some interviewers are better at selecting candidates, some salesmen sell more, and some people are more effective in a variety of everyday social situations; they are said to be more socially skilled. Effective and ineffective performances at any particular skill can be compared, and the social techniques which produce the best results can be isolated. This has been done for a number of professional social skills, and the social inadequacies in everyday life of different kinds of mental patients have been analysed. The social skills which are needed in politics have not yet been analysed by psychologists, but they would probably include establishing trust and a co-operative relationship, persuasion, negotiation, effective presentation of positions, etc. A number of different methods have been devised for training people in social skills, but to do this it was necessary to find out first which techniques of social training are most effective.

1   Training on the job is commonly done but seems to be ineffective. This could be a successful training method if an experienced tutor was in frequent contact with the trainee, gave him clear feedback on his mistakes, and suggested alternative behaviour. The tutor would have to be expert both at the skill in question and at the minutiae of social interaction.

2   We have been working with role-playing methods mainly for training interviewers and for treating mental patients who cannot deal with social situations. The procedures are that 1 / the main features of part of the skill are explained and a demonstration or film shown, 2 / the trainee role-plays with stooges, for seven to twenty minutes, 3 / a videotape of his performance is played back and discussed with him. Trainees go through a series of such exercises with different stooges, some of them

programmed to provide particular problems. Other exercises are used such as role-reversal and practice in aspects of non-verbal communication (Argyle 1969, chapter 10).

3   T-groups are widely used in American industry. Follow-up studies show that about 40 per cent of trainees show some improvement, but that about 10 per cent are disturbed by the experience and some have nervous breakdowns (Campbell and Dunnette 1968).

III   COMMUNICATION AND INTERACTION BETWEEN
       PEOPLE FROM DIFFERENT CLASSES AND CULTURES

In politics participants are often from different social classes within the same culture or from quite different cultures. This may give rise to various kinds of misunderstandings which will add to the difficulties created by real conflicts of interest, thereby making the resolution of political problems more difficult.

Information processing in interaction

Hall (1964) speaks of different cultures as 'inhabiting different sensory worlds' in the sense that they place varying emphasis on particular sensory input channels for the gathering of information. He suggests, for example, that Arabs, unlike Westerners, use the olfactory modality as an interpersonal distance-setting mechanism. Wober (1967) says much the same thing when he refers to Africans and Westerners as being different 'sensotypes.' Whenever individuals from different cultures meet – and this would certainly be the case within a political context – they will invariably attempt to obtain information about and from each other. Each will bring to bear a set of discriminations, or a cognitive style, which enables him to evaluate the other person, the ongoing interaction, and the information exchanged. Insofar as each actor's style reflects in part that of his parent culture, he will differ from that of his partner. Cognitive styles have been known to differ in several respects. First, people from different cultures may display varying cognitive complexity in that they use different numbers of independent dimensions in assessing people and things. Or they may use similar dimensions, but employ them in a different order, that is, some discriminations will be seen as more salient or important than others. Individuals may also differ in the extent to which they employ fine discriminations or simpler classifications. Prothro (1955) found that Arabs judge certain attitude statements as significantly more moderate than do Americans. In fact, several writers have referred to the overassertion and exaggeration found in spoken Arabic (Shouby 1951). Suleiman (1967) spells out the implications of these culture-bound forms of rhetoric for politics in a study in which he compares the speeches of Nasser and Eden over Suez. He points to the vagueness, repetition, exaggeration, and assertion which accompanied Nasser's pronouncements and goes on to argue that these features and Eden's understatement were largely responsible for the misunderstanding which arose between Nasser and Eden.

Finally, cultures may differ in terms of the degree to which certain dimensions are used independently of each other. Foa (1967) has written on the relationship between status and affect (i.e. liking) in traditional and modern cultures. He points out that whereas status is achieved in the West, in the Middle East it is ascribed, so that there is less need among Arabs for behaviour to change the status of a person. Therefore the differentiation between behaviour manipulating status and behaviour manipulating affect is less strong among Arabs than it is among Westerners; whereas giving status and giving liking are seen as distinct by us, among the Arabs these behaviours would tend to be seen as more or less similar.

Cognitive organization serves for coding outgoing messages and for decoding incoming messages. If the categorization used by the decoder is different from that used by the coder – and this would appear to be the case in communications between cultures – then the message received may be different from the message sent. But misperception may also occur where the cognitive organizations of participants are similar but where the sign does not have shared meaning or the same range of connotations for both parties. Apart from the obvious difficulties which arise when one or both parties adopt another language, it may be the case that the same word represents a different categorization of objects or events for different persons. Concepts such as small loan or University may represent rather different classes of objects. The same word or phrase may also have different emotional meanings for different groups (e.g., 'Negro,' 'demonstrator'). Lastly, the same word may be embedded in different intellectual constructions. Not only does the term 'democracy' evoke a wide variety of responses, it has been seen to signify widely differing political institutions. Danielian (1967) refers to cultures in which compromise connotes political stupidity and weakness rather than the beneficient (meet the person half way) features associated with it in the Anglo-American culture.

Conveying information in interaction

Whenever individuals meet they invariably communicate information to each other. They may signal their state or intention, transmit facts and opinions, and attempt to define and control the interaction. The means whereby they convey this information and the type and amount of information conveyed will vary among individuals and between contexts. Nevertheless, patterns of shared behaviour will be found throughout a culture, and these patterns may differ from those that exist in other cultures.

Differences in non-verbal communication
During an interaction information is relayed either verbally or through non-verbal channels (e.g., status or office communicated through clothing, posture, physical position, etc.). Cultures differ in their use of these channels. Hall (1964) has speculated at length on cross-cultural differences in interpersonal distance, and Watson and Graves (1966) have empirically validated some of his assertions concerning non-verbal behaviour among Arabs. They found that Arabs face each other more directly, sit closer, touch each other more, engage in more mutual looking, and talk slightly louder in interaction than do Americans.

        Little (1968) and Ingham (1969) have independently pointed to preferred seating positions and different personal distances in several cultures. Hewes (1955) has systematically described the world distribution of certain postural habits, and La Barre (1964) has discussed cultural variations in gestures. Clearly, when members of different cultures meet, the non-verbal behaviour they manifest, whether intentionally or in the form of 'leakage,' may be misconstrued by the other. The relevance of the study of non-verbal behaviour to the business of politics may be questioned: 'It is easy to ridicule the study of non-verbal behaviour as an abstruse, pedantic, and unimportant study by pure scientists. But I believe kinesiology is, on the contrary, one of the most important avenues for better understanding internationally. Consider, as one small example, how Chinese hate to be touched, slapped on the back, or even to shake hands; how easily an American could avoid offense by merely omitting these intended gestures of friendliness' (La Barre 1964). We would probably be misguided in arguing that the isolation and subsequent employment of a repertoire of non-verbal signals which connote friendliness and trustworthiness for another culture would consistently alter the course of political events, nevertheless we feel that non-verbal behaviour, inasmuch as it constitutes a form of interpersonal communication, could when correctly read lead to a more precise understanding of the intention of members of other cultures.

Different linguistic styles
There are also cultural variations in verbal behaviour, though these are really only of relevance to our discussion where someone injects his native linguistic style into his use of his partner's language. Lyman (1969) refers to the 'flatness of tone and equality of metre' after which the Nisei (first-generation Japanese Americans) strive. For the uninitiated this 'brings about wonder about what is "really" being said and in some instances suspicion of ulterior motives' (p.14). Bernstein (1959) has shown that different social classes in England speak in characteristically different ways. Working-class people, for example, ask more questions ('didn't I?'), fail to explain the background and assumptions of remarks, and make more use of personal pronouns than other classes. There may also be different conventions between groups with respect to time-sharing during conversation, tone, speech speed, the use of silence, etc., and these may affect the perceptions that members of these groups make of each other. There may also be miscommunication in an intercultural encounter because of different modes of disclosure and self-disclosure, the extent to which members enhance themselves in the presence of others, and the degree to which they are personal or formal. Bennett and McKnight (1966) show how differing expectations by people from different cultures may disrupt an engagement. They suggest that the status-conscious Japanese expect Americans, by virtue of the roles they reserve for them, to behave in a superior fashion. But Americans, being typically egalitarian, behave contrary to expectation. Since the Japanese find difficulty in responding to perceived superiors who behave as peers, they tend to retreat into a state (*enryo*) which impairs the course of the interaction.

Different rules and conventions

Though similar behaviour may occur in two cultures, the contexts and the rules governing it may be different. Ignorance of cultural rules may lead to ruptures in intercultural communication. For example, while talking business is permitted in both India and England, in India it is forbidden in a man's home. Moreover, cultures will emphasize certain norms, such as reciprocity versus responsibility and co-operation versus competition, and their members will hold to particular conceptions of what constitutes a legitimate compromise, a fair price, or an excessive demand. Very little research has been carried out into cultural variations in these aspects of negotiation. A study by Summers (1968) on cognitive conflict between Americans and Arabs did show that on the issue of American policy Arabs compromised less than Americans in their judgments. But here as elsewhere it is necessary to find out whether such behaviour is bound to particular issues or whether it represents some culture-specific set of dispositions independent of the issue.

Relationship between groups

There are numerous factors which may influence the course of a relationship between members of different groups. The traditional roles that each group has occupied vis-à-vis the other and the accompanying stereotypes each holds for the other will determine the approaches of the two parties. In addition, assumptions of superiority and the facts of disparate power, bargaining leverage, and political alignment may affect the interaction between members of different groups.

Training for culture-contact

Foa (1967) and Foa and Chemers (1967) have developed a model which relates status and affect to particular contexts in traditional and modern cultures. These observations, together with material derived from critical incident surveys, have been built into several 'culture assimilators' by Fiedler, Triandis, and their associates. Essentially, a culture assimilator is a self-instructional manual which is designed to train subjects to assimilate the social conventions operative in a target culture. Chemers (1966), for instance, found that Arab-American task groups guided by Americans who had been trained with an Arab culture assimilator registered superior task effectiveness and more favourable interpersonal relations (though not statistically significant) than did similar groups guided by Americans trained in irrelevant geographic material. Fiedler *et al.* (1971) reviewed the studies on the impact of this type of training on the functioning of heterocultural task groups guided by members with certain leadership styles.

An approach related to these investigations is to be found in the work of Danielian (1967) and Stewart (1966). They have concerned themselves with sensitizing Americans to the perspectives of other cultures by confronting them with a role-playing 'contrast-American' who has been programmed in the world view of a synthetic culture. His task is to confront the American with statements which counter the cultural assumptions (such as the belief in the efficacy of the democratic process) of his society. In this manner they have been able to generate a series of interactions which simulate the processes that Americans repeatedly encounter, namely that of cognitive conflict with members of other cultures.

Apart from efforts to instruct people in the conventions and perspectives of other cultures, there has recently been work on training in the non-verbal behaviour of various target cultures. Collett (1971) built the findings of Watson and Graves, and material provided by informants, into a program which was used to train Englishmen to employ Arab non-verbal behaviour. He found that Arab subjects preferred these culture-trained Englishmen significantly more often than they did control subjects who had been trained with irrelevant material on the Arab world.[3]

CONCLUSION

In this paper we have tried to show that the political process, because it involves communication between individuals and groups of people, is as much the domain of the social psychologist as it is that of the political scientist or economist. Social psychology therefore offers a complementary perspective and new research methods to the problem of understanding the social relationships involved in politics.

REFERENCES

ARGYLE, M. *Social Interaction*. London: Methuen [New York: Atherton], 1969.
ARGYLE, M., M. LALLJEE, and M. COOK 'The effects of visibility on interaction in a dyad,' *Human Relations*, 21 (1968), pp. 3–17.
ARGYLE, M., V. SALTER, H. NICHOLSON, M. WILLIAMS, and P. BURGESS 'The communication of inferior and superior attitudes by verbal and non-verbal signals,' *British Journal of Social and Clinical Psychology*, 9, pp. 221–31.
BARKER, R.G. and H.F. WRIGHT *Midwest and Its Children: the Psychological Ecology of an American Town*. Evanston, Ill.: Row, Peterson, 1955.
BENNETT, J.W. and R.K. MCKNIGHT 'Social Norms, National Imagery, and Interpersonal Relations,' in A.G. Smith, ed. *Communication and Culture*. New York: Holt, Rinehart and Winston, 1966.
BERNSTEIN, B. 'A Public Language: Some Sociological Implications of a Linguistic Form,' *British Journal of Sociology*, 10 (1959), pp. 311–26.

3 Readers interested in recent developments in training for culture-contact are referred to Wight's handbook on the subject and information available through SITAR (Society for Intercultural Training and Research), c/o Centre for Research and Education, PO Box 1768, Estes Park, Colorado 80517, USA.

172 Michael Argyle and Peter Collett

CAMPBELL, J.P. and M.D. DUNNETTE 'Effectiveness of T-group Experiences in Managerial Training,' *Psychology Bulletin*, 70 (1968), pp. 73–104.

CHEMERS, M.M. *et al.* 'Some Effects of Cultural Training on Leadership Heterocultural Task Groups,' *International Journal of Psychology*, I (1966), pp. 303–14.

COLLETT, P.R. 'Training Englishmen in the Non-verbal Behaviour of Arabs,' *International Journal of Psychology*, 6, 3 (1971), pp. 209–15.

DANIELIAN, J. 'Live Simulation on Affect-laden Cultural Cognitions,' *Journal of Conflict Resolution*, 11, 3 (1967), pp. 312–32.

FIEDLER, F.E., T. MITCHELL, and H.C. TRIANDIS, 'The Culture Assimilator: An Approach to Cross-cultural Training,' *Journal of Applied Psychology*, 55 (1971), pp. 95–102.

FOA, U.G. 'Differentiation in Cross-cultural Communication,' in L. Thayer, ed. *Communication, Concepts and Perspectives*. Washington: Spartan Books, 1967.

FOA, U.G., and M.M. CHEMERS 'The Significance of Role Behaviour Differentiation for Cross-cultural Interaction Training,' *International Journal of Psychology*, 2, 1 (1967), pp. 45–67.

GOFFMAN, E. *Asylums*. New York: Anchor Books, 1961.

– *Behaviour in Public Places*. Glencoe, Ill.: Free Press, 1963.

HALL, E.T. *The Hidden Dimension*. New York: Doubleday, 1964.

HEWES, G.W. 'World Distribution of Certain Postural Habits,' *American Anthropologist*, 57 (1955), pp. 231–44.

INGHAM, R. 'Cultural Variations in Social Behaviour,' Institute of Experimental Psychology, Oxford, 1969 (mimeo).

KENDON, A. 'Some Functions of Gaze Direction in Social Interaction,' *Acta Psychologica*, 26, 1 (1967), pp. 1–47.

LA BARRE 'Paralinguistics, Kinesics, and Cultural Anthropology,' in T.A. Sebeok *et al.*, eds. *Approaches to Semiotics*. Mouton: The Hague, 1964.

LITTLE, K.B. 'Cultural Variations in Social Schemata,' *Journal of personality and social Psychology*, 10 (1968), pp. 1–7.

LYMAN, S. 'Generation and Character: The Case of the Japanese Americans,' *University of Nevada* (1969).

MORLEY, I.E., and G.W. STEPHENSON 'Interpersonal and Inter-party Exchange: A Laboratory Simulation of an Industrial Negotiation at the Plant Level,' *British Journal of Psychology*, 60, 4 (1969), pp. 543–5.

PROTHRO, E.T. 'Arab-American Differences in the Judgement of Written Messages,' *Journal of Social Psychology*, 42 (1955), pp. 3–11.

SHOUBY, E. 'The Influence of the Arabic Language on the Psychology of the Arabs,' *Middle East Journal*, 5 (1951), p. 291.

SUMMERS, D.A., T.R. STEWART, and G.R. OCKEN 'Inter-personal Conflict in Heterocultural Dyads,' *International Journal of Psychology*, 3, 3 (1968), pp. 191–6.

SULEIMAN 'The Arabs and the West: Communication Gap,' *Il Politico*, 32, 3 (1967), pp. 511–29.

STEWART, E.C. 'Aspects of American Culture: Assumptions and Values that Affect Cross-cultural Effectiveness.' Pittsburgh: Graduate School of Public and International Affairs, 1966.

WATSON, O.M., and T.D. GRAVES 'Quantitative Research in Proxemic Behaviour,' *American Anthropologist*, 88 (1966), pp. 971–85.

WIGHT, A.R. *Cross-cultural Training: A Draft Handbook*. Estes Park, Colorado: Centre for research and education, 1969.

WOBER, M. 'Adapting Witkin's Field Independence Theory to Accommodate New Information from Africa,' *British Journal of Psychology*, 58 (1967), pp. 29–38.

PART FOUR

Computer simulations

HAYWARD R.ALKER, JR & CHERYL CHRISTENSEN

From causal modelling to artificial intelligence: the evolution of a UN peace-making simulation*

This paper is a progress report on joint efforts by ourselves and William Greenberg to explore further UN peacemaking efforts and prospects with the help of formal modelling techniques. As such, work began with the decision to write a 'statistical afterthought' to Ernst Haas's impressive review of the successes and failures of attempts to achieve collective security through the United Nations.[1] It was thought that such an effort might show how Haas's insights, many of them demonstrated with the use of cross-tabulations, could be strengthened and further tested through the use of multivariate causal modelling procedures. Given a multi-

*   We would both like to acknowledge the research support of the National Science Foundation through its Grant GS–2429 to the Center for International Studies at MIT and its continuing support of the Mathematical Social Sciences Board at whose workshop on Formal Analysis on International Systems some of the ideas contained herein were first conceived. Of the many additional contributors to our research, at least Lincoln Bloomfield, William Greenberg, and Ernst Haas must be mentioned.

1   Ernst Haas, *Collective Security and the Future International System* (Denver 1968). Familiarity with this monograph is assumed in the present discussion. Two independent efforts to redo the Haas monograph are by John G. Ruggie of the University of California, Berkeley, who also participated in the International Systems workshop mentioned in the acknowledgments, and by Mark Zacher, now at the University of British Columbia. J.G. Ruggie, 'Environmental Discontinuities and Collective Security: Simulating United Nations Intervention, July 1969,' and M.W. Zacher, 'United Nations Involvement in Crises and Wars: Past Patterns and Future Possibilities,' delivered at the American Political Science Association meeting, September 1970. With Joseph Nye of Harvard, Haas is himself extending his work to include the role of regional security organizations.

equation causal model, one could both better explain UN successes and failures and further study how the UN has modified its peace-making or peace-keeping practices as a result of these outcomes. Understanding how or why such an evolution – or devolution – in the UN system has taken place was clearly a prerequisite to Haas's goal of theory-based projections of possible UN futures.

'Progress' is no longer an easy word to use, whether we are talking of UN peace-making or of attempts to analyse UN political processes. Yet we feel we have learned a lot, gradually transforming our causal interpretations[2] into the analysis of shared cognitive processes. Having been influenced by the literature on precedent search in crisis decision-making,[3] more general studies of concept attainment,[4] and the concern with adaptive or maladaptive evolution in complex social systems,[5] we only gradu-

2   The best comprehensive treatments of causal analysis are Herbert Simon, *Models of Man* (New York: Wiley, 1957); H.M. Blalock, Jr, *Causal Inferences in Nonexperimental Research* (Chapel Hill: University of North Carolina Press, 1964); R. Boudon, *L'Analyse mathématique des faits sociaux* (Paris: Plon, 1967); H.M. Blalock Jr, and A. Blalock, eds., *Methodology in Social Research* (New York: McGraw-Hill, 1968); E.F. Borgatta, ed., *Sociological Methodology, 1969* (San Francisco: Jossey-Bass, 1970). For a review touching on economic, political, and psychological applications and procedures, see H.R. Alker Jr, 'Statistics and Politics: The Need for Causal Data Analysis,' in S.M. Lipset, ed., *Politics and the Social Sciences* (New York: Oxford University Press, 1970).

3   More specifically, discussions with Richard Snyder while at the MSSB Workshop on Formal Models, and with John Steinbrunner, Robert Beattie, and Lincoln Bloomfield at MIT about the CASCON system for computer-aided retrieval of information on actions taken in previous similar international crises; this program was eventually used in the fall of 1969 in the CONEX series of games. The related study is L.P. Bloomfield and A. Leiss, *Controlling Small Wars: A Strategy for the 1970's* (New York: Knopf, 1969). See section II below for more details.

4   In particular, discussions with Philip J. Stone at Harvard about Earl Hunt, Janet Marin and Philip Stone, *Experiments in Induction* (New York: Academic Press, 1966), and P.J. Stone, 'Computer Models of Human Information Processing Procedures' in H.M. Schroder and P. Suedfeld, eds., *Personality Information Processing Models* (New York: Ronald Press, forthcoming). For an overview of the 'artificial' intelligence and cognitive simulation traditions, perhaps the most relevant additional work is by a causal modeller, Herbert A. Simon, *The Sciences of the Artificial* (Cambridge: MIT Press, 1969). But see also L. Fogel, A. Owens, and J. Walsh, *Artificial Intelligence through Simulated Evolution* (New York: Wiley, 1966).

5   In particular the work of G. Sommerhoff, Herbert Simon, Karl W. Deutsch, D.T. Campbell as in part summarized in Walter F. Buckley's two books: *Sociology and Modern Systems Theory* (Englewood Cliffs: Prentice Hall, 1967); and *Modern Systems Research for the Behavioral Scientist: A Source Book* (Chicago: Aldine Press, 1968). Relevant computer simulation models that can be seen in such a perspective are reviewed in William Coplin, ed., *Simulation in the Study of Politics* (Chicago: Markham Press, 1968).

ally came to realize the limitations of even the most advanced forms of simultaneous equation non-linear, dynamic causal analysis. What has been gained is not a much better fitting model – although some improvement in explaining UN involvement has occurred – but a new and intuitively more satisfying way of causally analysing the diplomatic process in terms of precedent searches and of evolving sets of charter-like norms. Because our formulations are still rudimentary and our data not totally adequate for our purposes, we have in effect raised more questions than we have answered and become more consciously aware of different realms of potentially relevant variables. It is, nonetheless, a tribute to Haas's original study that his elementary data analysis helped suggest an extension along these new lines, which in retrospect appear to be quite consonant with his and our own original verbal conceptualizations of the collective-security process.

Thus an attempt to illustrate the relevance of Simon-Blalock causal modelling methodology to the representation and analysis of systematically conceptualized political processes has become an assault on – or better, an expansion or transformation of – this methodology. Although our current formulation can technically be thought of as a multilevel causal model or a synthesis of two modelling traditions, it is perhaps more enlightening to think of a paradigm shift as having occurred, at least in our own work.[6] Such has clearly already been the case in Herbert Simon's modelling efforts; therefore, we use his preferred term for the newer paradigm: artificial intelligence modelling. Given the gap that still remains between reality and our abstract model, the terms 'artificial' and 'simulation' seem both revealing of a new orientation and appropriately modest in our beginning efforts to summarize a complex set of diplomatic expectations and behaviours.

Even though a fuller version of our empirical findings will be published subsequently,[7] a historical reconstruction of the development of our simulation model may be of some general interest. It can help illustrate the cognitive blinders that paradigms can impose on those not conscious of them or their alternatives, the role of serendipity in empirical social research, and the real causes of, or reasons for, our choice of a hybrid concept attainment model for simulating UN peace-making activities. In conclusion, we shall try to show how both the causal and artificial

6 These phrases derive from Thomas Kuhn's provocative, *The Structure of Scientific Revolutions* (Chicago: University of Chicago Press, 1964). Relevant discussions of paradigm shifts occur, *inter alia*, in N.R. Hanson, *Patterns of Discovery* (Cambridge: Cambridge University Press, 1965).

7 In H.R. Alker Jr, ed., *Transnational Politics: Some Formal Analyses*, forthcoming.

intelligence traditions of model analysis suggest ways of making our new perspective a cumulative rather than merely a novel one.

I AN EARLY CAUSAL MODEL OF THE PEACE-MAKING PROCESS

In the spring of 1968, with the assistance of Lawrence Rose, Alker obtained, copied, transcribed to IBM cards, and retabulated Ernst Haas's McBee sort cards containing the codings that formed the data basis for Haas's original monograph. As suggested above, the intent was to develop a dynamic rather than a cross-sectional simultaneous equation process model as an example of politically relevant causal modelling. Haas's work seemed especially appropriate for this purpose for at least three reasons: 1 / it lent itself nicely to a process interpretation in the sense of Lasswell, Deutsch, Easton, or Simon;[8] 2 / at that time such a process orientation seemed consonant with a causal modelling approach; and 3 / computer programs existed at Stanford and MIT for the flexible construction of quantitative process variables from Haas's data.

The elements of a process perspective

A commitment to a process interpretation meant that somehow one should represent actors, with various perspectives concerning a collective-security dispute, using resources in different UN arenas (characterized by conditional or causal relationships) to take diplomatic actions leading to more or less satisfactory outcomes with longer run consequences or effects on the way future disputes would be handled.

Fitting nicely into such concepts, Haas's codings of disputes contained a number of suggestive classifications of disputants and their perspectives, for example, the issue involved (colonial, Cold War, other), the cognitions concerning hostilities (the likelihood or existence of civil or international hostilities), the bloc positions of parties to the dispute (bloc leader, small powers in opposing blocs, etc.), and the general power configuration of the period within the UN system (unipolar, bi-

---

8   Previous papers that have reviewed simulation models from such a perspective include: H.R. Alker Jr, and Ronald Brunner, 'Simulating International Conflict: A Comparison of Three Approaches,' *International Studies Quarterly*, 13, 1 (March 1969); H.R. Alker Jr, 'Decision-Maker Environments in the Internation Simulation,' in Coplin, *Simulation in the Study of Politics*; and H.R. Alker Jr, 'Computer Simulations, Conceptual Frameworks and Coalition Behavior' in S. Groennings *et al.*, *The Study of Coalition Behavior* (New York: Holt, Rinehardt, Winston, 1970).

polar, tripolar, or multipolar). In addition to consensus mobilization categories suggesting various roles for the Security Council, the General Assembly, the Secretary General, and the nations involved, actions were coded nominally but naturally in terms like 'inquiry,' 'cease fire order,' and 'collective conciliation' which have a clear basis both in the UN charter and in experience. Outcome codings included stopping hostilities, maintaining a truce, helping to settle or settling disputes. While no 'effect' categories were explicitly coded, many of Haas's findings intimated what they might be like: the surprising degree of UN success in early Cold War disputes followed by a partial avoidance of such issues, the declining effectiveness of certain mediation and conciliation procedures, the adaptive reliance in the tripolar period on unconventional consensus mobilization procedures, such as the 'balancing' of great powers by unaligned states they did not want to displease, or the permissive engagement of UN symbols through the office of the Secretary General.

Causal modelling as process modelling

If the appropriate quantifications could be obtained, prospects for causally catching most of these outcomes and effects also seemed relatively sanguine. Haas had argued that 'a causal understanding of why the UN succeeds or fails must attempt to link the [environmental] power distribution of the system, the consensual patterns which prevail [in reaching agreement on a course of instrumental action], and the type of issues to which they apply ...'[9] Furthermore, it seemed possible without the use of direct feedback relationships to conceptualize the evolutionary direction taken by the UN collective security system using a number of carefully constructed statistical interaction terms in a causal model.

If the UN had really evolved so that it responded to new and difficult disputes as if some guiding collectivity wanted to stop hostilities or even settle the dispute, then Sommerhoff's notion of 'directive behaviour' seemed a likely way of conveying the regulative thrust of an, at best, quasi-teleological collectivity.[10] If in certain environmental contexts different kinds or levels of involvement were more likely to be successful than others, and these kinds of actions were actually taken, then such a

9   Haas, *Collective Security*, p. 57.
10   This idea has subsequently been more fully and consistently explained in H.R. Alker Jr, 'Directive Behavior,' *Revue français de sociologie*, forthcoming. Although statistical interaction was central to Alker's 'The Long Road to International Relations Theory: Problems of Statistical Nonadditivity,' *World Politics*, 80, 4 (1966), pp. 623–55, a 'means-ends as a function of context' interpretation of interaction was not there clearly apprehended.

direction or collective purpose could be demonstrated. Statistically, when the Cold War threatened to diminish the effectiveness of involvements of type 1 as well as to lower the level of their employment, this would have meant that at the same time other kinds of involvement (call them type 2) would have been activated and perhaps even their effectiveness increased. Figure 1 suggests how this kind of directive behaviour could be represented with four variables plus two interaction terms.

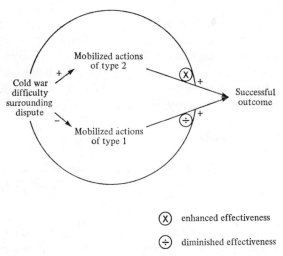

    Ⓧ   enhanced effectiveness

    ⊕̇   diminished effectiveness

Figure 1 An idealized version of adaptive peace-making in the face of cold war difficulties. In the figure, linear causal relations with positive magnitudes are symbolized ($x \xrightarrow{+} y$); analogously for negative effects: an interactive variable w may multiplicatively enhance ($x \xrightarrow{\otimes +} y$) or through division diminish the effects of x on y ($x \xrightarrow[w]{\oplus +} y$).

Problems of index construction

To prepare for the development and testing of such a model, the authors throughout 1969 undertook an intermittent but lengthy recoding and index construction exercise designed to quantify levels of dispute difficulty, consensus mobilization, involvement, and success. Perhaps the most significant but almost automatic recoding decision was not to try and get detailed information on the proposals, expectations, and preferences of major actors in each collective-security dispute. One reason for deciding this was that the expected output did not require it; Haas had also not systematically recorded such information, and doing so would have been terribly time consuming or maybe even impossible. In effect, this practice precluded the use of a disaggregated multiactor model, so that a number of rough approximations had to suffice. In retrospect another highly significant decision was to treat involvement and success as unidimensional variables and situational difficulty and consensus mobilization as bidimensional. Had a good set of multidimensional scaling or factoring programs been available throughout 1969 it is likely that some of these decisions would have been made differently.

The main variables used for the first causal application or test of the ideas suggested by figure 1 are given in table 1. Two different kinds of success – hostility stopping and dispute settling – are merged in a way that correlates about 0.65 with the involvement index. Although both the amount and the level of consensus mobilization were correlated about 0.70, an effort was made to catch both General Assembly and Security Council based mobilization effects with these concepts. Their quantifications were suggested by preliminary cross-tabulations and by the plausible hypothesis that the UN probably adapted to Cold War or great power induced Security Council vetoes by a greater reliance on the Secretary General and the General Assembly.

To many readers the precise codings in table 2 and the correlations derived from them must seem arbitrary. Using the flexible index construction capabilities of the SPSS system operating at the Stanford Computer Center,[11] we did try, however, to follow some general index construction goals or rules. The general goal was to find theoretically meaningful interval scale constructs that maximized intercorrelations, such as those mentioned above, for which prior hypotheses of relationship existed. Ordinal or interval scales were plausible in most such cases. Concepts such as UN involvement, dispute difficulty, consensus mobilization, and success seemed matters of degree; in some cases dichotomous dummy variables could suffice. And clearly another constraint also existed: the power of multiequation causal process models could not be fully utilized on a small sample of cases unless a number of interval variables with selective interactions formed the basis of the analysis.

A major effort was also made to break up Haas's fifty-five cases into more meaningful subunits because it seemed possible and desirable for both statistical and effect investigating purposes. With the help of Amelia Leiss, Ernst Haas, and John Gerald Ruggie, fifty-four of Haas's original cases – data for the omitted case, the Bay of Pigs, were lost – were split

11 A revised SPSS system is now generally available. Later index construction work in the same vein used the ADMINS system at MIT. See 'ADMINS Mark III-User Manual,' March 1970; see also Norman Nie *et al, SPSS (Statistical Package for the Social Sciences)* (New York: McGraw-Hill, 1970).

TABLE 1

Measures used in first causal analysis of UN attempts to stop hostilities and settle issues

Variable	Label	Description	Measurement Construction
X_1	DDIFIX	Dispute difficulty index	$\left(\begin{array}{l}\text{Participant has veto} = 1 \\ \text{or not} = 0\end{array}\right) + \left(\begin{array}{l}\text{Cold War issue} = 2 \\ \text{Colonial issue} = 1 \\ \text{other issue} = 0\end{array}\right)$
X_2	CWINIX	Cold War intensity index	$\left(\begin{array}{l}\text{Cold War issue} = 2 \\ \text{otherwise} = 0\end{array}\right) + \left(\begin{array}{l}\text{dispute beginning:} \\ \text{unipolar or multipolar} = 2 \\ \text{other period} = 0\end{array}\right)$ $+ \left(\begin{array}{l}\text{extent of inter-bloc conflict:} \\ \qquad\qquad \text{big power veto} = 3 \\ \text{small powers, } \geqslant 1 \text{ in different blocs} = 1.5 \\ \qquad \text{small powers, same bloc} = 0.5 \\ \qquad\qquad\quad \text{both unaligned} = 0\end{array}\right)$
X_3	EXHOST	Extent of hostilities	(civil or international war = 1, none = 0)
X_4	LCSMOB	Level of consensus mobilization (1st consensus)	(Concert (SC) = 5, permissive engagement with concert (SG and SC) = 4, balancing in SC = 3, permissive engagement with balancing in SC (and SG) = 3, balancing (GA) = 2, permissive engagement with balancing (SG and GA) = 2, majority will (GA) = 1, permissive enforcement (GA) = 1; inappropriate = 0)
X_5	ACSMOB	Amount of consensus mobilization (1st consensus)	(Majority will = 3, concert = 2, all permissive or balancing arrangements = 1, inappropriate = 0)
X_{10}	UNINV	UN involvement index	(no action = 0, inquiry, collective mediation or conciliation = 1; direct negotiations and/or referral to regional organization, single mediator, SG presence, committee of experts = 2; adjudication on ceasefire ordered = 4; true supervision established, enforcement, boycott, embargo, police force created = 8)
X_{15}	CSCESI	Combined success index	(no success = 0, bilateral or multilateral settlement and UN referral = 1; stopping hostilities = 2, UN helps settle or settles = 3)

into seventy-two separable disputes. As a result, better discrimination was possible among UN involvements in such long-term agenda problems as French colonial relations, Korea, Arab-Israeli confrontations, and the perpetuation of apartheid in South Africa. The new set of cases and our latest recordings of UN settlement successes and failures are exhibited in table 2.

TABLE 2

Collective security disputes before the United Nations, 1945–65

Dispute	Dates	Settlement outcome
I UNIPOLAR PERIOD, 1945–7		
1 Syria/Lebanon/France (withdrawal)	1946–6	Bilateral settlement*
2 Azerbaijan	1946–6	UN settles
3 Corfu channel	1946–6	UN helps settle
4 Spain (Franco government)	1946–6	Unsettled
5 Trieste	1946–7	Multilateral settlement
6 Balkans – 1	1946–	Unsettled
7 South Africa – India – 1 (race policies)	1947–	Unsettled
8 Palestine Partition – 1	1947–	Multilateral and unsettled
9 Suez/Sudan (revision of 1936 agreement)	1947–7	Bilateral settlement*
10 Indonesia	1947–50	UN helps settle; hostilities stopped
II BIPOLAR PERIOD, 1948–55		
11 Kashmir – 2	1948–	Unsettled; hostilities stopped
8+ Palestine partition – 2 (war)	1947–9	Unsettled; hostilities stopped
12 Czechoslovakia (coup)	1948–8	Unsettled
13 Hyderabad	1948–8	Unsettled
14 Berlin	1948–8	Bilateral settlement*
7+ South Africa-India – 2	1947–	Unsettled
8+ Israel border	1949–	Unsettled; hostilities stopped
15 Korean War	1950–3	UN settles; hostilities stopped
16 Withdrawal of KMT troops from Burma	1950–61	UN settles
6+ Balkans	1946–51	UN helps settle; hostilities stopped
17 Iranian oil nationalization	1951	Multilateral settlement
18 Moroccan decolonization	1951–6	Bilateral settlement
7+ South African Apartheid	1952–	Unsettled
18+ Tunisian decolonization	1952–6	Bilateral settlement
19 Guatemala	1954–4	Unsettled
20 Future status of Cyprus	1954–	Unsettled
18+ Algerian decolonization – 2	1955–	Unsettled
III TRIPOLAR PERIOD, 1956–62		
21 Suez	1956	Hostilities stopped; UN settled
22 Hungary	1956	Unsettled

TABLE 2—*continued*

Dispute		Dates	Settlement outcome
18+	Israel border	1949–	Hostilities stopped; unsettled
23	Syria/Turkey border	1957	Bilateral settlement*
20+	Future status of Cyprus – 3	1954–9	Bilateral settlement*
11+	Kashmir – 3	1948–	Hostilities stopped; unsettled
7+	South Africa-India – 3	1947–62	Unsettled
7+	South African Apartheid – 3	1952–	Unsettled
24	Lebanon/Jordan unrest	1958	Hostilities stopped; UN helps settle
25	Laos civil war	1959	Unsettled
26	Tibet	1959–62	Unsettled
27	Nicaragua/Honduras border	1960	UN settles
28	U-2 incident	1960	Unsettled
29	Thailand/Cambodia border	1960–1	UN settles
30	South Tyrol	1960–1	Unsettled
31	West Irian	1960–2	Hostilities stopped; UN helps settle
32	Congo – 3	1960–	Hostilities stopped; unsettled
33	Goa	1961	Unsettled
34	Bizerta	1961	UN helps settle
35	Kuwait/Iraq/UK	1961	Multilateral settlement
36	Cuban intervention in Dominican Republic	1961	Unsettled
37	Portuguese colonies (Angola)	1961–	Unsettled
38	Oman civil unrest – 3	1961–	Unsettled
18+	Algerian decolonization – 3	1955–62	Bilateral settlement*
39	Cuban missile crisis	1962–2	Bilateral settlement
40	UK/Venezuela border	1962	Bilateral settlement

IV MULTIPOLAR PERIOD, 1963–5

7+	South Africa Apartheid – 4	1952–	Unsettled
32+	Congo – 4	1960–3	Stops hostilities; UN settles
8+	Israel border	1949–	Stops hostilities; unsettled
37+	Portuguese colonies (all)	1963	Unsettled
41	Southern Rhodesia	1963–	Unsettled
42	Yemen civil war	1963–	Unsettled
43	Dominican intervention in Haiti	1963	Multilateral settlement*
44	Senegal/Portugal border	1963–	Unsettled
45	Malaysia/Indonesia	1963–	Unsettled
46	Aden/Yemen border	1964	UN helps settle
47	Stanleyville air rescue	1964	UN helps settle
48	Panama Canal	1964	Bilateral settlement*
49	Cambodia/South Vietnam/US (border incidents)	1964	UN helps settle
50	Cyprus civil war	1964–	Hostilities stopped; UN helps settle
51	Greece/Turkey (hostile acts)	1964–	Unsettled
38+	Oman – 4	1961–	Unsettled
52	India-Pakistan war	1965	Hostilities stopped; UN helps settle
53	US intervention in Dominican Republic	1965–	Unsettled
54	Gulf of Tonkin (US) North Vietnam	1965–	Unsettled

*   UN referrals to direct negotiations or regional organizations.

The first causal assessment

Elaborating the ideas in figure 1 in terms of the variables in table 2 led, after some preliminary testing, to a set of causal expectations like those in figure 2. The basic asymmetry between the two dispute difficulty variables is clearest in the assumed positive impact of the Cold War (CWINIX) and the resulting expectations of Security Council veto on General Assembly type mobilization efforts (ASCMOB). A modification from figure 1 is the assumption that Cold War issues are particularly solvable through the Security Council if and only if the consensus level is high too. Assuming the Cold War index to have a multiplicative effect on one kind of mobilized action and a divisional impact on another kind is another way of testing UN peace-making adaptability.

Note also the central role of a single involvement variable as a positive determinant of success. High consensus levels are assumed to facilitate, and difficulty levels to dampen, this positive relationship. Dispute characteristics, including difficulty levels and the existence of hostilities (EXHOST), are thus asumed only to have indirect effects on success or failure.

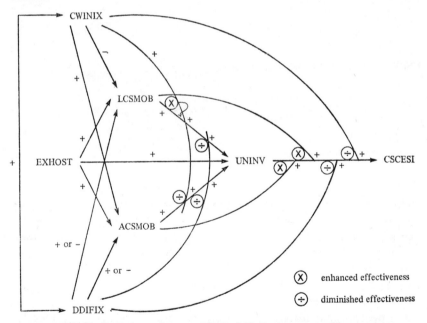

Figure 2 Hypothesized determinants of United Nations peace-making success. Arrow symbols including multiplicative and divisional interactions are explained in table 1; variable labels correspond to those in table 2.

Let us first emphasize the positive (i.e., theory confirming) aspects of the preliminary findings. The most generally valid aspect of the model is the strong positive causal chain from EXHOST to UNINV to CSCESI, that is, from the existence of hostilities to UN involvement to success in stopping hostilities or settling disputes. Furthermore, none of the situational or process variables had direct effects on success except through involvement. Trial and error led to an array of significant interactional effects that, in addition to involvement, accounted for 60 per cent of the variance in CSCESI. A respectable but not totally satisfying 39 per cent of the variance of UNINV was also explained.

After considerable rethinking, several aspects of the directive behaviour idea also became visible in the data. Consider the estimated equations – omitting the most insignificant links – for CSCESI and UNINV:

$$\text{CSCESI} = \text{UNINV} \left(0.35 + \frac{0.095}{\text{CWINIX} + 1} \right) + 0.051 \text{ LCSMOB} \times \text{CWINIX} + 0.044 \text{ LCSMOB}$$

$$\times (3.82 - \text{UNINV}) - \text{ACSMOB} \left(\frac{0.748}{\text{DDIFIX} + 1} \right) + u \qquad (1)$$

$$\text{UNINV} = -0.20 + 1.19 \text{ EXHOST} + \text{ACSMOB} \left[\left(\frac{1.95}{\text{DDIFIX} + 1} - c_1 \right) + \left(\frac{0.98}{\text{CWINIX} + 1} - c_2 \right) \right]$$

$$+ \text{LCSMOB} \left(1.02 - \frac{0.65}{\text{DDIFIX} + 1} \right) + 0.023(\text{LCSMOB} - 2.53) \text{CWINIX} + \sigma \qquad (2)$$

where $c_1 + c_2 = 0.80$

Looking first at equation 2 and refreshing our memories as to the variable definitions in table 1, we see that the debilitating effects of the Cold War on involvement are more complex than those associated either with the paradigm of figure 1 or the hypothesis set of figure 2. The Cold War thus seems to have attenuated the effects of high consensus on involvement but probably without reversing the sign of effect. Similarly, but more drastically, for those rare Cold War infected issues with some kind of great power concert (consensus levels above a threshold of 2.53), involvement is enhanced; in the more typical case of lower consensus levels, involvement is directly decreased by Cold War complications. Thus the route of relying on Assembly majorities more than on Security Council concerts seems to indicate a modest degree of UN adaptability when concerts have not been obtainable.

The estimates of why success was or was not achieved tended also to fit prior expectations, but with modifications and a number of threshold effects. UNINV has a large positive, direct effect that is only slightly diminished by high Cold War intensity. Also, as predicted, LCSMOB appears to enhance the effect of involvement on success but this appears true only for UNINV below 3.82, that is, short of major involvement.

Moving now to the negative side, two terms appear in the CSCESI equation that we had hoped would only relate to UNINV. In this sense, the causal hypothesis of figure 2 is not wholly supported. Thus we find the assumption of figure 2 – more involvement from LCSMOB when CWINIX is high – weakly but positively true of CSCESI. And with an unexpected minus sign, consensus amount qualified by dispute difficulty affects CSESI, in a sense partly destroying the positive dispute settlement effect of ACSMOB. Thus taking the ACSMOB (General Assembly) route involvement may work in such cases, but one should expect less effectiveness from resulting levels of involvement.

Even more disappointing was the breakdown in the anticipated alternating pattern of situational effects on the level and amount consensus mobilization variables. Consensus level responses are not inhibited by the Cold War, rather, they seem to be enhanced. The other dispute difficulty index, DDIFIX, does however, have a negative effect on consensus level, perhaps because the two dispute difficulty indices are so highly intercorrelated (c 0.60–0.70). And worse, nothing seems to affect the consensus amount variable except consensus level, which is clearly correlated with it in a definitional way.

Lessons from the analysis

It was our original intent to combine equations 1 and 2 and their causal antecedents in order to do compound path analysis.[12] This meant, for example, assessing the direct plus the indirect effects of the Cold War and other dispute/situational characteristics. Maybe the Cold War had not been as debilitating with regard to disputes actually introduced into the UN as popular interpretation would have it; moreover, adaptation to the interactability of such issues as the German or Korean settlements may have led to joint recognition of the difficulties of a UN role in Vietnam. It

12   This term derives from Sewall Wright. For an exposition, see Donald Stokes, 'Compound Paths in Political Analysis,' *Mathematical Applications in Political Science*, IV (Charlottesville: University of Virginia Press, 1969).

also meant looking at unexplained involvement levels to see if they represented choices peculiar to a particular situation yet still tending, as if by direction, to increase the chances of dispute settlement.[13] But there were enough disquieting findings and unsettled problems to prevent us from doing so.

Gradually a number of these problems became clear, more through self-criticism than through third parties, most of whom did not find the early expositional effort comprehensible enough to criticize. The shortcomings included:

1 Too great a collapse of involvement and success variables into unidimensional indices. Maybe this is why several terms caused CSCESI when they were supposed to cause UNINV. Adaptive or directive behaviour could also be better represented with a multiplicity of selectively activated diplomatic instruments.

2 The arbitrariness of and/or the incomprehensibility of SPSS and ADMINS index quantifications. If the general idea of trying to produce theoretically meaningful linear correlations was to be taken sincerely, then clearer, more defensible, and more unidimensional indicators were needed.

3 A drastic reconceptualization of consensus mobilization indices, perhaps in a unidimensional way. Greater reliance on broader amounts of numerical support, particularly in the Assembly, had been shown to help get around Cold War inhibitions of involvement, but it had also been shown to decrease high involvement success potential. Given the high intercorrelation of LCSMOB and ACSMOB, it did not seem possible, however, to sort out differential consensus responses to dispute/situational characteristics.

4 The degree of success in explaining involvement. The 'directive behaviour' approach at best seemed to suggest some interesting interaction terms. But the highly intercorrelated difficulty indices seemed to convey imperfectly the impact of dispute/situational characteristics.[14]

13 This idea was only fully articulated in UN terms in the fall of 1970 in Alker's, 'Directive Behaviour.'

14 Some of our puzzlement as to the relative superiority of $UNINV/(CWINIX + 1)$ versus $UNINV \times CWINIX$ type interactions and the different signs they tended to have become clearer in discussions with William Greenberg. For a denominator with a dummy variable, the two representations are indistinguishable. Otherwise, because $X/(1 + y) = X(1 - y + y^2 \ldots)$, they are highly intercorrelated. As result, it was decided to use only multiplicative interactions in the future without being able to claim complete confidence in their correct specification.

5   The inadequacy of the learning or evolutionary mechanisms in the 'causal model with interactions format.' After all – and this increasingly seemed the major flaw – there was no explicit feedback via learning or trial and error problem-solving from success or failure to future involvement decisions. It had no moving parts.

The ramifications of 5, which touch problems 1 and 4 above as well, only slowly became clear in the next phases of our work. Reading about learning theory models, thinking and talking about analogous evolutionary or decay processes as described by process theorists in the general systems theory literature, and the discovering breakpoints in the magnitudes of the regression coefficients before and after 1961 led us to think that some of the most important, and in some ways the most depressing, declines in UN effectiveness noted by Haas had not yet been accounted for.[15]

II   LEARNING THEORY MODELS OF PEACE-MAKING ACTIVITIES

Looking back over the next stages of our work, it seems clear that we were groping for a better, more dynamic model. Our set of causal mechanisms was too mechanical: there were too many ad hoc but statistically significant interaction terms. At best we had summarized change without modelling it; no internal states were changing to reflect adaptive or maladaptive involvement tendencies. Subsequent developments can be rationalized by – even if they were not consciously motivated by – a more dynamic learning theory or evolutionary perspective. Rather than look for traces of quasi-teleological behaviour directed towards a peace-making goal – stopping hostilities and settling disputes – we wanted a richer version of learning or evolutionary mechanisms and processes. We thought we could probably get a better explanation of involvement decisions if explicit feedback variables were included in the causes of involvement. Involvement predispositions could be more discriminantly studied if we stopped treating the variable as unidimensional and started thinking of different

15   Relevant general systems theory references have been noted in footnotes 5 and 8 above. Markov learning models had been called to our attention from a causal perspective by Pat Suppe's, *Set-Theoretic Structures in Science* (Stanford Book Store, 1967, mimeographed). See also Sternberg's review of mathematical learning theory in R.D. Luce *et al.*, eds., *Handbook of Mathematical Psychology*, 1963. Breakpoints – significant changes in causal structure – were found by Christensen in a term paper by Christensen and Greenberg, 'Alternate Models of UN Peace Keeping,' and in her presentation to the Vancouver IPSA Roundtable, spring 1970.

kinds of changeable involvement predispositions. A clearer mobilization index could be thought of as multiplying or translating some of these tendencies into practice. A better way to study what was positively learned from successes or negatively learned from failures would be to use both components of the success measure separately, that is, stopping hostilities and maintaining truces as one variable, and helping to settle or settling a dispute as another. Although their realization took over a year, from the spring of 1969 to the fall of 1970, we can discuss these developments in three stages: 1 / the use of simulation models to specify stochastic learning mechanisms; 2 / the rediscovery of non-stochastic precedent logistics as experience accumulators; 3 / the use of quantification scaling procedures to quantify ordinal mobilization, involvement, and success variables.

Simulation models of stochastic learning mechanisms

Almost simultaneously, Greenberg and Christensen started work on learning theory simulations,[16] but a number of similarities and divergencies occurred as their work progressed. Both models disaggregated involvement into eleven component actions – inquiry, collective mediation, ordering a ceasefire, etc. Both used thresholds in the success index to produce learning as to involvement probabilities. Christensen used Mosteller-Bush type stotostic learning mechanisms (see figure 3), while Greenberg used more sophisticated Bayesian learning theory.[17] Each had ways of involving new actions either by a simple random choice mechanism or, if an early effort failed, by going into the General Assembly. Both models implied a kind of positive approach and negative avoidance learning. Diplomatic actions that worked would be used more often, some were not tried, and especially those that failed were tried less often. Because simple learning theory models were still insensitive to the contextual features of a dispute – its environmental characteristics – several qualifying mechanisms were tried. Christensen allowed for exogenous or recom-

16 William Greenberg, *A Learning Model Simulation of United Nations Response to Crises* (unpublished MS thesis, MIT, August 1969). C. Christensen, flow charts for a UN simulation, July 1969. One of these flow charts is reproduced below; the related PLI program has been lost. A much revised version of the Greenberg simulation, taking into account recent developments, is forthcoming in Alker ed., *Transnational Politics: Some Formal Analyses*. Ruggie's previously cited work also started during the spring of 1969, coming to fruition during and after the summer of 1969.

17 For relevant references, see Sternberg, 'Stochastic Learning Theory,' and John Pratt, Howard Raiffa, Robert Schlaifer, *Introduction to Statistical Decision Theory* (New York: McGraw-Hill, 1965).

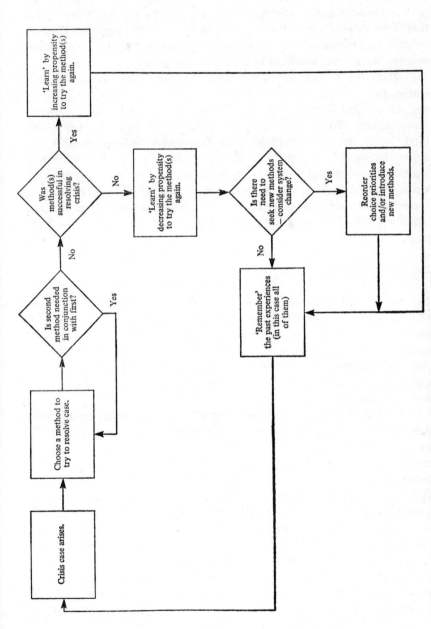

Figure 3 A 'conceptual' flow chart of collective security learning experiences.

puted involvement propensities in each different systematic period (uni-polar, bipolar, tripolar, multipolar). Greenberg used a regression equa-tion from dispute characteristics to UNINV to set a maximum level of possible involvement and then, using earlier aggregate involvement codings, interpreted this limit in disaggregated terms.

The press of time and some new ideas about precedent logics led Christensen and Alker to discontinue their simulation efforts in the antici-pation that Greenberg would finish his own similar and more exhaustive investigations. To us, Greenberg's dissertation showed that levels and kinds of involvement could be quite frequently predicted from a dis-aggregated model but that stochastic approaches that were not sufficiently attentive to contextual dispute characteristics were also not likely to prove strong 'learning' effects of the sort we were seeking. Greenberg's use of Bayesian methods also had a sleeper effect, which was only later realized when we started introducing a priori precedents into a precedent logic model.

The use of precedents as experience accumulators

In retrospect it is quite surprising how long it took us to see the relevance of precedents for determining UN involvement. When we did so, none of our first attempts to measure the effects of precedent produced very sub-stantial results. Nonetheless, a year later once new quantifications of success, mobilization involvement and precedent variables had been obtained, a 10 to 15 per cent improvement in predictions of involvement was achieved.

Like most ideas that redefine perspective or paradigms, the crystalli-zation of formal precedent logics as 'rules for accumulating experience in an action predisposing way' came in fits and snatches. During the academic year 1968–9, both of us had been exposed to Lincoln Bloom-field's work with Robert Beattie, Amelia Leiss, and John Steinbrunner. Alker had proposed weighted linear combinations of differences in char-acteristics for measuring dispute distances and proximities in CASCON, their precedent based information retrieval system. Christensen had been struck by the importance of precedents in experimental games with students and foreign policy elites which were designed to study how differing information conditions affected policy-making performance by national governments in international crises. Both of us had shared with Philip Stone the cognitive bias that made his discussions of work by Gregg and Simon, Hunt, Marin, and Stone on the use of cognitive hypotheses in concept attainment experiments particularly attractive.[18] And each of us had sensed the same kind of problems with the nearly context-free way in which the Christensen and Greenberg learning simulations had summarized what had been learned from attempts to resolve previous disputes. While a Bayesian approach seemed superior in that it relied on a priori action predispositions rather than a blank slate approach, these predispositions were too action specific and too context free.

Alker's discussions with Richard Snyder during the 1969 summer workshop – at the same time that work on the causal model of figure 2 was well underway and the stochastic model of figure 3 was just being implemented – led him to realize that a whole class of rules, or psycho-logics, might account for precedent choices. Debates as to whether Manchuria was or was not the relevant precedent for US and UN involvement in Korea or Munich the analogous justification for US involvement in Vietnam were recalled. The same point applied to UN involvement in cases like the Congo, where it was clear that Suez had been an important legitimizing and action predisposing precedent. Analogous to the concept attainment studies and Bloomfield's experiments, the key questions were, first, what are the logics, rules (or hypotheses) by which action predisposing precedents are determined, and, second, how are the logics changed by successful or unsuccessful applications.

18   In addition to the Bloomfield-Leiss volume cited in note 3, each of us had been exposed to a number of project related unpublished memos and reports. For those not familiar with the 'concept attainment' literature discussed in much greater length in the references of note 4, a brief description of some of the experimental and modelling work is provided here. It is also worth mentioning that Gregg and Simon in a sense parallel and precede our conversion from a non-cognitive stochastic process model to a cognitive process model of the same learning phenomena.
     Briefly, the experimenter tells the subject that in showing him various subjects he has a particular concept in mind. If, for example, the concept is 'blue and rectangular,' a blue pen would not be an instance but a blue book would (if seen in two-dimensional perspective). What one models is how the subject learns from his lucky and unlucky guesses what the actual concept is. Markov learning models with fixed transition probabilities (e.g., the probability of moving from an incorrect hypothesis to a correct one) and absorbing states (e.g., having the correct hypothesis) have been used by Bauer, Trabasso, and others to model this process. More cognitive approaches treat guesses as hypotheses, and model ways in which the subject might test and modify them vis-à-vis his new experience. Various modelling possibilities include the random selection of a new, as yet untried, hypothesis when an old one is incorrect, greater reliance on memory to recall whether the new hypothesis would have been consistent with previous replies by the experimenter, etc. Gregg and Simon's most impressive accomplishment, perhaps, is the 'derivation' of stochastic cognitive processing parameters.

Joint discussions with Stone and Greenberg helped in the elaboration of what these precedent logistics might be. Presumably Haas's dispute characteristics were a fair approximation of the main variables involved. One major option was whether to search for precedents in terms of simultaneous matches on as many dispute characteristics as possible or, in a sequential fashion, to match first on one characteristic and then, if that was correct, to go on to a second, etc. Thus, looking for a precedent to the Congo, should one look first only at those cases with civil wars and among those cases of these which involved colonial issues and among these cases those that did not directly involve a great power, etc? Such a search procedure – which we call lexicographic because of an analogous term in economic choice theory and dictionary construction practice – would in fact not discover the Suez crisis as a relevant precedent. Neither in this case would a 'maximum number of identical dispute characteristics' approach, if there was another earlier colonial issue involving domestic strife but no direct great power involvement. In retrospect, Alker's suggestions for CASCON matching rules that use weighted linear combinations of dispute characteristics can be seen to be a variant of the 'maximum match' approach. Other options included different lexicograph orderings and whether or not to consider only successful precedents or, if similar enough successful ones could not be found, unsuccessful precedents as well. The fact that a number of the disputes in table 2 were continued across periods suggested the obvious possibility that a good predictor and a partial explanation of continued heavy involvement might well be found in the previous involvement levels of the parent case. Another intriguing possibility analogous to the stochastic learning models was whether negative avoidance learning or positive approach learning was the proper way to define precedents.

Table 3 presents a number of 'proposed involvement' indices derived from a computer program written to implement difference precedent rules. The resulting not directly measurable precedents were construed as proposals and correlated with a revised overall involvement index UNIN2 created in the ADMINS system at MIT.[19]

19　Table 3 and equations 3 and 4 related to it are taken from Christensen and Alker's preliminary version of the present paper, delivered at the IPSA Vancouver Roundtable. Various combinations of these precedent variables were also explored in Christensen and Greenberg, 'Alternate Molds.'
　　Just as we were to learn the hard way that SPSS or ADMINS could not help us sufficiently to provide a satisfactory quantification of our indices, thus necessitating the use of Guttman-Lingoes non-metric multidimensional scaling programs, so it also became clear that neither ADMINS nor SPSS nor any other conventional social science oriented data analysis system could be used to construct precedent involvement variables because of the peculiar relational

TABLE 3

Some early precedent variables

PREC1   Find the last case which occurred in the current period and involved the same kind of issue. Let the value of precedent = UNIN2 + 1 for that precedent case. If no such case exists, let the value of precedent = 0.

CPREC1   Find the last case which occurred in the same period and involved the same kind of issue in which the action the UN took was successful (settled or helped settle the issue). Let the value of precedent = UNIN2 + 1 for that precedent case. But if no such case exists, let the value of precedent = 0.

PREC2   Find the last case which had the same level of bloc involvement and occurred in the same period. Let the value for precedent = UNIN2 + 1 for that precedent case. But if no such case exists, let the value of precedent = 0.

CPREC2   Find the last case which had the same level of bloc involvement and occurred in the same period, but where the UN's action was successful. Let the value of precedent = UNIN2 + 1 for that case. If no such case exists, let precedent = 0.

PREC3   PREC3 is generated by a short PL1 program which can vary the 'tree' it searches to find a precedent case. When it finds a precedent case, it assigns UNIN2 + 1 for that case as the value of precedent. If no such case is found, precedent = 0. In this case the program tried to match first to see if there was a parent case (the result of breaking a case into separate cases by period) and used it as the precedent if it existed. If no parent case existed, the program tried to match by period, existence of hostilities, level of bloc involvement, and issue. Each time it failed to find a match, it dropped a variable. The order of dropping was: bloc involvement, issue, period, existence of hostilities. If all variables were dropped without a match, the precedent score was 0.

PREC4   The method used is identical to that used in PREC3 except that the order of dropping variables is: issue, period, bloc involvement, existence of hostilities.

PREC5   The method used is identical to that for PREC4 except that there is no initial search for a parent case.

NPREC1   The program was modified so that it went through the tree initially looking for cases which were similar and in which the UN action taken was successful. If it did not find any such case, it then went back through the tree again and found the most similar case it could, regardless of success. The order of dropping was: period, bloc involvement, issue, existence of hostilities. A parent search was used at the beginning of each tree search.

NPREC2   The program was identical to that for NPREC1 except that the order of dropping was: issue, period, bloc involvement, existence of hostilities.

---

notions we were thinking in terms of. Thus a separate 'precedent logics' PL/I Computer Program was written by Christensen in order to generate indices derived from various such logics. This problem is probably typical of counter paradigm research. Fortunately, from this perspective, the new ADMINS system being programmed for the Multics Time-Sharing System at MIT will have the desired capability.

Our first findings in the winter of 1969–70 were mixed but not altogether discouraging. Most of the precedent variables did not correlate very highly with the involvement variable. Correlations in the 0.20s were about as high as we got. One of the main reasons for our limited success was our inability to discriminate among types of involvement and our failure to consider multiplying precedent based involvement proposals by actual or predicted consensus mobilization levels in order to get a better prediction for actual UN performance. Thus an obvious reason for many bad predictions was the inability of any UN organization to come to agreement on actions that it or someone else should take despite the presence, we presume, of a number of precedent linked involvement proposals.

Nonetheless, several results did suggest further inquiry. One was the strange, seemingly pathological, finding that negative precedents seemed to have positive effects. Put more correctly, correlations between involvement levels of contemporary cases and the involvement levels of their unsuccessful precedents were positive. One could get the impression that there were competing forces affecting the success or even the viability of the United Nations. 'Bad' precedents tended to create future failures or non-involvements and 'good' precedents pressured the UN to get involved in more disputes, stop hostilities, and, if possible, to settle the underlying issues as well. At a later date it became clear that the positive correlations between involvement levels and both successful and unsuccessful precedents could also be interpreted in terms of the more general precedent rule suggested above: find a similar enough successful precedent, if there is one; if not, act on the basis of a similar but unsuccessful antecedent case.

Christensen was also able to produce considerably better explanations of UNIN2 (a regrouped and requantified aggregate involvement index) along with a slightly better explanation of the overall combined success index used previously. Limiting herself to multiplicative interaction terms (for reasons given in footnote 14), she derived equations 3 and 4. The first of these accounted for 64 per cent of the variance in CSCESI and the second did almost as well for UNIN2: $R^2 = 0.56$. Omitting the obviously insignificant terms and putting standard errors below the coefficients, we have:

$$\text{CSCESI} = \underset{(\pm 0.25)}{0.69\,\text{UNIN2}} + \underset{(\pm 0.075)}{0.12\,\text{UNIN2} \times \text{LCSMB3}} - \underset{(\pm 0.04)}{0.06\,\text{UNIN2} \times \text{CWDFIX}}$$

$$+ \underset{(\pm 0.28)}{0.59\,\text{ACSMB3} \times \text{EXHST2}} - \underset{(\pm 0.17)}{0.25\,\text{LCSMB3} \times \text{EXHST2}} + u \qquad (3)$$

$$\text{UNIN2} = \underset{(\pm 0.22)}{0.33\,\text{ACSMB3}} + \underset{(\pm 0.20)}{0.49\,\text{LCSMB3}} - \underset{(\pm 0.07)}{0.15\,\text{LCSMB3} \times \text{ACSMB3}} - \underset{(\pm 0.28)}{0.57\,\text{ACSMB3}}$$

$$\times \underset{(\pm 0.55)}{\text{EXHST2}} + 1.23\,\text{EXHST} - \underset{(\pm 0.10)}{0.14\,\text{CWDFIX} \times \text{EXHST2}} - \underset{(\pm 0.29)}{0.43\,\text{DUM61}}$$

$$- \underset{(\pm 0.07)}{0.14\,\text{CPREC2}} + \sigma \qquad\qquad (4)$$

In these equations UNIN2, LCSMB3, ACSMB3, and EXHST2 are slight variants on UNINV, LCSMOB, ASCMOB, and EXHOST as defined in table 1; CPREC2 is defined in table 3 as the precedent suggested by the most recent successful UN involvement in the same period, with the same kind of bloc involvement as the present crisis. DUM61 is a dummy variable equal to 1 after 1961.

A number of similarities and differences can be found by comparing these equations with their earlier relative equations 1 and 2. Thus the direct, positive effect of hostilities on involvement and involvement on success is again clear. Some of the same Cold War effects are observable, but dispute difficulty terms were not considered, in part because of their multicollinearity effects on the estimation of Cold War related coefficients. Hostility related interactions, which Alker had failed to explore, are obviously quite powerful. Post-1961 involvement has decreased (possibly because of a basic shift within the UN multipolar power system, but also in part because of the UN financial crisis). Perhaps the most disturbing result is the significant and negative effect on involvement of recent successful intervention precedents. Again implicit breakpoints associated with the financial crisis may be part of the story. We suspect, however, a more serious problem: even when experts have coded the settlement of a dispute as having gone reasonably favourably (hostilities stopped, UN helped to settle), serious great power dissent can hinder deeper involvements in subsequent similar cases.

Whether we could catch this dissatisfaction and the associated decline in post-1961 involvement within a revised and generalized routine remained a question for further analysis. Clearly, a less arbitrary exclusion/inclusion rule had to be used with respect to interaction terms involving LCSMB3, ACSMB3, and DUM61 with or without thresholds. More fundamentally, we were still dissatisfied with the catch-all nature of equation 4. It would be a much clearer theoretical argument to say somehow that all situational effects, including the existence of hostilities and Cold War difficulties, were conveyed through the precedent ascertaining

200 Hayward R. Alker, Jr and Cheryl Christensen

process. And it was gradually becoming clear that mobilization variables, if more carefully reformulated, should be considered as multiplicative modifiers of the way precedent proposals for action affected actual involvements, not as independent causes of the involvements. Before any of these ideas could be tested in terms of a more general precedent generating routine, however, it seemed advisable, as noted above, to get less arbitrary and more discriminating measures of several success, involvement, and mobilization dimensions.

Index construction via quantification scaling

As we began to take seriously a commitment to try and summarize the effects of dispute characteristics through the precedent determination and application process, it became clear that, at least temporarily, we could avoid the difficult problem of how best to measure directly the Cold War difficulty or settlement difficulty of a dispute. These aspects of a dispute should be caught by the various interactions of dispute characteristics that go into the determination of precedent-based involvement proposals. Thus, during the summer of 1970, with the Greenberg's assistance, Alker proceded to implement a quantitification scaling program written by James Lingoes as part of a series of programs for the multi-variate analysis of contingencies.[20]

The basic idea of the program is to find those quantifications of two (or more) categorical variables that maximize the linear correlation(s) among them (a procedure we call metricization). Consider the possibility that two nominal variables cross-tabulate in a way that allows their row and column categories to be reordered and then assigned quantitative values so that the resulting row and column indices are nearly perfectly correlated. It certainly is not the case that such a result is inevitable.[21] A

20 Both MAC–2 and MAC–3 were tried and MAC–3 finally used. The programs (actually their predecessor) and some alternatives are best described in J.C. Lingoes, 'Multivariate Analysis of Qualitative Data,' *Multivariate Behavioral Research*, 3, 1 (1968), pp. 61–94. A review of the logic of bivariate quantification scaling, which was developed by C. Hayashi and others in Japan independently of Guttman and Lingoes' efforts is given in the appendix of Alker, 'Statistics and Politics.'
21 For the simplest case of two dichotomies the resulting correlation equals phi, which ranges between −1 and +1, depending on the marginals. The bivariate problem can be thought of in terms of maximizing a non-linear correlation ratio. For more than two polychotomies, this generalizes to something like maximizing a correlation or the average of all pair correlations. Thus even when non-linear relationships exist, variables are in effect transformed to their 'best' linearized form.

poor fit may have occurred, and the categories themselves may have been assigned numbers that violated a priori expectations as to their proximities and rankings. If such problems do not arise and the reconstructed correlations have approximately the magnitudes that were expected, it seems appropriate to say that a non-arbitrary, partly validated quantitative transformation of the original nominal, ordinal, or ordered-metric information has occurred. All the information available would be consistent with the hypothesis of truly quantitative variables underlying the observed qualitative distinctions and relationships.

Such was the strategy applied in an attempt to quantify the success, involvement, and consensus mobilization variables less arbitrarily. If there were few observations within a category or if a category could not clearly be distinguished from adjacent categories, then a merging or recoding of these categories could also be considered a legitimate procedure in attempting to derive our 'metricized' index values.

After a number of such efforts, it seemed that, as partly anticipated, involvement levels were clearly multidimensional – at least two dimensions were needed to summarize action/outcome relationships. A search began for a rationale for distinguishing among the eleven diplomatic action categories. Bloomfield's crisp review of recent diplomatic discussions of peace-keeping options in terms of coercive versus non-coercive actions gave us an appropriate answer: we could quite easily summarize these debates and discussions of these options in coercive versus non-coercive terms. In the charter there is even a suggestion that early forms of Security Council or General Assembly involvement might involve inquiry or the referral of negotiations, while latter or more serious levels of coercive or non-coercive involvement would consist of full-scale conciliation or mediation, ordering a ceasefire, enforcing it, or sanctioning its offenders. Ordering of involvement intensity and/or sequence are clearly implied.

This set of distinctions also reinforced our original feelings and ambiguous statistical evidence about the inadequacy of combining hostility, stopping or truce maintaining and dispute settling in a single index. A convincing argument could be made that if hostilities existed, coercive and non-coercive measures would be needed to stop them (e.g., mediation plus a ceasefire order). Then, if troops were not needed to maintain the ceasefire, non-coercive settlement procedures would normally be invoked. For non-violent disputes and even for some other violent ones (e.g., those in which a veto was likely) total reliance on presumably less effective non-coercive measures would be all that could be ventured.

The resulting quantifications or ordinally coercive and non-coercive involvement variables together with a hostility stopping/truce maintaining dichotomy and an ordinal success trichotomy surpassed prior expectations. Figure 4 shows how cross-tabulations of involvement and success variables – of means and ends, actions and their outcomes – produced modestly positive correlations when quantified. The analogous means-ends figure for coercive involvement and stopping hostilities has a correlation around 0.75. As we would expect, coercive and non-coercive involvement are slightly more highly related than hostility termination and success. Moreover, turning to the first part of table 4, it is quite gratifying to note that one of Haas's most difficult distinctions, between the UN helping to settle a dispute and actually settling it, does not show up as a very useful statistical distinction either. The same almost applies for the two upper levels of the coercive involvement index. The results were relabelled Metricized Non-Coercive InVolvement Index (Recoded), MNCIVR; Metricized Coercive INvolvement Index (Recoded), i.e., MCINVR; HOSTP1 (stopping hostilities or maintaining a truce); and Metricized SuCcess IndeX (Last), i.e., MSCIXL. An important piece of evidence is that we could not abstract additional orthogonal quantifications that were statistically significant, ordinarily meaningful, or highly intercorrelated from any of these variables. In an important sense, our desire for validated quantitative measurements of involvement and success had finally been satisfactorily accomplished.[22]

The quantification scaling of consensus mobilization introduced a more difficult challenge. In cross-tabulating it vis-à-vis our two new involvement and success variables, it was not possible to develop a clear set of interpretable results or expectations. More than one dimension of mobilization was extractable. Nonetheless, after some regrouping of categories, the first dimension of our quantification analysis, as summarized in table 4 (MCMOBL), finally came into focus. Security Council

22 Something more radical may have been achieved if these new quantifications
    adequately summarize the action to outcome phase of the collective security
    process without the use of non-environment interaction terms to account for
    previously discovered breakpoints in the success and involvement equations.
    If they do, then perhaps adaptive relations between diplomatic actions and
    situational characteristics as they affect outcomes have been entirely shifted
    back to the preinvolvement phase by the introduction of not directly measur-
    able precedent variables. This means directive behaviour is evidenced only
    when dispute characteristics statistically interact in the choice of action pro-
    posals and during the process of trying to get consensus support for such
    proposals. As a matter of fact, only such an assumption of linear situation
    independent means/outcomes relationships is consistent with the assumptions
    of the quantification scaling procedure. Compare the models of figures 1, 2, 5,
    and 8 or their related equation systems to explore this point further.

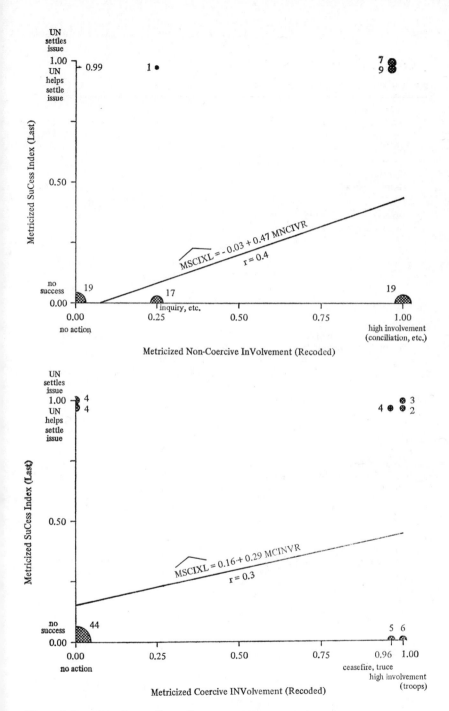

Figure 4 Quantification scalings of MSCIXL versus MNCIVR, MCINVR.

TABLE 4

Key variables in the Alker-Christensen UN peace-making simulation

Variable labels and names	Variable categories and values	Comments
A OUTCOME VARIABLES		
1 HOSTP1 (stopping hostilities on maintaining truce)	yes = 1.000 no = 0.000	as with MSCIXL, MCINVR, MNCIVR. Derived from a means-ends quantification scaling procedure
2 MSCIXL (metricized last recoded success index)	no success, bi-lateral or multi-lateral settlement not on the basis of UN referral = 0.000 UN helps settle = 0.990 UN settles issues = 1.000	
B ACTION VARIABLES (INVOLVEMENTS AND CONSENSUS MOBILIZATION)		
3 MNCIVR (metricized non-coercive involvement index, recoded)	no coercive action = 0.000 committee of experts, inquiry, referral of negotiations (neg. ref.) = 0.326 SG presence, mediation, conciliation, adjudication = 1.000	For both MNCIVR and MCINVR more than one action was observed; therefore, each dispute is coded in terms of the level of coercive UN action taken in it. Original action categories and the coercive/non-coercive distinction are charter based
4 MCINVR (metricized coercive involvement index, recoded)	No coercive actions = 0.000 Ceasefire ordered, truce established = 0.965 Police force, enforcement boycott, embargo = 1.000	
5 MCMOBL (metricized consensus mobilization level)	Inapplicable, none = 0.000 Majority will, permissive engagement with majority will = 0.778 Great power concert in SC = 0.918 Permissive engagement with concert = 0.946 Balancing in GA, permissive engagement with SG = 0.986 Balancing in SC, permissive enforcement by SG = 1.000	Categories are from Haas. Metric scores are from quantification scaling procedures

TABLE 4—*continued*

Variable labels and names	Variable categories and values	Comments
C ACTION PROPOSALS (OR GOAL AND SITUATION SPECIFIC PRECEDENTS)		
6 SXVCIP (success validated coercive involvement precedent)	Same as MCINVR except when modified by forgetting or extinction.	Derived from precedent determination routine with HOSTP1 (or MSCIXL) as a criterion (applies also to proposals 7 to 9 inclusive)
7 HTVCIP (HOSTP1 validated coercive involvement precedent)	Same as MCINVR except when modified by forgetting or extinction.	
8 SXVNCP (success validated non-coercive precedent)	Same as MNCIVR except when modified by forgetting or extinction.	
9 HTVNCP (HOSTP1 validated non-coercive precedent)	same as MNCIVR except when modified by forgetting or extinction	
D SITUATION (DISPUTE) CHARACTERISTICS		
10 EXHOST (extent or nature of present or recent hostilities)	no hostilities = 0 civil war = 1 international hostilities = 2	nominal variable used in precedent routine (applies also to characteristics 11 to 14 inclusive)
11 UNORGA (UN organ involved in case)	Security Council (SC) or both SC and GA = 1 GA or International Court (ICJ) = 2	
12 BLCONF (extent of inter-bloc conflict)	Veto power involved = 1 small powers in opposing blocs = 2 small powers one aligned, one not = 3 small powers within same bloc = 4 unaligned small powers = 5	
13 ISSUE (type of issue involved in case)	Colonial = 1 Cold War = 2 Other = 3	
14 PERIOD (period of case; for cases broken down into separate periods, this will change)	Unipolar-period = 1 (1945–7) Bipolar-period = 2 (1948–55) Tripolar-period = 3 (1956–62) Multipolar-period = 4 (1962–5+)	
15 EXHST2 (existence of a record of civil or international hostilities)	yes = 1.000 no = 0.000	used in regression equations

TABLE 4—continued

Variable labels and names	Variable categories and values	Comments

E   PRECEDENT LOGICS: RULES FOR DETERMINING SITUATION-RELEVANT ACTION PROPOSALS

16	MODERULE: basic rule for determining precedent cases, including (ordered) dispute characteristics	LEX, ROT or MAX, e.g., LEXMIN3EUBIP means search for precedents lexicography; first match on EXHOST, then UNORGA, then BLCONF, then ISSUES, then PERIOD. At least E, U and B should match for a precedent to be declared.	Precedents may be found either by a lexigraphical, non-lexicographical (MAX) or mixed (ROT) matching of dispute characteristics
17	MIN (the minimum number of matches required before a precedent is declared)		The valuables used in checking for precedents are principally 10–14 plus a success criteria such as HOSTP1 or MSCIXL > 0.5.
18	IDAGR (index of importance of identification number agreement)	IDAGR $= 1$ if previous period version of same conflict is to be considered a dominating successful (or unsuccessful precedent) otherwise $= 0$	Several cases, e.g., the Middle East and Apartheid in South Africa, have been listed as separate cases in different periods but with the same ID numbers.
19	SUC (index of importance of second search for non-successful precedents)	If SUC $= 1$, then such a search will be made if no successful precedents have been found.	Again an option in determining how precedents are to be redefined.

F   RULES FOR REDEFINING PRECEDENTS (SYSTEM CHANGE OR EFFECTS GENERATING VARIABLES)

20	RATE (parameter of forgetting model)	If RATE $= 1.0$, then no memory exists; slower learning is associated with higher RATES.	This is relevant to the modification of expected coercive or non-coercive involvement levels and maybe also to expected MCMOBL values.
21	NEXT (the number of successful intervening disputes before a successful precedent is extinguished.	NEXT $\geqslant 1.0$	This allows a redefinition of the precedent case.
22	SHOT (number of times a success must occur before Charter norms are considered revised)	SHOT $= 1$ is currently only implemented option	One-shot learning is probably the most "powerful" norm revision mechanism in the model

concert clearly does better than a General Assembly majority in evoking involvement or success. The creative use of the Secretary General's office and third world balancing effects on hesitant great powers are also seen to have been worth an effective mobilization level score. No wonder actions mobilized through the Secretary General's office have evoked such controversies over the literal meaning of the charter.

III   AN ARTIFICIAL INTELLIGENCE MODEL OF UN PEACE-MAKING

Consolidating the above insights into a new, rough, unitary approximation of a collective decision process involved exciting, sometimes frenetic activity.[23] A new computer program was needed to include and help choose among the precedent determination options that we already knew we needed. And, as often is the case when writing such programs to taste rather than using 'canned' programming packages, some new modelling ideas emerged. If we could see where we were going in choosing precedent logics by determining which one predicted best using newly quantified involvement variables, taking consensus mobilization into account, it was not completely clear whether we had satisfactorily answered the question we had asked before. How are these logics or the precedents they discover changed by successful or unsuccessful applications?

Even if our course was largely determined, we were still not sure where and when we would arrive. The growing realization that we were now trying more explicitly to model the complex ways in which collectivities apply and change both norms and expectations produced a deepening sense of humility as to how well we would succeed given the relative simplicity of our programming elements. This feeling of doubt complemented our excitement over our conversion (through the in-depth examination of attempts causally and interactively to interpret statistical cross-tabulations) to the artificial intelligence paradigm.[24]

23   In addition to Christensen's imminent departure for London and Kampala, Alker was to give a paper on 'Quantitative Methods for Political Analysis' for the September 1970 meetings of the International Political Science Association in Munich. Most of the results of this section were first reported publicly at that time. During July and part of August William Greenberg then assumed a more active role as programmer, discussant, and suggestion-maker. Some of the reformulations of the present section also reflect responses to a number of public presentations of the essential ideas of the Alker-Christensen model.
24   Particularly in the perspective of Fogel, Simon, and D.T. Campbell, a key element of an artificial intelligence model is the use of evolution-like mechanisms for the modification of programs of activity in more or less efficient directions, with concomitant effects on their survival chances. It is probably

In what is still an ongoing effort, we report here three stages of further analysis: 1 / a second attempt to find realistic action proposals using precedent logics; 2 / the filling out of the concept attainment or artificial intelligence paradigm with a provisional higher level model of system norms and systems evolution; 3 / current reflections on the successes and failures of our artificial intelligence approach. (Have we really progressed from causal modelling to artificial intelligence?)

A second test of precedent logics

An incomplete but suggestive flowchart for the current PRECEDENT computer program is given in figure 7 below, but in order for it to be comprehensible, the reader must be introduced to the options it contains. After several modifications during the design phase, it was decided to allow the use of up to five dispute/situational characteristics in searching for and applying precedents. In the PRECEDENT program and in table 4 these are given the abbreviated labels EXHOST (the existence of hostilities), UNORGA (UN organ or organs involved), BLCONF (extent of bloc conflict), ISSUE, and PERIOD. Ties in matching levels are always to be resolved in favour of the most recent successful (or unsuccessful) precedent case. The dominance of a successful parent case in determining subsequent involvements can be assumed when ID numbers agree (IDAGR = 1). The option of a second search through antecedent data if a successful precedent has not been found is symbolized by a SUC parameter. Any intermediate value of HOSTP1 or MSCIXL (metricized hostility stopping and settlement success indices) can be used as a success or failure threshold. One metricized coercive involvement index and two metricized noncoercive involvement indices – only the more justifiable one is included in figure 4, table 4, and the present model – are treated as program inputs. Both lexicographical (LEX) and maximum match (MAX) precedent determination rules (called MODERULES) are allowed, as well as a mixed rule (labelled ROT) allowing lexicographic discrimination among precedents with an equal number of matching characteristics.

more accurate to describe our own change of heart towards such an approach as primarily a transformation in our UN modelling style. Although at least one of us had been committed to the casual modelling approach for years, each of us had been deeply impressed by the modelling approaches of these authors as well as those of Robert Abelson, Kenneth Colby, and Joseph Weizenbaum. What was profound about the step-by-step process described here was the implied gradual undermining, or reformulation, of the widely shared causal modelling perspective.

Given the small number of possible precedents, a minimal lexicographic or maximal match requirement of two or three corresponding dispute characteristics (MIN = 2 or 3) often meant that no precedents of that degree of similarity existed. Therefore Alker introduced the residual precedent determination option of using a weighted average of previous involvements, not contextually defined.[25] At an even later date, Alker and Greenberg included a correlation and regression calculation option so as to be able to compare HOSTP1 or MSCIXL precedents, possibly multiplied by consensus mobilization scores (MCMOBL), with actual involvement decisions.

Given all the above options the PRECEDENT routine was bound to work better, although perhaps not in a statistically significant way because of the equally numerous additional degrees of freedom introduced. Nonetheless, without the MCMOBL multiplication option, correlations between hostility termination or settlement success validated action proposals (HTVCIP, HTVNCP, SXVCIP, SXVNCP) and metricized coercive and noncoercive UN involvements (MCINVR, MNCIVR) jumped from the previous 0.15–0.25 range to a more respectable 0.30–0.40 range, with coercive involvements being easier to predict, probably because of the previously noted galvanizing effect of the existence of hostilities.

The lexicographic mode of precedent determination used exclusively in Christensen's earlier runs also proved to be superior to either the maximum match approach (LEX versus MAX) or a mixed approach (LEX versus ROT).[26] More correctly, when used with a minimum match requirement of 2 or 3, almost all LEX orderings of dispute characteristics did better by about 0.10 than the corresponding MAX or ROT alternatives. The clearly helpful minimum match threshold requirement (MIN = 2, 3 or 4) also

---

25 This is a direct 'distributed lag' generalization of Christensen's earlier discovery of first order autocorrelation in involvement sequences. A relevant exposition is contained in J.W. Forrester, *Industrial Dynamics* (Cambridge: MIT Press, 1961), appendix E.

26 Unfortunately this occurred a year after Alker had suggested a MAX type approach to Beattie and Bloomfield for the CASCON system. Technically this was not a perfect test of the lexicographic alternative to Alker's original weighted maximum approach for several resons: 1 / Bloomfield and Beattie were working with a much greater set of situational and action variables and a smaller set of coded precedent cases on US involvement in third world disputes; 2 / Bloomfield and Beattie were trying to predict to recommended involvements derived from a post mortem analysis; 3 / the MIN option makes it harder to distinguish a lexicographic ordering from a matching one. It is worth noting that Beattie and Bloomfield eventually chose a cluster analysis procedure over Alker's weighted MAX type proposal. It appears that most such procedures are versions of a MAXMIN precedent seeking rule.

combines elements of both an ordered and a maximum match approach.

A summary of most of this discussion is conveyed by the schema of figure 5, some of whose aspects we have not yet explained. As the figure suggests, we have found a particular lexicographic ordering of dispute characteristics (EUBIP, which means check EXHOST before UNORGA before BLCONF before ISSUE before PERIOD and, in the LEX mode stop matching with the first mismatch) to be the most efficient involvement predictor. It works the best when the first three matches are required (MIN = 3) and when a second round search is made for unsuccessful precedents if no similar enough successful ones have been found (SUC = 1).

Uncertainty on this matter still exists, however, because other precedent search orders, such as LEXMIN2EUIBP, do as well in predicting coercive involvements. Furthermore the same MODERULE does not always do the best for each involvement type when we use either HOSTP1 or MSCIXL as learning reinforcers. There is now, however, considerable evidence that the PERIOD variable so important in Haas's theoretical analysis, the stochastic simulation of figure 3, and the computation of CPREC2 and DUM61 used in equations 3 and 4 is not as decisive as we had earlier anticipated.[27] A third reason for being very tentative about a LEXMIN3EUBIP rule for precedent search activities is that the results just presented, although they produce correlations of 0.60 and 0.75 with noncoercive and coercive involvement when multiplied by the metricized concensus mobilization index, depend on a whole new host of assumptions and model mechanisms.

System norms and systems evolution

To be a real process model, the schema of figure 5 should include ways in which success and failure outcomes modify subsequent system performance. This is what Lasswell among process theorists means (in part) by the category of systemic 'effects.' In another phraseology, the model should contain the seeds of its own renewal or destruction: 'feedback' or

27 The unipolar-multipolar distinction as a single nominal variable, of course, does not catch all of what Haas or we mean by PERIOD. It may still be very significant in determining what kinds of disputes do and do not come to the UN, a matter we have here wrongly treated as exogenous. It also may be important as a summarizing concept for explaining new kinds of involvement or concensus mobilization activities. Like evolutionary improvements or randomly selected new hypotheses in concept attainment studies, these innovations are treated essentially as non-precedented and exogenous in the scheme of figure 5.

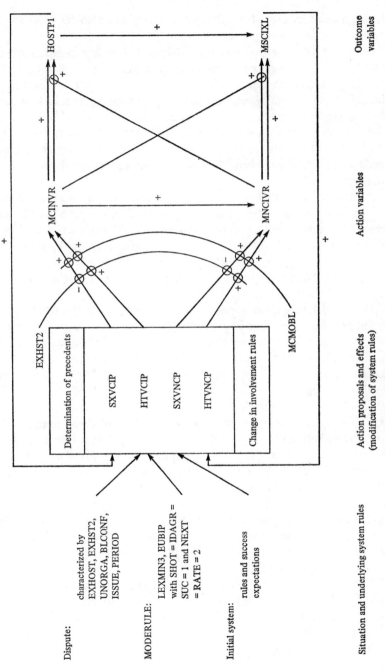

Figure 5 An artificial intelligence model of United Nations' peace-making.

endogenous system change mechanisms. These can also be considered second-level causal mechanisms.

Similarly, to be a real concept attainment learning model, such a formulation as we have now described should contain explicit rules both for finding precedents and modifying their involvement implications. Thinking of precedents as action proposals, our model should first say how such concepts, or hypotheses, are actually attained. This we have tentatively answered with the precedent logic LEXMIN3EUBIP, SUC $= 1$, IDAGR $= 1$. But we also have to describe how this rule or its derived precedents are modified through successful or unsuccessful invocation experience.

As we applied model versions like those described above and looked at their deviant cases it seemed that they worked better for a middle set of cases. There were no apparent precedents for the early cases, and the predicted involvements for later cases were often too high, because for most of the later disputes somewhere in the past there was a similar case in which the UN had been involved, perhaps even succeeding in stopping hostilities or in helping to settle the dispute.

Our model lacked an a priori set of proposals for involvement in different kinds of disputes; to be treated like other precedents these proposals should have expectations of their likely success or failure associated with them. The model had an extremely simple learning theory: one-shot collective learning. Successful precedents were external. Both assumptions were clearly wrong.

Good textbook discussions and Haas himself have emphasized that the UN charter is an attempt to revise League of Nations involvement rules on the basis of its failure to avoid the second world war (the Japanese conquest of Manchuria, the Italian conquest of Ethiopia, German and Russian invasions of Poland, German occupation of Czechoslovakia, and the Russian conquest of Finland are often cited as such failures). The essential need for co-operation among the winning great powers in the second world war has also been enshrined in their Security Council veto power. As any diplomatic historian knows, the idea of relying on a great power concert in shaping collective-security decisions predates the UN; it predates the League as well.

Thus one of the most obvious but still exciting and not yet well-specified 'rediscoveries' in this continuing attempt to model UN peace-making processes was the essential role of charter norms and expectations as initial precedents. As residual action proposals, they help suggest when, and in what kinds of disputes, high coercive involvement is to be expected and, equally roughly, which of such involvements are likely to be successful.

Figure 6 represents Alker's first interpretation of these norms and expectations in terms of Haas's dispute/situational characteristics. In applications of a revised PRECEDENT program, each of ninety charter precedents was treated as a 'preprecedent,' coming before actual cases of UN action or inaction experience. (Ignoring PERIOD, these ninety preprecedents cover all kinds of cases derivable from combinations of 5 BLCONF, 2 UNORGA, 3 ISSUE and 3 EXHOST possibilities: $5 \times 2 \times 3 \times 3 = 90$. At first, relying mostly on pieces of the charter plus the most outstanding historical cases, Alker had missed the program-like aspect of figure 6 by introducing only ten to eighteen of such possibilities.

The UN collective security system can be described in terms of its essential operating norms. Thus the set of initial system norms in figure 6 should be considered a major additional input to the schema of figure 5 and the PRECEDENT routine briefly charted in figure 7. With revisions, they can describe the effects of both exogenous and endogenous model change as system norms are learned or forgotten, evolved or extinguished. In concept attainment terms, our current model says there are ninety kinds of situation-specific action proposals (grouped into eight 'boxes' in figure 6) that piece by piece are being modified by success and failure experiences. At an abstract level, figure 6, as updated, represents a changing program for involvement, a complete set of action rules. The fuller model, in response to new, exogenous, quasi-random data inputs, changes most distinctly through one-shot learning from any involvement success. For those familiar with the artificial intelligence models of Simon or Fogel *et al.*, the parallels with their artificial intelligence models of evolving problem-solving procedures should be striking.

From this and other perspectives, ours was clearly too optimistic a model. Figure 5 indicates how forgetting and extinction mechanisms were subsequently added to previous PRECEDENT specifications. Current limited experience suggests that such modifications are an improvement over earlier versions. Within the limitations of a one-shot learning approach (SHOT = 1), unsuccessful precedent applications were then assumed to diminish by half (RATE = 2) the proposed involvement levels. If such forgetting was not sufficient and the same earlier successful precedent was again unsuccessfully invoked, then a second failure would lead to the extinction of the successful precedent (NEXT = 2).

Surely these improvements are simple versions of any learning process, let alone a complex, non-isolated group process like parlia-

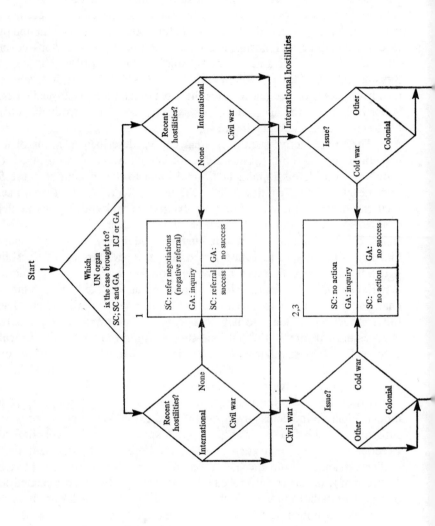

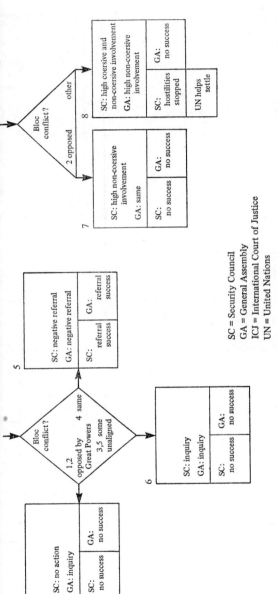

Figure 6 An initial program of United Nations' peace-making. Boxes 1 to 8 contain a priori estimates of likely involvement levels; beneath them are expected success levels. This chart suggests a UEIBP precedent rule, but is also consistent with LEXMIN3EUBIP.

SC = Security Council
GA = General Assembly
ICJ = International Court of Justice
UN = United Nations

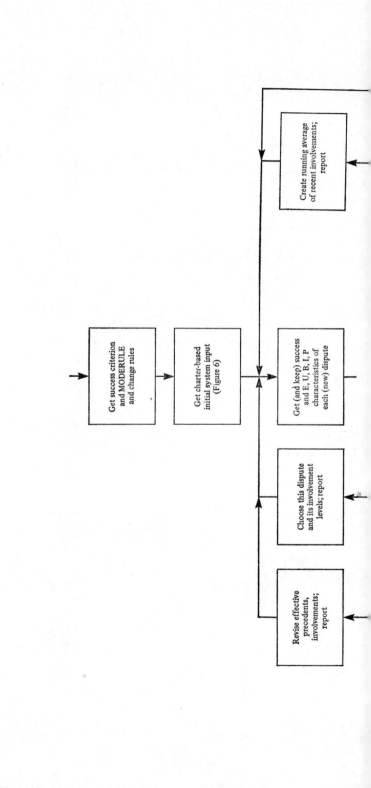

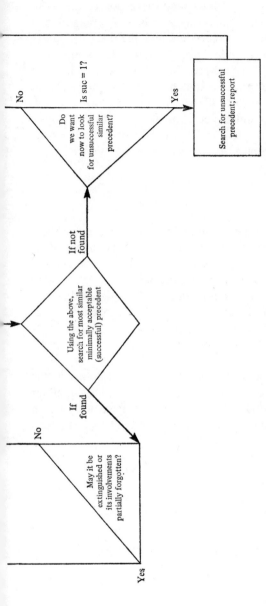

No

Do
we want
now to look
for unsuccessful
similar
precedent?

Is suc = 1?

Yes

Search for unsuccessful
precedent; report

If not
found

Using the above,
search for most similar
minimally acceptable
(successful) precedent

If
found

No

May it be
extinguished or
its involvements
partially forgotten?

Yes

Figure 7 A macro flow chart for determining precedents and changing involvement rules. Programming of this model for the 360/65 has been done in PL1 by William Greenberg,

218 Hayward R. Alker, Jr and Cheryl Christensen

mentary diplomacy. Figure 8 gives an intriguing suggestion of the particulars of such a model and is useful in determining its strengths and limitations. It is based on success precedents and the LEXMIN3EUBIP MODERULE. Except for the controversial implications of Haas's judgment that Korea was a UN 'success,' it has the beginnings of plausibility. Not the least of its virtues is the impression that figure 8 and others like it begin to reproduce evidence as to when Charter norms may have evolved. They help pinpoint changes and, unlike causal models, help explore topics such as the implications for the operative Charter of Korea, Suez, or the Congo. Such topics have long been at the centre of attention of many non-formal theorists.

How far have we progressed?

A historical recounting like the one we have just completed encourages the reader to argue whether or not any real progress has been made. Presenting only the model of figures 5, 6, and 7 would not have allowed this posibility. Thus a serious argument for the virtues of the present approach is still required. One important point has been suggested: figure 8 suggests a whole new realm of potentially explainable phenomena as well as potentially falsifying data. Diplomatic debates over charter interpretation and relevant precedent disputes have yet to be systematically analysed.

A comparison of action and outcome causal interrelations in the present hybrid model with earlier causal interpretations, such as equations 1, 2, 3, and 4 is also in order. Although their coefficients have not yet been stably estimated, equations 5 to 8, derived from figure 5, allow some such juxtapositions.

$$\text{MSCIXL} = C_1 + a_1\text{MNCIVR} + a_2\text{MNCIVR} * \text{MCINVR} + a_3HOSTP1 + u_1. \tag{5}$$

$$\text{HOSTP1} = C_2 + a_4\text{MCINVR} + a_5\text{MNCIVR*MCINVR} + u_2. \tag{6}$$

$$\text{MNCIVR} = C_3 + a_6\text{MCINVR} + [a_7\text{EXHST2*HTVNCP} + a_8(1\text{-EXHST2})\text{SXVNCP}]*\text{MCMOBL} + u_3. \tag{7}$$

$$\text{MCINUR} = C_4 + [a_9\text{EXHST2*HTVCIP} + a_{10}(1\text{-}\text{EXHST2})\text{SXVCIP}] \text{MCMOBL} + u_4. \tag{8}$$

Certainly an interesting twist is given to the present model by its implied flexibility in goal redefinition. If hostilities have recently existed, then

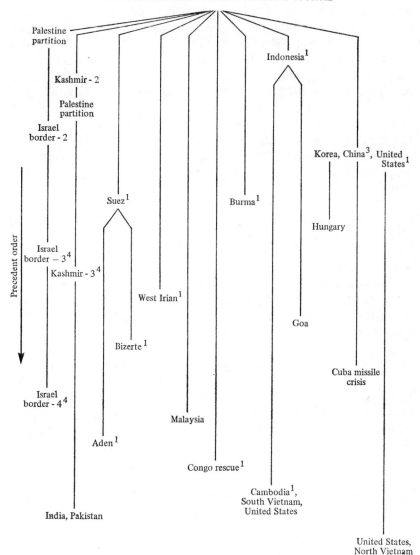

CHARTER PRECEDENT [1,2]

FOR GENERAL ASSEMBLY AND SECURITY COUNCIL

Palestine partition

Kashmir - 2

Palestine partition

Israel border - 2

Indonesia[1]

Korea, China[3], United States[1]

Precedent order

Israel border — 3 [4]

Kashmir - 3 [4]

Suez[1]

Hungary

West Irian[1]

Burma[1]

Goa

Bizerte [1]

Israel border - 4 [4]

Cuba missile crisis

Malaysia

Aden[1]

Congo rescue[1]

India, Pakistan

Cambodia[1], South Vietnam, United States

United States, North Vietnam

Figure 8 Charter application and charter evolution: cases involving international hostilities on colonial and other issues by non-opposed powers. 1: cases judged to have been at least in part settled by the United Nations. 2: charter precedent is high coercive and non-coercive involvement by the SC (with success in stopping hostilities and settling issues) and high non-coercive but not successful GA involvement. 3: this case is a violation of charter expectations. 4: this case would no longer be governed by a weakened successful involvement precedent if the NEXT parameter being employed is 2.

precedents relevant to hostility-stopping dominate; if recent hostilities are not a factor, then dispute settlement procedures are the most appropriate precedent proposals. Turning to variance explained considerations, preliminary indications are that hostility-stopping by an interactive combination of both coercive and non-coercive involvements will have an R^2 approximating 0.70, that is, better than the variance explained by either equation 1 or 3. Explaining success or failure in settling disputes is more difficult, however. Interaction terms involving situation characteristics may not be needed, thus dramatically simplifying the later parts of the PRECEDENT model, while validating a key assumption of the quantification scaling procedure. The two-part representation of dispute handling efforts will then be more fully justified.

But at a more profound level, it is not completely fair to say we have succeeded in justifying a paradigm conversion. Recall the ambiguity of statements that we have either assaulted, transformed, undermined, or modified the causal modelling or stochastic learning traditions in the UN peace-making context. A constructive interpretation would stress the modification aspect. Thus our second level, simple learning, forgetting and extinction model is clearly mechanistically causal. Its main virtue is that it helps explain changing parameters in previously fixed causal links going from dispute to action, thus possibly accounting for some of the more striking previously discovered interactions of the mobilization involvement type, depending on dispute difficulty characteristics.

The new model can also be interpreted in stochastic learning terms. Our most serious mistake was not listening more seriously to the intimations of either the period specific involvement assumptions of the Christensen simulation model (figure 3) or the context limiting-involvement Bayesian (a priori) reasoning of the Greenberg simulation. A better learning simulation would be one that learned or forgot not eleven action predispositions, but ninety context-specific charter-based preprecedents. Only a larger number of 'internal states' are needed to capture related changes from a stochastic learning perspective.

As far as they go, these arguments are probably correct. But perhaps the best reason for continuing to work mainly in the artificial intelligence tradition is so that the insights of the other clearly relevant approaches will be used as well.

1   We shall continue to try to use the statistical estimation and testing procedures that are great strengths of the stochastic learning and causal modelling approaches. New statistics need to be developed for many of the methods we are using, but some of the old ones, such as ways to determine whether an interaction term makes a statistically significant

contribution to explaining MSCIXL, can still be very useful. New work on estimating the effects of unmeasured variables, such as action proposals, could also prove helpful.

2   A number of intriguing modifications are possible with modest enrichments of the learning mechanisms mentioned above. Maybe different judgments as to success or failure could be incorporated into the learning or evolution process. Thus a Troika or triple-requisite evolutionary mechanism would say that only if most Communist, American-allied and non-allied nations felt an action to have been a success would charter evolution occur. Such is not an unrealistic empirical hypothesis for the current period. Other, perhaps more parsimonious organizations of our ninety different kinds of involvement situations are certainly worth exploring. Outcomes that change more than one of these at a time or even modify the precedent determination rule can at least be contemplated. More estimation and validation work on second level learning and forgetting mechanisms as well as latent contextual predispositions is clearly needed.

Perhaps the most intriguing idea associated with a mechanistic causal perspective in the present context is as follows: There are what metaphorically might be called interacting forces of light and darkness, each respectively pressuring the UN towards growth and extinction. Such a perspective might seem hopelessly metaphysical were it not obvious that aspects of it occur throughout the empirical examples of the present paper. In Haas's work such forces could be discovered in action to outcome cross-tabulations that vary with systemic period or context. Figures 1, 2, and 3 progressively enrich this idea through the use of continuous variable interactions and flow chart logics. A blank slate precedent learning model which maps complex interactive ways in which good and bad preprecedents combine with constant causal mechanisms and fluctuating case inputs is an obviously relevant extension. The full-fledged schema of figure 5 is a profound multilevel generalization, yet an incomplete realization of the idea behind figure 1. Surely overall tendencies and capacities of alternate specifications of these schemata are worth further conceptual and empirical work.

3   But from a process perspective, some of the most intriguing research possibilities are most easily discussed in normative-cum-empirical artificial intelligence terms. What charter modifications might work (better) in the future? Are there any other norms than those which are currently operative that might have evolved or have been consistent with different orderings of historical experience? If nation-specific 'satisfactions' were substituted for scholarly judgments of objective 'success,' how different would the charter system look from the one that actually evolved? Would

there still be any norm overlap? Joseph Weizenbaum has commented that
our current model contains something like a teaspoon of artificial intelligence. We agree. Bureaucratic or institutional learning is sometimes
tortured, always slow and oversimplified.[28] But could not a much deeper
understanding of the collective security process be obtained by the interaction of several representative but different belief systems?

Surely the UN, with its charter-based capabilities and limitations,
could not have prevented the second world war. The Germans were a
great power and could have vetoed unattractive actions if they had felt it
necessary to remain in the League. Under the present charter the UN could
at best have prevented the rape of Ethiopia because Italy was not considered a great power. Are there revisions in charter-based norms that
might have led the League or the UN to a better record? Are current norms
and precedent determination procedures optimal for handling likely future
disputes? With or without the Veto?

The greatest success of the artificial inteligence approach for us has
been a new consciousness of model-reality linkage possibilities. Each of
the three modelling traditions we have explored can contribute to answering some of the questions we have asked above if its advocates recognize
the same complex, multilevel norm-modifying political process that has to
date characterized the UN peace-making process.

REFERENCES

ALKER, HAYWARD R. JR 'Computer Simulations, Conceptual Frameworks and
    Coalition Behavior,' in S. Groennings, ed. *The Study of Coalition
    Behavior*. New York: Holt, Rinehardt, Winston, 1970.
–   'Decision-Maker Environments in the Inter-Nation Simulation' in
    William Coplin, ed. *Simulation in the Study of Politics*. Chicago:
    Markham Press, 1968.
–   'Directive Behavior,' *Revue Française de sociologie* (forthcoming).
–   'The Long Road to International Relations Theory: Problems of
    Statistical Nonadditivity,' *World Politics*, 80, 4 (1966), pp. 623–55.
–   'Statistics and Politics: The Need for Causal Data Analysis' in S.M.
    Lipset, ed. *Politics and the Social Sciences*. New York: Oxford University
    Press, 1970.
–   *Transnational Politics: Some Formal Analyses*. Forthcoming.
ALKER, HAYWARD R. JR and RONALD BRUNNER 'Simulating International

28 See Robert Axelrod, 'Learning as a Political Process' (unpublished manu-
    script) for more thoughts along these lines. Axelrod and Mathew Bonham and
    Michael Shapiro are themselves working on US precedent determination
    simulations of the foreign policy crisis decision-making process.

Conflict: A Comparison of Three Approaches,' *International Studies Quarterly*, 13, 1 (March 1969).

AXELROD, ROBERT 'Learning as a Political Process,' mimeographed.

BLALOCK, H.M. JR *Causal Inferences in Nonexperimental Research.* Chapel Hill: University of North Carolina Press, 1964.

BLALOCK, H.M. JR and A. BLALOCK, eds. *Methodology in Social Research.* New York: McGraw-Hill, 1968.

BLOOMFIELD, L.P. and A. LEISS *Controlling Small Wars: A Strategy for the 1970's.* New York: Knopf, 1969.

BORGATTA, EDGAR F., ed. *Sociological Methodology, 1969.* San Francisco: Jossey-Bass, 1970.

BOUDON, R. *L'Analyse mathématique des faits sociaux.* Paris: Libraire Plon, 1967.

BUCKLEY, WALTER F. *Modern Systems Research for the Behavioral Scientist: A Source Book.* Chicago: Aldine Press, 1968.

BUCKLEY, WALTER FREDERICKS *Sociology and Modern Systems Theory* Englewood Cliffs, NJ: Prentice-Hall, [1967].

CHRISTENSEN, C. and W. GREENBERG 'Alternate Models of U.N. Peace Keeping.' Delivered at the Vancouver International Political Science Association Roundtable, 1970.

COPLIN, WILLIAM, ed. *Simulation in the Study of Politics.* Chicago: Markham Press, 1968.

FOGEL, LAWRENCE J., ALVIN J. OWENS, and MICHAEL J. WALSH *Artificial Intelligence through Stimulated Evolution.* New York: Wiley 1966.

GREENBERG, WILLIAM 'A Learning Model Simulation of United Nations Response to Crises,' unpublished MS thesis, MIT, August 1969.

HAAS, ERNST *Collective Security and the Future International System.* Denver: University of Denver, 1968.

HANSON, N.R. *Patterns of Discovery.* Cambridge: Cambridge University Press, 1965.

HUNT, EARL, JANET MARTIN, and PHILIP STONE *Experiments in Induction.* New York: Academic Press, 1966.

KUHN, THOMAS *The Structure of Scientific Revolutions.* Chicago: University of Chicago Press, 1964.

LINGOES, JAMES CHARLES 'Multivariate Analysis of Qualitative Data,' *Multivariate Behavioral Research* (November 1967).

NIE, NORMAN et al. *Statistical Package for the Social Sciences.* New York: McGraw-Hill, 1970.

PRATT, JOHN, HOWARD RAIFFA, and ROBERT SCHLAIFER *Introduction to Statistical Decision Theory.* New York: McGraw-Hill, 1965.

RUGGIE, J.G. 'Environmental Discontinuities and Collective Security: Simulating United Nations Intervention,' mimeographed.

SIMON, HERBERT *Models of Man.* New York: Wiley, 1957.

– *The Sciences of the Artificial.* Cambridge, Mass.: MIT Press, 1969.

STERNBERG, SAUL 'Stochastic Learning Theory' in R.D. Luce *et al. Handbook of Mathematical Psychology*, II. New York: Wiley, 1963.

STOKES, DONALD 'Compound Paths in Political Analysis,' *Mathematical Applications in Political Science*, IV. Charlottesville: University of Virginia Press, 1969.

STONE, PHILIP J. 'Computer Models of Human Information Processing Procedures' in H.M. Schroder and P. Suedfield, eds. *Personality and Information Processing*. New York: Ronald Press, 1971.

SUPPES, PATRICK COLONEL *Set-Theoretic Structures in Science*. Stanford: Institute for Mathematical Studies in the Social Sciences, Stanford University, 1967.

ZACHER, M.W. 'United Nations Involvement in Crises and Wars: Past Patterns and Future Possibilities.' Paper delivered at the American Political Science Association meeting, September 1970.

Political coalitions
and political behaviour:
a simulation model

I INTRODUCTION

Social science research increasingly points to the fact that a global explanation of political change requires the simultaneous consideration of a
rather large number of variables. Although analytical methods for multivariate procedures have been developed at a rapid pace, difficult problems
remain to be solved, especially with regard to interactive dynamic processes.

For many scholars, the quality of concrete political life cannot possibly be represented by a formal model; they argue that only some broad
guiding lines may be systematized and that any historical situation is the
result of a multitude of specific events which cannot be expressed in terms
of regularities. However, it is tempting to assume on the contrary that if
a given historical situation appears to have a unique quality, it is because
we are not able to handle satisfactorily the interaction of a large number
of such regularities. When many variables interact, their very number
may make use perceive successive outcomes as qualitatively different.
But if we could disentangle the factors which determine the state of the
social system within which these outcomes are observed, the latter's
singular features might well appear as variations on the same theme. Two
seemingly qualitatively different historical cases could, in fact, be the
result of variations in the initial conditions of identical variables, the
general laws relating these variables remaining unchanged.

But we can do more than speculate about such a possibility; we can test by experimenting with complex multivariate models, computers, and simulation techniques. Such is the purpose of the simulation model presented here. More specifically we intend to describe 1 / alliance building, stability, and breakdown among social actors, and 2 / the changes of some properties and relations which characterize these social actors and link them to one another.

Although the goal of this paper is to construct a general framework for the analysis of processes at different historical periods and places, past as well as present, it is focused on a particular series of events: those connected with the general uprising which occured about 1780 in some regions of what is now known as Peru and Bolivia. These events having been described elsewhere, no new account of them will be given here.[1] The model is intended to reproduce some of the political events which developed in those areas at that time. As the particular features of the political space showed significant regional variations, it is expected that the model will be able to describe these variations when the differing initial conditions in the various regions are fed into the computer program. The model, which is of the 'all computer' type[2] has been programmed for computation and is presently under experimentation. It is sensitive to variations of initial conditions. The variations are similar to those which occurred in the historical case studied, so that these experiments may be considered as stages in a step-by-step validation process. Further experimentation with the model is envisaged for other cases.[3]

Numerical analysis of complex models, always raises the question of the precision of the data employed either as inputs or to validate outputs. But complex models should not be burdened with more stringent requisites than those asked of other methods of social research. As they stand now I think we must consider complex models complementary tools to other procedures of social sciences, especially useful in interpreting the dynamics of a complex set of events.

My basic aim is to construct models compatible with data obtained through detailed case studies. The shortcoming of such an approach is that the usual statistical validation procedures are not always easily ap-

1   See Oscar Cornblit, 'Society and Mass Rebellions in XVIIIth Century Peru and Bolivia,' in R. Carr, ed., *Latin American Affairs* (Oxford: Oxford University Press, 1970), pp. 9–44.
2   For a discussion of the different types of models see H. Guetzkow, 'Simulation in International Relations,' in William Coplin, ed. *Simulation in the Study of Politics* (Chicago: Markham Publishing, 1968).
3   For an examination of some numerical results of the model see Oscar Cornbilt, *Cambio Político en Cuzco y Oruro a fines del siglo XVIII: un estudio comparado de simulación* (Buenos Aires: Instituto Di Tella, 1970).

plicable. On the benefit side, on the other hand, we must consider that, as a result of the approach used in collecting and interpreting the data, one obtains a more balanced combination between the amount of data employed to describe the state of societies and the quality of the analysis linking these data through a system of explicitly stated hypotheses.

II   GENERAL DESCRIPTION OF THE MODEL[4]

The conditions prevailing in 1780 in the regions we are studying are described by the following variables:

a   Social actors. An actor may be a set of individuals, an institution, or any other social unit which is considered relevant for the interpretation and explanation of events. The set of social actors selected depends upon the hypothesis considered. Twenty-two social actors are employed in this particular study.

b   Actor properties. They describe charcteristics of a given social actor. Here twenty characteristics are considered so that each actor is characterized by a property vector of twenty components.

c   Actor relations. They describe different types of dyadic relations among actors. The relations are expressed by means of square matrices. The number of matrices is five, each one of twenty-two rows and columns.

In this particular model, there are no societal variables, although they are implied by actor variables and expressed through exogenous influences.[5] For instance, tax structure is not used as an explicit variable. If considered, it would belong to the area of social controls and would be introduced specifically as a characteristic of the society in question. Nevertheless its influence is expressed partially through the matrix of economic relations whose symbol is ARMIN(i,j), since the actor called 'new bureaucracy' has negative values in the appropriate relation with other actors such as mineowners, big landowners, etc.

Within the model, the variables are of two kinds: exogenous to and endogenous. Initial conditions are also given exogenously. The exogenous variables can vary exclusively as a result of information supplied from

4   The basic structure of the model is based on more general previous elaborations. See Oscar Cornblit, Torcuato Di Tella, and Ezequiel Gallo, 'A Model of Political Change in Latin America,' *Social Science Information*, 7, 2, pp. 13–48, and Oscar Cornblit, *Conflicto, Cooperación y Cambio. Interpretación Formal de un Modelo de Cambio Social para América Latina* (Buenos Aires: Centro de Investigaciones Sociales, Instituto Di Tella, 1967).

5   In the general case referred to in the previous models, societal variables are also part of the model.

outside the system of hypothesis. The endogenous variables have two possible sources of variation: because of the internal operation of the model, or because of external events supplied as additional information.

The purpose of starting experimentation and validation with a short-run type model, and then increasing the time span step by step is on the one hand to reduce as much as possible the variables which change within the period, and on the other to change constants into variables in a stepwise fashion, thus in a sense approximating the conditions of controlled experiments.

Not being able to control experiments in as neat a way as in the physical sciences is, of course, a crucial obstacle to experimentation in the social sciences. But keeping the number of variables significant for the analysis of change in the period considered as low as possible increases the possibility of finding similar situations in which the same kind of model may be applied and tested. In fact, if the model were able to provide acceptable interpretations of events in a wide number of different situations, its validity would increase. We are thus using an initial set of few variables, which in subsequent models are to be refined and enlarged. This refining and enlarging should be the result of the confrontation of the output of the model with the real world. This means improving both the measurement of the variables and the equations which relate them. On the other hand the measurement of variables with the classical requirements of validity and reliability should be considered within the whole structure of the model and not only as a procedure which refers exclusively to measurement. If every model may be considered in fact as a pair of models, one referring to measurement and the other one to derivation,[6] reliability of measurement (or indicators) should not be analysed exclusively in the measurement model but also in that from which it is derived, through its outputs.

d   Hypotheses on coalition building. A set of rules are given to build coalitions of actors on the basis of relation matrices.

e   Hypotheses on endogenous changes in the magnitudes of property vectors and relation matrices. This group of hypotheses is expressed through a set of behaviour equations which link variations of some variables to variations in others.

Dynamically the model behaves as follows. On the basis of the initial data and the rules of coalition formation, a first set of coalitions is formed. Then, through the operation of the behaviour equations, shifts are produced in the values of the vectors describing the properties of actors and

6   Cf. Oscar Cornblit, 'Modelos, Teorías y Medición en Sociología' (Buenos Aires: Departamento de Sociología, 1962), pp. 18–19 (mimeo).

in the entries of the matrices describing their relations. New coalitions are then calculated applying the corresponding rules, and so forth. At the beginning of each major period of the dynamic process, information on exogenous variations is provided to the system.

There are four sets of behaviour equations which essentially represent an iteration of the same system of behaviour equations. Each group of behaviour equations feeds back into the process of coalition building and is linked at the same time to the next group of behaviour equations. The whole process is described schematically in figure 1.

III DESCRIPTION OF THE SPECIFIC CONTENT OF THE MODEL

1 *Social actors*

Twenty-two actors are considered in this particular application of the model. Obviously any other number of actors could be employed, the only limit being the storage capacity of the computer. Specifically the actors are:

1 merchants
2 mineowners
3 big landowners
4 owners of textile mills
5 old bureaucracy
6 new bureaucracy
7 principal chiefs of Indian communities (Curacas)
8 local secular higher clergy
9 local secular lower clergy
10 local regular higher clergy
11 local regular lower clergy
12 original Indians
13 foreign Indians
14 urban middle classes
15 officers of the armed forces
16 Indian aristocracy
17 white aristocracy
18 Corregidores (a special kind of colonial official)
19 crown
20 second chiefs of Indian communities
21 charismatic leaders
22 medium and small rural landowners

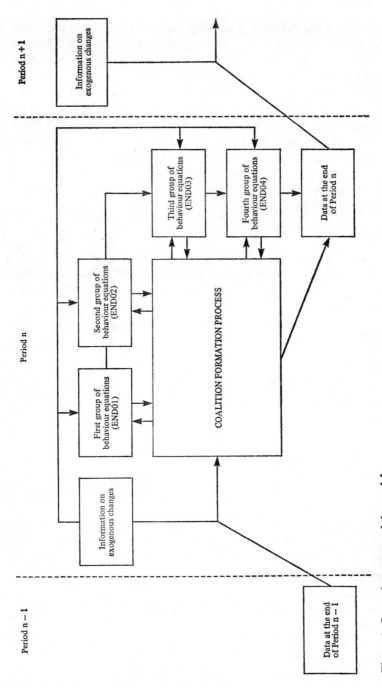

Figure 1 General structure of the model.

As may be seen the criteria used to differentiate actors are varied, although the highest proportion identifies occupational sectors within social strata. In more modern settings political parties might be part of the actor set.

2 *Properties of actors*

Each set of properties of an actor can be mathematically represented as a vector. The following list gives the twenty properties which characterize each actor, together with their symbolic representation.

1   Organizational weight. WOR Measures the degree to which an actor has potential influence, that is, capacity to introduce desired changes into society. It takes into account the population of the actor, its economic status, its prestige, its resources, its strategic centrality and specially its organization. Exogenously, the organizational weight depends on other characteristics of the society, for instance, general level of participation or legitimacy of the social system, but the influence of the latter is not explicitly stated within the structure of the model.

2   Alertness weight. WOM This variable takes into account the same components as the previous one except that of organization. Instead, it includes the degree of social alertness of the actor.

3   Propensity to violence FAVIOL This variable describes the degree of violence with which the actor tends to express himself.

4   Alienation ANOM This variable is also sometimes called anomie, because it includes many features which are frequently conceived as being components of this last term. It includes the concept of dissonance in norms, powerlessness, meaninglessness, self-estrangement, isolation, lack of solidarity, lack of definition of the situation, and uncertainty.[7] We conceived of alienation as a type of response of an individual or a group of individuals to the social system to which he or they belong, a fact which should be remembered when examining the influence of the variable in the behaviour equations.

5   Evaluation of 'mobilization' EVLMOV Measures the degree to which mobilizationism is valued positively as a mode of participation. Mobilizationism is a mode of participation which uses mass mobilization as a strategic persuasive element in decision-making. The model calls for only two forms of participation: elitism and mobilizationism. Whatever gains are obtained by one are lost by the other. This is a reasonable assumption

7   For a discussion of some of these terms see, for instance, Melvin Seeman, 'On the Meaning of Alienation,' *American Sociological Review*, 24 (December, 1959), pp. 783–91. For a critical consideration of the concept see Daniel Vidal, 'Un cas de faux concept : La notion d'aliénation,' *Sociologie du Travail*, 1 (janvier-mars 1969), pp. 61–82.

for the society considered in this particular application. In subsequent formulations other forms of participation such as associationism or referendism will be considered.

6   Counterideology CNTRID Measures the degree to which the actor holds an ideology which is against the basic tenets of the existing social system. This variable also measures the degree of support of the existing social system by allowing the possibility of negative values.

7   Social organization ORGZON Measures the degree to which the actor is organized for concerted action in organizations in which he or it shares an important part of the control.

8   Prosperity PRSPER Measures the degree to which the economic situation of the actor is prosperous, compared with its usual expected level.

9   Social alertness MOVSOC Measures the degree to which the actor is alert and able to respond to the impact of new influences. It should be clear that possession of this capacity does not mean that the actor is mobilized as a participant.[8]

10   Status incongruence INSTT Measures the degree to which ranking of individuals differs in significant dimensions.

11   Economic security SEGECO Measures the degree to which sources of income, whatever their origin, are secure.

12   Religiosity RELIG Measures the influence of religion or other moral system not based on a short-run pragmatic view of life; in other words, it measures the postponement of immediate in favour of future gratifications.

13   Communications with the rest of society COMNIC Measures the degree to which the actor communicates through any kind of contacts with the rest of the actors in the society.

14   Horizontal mobility MOVHOR Measures the degree to which the individual members of the actor move from one geographical place to another where conditions of life are significantly different for him, or where adjustment is not a smooth process.

15   Economic status STTECO Gives the mean annual income of individuals belonging to the actor.

16   Social prestige PRESOC Measures respect, honour, and deference received from others.

17   Strategic centrality of position CENEST Measures the degree to

8   This concept is somewhat related to *mobilization*, but should not be confused with it. Two discussions of the concept of mobilization may be found in K. Deutsch, 'Social Mobilization and Political Development,' *American Political Science Review*, 55, 3 (September 1961), pp. 493–514, and G. Germani, 'Los Procesos de Movilización e Integración y el Cambio Social,' *Desarrollo Económico*, 3, 3 (October 1963).

which the normal functions which the actor performs (social, economic, cultural, technical) give it preferential access to power, decision-making, the elaboration of belief-systems, or any other point of the social system of marked relevance.

18 Gross weight WOB Measures the degree to which an actor looms large in society as a consequence of its numbers, economic status, prestige, resources, or strategic centrality. As may have been noted, neither organization nor social mobilization are included here.

19 Evaluation of social welfare of lower classes EVBIBA Measures the degree to which the actor regards positively the welfare of the lower sectors of society.

20 Class CLASE Measures only one of the several possible criteria for assigning a position in the class hierarchy to an individual. Any pure or mixed criterion may be applied, and ultimately the problem boils down to the specific determination of the class situation of each particular actor. In this version of the model only two possibilities for class membership are allowed: low and high class.

3 Relations of actors

Dyadic relations among actors are described by means of the following matrices:

I   Matrix of communications COMUN (i,j) For any two actors this gives the amount of communication flowing between them. The matrix is symmetrical, the amount of communication flowing from actor i to actor j being considered the same as that flowing from actor j to actor i.

II   Matrix of menaces AM (i,j) For any two actors this gives the degree to which actor j expects that its well-being may deteriorate in the near future as a consequence of actions emanating from actor i.

III   Matrix of ethnic differences DIFET (i,j) For any two actors each entry of the matrix gives the amount of ethnic distance existing between them. The matrix is symmetrical.

IV   Matrix of agreement of interests ARMIN (i,j) This matrix gives the degree of harmony or antagonism of interests resulting from similarities or differences in 1 / economic interests with respect to markets, 2 / use of authority, 3 / access to means of production or distribution. These variables are mostly those separating owners or managers from workers and monopolist sellers or buyers from customers.

The relation matrix which includes several kinds of interests tries also to reflect the effect of the overlap between actors. For instance, every dependence relation contains a measure of both co-operation and conflict,[9] and at different periods of time each of the partial components may vary in relevance. However, no difference is made between an objective and perceived harmony (or antagonism) of interests. It would, of course, be very useful to separate both components, difficult as it might be in many cases. This would provide the model with more refined and flexible possibilities of analysis. In this presentation we shall restrict ourselves to the simpler matrix in order not to complicate the numerical analysis.

This matrix is not usually symmetrical, although this may occur. The perception of conflict (or harmony) of interests is normally not the same for both elements of the relation.[10] Possibly there is a long-run tendency for interest matrices to become symmetrical. This could verify a Marxian conception of class concsiousness formation.

In the case of authority conflicts, we make no distinctions as to types, as for instance in Weber's classical typology.[11] Here again, although no explicit reference is made to types of authority, the fact that actors claim authority on conflicting legitimacy bases is reflected in the matrix of interest relations. For instance, crown and charismatic leaders should have negative entries, as long as charismatic leaders' claims to authority lie outside the legitimacy of the crown.

v   Matrix of attractions ATR (i,j) This matrix measures the attraction which actor i exerts on actor j. Menaces, ethnic differences, and agreement of interests enter into its calculations. But there are other components of attractions which are not explicitly stated in the model so that its initial values cannot be obtained solely by means of the initial values of the relevant matrices. One must remember also that variations in the values of such matrices affect the values of attractions and that these variations might arise out of exogenous sources.

When operating the model after relational matrices are calculated endogenously. They are given at each point of the process where they are constructed.

4   Process of coalition building

In this section we shall give a brief verbal description of the main features of the process of coalition formation. It will be followed by detailed formalized description.

9   This theme is examined by S. Ossowski in *Class Structure in the Social Consciousness* (London: Routledge and Kegan Paul, 1963), chapter x.
10   Ossowski considers that all reactions of antagonisms are symmetrical. But it is not evident why it should be so except as a limit case. *Ibid.*, p. 149.
11   Cf. Max Weber, *Wirtschaft und Gesellschaft* (Tübingen: J.C.B. Mohr [Paul Siebeck], 1956), p. 144.

Let us consider that two actors are members of the same coalition when they join forces in acts which have the purpose of obtaining greater influence on the higher centres of political decision-making. This does not mean that both are contending for positions in the political decision-making apparatus. One actor might value government political positions, while another might be fighting for the alteration of certain control levers of society. In many cases one or more actors may have no opinion about certain areas of conflict, so that the opinion of the coalition will in fact be the opinion of only a subset of its membership. As we shall see, the model allows for the possibility that some actors will become members of several coalitions at the same time. Indications that two actors are totally or partially members of the same coalition, although varied, might be expressed, for example, by voting the same alternative in a referendum, fighting on the same side in a civil war, answering similarly questions in a survey.

The principal steps in the process of coalition formation are as follows:

I   Selection of leading actors Some of the actors are selected as potential leaders of coalitions in an attempt to reflect the fact that in real political life certain groups of individuals act as nuclei around which cluster wider circles of the population. To be able to play the role of leader an actor has to fulfil certain conditions. In this particular application we have not tried to separate what might be considered the leadership quality within an actor from his more passive characteristics. Other applications might use this distinction. We have not used either a breakdown by political parties, since there were none at the time and place considered, but they could easily be introduced into the simulation and considered as actors with leadership possibilities.

II   First-order coalitions First-order coalitions of only one leader and one or more non-leader actors are first constructed. Two basic criteria for obtaining coalitions are attractions among actors and menaces. This last factor assumes that actors threatened by a common or allied menace will try to join forces to face it. The two processes interact with each other to increase the size of coalitions.

III   Higher order coalitions Once all possible first-order coalitions are calculated they become the building blocks on which higher order coalitions are constructed. A coalition is of order n if n leading actors belong to it; a coalition is of higher order if the number of leading actors which belong to it is greater than one. At each particular time period the process of coalition-building stops when there is no possibility of forming new coalitions. Throughout the coalition-building cycle, and between cyles the behaviour equations are used to aggregate or disaggregate actors and leaders.

5   Behaviour equations

The behaviour equations specify how changes in menaces, evaluation of mobilizationism, communication, anomie, propensity to violence, evaluation of social welfare of the lower classes, and attractions are produced. They are as follows:

I   Menace The menace which an actor (or a coalition) exerts on another actor (or a coalition) increases with the weight of the menacing actor (or coalition) and with the propensity to violence. It decreases with the amount of communication either between both terms of the relation or between the menaced actors and officers of the armed forces. The magnitude of change in menace is affected by ethnic difference, class membership, conflict of interests, and by the previous attractions of both terms of the relation. It is also altered by the degree of prosperity of the menaced actors, by their counter-ideology, status incongruency, and economic security.

II   Evaluation of mobilizationism The evaluation of an actor's mobilizationism increases with the level of menaces coming from other actors and with the growth of social alertness against social organization. The measure is also affected by previous menaces, by the attraction between menacing and menaced actors, by class membership, and by the level of prosperity, counter-ideology, economic security, and status incongruency of the actor whose evaluation of mobilizationism is being calculated. Finally, coalition membership also affects evaluation of mobilizationism since the opinions of non-leader are adjusted to those of leaders.

III Communication Being members of the same coalition increases communication between actors, while an opposite effect results from contrary conditions.

IV   Alienation Alienation increases with social mobilization against social organization and with horizontal mobility. It decreases with economic security, prosperity, and communication. Religiosity puts an upper bound to the value of alienation.

V   Propensity to violence Propensity to violence increases with alienation, counter-ideology, evaluation of mobilizationism, and growth of the weight of the coalition to which the actor belongs. It is negatively affected by prosperity. Menaces also affect this variable in a way which varies with class membership. Class also affects the impact of the other variables.

VI   Evaluation of social welfare of the lower classes This variable depends strongly on class membership. If the actor belongs to the lower classes the variable increases with social mobilization and with evaluation of mobilizationism. For higher class actors it increases with menaces coming from other high-class actors. (It should be remembered that in this version of the model we have divided the class structure into only two groups: lower and higher classes.) Prosperity, economic security, counter-ideology, and status incongruency affect the variable.

VII Attraction Attraction increases when menace, evaluation, and ethnic differences decrease. It increases with increasing harmony of interests.

IV FORMAL DESCRIPTION OF THE MODEL

1 *Choice of leaders*

The first step in the process of coalition-building is the selection of those actors fulfilling the required conditions to become leaders.
Symbols

LID   the set of leading actors
NLID   the set of non-leading actors
.e. 'belong to.' Thus, 'actor *i* belongs to the set of leading actors' will be written *i.e.* LID
.gt. greater than
.lt. less than
.ge. greater or equal to
.le. less than or equal to
.or. the greatest of
.and. the smallest of
PAR1 parameter 1

Conditions to be leader
An actor *i* is considered to be a leader if any of its following properties is greater than a specified parameter: counter-ideology (CNTRID), social prestige (PRESOC), status incongruency (INSTT), economic status (STECCO), strategic centrality (CENEST), social organization (ORGZON). In symbols:

i.e. LID if and only if one of the following conditions is true:
CNTRID*i* .gt. PAR1
PRESOC*i* .gt. PAR2
INSTT*i* .gt. PAR3
STECCO*i* .gt. PAR4
CENEST*i* .gt. PAR5
ORGZON*i* .gt. PAR6

2   *First-order coalitions* (order one coalition)

A coalition is of order one if, and only if, only one leader belongs to it.
The first step in the construction of first-order coalitions is accomplished
by obtaining what is defined as a primitive coalition: a coalition of order
one to which not more than one non-leader actor belongs.

Formation of primitive coalitions
Given leader actor i and non-leader actor j, or in symbols

> *i.e.*   LID
> *j.e.*   NLID,

we say that i and j belong to the same coalition COALn if:
1   ATR(i,j).gt. PAR1. (This PAR1 has nothing to do with that used for
the choice of leading actors. Within the same process we number the
parameters from 1 up. Whenever two parameters receive the same value it
will be stated explicitly.)
2   ATR(i,j).ge.ATR(i,m) for every m, m being another non-leading
actor fulfilling condition 1.
3   If conditions 1 and 2 have been fulfilled by more than one non-
leader, say non leaders j, m, and f, then it is true that

> WOBj.*gt*.WOBm
> WOBj.*gt*.WOBf.

4   If this still leaves more than one non-leader as a possible member of
the coalition COALn, one of them is chosen at random. We may then write
$i,j.e.$ COALn. These conditions express, first, that no coalition may be
formed without the participation of a leader actor, second, that two actors,
one leader, and a non-leader will belong to the same coalition if 1 / the
leader attracts the non-leader with a sufficiently high intensity (intensity
which is expressed through PAR1 of condition 1); 2 / the intensity of
attraction exerted by the leader over the non-leader is greater than or
equal to the attraction exerted over the same non-leader by any other
leader; and 3 / when more than one non-leader actor fulfils the previous
conditions that with the higher gross weight is incorporated.
      The process of coalition formation is continued for every actor leader
i and every non-leader actor j.

Weight with which actors enter coalitions
The process just described gives no indication of what proportion of each
actor will enter into each coalition. This proportion is expressed by means
of organization weights, nobilization weights, and gross weights.

Weights of leader actor i in COALn (primitive)
If i is a leader, the weight with which he enters COALn is the sum of weights he had at the beginning of the process of coalition formation. In symbols:

If $i.e.$LID and $i.e.$COALn
WORi in COALn = WORi at the beginning of the process.
WOMi in COALn = WOMi at the beginning of the process.
WOBi in COALn = WOBi at the beginning of the process.

Weights of non-leader actor j in COALn (primitive)
Non-leader actors do not necessarily enter coalitions with all their weights. This allows for the possibility that a non-leader actor will become a member of several coalitions in different proportions. The proportion of the weights which enter each coalition is obtained through the calculation of the following two coefficients called DISMAX and DISMED.

DISMAX calculates the distribution of the weight of non-leader j among those leader actors with a sufficiently high attraction. This high attraction is represented by a parameter called PAR1, and so is the coalition.

Let us now define some of our symbols. SUMn means 'sum over n of ...' For instance SUMh ATR(h,j) means the sum of the attraction which all actors h exert on actor j. / means division, as in an arithmetic operation. DISMAX (j,i) means the distribution coefficient DISMAX of non-leader actor j in the coalition to which leader actor i also belongs. Bearing this in mind we may define DISMAX (j,i) as follows. Given $i,j.e.$ COALn and $h.e.$LID such that ATR$(h,j).ge.$ PAR1,

$$\text{DISMAX } (j,i) = \text{ATR}(i,j)/\text{SUM}h \text{ ATR } (h,j).$$

It should be clear that DISMAX represents the relative strength with which leader i is able to incorporate non-leader j, relative to the forces exerted by other leaders who are able to exert an attraction over non-leader j with a sufficiently high magnitude, a fact which is expressed by the parameter PAR1. Nothing is said, at least at this stage, about the possibility of non-leader j also being incorporated into another coalition COALr to which leader h, fulfilling the condition

$$\text{ATR}(h,j).ge.\text{PAR1}$$

might belong.

The second coefficient, DISMED, performs a somewhat similar function; it distributes the weights of non-leader j among those leaders whose attraction is more than PAR1 when compared to those whose attraction is more than another parameter PAR2, provided that

$$\text{PAR1}.ge.\text{PAR2}.$$

Using the symbols introduced before, DISMED is defined as follows. If

$j.e.$NLID
$i.e.$LID such that ATR$(i,j).ge.$PAR1
and $k.e.$LID such that ATR$(k,j).ge.$PAR2,
DISMED$(j,i) = [$SUMiATR$(i,j)]/[$SUMkATR$(k,j)]$.

It should be remembered that DISMED(j,i) represents symbolically the distribution of non-leader j in all those i which satisfy the stated conditions.

Once having calculated these two coefficients, we may define another coefficient called DISTR(j,i) through the formula

DISTR$(j,i) = f[$DISMAX(j,i), DISMED$(j,i)]$.

This function may have different forms, depending on the hypotheses being tested, with respect to the proportion of each non-leader actor which enters into each coalition.

Once having calculated this parameter, the weights with which non-leader j enters coalition COALn to which leader i belongs are:

PORRji = WORj * DISTR(j,i)
POMRji = WOMj * DISTR(j,i)
POBRji = WOBj * DISTR(j,i).

We define PORRji as the 'remaining organization weight of non-leader j in COALn to which leader i belongs,' or the 'remaining weight of j in i,' it being understood that it describes the weight with which non-leader j enters COALn. The symbol * is used for multiplication. Similar meanings are given to symbols POMji and POBRji.

In the simple case in which it is supposed that

DISTR$(j,i) = f[$DISMAX(j,i), DISMED$(j,i)] = $ DISMAX(j,i) * DISMED(j,i),

then in fact DISTR(j,i) can be calculated directly without calculating the two intermediate coefficients. This can be easily seen by expressing the product in terms of the definitions of each coefficient.

DISMAX(j,i) * DISMED(j,i)
$= [$ATR$(i,j)/$SUMhATR$(h,j)]/[$SUMhATR$(h,j)/$SUMkATR$(k,j]$, where
ATR$(h,j).ge.$PAR1
ATR$(k,j).ge.$PAR2.

By eliminating SUMhATR(h,j) which is both in the numerator and denominator, we obtain

$$\text{DISTR}(j,i) = \text{DISMAX}(j,i) * \text{DISMED}(j,i) = \text{ATR}(i,j)/\text{SUM}k\text{ATR}(k,j).$$

Free weights

After a non-leader j has been incorporated into coalition COALn with what we call 'remaining weights' PORRji, POMRji, and POBRji, that part of the weight which has not entered into the coalition will be called 'free weight,' and will be denoted by the symbols PORLj, POMLj, and POBLj.

In general at any stage of coalition formation we define free weights as those weights of actors which do not belong to any coalition. We could say then that before the beginning of the process of coalition formation free weights are equal to original weights, or that all weights are free. Formulae to calculate free weights are as follows:

$$\text{PORL}j = \text{WOR}j - \text{SUM}i\text{PORR}ji$$
$$\text{POML}j = \text{WOM}j - \text{SUM}i\text{POMR}ji$$
$$\text{POBL}j = \text{WOB}j - \text{SUM}i\text{POBR}ji.$$

It is clear that if j does not belong to any coalition

$$\text{PORL}j = \text{WOR}j$$
$$\text{POML}j = \text{WOM}j$$
$$\text{POBL}j = \text{WOB}j.$$

After this step has been completed we can proceed to the construction of coalitions of order one which may have more than two members.

Formation of derivative coalitions of order one

Let us define derivative coalitions as those coalitions comprising more than one non-leader. Should a coalition have only one leader actor it is called 'derivative coalitions of order one.'

Transient reduced matrices of attractions

The first step at this stage is to construct an attraction matrix corresponding to the primitive coalitions just obtained. This matrix of attraction requires entries relating actors to actors, actors to coalitions and coalitions to coalitions.

If we arrange the column and the row orders in the matrix of attraction so as to put first the coalitions and then the actors and if we agree to call at this stage a leader actor a 'coalition' even if he is alone, the resulting matrix of attractions will have the following structure (figure 2).

Coalitions   Non-leader actors

Sector A	Sector B
Sector C	Sector D

Coalitions (left vertical label, top) / *Non-leader actors* (left vertical label, bottom)

Figure 2 Transient reduced matrix of attraction corresponding to primitive coalitions.

Sector D has the same entries as the initial matrix of attractions. Sectors A, B, and C have to be calculated, although those parts of these sectors which include coalitions formed only by leaders to the exclusion of non-leaders are the same as the corresponding entries in the initial attraction matrix. The corresponding formulae for each sector are the following:

SECTOR B First let us note that the symbol PORRji.or.POMRji means 'the greatest of remaining organization weight and mobilization weight in COALs to which leader i belongs.' Alternatively, we may also write

(PORR.or.POMR)ji.
Bearing this in mind we can write
ATR(COALn,j)
= [SUMs(PORR.or.POMR)si $*$ ATR(s,j)]/SUMs(PORR.or.POMR)si,

s being a member of COALn to which leader i belongs (in particular s may be equal to i), or $s.e.$ COALn. There is also a restriction on the values which s is allowed to take. If non-leader actor j is already member of COALn, then $s \neq j$ and $s \neq i$ (i being the leader actor in COALn).

SECTOR A Having thus defined ATR (COALn, j) it is easier to define entries in sector A. Attractions between coalitions are simply obtained as weighted averages of attractions between coalitions and actors.

If m belongs to COALh to which leader h belongs

ATR(COALn, COALh)
= [SUMmATR(COALn,m) $*$ (PORR.or.POMR)mt]/SUM(PORR.or.POMR)mt.

SECTOR D As already stated the values in sector D are obtained directly from the entries in the initial attraction matrix between actors.

SECTOR C is calculated in the same way as sector B. The matrix of attraction has to be calculated each time a new set of coalitions is formed; let us call it 'transient reduced matrix of attraction' (TRMATR). The word transient refers to the fact that these matrices are calculated only as auxiliary matrices for the calculation of coalitions. The word reduced refers to the fact that attraction between coalitions and actors is smaller than it should be because not all intervening actors are included in the calculation.

Calculus of coalitions on the basis of TRMATR

Once the transient reduced matrix of attraction corresponding to primitive coalitions has been formed, it is used to repeat the process employed to obtain the primitive coalitions, with the proviso that the role previously played by leader actors is now played by primitive coalitions, it being understood that isolated leaders are considered primitive coalitions of only one member. New coalitions are thus obtained. As before DISMAX, DISMED, and DISTR are calculated by means of the same procedure and finally the weight of the non-leader actors being incorporated to the coalitions are obtained through the formulae:

$$\text{PORR}ji = \text{PORL}j * \text{DISTR}\ (j,\text{COAL}n)$$
$$\text{POMR}ji = \text{POML}j * \text{DISTR}\ (j,\text{COAL}n)$$
$$\text{POBR}ji = \text{POBL}j * \text{DISTR}\ (j,\text{COAL}n),$$

where i of PORRji is leader actor i which belongs to COALn, etc., and where DISMAX is the coefficient of distribution of non-leader j among all coalitions which attract j more than or at least as much as PAR1. DISMED has a meaning analogous to that given in the formation of primitive coalitions; the same applies to DISTR.

Finally, to calculate the free weights of actors which are non-leaders we use the formulae:

$$\text{PORL}j = \text{PORL}j - \text{PORR}ji$$
$$\text{POML}j = \text{POML}j - \text{POMR}ji$$
$$\text{POBL}j = \text{POBL}j - \text{POBR}ji$$

It is clear that PORLj, POMLj, and POBLj to the right of the equal signs are the previous free weights which were obtained as a consequence of the formation of the primitive coalitions. Those to the left of the equal signs are the free weights following the formation of new coalitions.

Iteration of the procedure
On the basis of the coalitions just obtained, new transient reduced matrices
(TRMATR) are calculated by repeating the procedure used for the construction of the previous TRMATR. Using the new TRMATR as base, a new
round of derived coalitions of order one is obtained, and the corresponding PORR*ji*, POMR*ji*, POBR*ji*, PORL*j*, POML*j*, and POBL*j* are calculated.

This process of building derivative coalitions of order one is continued until it is not possible to incorporate more non-leader actors to the
coalitions. At this stage another criteria for the building of coalitions is
introduced: menaces.

Derivative first-order coalition building
through menaces
Thus far the basic criteria for building coalitions were a certain similarity
of interests, ideology, evaluations of control procedures in society, etc.
But, in addition, actors may also join forces because of threats of various
kinds, which must now be combined with the existing affinities. The first
step is to define a new matrix of attraction between coalitions and actors
to be called 'augmented matrix of attraction.'

Augmented matrix of attraction
This new matrix corresponds to the last set of coalitions obtained and
reflects attractions between actors, between actors and coalitions, and

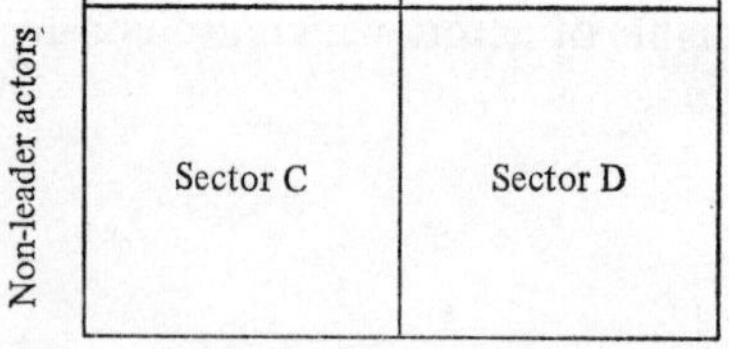

Figure 3 Augmented matrix of attraction.

between coalitions. As before, arranging the column and the row order in
the matrix so as to put the coalitions first and then the actors, we obtain
four sectors: A, B, C and D (figure 3). The formulae for each sector are:

SECTOR A Let us consider any two coalitions, COALm and COALn, i being a leader actor in COALm, h a leader actor in COALn, s any actor in COALm, and t any actor in COALn. Then

ATRAUM(COALm, COALn)

= [SUMtATR(COALm,t) $*$ (PORR.*or*.POMR)th]/

[SUMt(PORR.*or*.POMR)th].

And

ATR(COALm,t)

= [SUMs(ATR(s,t) $*$ (PORR.*or*.POMR)si]/[SUMs(PORR.*or*.POMR)si],

where $s \neq t$.

As indicated by the formulae, attraction between actors in the same coalition is not excluded. The only impossibility is attraction of an actor to the self.

SECTOR B Here we calculate the attraction between coalitions and non-leader actors. Let COALm be any coalition whatsoever and j any non-leader actor. Let s be any actor in COALm (leader or non-leader), and let i be a leader belonging to COALm. Then

ATRAUM(COALm, j)

= [SUMs(ATR(s,j) $*$ (PORR.*or*.POMR)si]/[SUMs(PORR.*or*.POMR)si],

where $s \neq j$. The observations made in the previous case apply here as well.

SECTOR C Let us consider any j such that $j.e$.NLID and any COALm, with $i.e$.LID and $i.e$.COALm and s any actor whatsoever belonging to COALm. Then

ATRAUM(j,COALm)

= [SUMsATR(j,s) $*$ PORR.*or*.POMR)si]/[SUMs(PORR.*or*.POMR)si]

$*$ (PORL.*or*.POML)j[(WOR.*or*.WOM)j],

where $s \neq j$

In this case the attraction exerted by non-leader j is weakened because of the fact that his free weights have decreased when compared with the original ones. (In some cases the weights might, however, be the same.)

SECTOR D This sector records the attraction among non-leader actors. Their formula is as follows.

Let $j.e$.NLID and $f.e$.NLID, then

ATRAUM(j,f) = ATR(j,f) $*$ (PORL.*or*.POML)j/[(WOR.*or*.WOM)j].

Once again the attraction is reduced because of the diminishing effect of free weights. The other matrix needed at this stage is the 'augmented matrix of menace' corresponding to the last set of coalitions obtained.

Augmented matrix of menace
The formula corresponding to the four sectors is as follows:

SECTOR B As before let us call i an actor such that $i.e.$LID and $i.e.$COALm and s is the generic symbol for any actor whatsoever such that $s.e.$COALm. If $j.e.$NLID, then

AMAUM (COALm,j)

$= [$SUMsAM(s,j) $*$ (PORR.or.POMR)$si]/[$SUM$s($PORR.or.POMR$)si]$,

where $s \neq j$.

SECTOR C The formula for this sector is similar to the formula calculated for attraction. Let $j.e.$NLID $i.e.$LID *and* $i.e.$COALm s any actor whatsoever belonging to COALm. Then

AMAUM$(j,$COAL$m)$

$= [$SUMsAM(j,s) $*$ (PORR.or.POMR)$si]/[$SUM$s($PORR.or.POMR$)si]$

$* [($PORL.or.POML$)j/($WOR.or.WOM$)j]$.

In other words the menace from the part of the actor acting freely has been reduced in proportion to the remaining free weight.

SECTOR A This sector records menaces between coalitions. Let s be any actor whatsoever belonging to COALm and t any actor whatsoever belonging to COALn. If $i.e.$LID and $i.e.$COALm $h.e.$LID and $h.e.$COALn. Then

AMAUM(COALm,COALn)

$= [$SUMtAM(COALm,t) $*$ (PORR.or.POMR$)th]/$
$[$SUM$t($PORR.or.POMR$)th]$.

It should be noted that provided $s \neq t$ AM(COALm,t) is calculated with the same formula as AMAUM(COALm,t) in sector B, but there is no restriction on t, in the sense that it refers to either leaders or non-leaders.

SECTOR D Finally let us calculate the fourth sector in the augmented matrix of attraction.
Let $j.e.$NLID and $f.e.$NLID. Then

AMAUM(j,f) $=$ AM(j,f) $*$ $[($PORL.or.POML$)j/($WOR.or.WOM$)j]$.

Note that there is a clear distinction among sectors A and B on the one hand and C and D on the other. Sectors A and B represent menaces arising out of coalitions or leaders, while C and D represent menaces arising out of non-leader actors. In the case of coalitions (or in the limiting case of leader actors) menaces are weighted by the participation of each actor in the coalition. But the coalition as a whole does not increase its level of menace because of its size or any other agglomeration effect. The size effects will be considered when we introduce the behaviour equations.

Note also that menaces of non-leader actors are diminished proportionally to their reduction in free weights. Of course their influence is exerted through the coalitions to which they belong. In the extreme case, when there is no remaining free weight, all influence is exerted through coalitions, none as a free actor.

Calculation of derivative first-order coalitions
through menaces

The augmented matrices, which calculate both attraction and menace can now be used to obtain the new coalitions. In what follows we shall designate with a capital letter (H, for instance) any row or column component of the augmented matrices. Such capital letter designates either a coalition (which includes also leader actors which have not built a true coalition with another non-leader actor) or a non-leader actor. Let $j.e.$NLID such that PORLj $.gt.0$ or POMLj $.gt.0$. If there exists an H, such that AMAUM $(H,j).gt.$ PAR1 (PAR1 being another new parameter not defined until now) and if there exists a COALm which satisfies the following conditions

| ATRAUM(COALj)$.ge.$PAR2 | 1 |
| ATRAUM(H,COALm)$.le.$PAR3 | 2 |

and if

ATRAUM(COALm,j)$.ge.$ATRAUM(COALn,j)

for every COALn which fulfils conditions 1 and 2 then

$j.e.$COALm.

We obtain thus a set of COALm which fulfils all the stated conditions and to which j belongs. Now we need a coefficient of distribution to allocate the free weight of j among the coalitions COALm obtained. Let us suppose that there are n coalitions COALM which fulfil the stated conditions. Let us designate by i the leader actor which belongs to COALm, and as before, let us use PORRji to designate the organization weight with which j enters in COALm of which i is leader. Since, once incorporated into the coalition, this weight will be added to the organization weight of j already incorporated in COALm (which might be eventually 0), we shall use the same symbols to indicate the organization weight being incorporated to COALm, that already in it, and the new total achieved. The same applies for mobilizational weight and gross weight. Then

PORRji = PORLj/n
POMRji = POMLj/n
POBRji = POBLj/n.

This results from the fact that all attractions exerted by COALm on j are equal because of conditions 3, and that consequently the distribution is equal among all coalitions.

In the process of experimentation the set of three parameters PAR1, PAR2, and PAR3 may be varied widely. A possible set might be

PAR1 = 6
PAR2 = 3
PAR3 = − 5.

Other possible sets might be

$(9,2, -3); (8,3, -4); (7,3, -4); (6,3, -5).$

Another possibility is to make PAR2 and PAR3 dependent on the values of PAR1. Thus

PAR2 = f(PAR1)
PAR3 = g(PAR1).

The new functions f and g, which have not been defined previously, decrease with increasing values of PAR1; in other words an actor is assumed to be more willing to join a coalition when faced with increasing menaces from other actors.

Such are the basic rules by which first-order coalitions are built.

3   Coalitions of higher order

The order of a coalition is given by the number of leader actors belonging to it. To say that a coalition is of a higher order is to say that it is of an order higher than one.

As in the process of coalition-building of first order, two basic criteria for coalition formation are employed: attraction and menace.

Let us describe first the way coalitions of higher order are constructed through the exclusive operation of attraction and, second, how the effect of menace is added to the process.

Coalitions of higher order built through attraction
The attractions to which the following formulae refer, are those of the last augmented matrix of attractions.

As before we use COAL*m*, COAL*n*, COAL*r* to designate coalitions. The symbol with which a coalition is denoted does not indicate its order, although at the beginning of the process of coalition-building of higher order, the coalitions with which we operate are of order one. Let COAL*m*, COAL*n* be any two coalitions. Let both

    ATRAUM (COAL*m*, COAL*n*),*ge*.PAR1   1
    ATRAUM (COAL*n*, COAL*m*).*ge*.PAR1   2

(PAR1 is here another parameter defined independently from the others.) Let us define

    ATRAUM″(COAL*m*,COAL*n*)
    = ATRAUM(COAL*m*,COAL*n*) + ATRAUM(COAL*n*,COAL*m*).

It follows that:

    ATRAUM″(COAL*m*,COAL*n*) = ATRAUM″(COAL*n*,COAL*m*).

Let

    ATRAUM″(COAL*m*,COAL*n*).*gt*.ATRAUM″(COAL*m*,COAL*r*)

for every other COAL*r* satisfying conditions 1 and 2 and

    ATRAUM″(COAL*m*,COAL*n*).*gt*.ATRAUM″(COAL*n*,COAL*s*)

for every other COAL*s* satisfying conditions 1 and 2.
Then

    COAL*m*, COAL*n* .*e*. COAL*k*

whose order is equal to the sum of the orders of COAL*m* and COAL*n*.

In case the process is not able to select one coalition that would satisfy conditions 1 and 2, a random process is used to form the new coalition COAL*k*.

The PORR*j*, POMR*j*, and POBR*j* of the actors now belonging to the new COAL*k* are obtained by the sum of their corresponding PORR*j*, POMR*j*, and POBR*j* in each of the previous coalitions COAL*m* and COAL*n*.

Once all the possible coalitions of order two or less are obtained, a new augmented matrix is calculated. In a more general way, if COAL*m* and COAL*n* are the two coalitions of highest order obtained in the previous cycle of coalition formation, the process stops when all possible coalitions of order equal to the sum of orders of COAL*m* and COAL*n* or less are obtained, each new coalition being built exclusively out of two immediately preceeding coalitions.

The rules used to calculate attraction in each of the sectors A (attractions between coalitions), B (attractions exerted by coalitions on non-leader actors), C (attractions exerted by non-leader actors on coalitions), and D (attractions exerted by non-leader actors on non-leader actors) are the same as those given for coalitions of order one.

To this new augmented matrix of attractions, we apply the rules just given for the formation of higher order coalition through attractions, and let the process iterate until no new coalition of higher order may be constructed.

As is evident from the formulae, it is not necessary to examine the incorporation of non-leader actors to the new coalitions of higher order. If they have not been incorporated already to order one coalition, they will not be incorporated to the higher order coalitions, because the attractions exerted on them by the latter are always a convex combination of the previous lesser order coalitions, provided the same parameters are used in both cases.

Coalitions of higher order built through menace
To construct these coalitions we need as before the augmented matrices for both menaces and attractions. Although the possibility of incorporating non-leaders in the higher order coalitions formed through menace remains open, we shall not concern ourselves with this process now, the procedure being similar to that of incorporation of non-leaders to first-order coalitions. But this possibility must, of course, be taken into consideration in the general computation.

As before, a capital letter (for instance, H) is used to designate either any actor or a coalition of any order whatsoever. COAL*m*, COAL*n*, COAL*r* designate coalitions of any order. Let there be an H and an R such that both

AMAUM $(H, \text{COAL}m).gt.\text{PAR}1$ 1
AMAUM $(R, \text{COAL}n).gt.\text{PAR}1$ 2

(PAR1 being a new parameter defined independently from the previous ones), and both

ATRAUM $(H, \text{COAL}n).lt.\text{PAR}2$ 3
or

AMAUM $(H, \text{COAL}n).ge.\text{PAR}1$ 3a
ATRAUM $(R, \text{COAL}m).lt.\text{PAR}2$ 4
or
AMAUM $(R, \text{COAL}m.ge.\text{PAR}1,$ 4a

with the possibility of $R = H$ not being excluded. As before, PAR2 is a new parameter.

And let both

ATRAUM $(\text{COAL}m, \text{COAL}n).gt.\text{PAR}3$ 5
ATRAUM $(\text{COAL}n, \text{COAL}m).gt.\text{PAR}3,$ 6

where PAR3 $= h$ (PAR1), and where h is a decreasing function of PAR1. If both

ATRAUM″ $(\text{COAL}m,\text{COAL}m).ge.\text{ATRAUM}''(\text{COAL}m,\text{COAL}r)$ 7
ATRAUM″ $(\text{COAL}n,\text{COAL}m).ge.\text{ATRAUM}''(\text{COAL}n,\text{COAL}s)$ 8

COALs and COALr being two coalitions which satisfy the previous conditions 1 to 6. Then it is true that

COALm, COALn $.e.$ COALk,

the order of COALk being equal to the sum of the orders of COALm and COALn.

If there were more than two coalitions which fulfilled the whole set of eight conditions, the coalitions selected to form part of the new coalition COALk would be those two whose AMAUM in conditions 1 and 2 is higher. If there are more than two coalitions fulfilling this condition, the selection is done through a random process.

All the remaining organization, mobilization, and gross weights in the new coalitions are obtained by simply adding the coalitions being incorporated.

Among the many possible combinations of values for the parameters, one could use the following:

PAR1 (in the process through attractions) $= 6$
PAR1 (in the process through menaces) $= 6$
PAR2 (idem) $= 0$ (if independent from PAR1).
PAR3 (idem) $= 0$ (if independent from PAR1).

V   GENERAL DESCRIPTION OF THE BEHAVIOUR EQUATIONS

There is no space in this paper to give a detailed formal description of the behaviour equations. The previous discussion of coalition formation illustrates the simulation approach used and an interested reader could refer to a full description of the behaviour equations available elsewhere.[12]

As mentioned previously the behaviour equations, although influencing the process at different stages through different sets of equations, represent essentially the same set of equations. For convenience they are separated into four subsets, labelled ENDO 1, ENDO 2, ENDO 3, and ENDO 4.

1 Endo 1 Increase of menace due to clustering effects

These clustering or agglomeration effects are due to the fact that whenever two or more actors form a coalition the other actors which have a certain degree of conflict with them will feel more threatened. We need two new concepts at this point; 'the political weight of a coalition,' and the 'increase of political weight of a coalition.'

The political weight of a coalition is defined as the sum of all the remaining organization or mobilizational weights of the actors belonging to the coalition, with the condition that for each actor only the highest of the two is considered. For instance, if s designates the memberships of coalition COALm, then the political weight of COALm, symbolized by WOPm, is

$$\text{WOP}m = \text{SUM}s(\text{PORR}.or.\text{POMR})s.$$

The increase of political weight of the coalition compares its present political weight with the disaggregated condition before the construction of the coalition. When an actor does not participate in a coalition, only its organization weight counts, because it reflects the possibility given to the actor of influencing effectively, through some kind of organized action, the course of events. When an actor becomes party to a coalition, the organization capacity of the other members of the coalition is now at his service, and the potential influence of its mobilizational weight becomes effective. This is why the political weight of a coalition is calculated by adding the mobilizational or organizational weights, whichever is higher. Thus, the increase of political weight is obtained by subtracting from the political weight of the coalition the organized weight of its component members.

$$d\text{WOP}m = \text{SUM}s(\text{PORR}.or.\text{POMR})s - \text{SUM}s\text{PORR}s$$
always with $s.e.\text{COAL}m$

12 The behaviour equations appear in the original version of this paper presented at the Vancouver Round Table; they are available from the author.

Given these considerations we can describe the increase of menaces from clustering effects and outline the assumptions included in the equations of the ENDO 1. subject.

The menace which a coalition exerts over an actor or a coalition increases when the relative political weight of the coalition increases, provided the attractions exerted by the menacing coalition is low or provided the ethnic differences or conflict of interests are high. If predisposition to violence on the part of the menacing coalition is high, menace increases, while the opposite effect results from a high communication.

The last step in ENDO 1 is to distribute the increases of menaces among the individual actors. This is done in two parts. In the first part, each of the actors being members of a COAL*m* increase their menace in proportion to their participation in the coalition, while the menaced actors also distribute the menacing effect proportionate to their participation in the coalition.

2   ENDO 2 *Increases of several kinds of variables*

In this subset we differentiate two kinds of increments – exogenous and endogenous – acting as causal factors on the side of the independent variables to produce a variation in the dependent variables. The dependent increments are all endogenous.

Increment of evaluation of mobilizationism
In the case where actor *j* belongs to the lower classes, its evaluation of mobilizationism increases with the increase of menaces from actors of the higher classes. The magnitude of this increase depends on the previous level of menace or attraction from the same source. If attraction was high or menace low, the effect of the increase of menace is weak. Another cause for an increase of mobilizationism is an increase of social alertness relative to the increase of social organization.

When an actor belongs to the higher classes, his evaluation of mobilizationism decreases when menaces from the lower classes increase. This decrease is dampened by the magnitude of the attractions previously exerted by the actor on those menacing him, dampened also by the menace formerly exerted by the menacing actor. Furthermore, low prosperity or high counter-ideology on the part of the actor reduces the magnitude of the decrease of evaluation of mobilizationism. On the contrary, evaluation of mobilizationism increases when menace from high-class actors increases. Previous levels of attraction and menace have a similar effect on the magnitude of the increment as those described for the lower class actor.

Adjustment of evaluation of mobilization of non-leaders to leaders

Whenever a non-leader actor and a leader belong to the same coalition the former's evaluation of mobilizationism shifts towards that of the leader. This occurs in first-order coalitions. Because a non-leader may be a member of several first-order coalitions, with different weights, his total adjustment is a weighted average of each adjustment. The velocity of adjustment depends on changes in the prosperity of the non-leader, on whether his evaluation of mobilizationism is higher or lower than that of the leader, and on his class membership. When the evaluation of the mobilizationism of the non-leader is lower than that of the leader, and when prosperity has a downward tendency, adjustment is quicker. Opposite effects occur when the non-leader's evaluation of mobilizationism is higher than that of the leader and when there is a downward trend in prosperity. An increase in prosperity tends to reduce the influence of the leader; belonging to the higher classes has a similar effect.

Changes in the value of communication
Changes in communication among actors are produced endogenously, according to whether or not one belongs to the same coalition. Belonging to the same coalition increases communication; a decrease results from the opposite situation. The measure, of course, has to be obtained through a weighted average of all coalitions for which the increments of communication are calculated.

Changes in the value of alienation
Alienation increases with social alertness relatively to the degree of social organization and with horizonal mobility; it decreases with economic security, prosperity, and greater communication with the rest of society. If religiosity is high, alienation has a fixed upper limit.

Changes in propensity to violence
We differentiate two cases sharply, depending on class membership. When the actor belongs to the lower classes, his propensity to violence increases with the combined interaction of counter-ideology and alienation with the combined interaction of increases in evaluation of mobilizationism and in mobilization weight. The propensity to violence is also positively related to the belonging to a coalition of high political weight (provided the evaluation of mobilizationism of the actor is high). It decreases with prosperity.

When the actor belongs to the higher class the likelihood of favouring violence decreases with an increase in menace from lower class actors but increases when the menace is from higher class actors. It decreases with prosperity.

Changes in the evaluation of social welfare
of lower classes
When the actor belongs to a low class his evaluation of social welfare of the lower classes increases with social alertness and with evaluation of mobilizationism. If the actor belongs to the higher classes his evaluation of social welfare of the lower classes increases with increasing menaces from higher class actors.

Changes in the matrix of attraction
The entries in the matrix of attraction between actors change according to a formula which states that attraction exerted by actor i on actor j increases with increasing harmony of interests and decreases with increasing menace from actor i on actor j, and with increasing dissimilarities in the evaluation of mobilizationism, of social welfare of the lower classes, of propensity to violence and of counter-ideology, as well as with increasing ethnic distance.

3   ENDO 3 *Feedback effects of coalition membership*

The equations used to measure feedback represent what we might call the maturity effects of the coalition-building process. It consists essentially of the same process described in ENDO 2, but here only endogenous increments and adjustment processes are considered. We will not describe the assumptions because they are simply those of the ENDO 2 process already presented, starting in this case by the operation of adjustments within coalitions.

4   ENDO 4 *Increase of menaces because of changes in other variables*

In ENDO 1 we described clustering effects on the value of menaces. Let us now describe the influence of changes of values in the propensity to violence and communication in relation to changes in prosperity, counter-ideology, ethnic differences, and interest harmony. The following proposition states the hypothesis:
     The menace an actor i exerts on an actor j increases when the likelihood of actor i resorting to violence increases. This increment is reinforced if i belongs to the lower classes and if the previous attraction exerted by

the menaced actor was low. In addition, low prosperity, low economic security, and high counter-ideology, as well as status incongruency, reduce the perception of menace in the higher classes, while high ethnic distance and low harmony of interests have an opposite effect.

VI PROCESS SEQUENCE OF THE MODEL

We may now conclude by showing how the different parts of the formal description interact in the actual simulation. Several alternatives being possible, let us take one as an example.

The process starts with information about the values of matrices and vectors in the previous period, together with the exogenous changes produced at the beginning of the period. In the case of the initial period, all values are exogenous. On the basis of the values of the previous period plus the changes introduced at the beginning of the new period one obtains new values for the matrices and vectors. With such data the process of coalition-building is pursued in the following sequence.

1   Selection of leader actors.
2   Primitive first-order coalitions (through attractions).
3   Derivative first-order coalitions (through attractions) until there is no further possibility of constructing more first-order coalitions through attractions.
4   First-order coalitions through menaces. If a new coalition is obtained the sequence goes to 5.
5   First-order coalitions through attractions. Steps 4 and 5 then alternate until there is no further possibility of constructing more coalitions of first order.
6   At this step the ENDO 1 process operates to introduce changes in menaces because of agglomeration effects. These changes are added to the previously existing matrix of menaces.
7   The next stage is to build coalitions of higher order through attractions until there is no possibility of creating a new coalition by means of attractions.
8   Coalitions of higher order are constructed by adding non-leaders through menaces. This is done by testing the incorporation of non-leaders to already built coalitions through menaces. If the structure of the coalitions is altered, stage 7 is repeated. Then again 8 follows and the two stages alternate until no new coalition is formed.
9   Coalitions of higher order are built, on the basis of the previous coalitions, through menaces. If new coalitions are formed the process

returns to 7 and goes on cycling from 7 to 9 and back until there is no possibility of building new coalitions. At this stage coalition-building stops.

10 ENDO 2 operates now on the basis of exogenous changes of variables and of endogenous changes produced by ENDO 1. Changes produced by ENDO 2 are incorporated in vectors and matrices. At the end of ENDO 2, the whole process of coalition building from 1 to 7 is repeated starting again with a complete disaggregation of actors. This represents a transition from the set of coalitions formed in the first block of coalitions before the behaviour equations had exerted their influences, to the coalitions resulting from the operation of the second set to behaviour equations.

11 ENDO 3 operates to represent the influence of the previously formed block of coalitions on the values of vectors and matrices. This in turn leads back to a new block of coalition building through the processes described from steps 1 to 9.

12 ENDO 4 operates to produce another block of coalitions calculated to represent the last consequences of the perturbation process produced exogenously at the beginning of the period. Then the sequence goes on to the next period, where information about exogenous changes is received and so on ...

REFERENCES

CORNBLIT, OSCAR *Conflicto, Cooperación y Cambio, Interpretación Formal de un Modelo de Cambio Social para América Latina*. Buenos Aires: Instituto di Tella, 1967.
– *Cambio Político en Cuzco y Oruro a fines del siglo* XVIII: *un estudio comparado de simulación*. Buenos Aires: Instituto Di Tella, 1970.
– 'Mass Rebellions in XVIIIth Century Peru and Bolivia,' in R. Carr, ed. *Latin American Affairs*. Oxford: Oxford University Press, 1970.
– *Modelos, Teorías y Medicion en Sociología*. Buenos Aires: Departamento de Sociología, 1962, pp. 18–19.
CORNBLIT, OSCAR, TORCUATO DI TELLA, and EZEQUIEL GALLO 'A Model of Political Change in Latin America,' *Social Science Information*, 7, 2 (April 1968), pp. 13–47.
DEUTSCH, K. 'Social Mobilization and Political Development,' *American Political Science Review*, 55, 3 (September 1961), pp. 493–514.
GERMANI, G. 'Los Procesos de Mobilización e Integración y el Cambio Social,' *Desarrollo Económico*, 3, 3 (October 1963).
– 'Urbanización, Secularización y Desarrollo Económico,' *Revista Mexicana de Sociologia*, 25, 2 (May-August 1963), pp. 625–46.

GUETZKOW, H. 'Simulation in Internation Relations,' in William Coplin, ed. *Simulation in the Study of Politics.* Chicago: Markham, 1968.

OSSOWSKI, STANISLAW *Class Structure in the Social Consciousness.* Translated from the Polish by Sheila Patterson. London: Routledge and Kegan Paul, 1963.

SEEMAN, MELVIN 'On the Meaning of Alienation,' *American Sociological Review*, 24, 6 (December 1959), pp. 783–91.

VIDAL, DANIEL 'Un Cas de faux concept : La notion d'aliénation,' *Sociologie du travail*, 1 (janvier-mars 1969), pp. 61–82.

ALLAN L.PELOWSKI

An event-based simulation of the Taiwan Straits crises*

INTRODUCTION

The research reported in this paper was undertaken for two main reasons: first, partially to test a model of crisis development based primarily on the works of Charles McClelland et al. (1965), Robert C. North (1969), and Paul Smoker (1969); and second, to explore some of the advantages and limitations of what can be called 'event-based simulation.' After examining the theoretical and statistical underpinnings of the model, we outline the model itself and assess its performance relative to McClelland's study of the Taiwan Straits confrontations, 1950–64. In a concluding section, some suggestions for improving and expanding the model are offered.

THEORETICAL BASE

Event-based simulation, as a form of computer experimentation,[1] attempts to represent referent (or 'real') systems by 'entities' which, according to specified attributes and structures, perform selected actions

*   This research has been supported in part by the Simulated International Processes Project, Northwestern University (NU ARPA SD-260), and has benefitted from criticism by Paul Smoker and Mike Leavitt.
1   The term 'event-based simulation' as used in this paper refers to a set of terms (e.g., entity, attribute, structure, and event) which together provide a 'translation language' in going from verbal and statistical theory to computer programs. As in other forms of simulation (equation-based, man-machine,

with respect to their environments. An entity may be any unit of theoretical interest (e.g., decision-makers, nations, coalitions of nations, small-groups, etc.) that is capable of generating activity with respect to occurrences in its environments. Entities are thought to have an infinite number of attributes – the measurable properties of entities that can be used in the description and comparison of systems under study. The structure – relatively stable sets of interrelationships among entities – is composed of energy and information processing rules which serve to limit some kinds of activity and to reinforce others.[2] Either in a deterministic or probabilistic fashion,[3] combinations of attributes and structure are said to cause the actions and interactions of the various entities in the system. Particular spatio-temporally-located outcomes of such activity are called events. An event may be thought of as an entry in the gestalt which stimulates or otherwise activates the entities. This set of terms provides the experimenter with a meta-theoretical language suitable for translating his substantive theory and associated parameters into operating computer programs, provided of course that some homomorphy of meanings can be developed between the two sets of terms.

In the empirical study of the Taiwan Straits crises by McClelland *et al.* (1965), the entities are the four principal nations involved – Mainland China (PRC), the Soviet Union (USSR), Taiwan (TAI), and the United States (USA). Over the fifteen-year period of the crisis, from 1950 to 1964, each of these entities carried out directed activity with respect to one another. The form and content of this activity was found to depend (probabilistically) upon each entity's involvement in the situation (an attribute), and upon the occurrence of particular types of activity[4] in the

analogue, etc.), an attempt is made to gain control over an otherwise intractable situation such that experimental interventions into the modeled entities, attributes, etc., can be traced out in some greater detail than in referent-system empirical studies.

2   For detailed examples of how such terms have been built into computer languages and simulations, see SIMSCRIPT Reference Manual (1967) and Naylor *et al.* (1966), especially pp. 278–90.

3   The model developed in this paper is probabilistic in the sense that entities, attributes, and structures are 'sampled' with variously distributed random numbers. This technique gives some variability of outcomes across different runs of the same model. Simulations that produce identical outcomes each run are deterministic in the sense that particular combinations and sequences of entities, attributes, and structures are used in the same way to produce activity in each run. The concept of 'reliability' is appropriately applied to the former kind of simulation but not to the latter.

4   McClelland and his associates (1964, 1965, 1968) have developed and applied a typology of actions based on some twelve to eighteen action-types. These types are really categories of verbs that are of supposed relevance in the reporting of international transactions, both in the press and in scholarly literature. From the basic verb categories several exclusive subsets of com-

various stages of the crisis situation[5] (a structure). McClelland's coding scheme for action data[6] in this study utilized a theoretical framework of attributes and structure which has received a good deal of attention in the various fields of the social sciences.[7] This framework incorporates the variables 'degree of goal-involvement' of the entities in the situation, 'degree of threat' to those affected goals, and 'decision-freedom,' or the degree to which time is perceived as a constraint on the decision processes. As we discuss the modelling assumptions (below) which are based on this theory, we shall be thinking of crisis as a social situation that 1 / threatens the higher-priority goals of the actors involved, and 2 / restricts the amount of time available for decision before the situation becomes transformed.[8]

Assumptions

Glenn Paige (1969), Robert C. North (1969), Paul Smoker (1969), and Charles Hermann (1969), along with McClelland (1965, 1961), have investigated the decisional outputs of national decision-makers in

binations of actions can be constructed and used in statistical analyses. McClelland (1965, p. 93) has presented action data in terms of three such subsets – positive or co-operative acts, noise-making or neutral acts, and negative or non-co-operative actions. Co-operative actions include the use of verbs like 'agree,' 'support,' 'withdraw,' and 'propose.' Neutral acts are coded for verbs like 'demand,' 'warn,' 'deny,' and 'accuse.' Non-co-operative actions include 'force' and 'attack,' each of these latter categories referring to concrete physical coercive acts.

5 A 'stage' for McClelland *et al.* is a 'characteristic information level' or 'relative uncertainty' index value associated with the relative spread or concentration of types of actions in the period of crisis development and resolution. A given crisis may be divided into stages then if characteristically different mixes of actions occur for all actors over time, i.e., if the relative variety of acts takes on discontinuous values for different subintervals.

6 Action data were coded by McClelland *et al.* from reports in the *New York Times* and the London *Times*, with supplementary information from the *South China Morning Post*, the *Japan Times*, and the *Foreign Broadcast Information Service White Books*. For the Taiwan situation, the total number of acts coded into action types was over 2,000. The intercoder reliabilities reported by McClelland (p. 33) were generally above 0.81 for the eighteen action-types. We would thus expect that the aggregate categories – co-operative, neutral, and non-co-operative – would have even higher reliabilities, but these figures are not reported by the authors.

7 In psychology see Frye and Stritch (1964), Albers (1966), and Festinger (1964); in sociology the works by Barton (1970), Baker and Chapman (1962), and Lanzetta (1955). Most other works cited in this paper are found in the political science literature.

8 Adopted from Hermann (1969), p. 29. Hermann includes the variable 'degree of anticipation' in this set along with the others. I have not included it because the Taiwan situation occurred for a period of fifteen years in which surprises were probably ubiquitous, but for which no data are available.

crisis situations. In his study of the Korean decision from a USA decision-maker's perspective, Paige found that goal-involvement and the priority attached to goals is positively related to the other crisis variables. That is,

H_1 the greater the crisis and the greater the past record of non-avoidant responses to crisis, the greater the propensity towards making an additional non-avoidant response, and the greater the priority assigned to affected goals (Paige 1969, pp. 375, 469).

North stated a similar relationship between degree of involvement and the degree of threat; namely, that

H_2 the higher the initial involvement of the actors, the higher the probability that actors will seek threats, respond with counter-threats, and acts of violence will increase (North 1969, p. 53).

With respect to the relationships between time and threat, North also argued the interaction suggested by Paige.

H_3 As the threat-counter-threat process intensifies, time will become more salient to the actors and they will become increasingly concerned with shorter range issues at the expense of longer range possible outcomes.

This latter proposition has been stated somewhat differently by Albers (1966), Thompson and Hawkes (1962), and by Langer et al. (1961), who argue on the basis of their individual and small-group studies that increased stress produces a constricted future outlook, that increased danger produces a significant overestimation of how fast time is passing, and that perceived time pressures increase the goal-involvement felt by the actor.

Both Smoker and McClelland et al. have explicitly brought time into empirical investigations of decisional outputs in crises involving nation-entities. Smoker argues from his time-series analysis of Sino-Indian message-transmission that increases in the numbers of messages (and presumably in their threat context as perceived by the receiver) results in a 'lock-in effect,' which is closely similar to North's threat-counter-threat argument in H_3. As we shall see later in this paper, McClelland also found a great increase in activity (especially concrete physical acts of violence and coercion) during times of severe decision-constraints. Similar results have been reported by several of North's associates in their analyses of the first world war crisis messages (Holsti et al. 1964, Zinnes 1968). All of these studies suggest that threat, goal-involvement, and time-constraints are bound up together in a cybernetic escalatory process which results in the breakdown of 'normal' internation exchange and interaction.

From their studies of the Taiwan Straits (1965) and the Berlin situation (1968), McClelland *et al.* argue that there is also a de-escalatory process at work which reduces perceptions of threat, decreases time-constraints, and leads to goal-disengagement. This notion is expressed by McClelland as follows:[9]

H_4 Experience with previous encounters in crisis will increase the likelihood of successful resolution in each successive encounter (McClelland 1961, p. 188; McClelland *et al.* 1965, p. 53; McClelland 1968, p. 184).

It is not clear from these studies whether the de-escalation results from either co-operative initiatives, 'routinizing' behaviour, or from some combination of several other factors (exhaustion, internal pressures in each nation, other internation occurrences). As this problem must be made explicit if the simulation is to work at all, we have initially assumed that each party will build up the threat-counter-threat syndrome, but that each threatening action will increase the probability that both sides in the crisis will begin initiating co-operative actions.

All four propositions taken together suggest a model of crisis which produces decisional outputs from the interactions among 1 / initial goal-involvement, 2 / perceptions of threat to these goals, 3 / the action-reaction syndrome of threat-counter-threat, and 4 / a 'cooling off' or de-escalatory process based on experiences with previous encounters in crisis. Before we develop this model of crisis in greater detail, we shall present the initial data base for the three variables, goal-involvement, threat, and decision-freedom.

STATISTICAL BASE

From the action data presented by McClelland *et al.* (1965), we were able to construct a set of discrete probability distributions describing the attributes and structure of the Taiwan Straits crises (Tachens, Quemoy). The goal-involvement variable is measured by the relative proportions of the total activity undertaken by each entity – the four nations and the two coalitions among them – as an average of the entire period of crisis (1950–64).

9 The proposition is worded as in the 1961 study, but essentially the same idea is conveyed in the other studies as well. The 1965 study discusses the PRC's 'learning' from experience, and the 1968 study relates de-escalation to 'routinization' of the behaviour in the Berlin situations.

264   Allan L. Pelowski

We note in table 1 that while the USSR had a fairly small share of total activity in the crises, each coalition of nations developed a nearly equal number of actions (i.e., USSR-PRC took 1,472 actions versus 1,157 for the USA-TAI). The PRC developed more than twice as many actions as any other nation, with the USA and TAI together generating 44 per cent. This table does not tell us the relative proportions of activity occurring in different subintervals (i.e., years) of the crisis, nor each entity's proportion of activity in the subintervals. These estimates are given below in conjunction with McClelland's action-types and crisis stages.

TABLE 1
Goal-involvement (N = 2629)

Entity	Proportion*
USSR	0.04
PRC	0.52
USSR – PRC	0.56
USA	0.19
TAI	0.25
USA – TAI	0.44
TOTAL	1.00

* Of total activity for the entire period on an average.
SOURCE McClelland *et al.* (1965), p. 46.

The degree of threat contained in a particular action can be inferred from McClelland's threefold classification of actions.[10] In table 2, the 'non-co-operation' action category refers to the (reported) carrying out of concrete, physically threatening acts such as 'arrest,' 'seize,' 'kill,' 'injure,' 'bomb,' 'sink,' and the 'employment of military force against.' The 'neutral' or noise-making category refers to verbs like 'contradict,' 'censure,' 'blame,' 'insist,' 'require,' and 'admonish.' The 'co-operation' or positive action category includes such things as 'give consent,' 'acquiesce,' 'approve,' and 'retreat.' Without trying to make fine gradations of threat (i.e., between seize, injure, and arrest) within each category, we have assumed in the simulation that the categories can be ranked in terms of 'high threat,' 'low threat,' and 'no threat.' In terms of the reported adequacy of McClelland's coding scheme,[11] this is probably a highly reliable assumption.

10   The threefold classification used in the simulation represents aggregates of twelve of the McClelland categories. See note 4 for other verb subcategories.
11   See note 6.

On the basis of several statistical analyses of the action data, Mc-Clelland was able to divide the fifteen-year period of the crisis into five 'typical' stages or subintervals of activity, each representing a characteristic action-mix or concentration of types of action.[12] These have been labelled 'non-crisis,' 'pre-crisis,' 'crisis,' 'post-crisis,' and 'inter-crisis.' With the exception of the inter-crisis stage, each of the other four stages occurred twice during the fifteen-year period of activity in the Taiwan Straits.[13] In table 2 the entries under each stage represent the probabilities that particular types of actions occurred in each stage, where the different occurrences of non-crisis, pre-crisis, and post-crisis have been combined. Note that in this table the entities are the two-nation coalitions rather than the individual nations. This selection was made because of the difficulty of making the probability estimates for all four nations separately over each action-type and stage from the data given in the McClelland study.[14]

We note again that the entries in table 2 tell us neither how many actions of each type occurred in each stage nor the different propensities for action in the different occurrences of four of the stages. While we do know the total (N) of actions taken for the entire period (2,629), the probability estimates in table 2 take no account of the distributions of acts across the five categories. This means that numbers of acts, as opposed to the probability of undertaking a type of action in a given stage, are lost in the entries. This omission was deliberate insofar as the overall goal of the simulation was to replicate as closely as possible the pattern and magnitude of actions taken over the time span of the Taiwan Straits confrontations. The entries thus provide a loose estimate of propensities for action which serves to build the first stage of the model, but which avoids a simple tautology with the referent system.

Also, it should be noted that neither table presents data that distinguish initiatives from responses in the actions of entities. Given our

12 McClelland *et al.* (1965) carried out some five different statistical analyses of the raw magnitudes and frequencies of types of actions. These included the 'relative uncertainty' measures (see note 5) from which the stages of crisis were derived, as well as factor-analysis, standardization of data, chi-square analyses of differences, and the analysis of deviations. Since each method presented this author with somewhat different pictures of the crisis, the probability estimates in table 2 must be seen as tentative and partly as judgments.
13 Non-crisis (January 1951 to December 1952; January 1961 to December 1962), pre-crisis (January to June 1954; January to June 1958), crisis (July 1954 to June 1955 – Tachens; August to October 1958 – Quemoy), post-crisis (July to December 1955; November 1958 to April 1959), inter-crisis (July 1956 to June 1957).
14 Raw magnitudes of actions for particular nations were not reported for some of the time points of the crisis.

TABLE 2
Probabilities for types of action in five stages

Coalition	Action-type	Degree of threat	Non-crisis	Pre-crisis	Crisis	Post-crisis	Inter-crisis
USSR-PRC	Non–co-operative	High	0.1	0.2	0.8	0.2	0.2
	Neutral	Low	0.3	0.5	0.1	0.3	0.5
	Co-operative	None	0.6	0.3	0.1	0.5	0.3
USA-TAI	Non–co-operative	High	0.2	0.3	0.7	0.3	0.3
	Neutral	Low	0.3	0.6	0.2	0.2	0.4
	Co-operative	None	0.5	0.1	0.1	0.5	0.3

SOURCE McClelland, et al. (1965), pp. 48–50, 55, 63, 67–68, 70–71.

theoretical assumptions about action-reaction and threat, and about the relations between goal-involvement and threat, we can see that this distinction will have to be made explicit in the simulation. Since McClelland did not report his data in a way that would allow a direct estimate of action versus reaction, we will be making hypothetical assumptions about goal-involvement, degree of threat, and decision-freedom as they relate to action-reaction, the adequacy of which can then be tested in the comparison of simulation outputs with the patterns and magnitudes reported by McClelland.

Most of the action data presented by McClelland et al. are divided into yearly intervals, with some monthly data given around the periods of intense activity (i.e., the crisis stage). With this basic series length of fifteen data-points, it was not feasible to estimate decision-freedom through time-series analyses as employed by Smoker (1969).[15] Nor was it possible to make the estimate on the basis of ratios between initiatives and responses since this distinction is not reported in the study. However, with certain assumptions based on the propositions and original data in the two tables, we have developed parameter estimates of decision-freedom which are based on the relationships between goal-involvement and degree of threat. We assume that the greater the goal-involvement (as in table 1) and the greater the probability of taking a threatening action (as in table 2), the less the decision-freedom. This assumption combines propositions H_2 and H_3 and gives us an indirect way of estimating decision-freedom from the two variables threat and goal-involvement.

15 Smoker used trend-removal and serial correlation techniques to estimate the relative predictability of message-sending. He argued that the degree of predictability as measured by the auto-correlations of data from which trends had been removed was directly related to the 'lock-in' syndrome of action-reaction.

Briefly, in table 3 below we have assumed that if an action is reciprocated in another action, then the time-lag between the initiative and the response will depend upon initial goal-involvement as read from table 1 and upon the stages of crisis and their associated threat values (as read from the columns of table 2). We consider five combinations of pairs of action-types and three combinations of nation-pairs. The entries in the matrix refer to the numbers of cycles of the simulation before a response is called for.

TABLE 3

Decision-freedom times

Action-pair	USSR – USA	TAI – PRC	TAI – USSR or USA – PRC	Average waiting time
Co-operation-co-operation	8	3	6	5.7
Non-co-operation-non-co-operation	5	2	4	3.7
Neutral-Neutral	15	10	12	12.3
Some co-operation	12	88	10	10.0
Some non-co-operation	10	5	8	7.7

The absolute magnitudes of waiting times in table 3 are not so important as the relative ratios between times. Note, for example, that response times for full non-co-operation (i.e., where both actors choose highly threatening actions) are approximately one-third faster than for full co-operation. This difference is consistent with proposition H_3, although whether or not the ratio should be exactly that value is, of course, open to question. Note, too, that co-operation-co-operation interactions are faster than either neutral-neutral actions or mixed actions (i.e., where the two acting nations choose different threat content). We assume this ratio to be consistent with proposition H_4, which relates to the de-escalation of the threat syndrome. Also, we have assumed that pairs of actions with some non-co-operation would draw faster responses than actions with some co-operation, although neither of these mixed pairs would be faster than the two pure types. We have let neutral-neutral pairs have the slowest response times – assuming in effect that the 'noise-making' actions of either side, while involving some degree of threat, would still leave considerable decision-freedom beyond that of other action-pairs.

The timing matrix produces a bias in the direction of a threatcounter-threat reaction spiral, which, in conjunction with the entries in tables 1 and 2, should 'drive' the simulation model into producing a greater number of high threat actions than of low threat or mixed co-operative actions. Whether this expectation holds, and whether the action patterns reported by McClelland can be replicated with the model will depend upon the explicit interrelationships between the initial data and the theoretical assumptions as they are built into the simulation.

OUTLINE OF THE MODEL

In general, the model we are about to outline follows a five-step flow of activities involving 1 / the selection of pairs of nations from the probability distribution associated with the involvement of the entities, 2 / checking to see if the selected pair is 'legal,' that is, if the pairs are not in the same coalition, 3 / selecting an action to be taken by each nation on the basis of the stage of crisis that the model is in, 4 / checking to see if the selected actions are full non-co-operative, full co-operative, full neutral, or mixed, and 5 / placing the selected actions on an appropriate waiting list for further responses according to the timing matrix. The selections of nation-pairs and actions is by random numbers whose distributions are specified in the goal-involvement and degree-of-threat tables.[16] All five steps together create what we have called events: the specific actions that are placed on a waiting list for future access according to the timing assumptions in table 3. Each event can be considered to be an action-type that has associated with it a specific time t. When the simulation has cycled t times, the event is called from the list and is then used to determine the entry-point into the columns of the threat matrix, that is, whether the next selection of actions should be at probabilities of non-crisis, pre-crisis, crisis, post-crisis, or inter-crisis. High-threat actions, when called from the list for processing, would serve to move the model towards the crisis stage unless the model were already operating there, in which case the next selection of actions would occur at crisis probability values. Assuming that the model is in a crisis stage selection of actions, and assuming that a full co-operation action-pair were then selected (i.e., with probability of 0.1), the simulation would move into the post-crisis probability values for the next cycle. A noise-making or neutral event would not move the model except in the cases of non-crisis and post-crisis, where such an event would push the simulation into pre-crisis or inter-crisis, respectively. In this sequential fashion events pile up on the list waiting to activate the entities at one or another of the stages of crisis. As such, the model has an operating characteristic of goal-

16 The random number generators and the list are features of a simulation package called SPURT (1968), written in FORTRAN IV for the CDC 6400 computer, and which can be used in conjunction with user-written event-based simulation programs. SPURT also contains various statistical subroutines, analogue simulators, and output routines that have general relevance.

involvement, threat, and time, plus interactions among them, which attempts to embody the theory and assumptions as outlined in the first section of this paper. Table 4 summarizes the relationships between events called from the list and the five stages of the crisis model. The columns of the table refer to the position of the model at time t and the rows to the effects of events called at time $t + n$, where n is an entry in the timing matrix.

TABLE 4

The action-selection operating characteristic of the simulation model. Entries in the table are the effects of events called from the list

Effect of event $t + n$	Position of model at t				
	Non-crisis	Pro-crisis	Crisis	Post-crisis	Inter-crisis
Co-operation	remain	go to non-crisis	go to post-crisis	remain	go to non-crisis
Non-co-operation	go to pre-crisis	go to crisis	remain	go to inter-crisis	go to pre-crisis
Noise-making	go to pre-crisis	remain	remain	go to inter-crisis	remain

Let us take the model through two cycles from the time of initial start-up. First, two nations are selected according to the goal-involvement probability values. Each nation then generates an action in the non-crisis stage. Let us assume that one action selected is in the noise-making category and the other in the co-operation category. This action-pair then is stored on the waiting list according to the times associated with 'some co-operation' as in table 3, row 4. If the two nations selected had been the USA and PRC (with probabilities of 0.19 and 0.52 respectively), then the stored event would go on the list at time 10. The model would then recycle and choose two more nations and actions. Let us say that the USSR and TAI are selected and that they generate a full non-co-operation action-pair. This selection would occur in the non-crisis stage since the stored event $t = 10$ has not yet influenced the selection process. The new USSR-TAI event would then be stored at time 4 on the list, and again the model would recycle. The result of the two cycles would be a model in non-crisis with two events on the list, one waiting for cycle 4 and the other waiting for cycle 10. At cycle 4 an interaction would occur between degree of threat and the new selection: the non-co-operation event would change the selection values from non-crisis to pre-crisis. If the model were operating at crisis probabilities in cycle 9, the effect of the full co-operation event would be to change selection values to post-crisis. In this way an entity's involvement in the situation leads to the mobilization of initiatives and responses, the build-up of stored events, and interactions among the three variables.

In order to simulate Paige's proposition (H_1), relating involvement to goal-priorities, the initial selection of nation-pairs in each cycle was made dependent upon the degree of threat distributions in the stages of crisis. This was estimated through the use of normally distributed random numbers across the range of each nation's goal-involvement score. This means that nations with higher involvement scores (i.e., PRC, TAI) would be selected with higher probability as the crisis progressed up to crisis. For the non-crisis and post-crisis stages, each nation would be selected according to the initial values in table 1.

North's proposition (H_2) relating goal-involvement to threat is contained in the relation between the normally distributed involvement scores and the probability values associated with degrees of threat under each portion of the curve: the higher the involvement of an entity, the greater the likelihood of choosing actions with high threat. H_3, the proposition relating threat to timing, is built into the timing matrix assumptions which have their impact on the operating characteristic of the model (i.e., by speeding up responses to high threat). The dampening effects of H_4 through co-operative actions are contained in the operating characteristic as well; here we have let co-operative actions have intermediate response-times and a dampening effect through such events' capacity to move the model to non-crisis and/or post-crisis. For this latter assumption we take the theoretical position that co-operative actions will get responses quicker than the noise-making activities but slower than the high-threat non-co-operative activities.

Although the assumptions contained in this model are relatively simple, it might be useful if the reader would trace out the selections and decisions as summarized in the following block-diagram (figure 1). Note that the model is composed of a main program at the start of the model and four subroutines, each performing part of the selection process. The first subroutine selects the nation-pair and the other three choose actions depending upon the particular nation-pair and then load the events onto the list for a new cycle.

EVALUATION OF THE MODEL

The outputs from the model include 1 / the number of co-operative actions generated, 2 / the number of non-co-operative actions, and 3 /

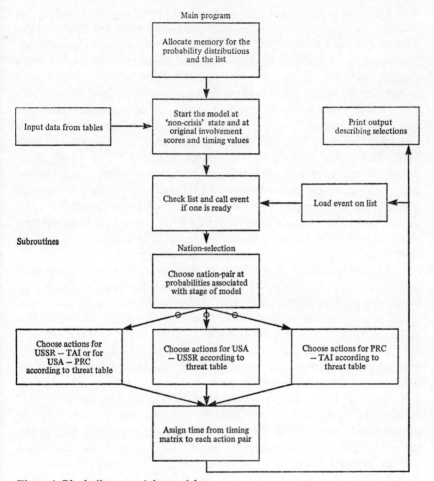

Figure 1 Block diagram of the model.

the number of noise-making actions for each run. McClelland *et al.* (1965, p. 55) have reported data similar to these over the fifteen-year period of the Taiwan Straits interactions. In the comparison of simulation outputs with the referent system study, we are concerned with testing the null expectation that the model-generated actions will not correspond significantly to events generated in the Taiwan Straits as coded and reported by McClelland *et al.*

The testing procedure employed ten simulation runs of identical structure, but with the random number generator being reset each run to provide variation in actor and action selection. For all ten runs the original data are those reported in tables 1 to 3. The probability distributions describing the attributes and structure of the entities were left constant: the goal-involvement, threat, and timing values were not changed by any feedbacks in the simulation. Insofar as McClelland's data show two crisis peaks (1955, 1958) and three depressions (1952, 1956, 1960), as illustrated in table 5, the simulation was allowed to run until such time as two peaks and three depressions were obtained. Each run of the model produced such a configuration in approximately 1200 cycles of operation. The ten sets of output were then averaged, standardized,[17] and correlated[18] with McClelland's variables. Since McClelland reported fifteen yearly datapoints for the three variables, an aggregation of simulation outputs was necessary before the correlations could be computed. This was accomplished by adding together every successive set of ninety simulation datapoints, leaving us with an effective N of 14 for making the cross-systems comparisons.[19] The raw data values are reported in table 5. Note that the simulation variables are averages of the ten runs.[20]

Our evaluation of the model in relation to the McClelland variables will focus on the concepts of convergent and discriminant validity as developed by Campbell and Fiske (1970) in their work on the multivariable-multimethod matrix. This approach to evaluation emphasizes not only the degree of correspondence between model and referent system (Guetzkow 1968) (Smoker 1969), but also the degree to which the correspondences across similar variables are higher than those between different but essentially incomparable variables. In other words, this approach demands that validity coefficients be compared to the 'non-sense' coefficients between dissimilar variables, so that convergence and discrimination can be used as checks on one another. In order to accomplish the evaluation, the eight variables in table 5 have been intercorrelated and are presented in table 6 in the multivariable-multimethod form.

Looking first to the monomethod, multivariable quadrants, we note immediately that the intercorrelations among the variables in the McClelland study are much higher than for the same intercorrelations in the simulation variables. On an average the McClelland variables correlate

17 The z-score transformation was used for plotting convenience; this does not affect in any way the correlations obtained.
18 Simple Pearson-product correlations were performed to estimate the relative strength of the various interrelationships between the two systems.
19 Alternatively, we could have selected every nth data-point for comparison, but since the McClelland data were already aggregated into yearly intervals, we chose this method.
20 The standard deviations across runs (because of the resetting of the random number generator) were all within the 0.05 to 0.10 range of error. The shapes of the outputs across different runs were approximately the same.

TABLE 5

Raw data values for co-operation, non-co-operation, and noise-making from the simulation and from the McClelland study (p. 55). (*mcc* indicates McClelland variables, *sim* indicates the simulations)

Time* Period	(1) Co-operation		(2) Non-co-operation		(3) Noise-making		(4) Total**	
	mcc	*sim*	*mcc*	*sim*	*mcc*	*sim*	*mcc*	*sim*
1950	0	10	71	50	30	23	101	83
51	3	12	26	42	24	50	53	104
52	0	10	14	82	14	32	28	124
53	0	10	16	56	14	30	30	96
54	4	10	206	102	95	94	305	206
1955	35	24	217	102	169	172	421	298
56	6	20	95	80	95	64	196	164
57	2	8	92	90	25	92	119	190
58	53	26	259	124	222	176	534	326
59	7	34	118	156	35	68	160	258
1960	2	58	88	108	37	64	127	230
61	0	42	14	94	30	50	44	186
62	0	32	16	32	26	62	42	126
63	0	10	16	16	14	32	30	58
TOTALS**	112	306	1248	1134	830	1009	2190	2449

* Refers to McClelland's yearly reported data and to aggregated simulation data.
** Total number of actions summed for each set of variables.

TABLE 6

Intercorrelations between McClelland and simulation variables

	McClelland variables				Simulation variables			
	(1)	(2)	(3)	(4)	(1)	(2)	(3)	(4)
1	100							
2	81	100						
3	94	90	100					
4	91	97	97	100				
1	**11**	06	09	08	100			
2	45	**64**	47	57	44	100		
3	91	89	**92**	93	15	53	100	
4	76	83	77	**83**	48	86	86	100

KEY   Variable 1 Co-operation $N = 14$* Coefficients have been multiplied by 100.
           Variable 2 Non-co-operation
           Variable 3 Noise-making
           Variable 4 Total Actions
* If significance levels were strictly appropriate (which they are not) coefficients above 0.50 would be 'significant' at 0.05. (Bold face coefficients represent the cross-method, same-variable validity coefficients.)

at 0.91, while the simulation variables correlate at only 0.55. This means that the study by McClelland *et al.* has produced a coherent picture of crisis which is not matched in the simulation outputs.

Second, shifting now to the multimethod quadrant (i.e., the bold face coefficients), we note that the correspondences between like variables across the two studies range from 0.11 (co-operative actions) to 0.92 (noise-making actions), with non-co-operation (0.64) and the total actions comparison (0.83) in between. We might be quite happy with this degree of correspondence were it not for the inability of these coefficients to distinguish themselves from the other non-sense coefficients in the same quadrant. In each row of this quadrant we see that none of the validity coefficients are much higher, if at all, than other coefficients which measure the cross-variable, cross-method shared variance. This points out in another way the lack of 'connectedness' in the simulation world as compared to the high coherence in the McClelland data.

On the other hand, we note that the total actions comparisons (variable 4) have approximately the same 'shape' across variables within each study. The McClelland total actions variable correlates 0.91, 0.97, and 0.97 with the McClelland co-operative, non-co-operative, and noise-making variables respectively. The simulation total actions variable has correlations of 0.48, 0.86, and 0.86 with its other variables. This means that while the simulation world is more loosely connected, in each study the co-operation variable is somewhat of an outsider with respect to variance shared with other variables. The low correlation between simulation co-operation and McClelland co-operation ($r = 0.11$) indicates that each variable is deviant in a different way in each study. An investigation of each co-operation variable in table 5 will reveal that 1 / the simulation produces much more co-operation than did the McClelland codes, and that 2 / the peak of co-operation in the simulation occurred two years later than the peak of co-operation in the McClelland study [i.e., in the referent system, co-operation reached its highest point during the Quemoy (1958) crisis, but in the simulation, co-operation kept building up until 1960]. The plot of these two variables (figure 2) illustrates this lagging of simulation co-operation behind referent system co-operation after 1958.

The lack of fit between the two variables probably results from a combination of errors in the original modelling assumptions about 1 / the response time for co-operative actions, 2 / probability-values associated with co-operative action selection, or 3 / the operating characteristic which drives the model towards the non-crisis or post-crisis stages. But whether or not this represents error in assumptions depends upon further

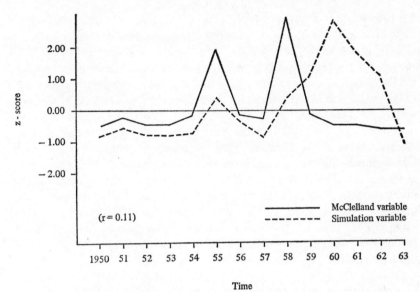

Time

Figure 2 Comparison of the incidence of co-operative action in the McClelland study and in the simulation.

theoretical and methodological assumptions. We might suspect for example that McClelland's proposition (H_4) is in error itself, or that errors were made in the translation of this proposition into the computer program. Going further out on a limb, we could as well hypothesize that McClelland's data are wrong with respect to the occurrence of co-operative actions. Whatever the explanation, it is clear that any linear change in the simulation co-operation routines will not suffice to correct the lack of fit. This is because the first nine data-points match quite closely while the last five do not. A linear change correcting the lack of fit after 1958 would only reduce the correspondence before 1958.

Given that convergent validity for the non-co-operation, noise-making, and total actions comparisons is reasonable, but that discriminant validity is low because of the lack of coherence in simulation versus high coherence in the referent system, a further validity experiment was carried out. The co-operation parameters were adjusted in the attempt to gain a closer fit with the McClelland variable. The involvement variable was left as is in table 1. The operating characteristics as in table 4 were also left alone. We hypothesized that responses to co-operative actions would be as fast as responses to non-co-operative acts – giving the full co-operation row in the timing matrix (table 3) values equal to those for full non-co-operation. The simulation was then run as before (i.e., for ten runs of three depressions and two peaks each), and the results were compared to those produced with the original assumptions.

The results of this validity experiment were encouraging. The strength of the relationship between simulated co-operation and McClelland's variable increased from 0.11 to 0.63. Also, the overall coherence of the simulation world with all four variables increased from 0.55 to 0.67, with the increase resulting from a better-fitting co-operation variable. We were able to conclude from this experiment that the McClelland *et al.* reconstruction of the Taiwan Straits situation was better replicated with fast response-times for the co-operative actions. However, the experimental change in parameters also produced significantly greater numbers of co-operative actions than in the first runs (845 versus 306), and these new magnitudes were even further away from the McClelland numbers (sum = 112) than before. Thus, in order to bring these two systems closer together we will probably need greater theoretical detail along with more flexible and possibly complex models of that theory.

SUGGESTIONS AND CONCLUSIONS

The event-based simulation developed in this paper was moderately successful in replicating the McClelland *et al.* (1965) data on actions taken in the Taiwan Straits, 1950–64. The model developed dynamic relationships between the variables, 'goal-involvement,' 'degree of threat,' and 'decision-freedom' as measured by response-time. The entities in the model were four nations and two coalitions among them. The structure of the simulation followed McClelland's categories for action-types and stages of the simulated crisis. The operating characteristic of the model provided working relationships between the initial data and the categories of structure. The overall fit between the two systems was improved through experimentation on the parameters associated with co-operative actions and response-times. The average correlation between co-operation, non-co-operation, and noise-making was improved from 0.55 to 0.67 with these changes; but this figure was still considerably lower than the average correlation in the referent system $r = 0.91$.

As a technique in computer experimentation on political systems, event-based simulation appears to offer some advantages over equation-based models.[21] First, the entities, attributes, and structure remain in a disaggregated state, which allows for more direct and specific experimental intervention. Second, experimental changes can be traced to

21   Regression equations and difference equations especially.

specific parts of the program since the entities, attributes, and structure are not bound up together in multivariate equations. Third, complex systems not solvable by direct mathematical algorithms can be at least indirectly assessed for validity and reliability by means of event-based simulation. However, event-based modelling also can lead to some difficulties not found in equation-based simulations. These can be generally associated with the necessity of translating verbal and statistical theory into the language of event-based modelling. Quite often, where an explicit parameter estimate will suffice for the equation-builder, some number of less explicit theoretical assumptions will be made by the event-based modeller in his effort to 'get the thing running.' In event-based simulation research we are not always sure whether an inconsistent theory has been translated correctly, or whether a consistent theory, having been translated incorrectly, appears as though it were inconsistent to the modeller (Krend 1970, Pelowski 1969).

The difficulties of translation can be overcome partially through several complementary means. First, the whole operation of social system modelling could be speeded up and rendered more flexible in an on-line, interactive computer environment. This would allow nearly immediate feedback from model to modeller about the effects of his assumptions and would permit rapid corrections if necessary through the interactive interface. Second, in the translation of verbal theory to computer programs a 'modular' approach may improve the degree of homomorphism between the two languages (Smoker 1970b, Pelowski 1969). If different subsets of the theory to be translated seem to be better developed than others, or if contending theories about similar phenomena exist, 'modules' (or 'submodels') of those relationships can be constructed, possibly linked to one another, and replaced when different theories and subsets thereof have been more fully articulated. Third, and perhaps more important, the criteria for event-based simulation validity and reliability need to be more adequately worked out (Smoker 1969b, Raser *et al.* 1970). Most validity studies of simulations have been of the convergent type; the assumption is usually that the referent system is in some sense already 'valid,' and that the model must therefore be manipulated to improve its correspondences. A complementary view of validity has been put forth by Smoker and Raser *et al.* They argue that we may wish to consider the model to be valid and then to effect changes in referent systems to improve their correspondence. The criteria and epistemological assumptions underlying either or both of these notions of validity deserve a fuller explication in the modelling of social systems – an activity where techniques, theory, and values often come into direct and explicit contact.

278   Allan L. Pelowski

REFERENCES

ALBERS, ROBERT J. 'Anxiety and Time Perspectives,' *Dissertation Abstracts*, 26 (1966).
BAKER, GEORGE W. and DWIGHT W. CHAPMAN, eds. *Man and Society in Disaster*. New York: Basic Books, 1962.
BARTON, ALLEN H. *Communities in Disaster: A Sociological Analysis of Collective Stress Situations*. Garden City, NY: Anchor Books, 1970.
CAMPBELL, DONALD T. and DONALD W. FISKE 'Convergent and Discriminant Validation by the Multitrait-Multimethod Matrix,' in Gene F. Summers, ed. *Attitude Measurement*. Chicago: Rand-McNally, 1970.
FESTINGER, LEON *Conflict, Decision and Dissonance*. Stanford, Calif.: Stanford University Press, 1964.
FRYE, ROLAND L. and THOMAS M. STRITCH 'Effects of Timed versus Non-timed Discussion upon Measures of Influence and Change in Small Groups,' *Journal of Social Psychology*, 63 (1964), pp. 139–43.
GUETZKOW, HAROLD 'Some Correspondence Between Simulations and "Realities" in International Relations,' in Morton A. Kaplan, ed. *New Approaches to International Relations*. New York: St. Martin's Press, 1968.
HERMANN, CHARLES F. *Crises in Foreign Policy: A Simulation Analysis*. Indianapolis: Bobbs-Merrill, 1969.
HOLSTI, OLE R., RICHARD A. BRODY, and ROBERT C. NORTH 'Theory and Measurement of Interstate Behavior: A Research Application of Automated Content Analysis,' Studies in International Conflict and Integration, Stanford University, May 1964. (Mimeographed.)
KREND, JEFFREY 'A Reconstruction of Oliver Benson's "Simple Diplomatic Game," ' Simulated International Processes Project, Northwestern University, March 1970. (Mimeographed.)
LANGER, JONAS, S. WAPNER, and H. WERNER 'The Effects of Danger Upon the Experience of Time,' *American Journal of Psychology*, 74 (1961), pp. 94–7.
LANZETTA, J.T. 'Group Behavior Under Stress,' *Human Relations*, 8 (1955), pp. 29–52.
MCCLELLAND, CHARLES A., DANIEL P. HARRISON, WAYNE R. PHILLIPS, and ROBERT A. YOUNG 'The Communist Chinese Performance in Crisis and Non-crisis: Quantitative Studies of the Taiwan Straits Confrontations, 1950–1964,' Behavioral Sciences Group, Naval Ordnance Test Station, China Lake, California, 14 December 1965.
– 'Access to Berlin: The Quantity and Variety of Events, 1948–1963,' in J. David Singer, ed., *Quantitative International Politics*. New York: Free Press, 1968.
– 'The Acute International Crisis,' *World Politics*, 14 (October 1961).
NAYLOR, THOMAS H., JOSEPH L. BALINTFY, DONALD S. BURDICK, and KONG CHU *Computer Simulation Techniques*. New York: Wiley, 1966.

NORTH, ROBERT C. 'Recommendations for Research on China,' Office of Naval Research, Technical Report no 3, 21 March 1969.

PAIGE, GLENN D. 'The Korean Decision,' in James N. Rosenau, ed. *International Politics and Foreign Policy*. New York: Free Press, 1969, pp. 461–72.

PELOWSKI, ALLAN L. 'An Approach to Stimulation Module Construction in International Relations,' Simulated International Processes Project, Northwestern University, August 1969. (Mimeographed.)

RASER, JOHN R., DONALD T. CAMPBELL, and RICHARD W. CHADWICK 'Gaming and Simulation for Developing Theory Relevant to International Relations,' Western Behavioral Sciences Institutes, Northwestern University, and the University of Hawaii, 1970. (Mimeographed.)

SIMSCRIPT Reference Manual, Control Data Corporation, Palo Alto, California, 1967.

SMOKER, PAUL L. 'International Processes Simulation: An Evaluation,' Northwestern University, 1970. (Mimeographed.)

– 'International Relations Simulations: A Summary,' Northwestern University, 1970b. (Mimeographed.)

– 'A Time-Series Analysis of Sino-Indian Relations,' *Journal of Conflict Resolution*, 2 (June 1969).

– 'Social Research for Social Anticipation and Creation,' *American Behavioral Scientist*, 6 (July-August, 1969b), pp. 1–13.

SPURT (Simulation Package for University Research and Teaching): A Description of SPURT, Revision E, Vogelback Computing Center, Northwestern University, August 1968. (Mimeographed.)

THOMPSON, JAMES D. and ROBERT W. HAWKES 'Disaster, Community Organization, and Administrative Process,' in George W. Baker and Dwight W. Chapman, eds. *Man and Society in Disaster*. New York: Basic Books, 1962.

ZINNES, DINA A. 'The Expression and Perception of Hostility in Prewar Crisis, 1914,' in J. David Singer ed. *Quantitative International Politics*. New York: Free Press, 1968. Pp. 85–158.

MICHAEL R.LEAVITT

Markov processes in international crises: an analytical addendum to an event-based simulation of the Taiwan Straits crises

As Naylor *et al.* (1966, p. 6) have stated, one reason to simulate a system occurs when 'the observed system may be so complex that it is impossible to describe it in terms of mathematical equations for which it is possible to obtain analytic solutions which could be used for predictive purposes.' What is impossible at first glance may not only become possible, but quite valuable after a study of the situation. If simulation is a vehicle for studying a system which seems analytically insoluble at first, then it follows that a result of the simulation itself might be enlightenment as to the possibilities of its use for subsequent analytical solution.

In the previous chapter by Pelowski, the stages of crisis (non-crisis, pre-crisis, crisis, post-crisis, and inter-crisis) were necessary constructs for determining the distribution of variables of interest to him: frequency of co-operative, non-co-operative, and neutral (noise-making) actions. Yet an equally interesting research question might well be the frequency with which the system found itself in periods of crisis (and the associated stages). These results were not reported by Pelowski because they were not immediately relevant to his research questions. The data are, however, available, not only in the computer output of the simulation runs but in the McClelland study (1965) on which the simulation was based. The research question to be dealt with in this note is, how accurately can an analytical model coincide with the simulation and/or referent data on the frequency with which the system is in one of the five stages of crisis.

The research was prompted by an examination of Pelowski's table 4: 'The action-selection operating characteristics of the simulation model.' In this table, the effects of the three kinds of action (co-operation, non-co-operation, and 'noise-making') are described when they occur in each of the five stages of the system. For example, the effect of a co-operative act in non-crisis is to leave the system in a state of non-crisis; the effect of non-co-operation during non-crisis, however, is to move the system to pre-crisis. This suggests a five-state Markov process, a process in which the state of a system at a given time point is dependent at most on its state at the immediately preceding time point.

Not only does Pelowski tell us what the effect of each action is at each stage, he also gives us the probabilities of each action at each stage (table 2). For example, the probability of the USSR taking a co-operative action during a non-crisis stage is 0.6. In order to construct a Markov chain, we need to know the probabilities associated with going from each stage to every other stage in the next time point, and these probabilities are derivable from tables 1 and 2 as follows. Table 2 provides a separate set of 'action-probabilities' for each coalition, USSR-PRC and USA-TAI. Table 1 gives us the probabilities of one coalition or another taking action. Thus it is necessary to multiply the action probabilities of the USSR-PRC coalition and the USA-TAI coalition taking action (0.56 and 0.44 respectively) by the probability that each would take a particular action at a particular stage, to arrive at the overall 'expected' probability. In the example above, the probability of the USSR or PRC taking a co-operative action during a non-crisis period was 0.6, while the probability that the USA or TAI would take that action at that stage was 0.5. Hence the expected probability was 0.556 (0.56 × 0.6 + 0.44 × 0.5 = 0.556). Combining tables 2 and 4 as described above, we can arrive at a matrix of transition probabilities, that is, the probabilities of going from any one stage to another. This matrix is presented in table A.

In the example in the previous paragraph, it was shown how the upper left-hand element of the transition matrix was derived. The probability of going from a non-crisis situation to a non-crisis situation is defined as the probability of having a co-operative action which is equal to 0.556.

TABLE A

Simple transition probabilities for the five-stage model

	Non-crisis	Pre-crisis	Crisis	Post-crisis	Inter-crisis
Non-crisis	0.556	0.444	0	0	0
Pre-crisis	0.212	0.544	0.244	0	0
Crisis	0	0	0.900	0.100	0
Post-crisis	0	0	0	0.500	0.500
Inter-crisis	0.300	0.244	0	0	0.456

Any other kind of action would move the system to pre-crisis. Since probabilities must sum to 1, the probability of going from non-crisis to pre-crisis, then, is $1.000 - 0.556$, or 0.444. The other elements of the transition matrix were created in the same way.

It may be noted that, as is necessary, the above matrix is a regular, stochastic matrix: it is regular because no elements are negative, and it is stochastic in that the number of rows equals the number of columns, and the sum of the elements in each row equals 1. It can be proved that as you take successive powers of a regular, stochastic matrix, it will approach and eventually equal another matrix with the following properties: 1 / all rows of that matrix will be equal; 2 / all elements of that matrix are positive; and most importantly 3 / each row is a vector called the *fixed point* of the initial matrix with the property that if that vector is multiplied by the matrix, the result is simply the fixed-point vector itself (Kemeny, Snell, and Thompson 1957, p. 219). The substantive interpretation of the fixed-point vector is that it represents the final distribution of states of the system. The transition matrix was a five-by-five matrix of probabilities of going from each state to all other states in the next time period. The fixed-point vector has five elements, which are simply the final percentages of time which the system spends in each of its five states. For the above example, the fixed-point vector is $(0.12, 0.17, 0.51, 0.10, 0.10)$. In other words, if the system acted on the assumptions stated above, it would spend 12 per cent of its time in non-crisis, 17 per cent of its time in pre-crisis, 51 per cent in crisis, 10 per cent in post-crisis, and 10 per cent in inter-crisis.

Thus, we have arrived at an analytical solution to the question (not Pelowski's) of frequencies of time spent in each stage. The figures above do not, however, coincide either with those found by Pelowski or by McClelland; these were $(0.30, 0.20, 0.18, 0.21, 0.11)$ and $(0.44, 0.11, 0.14, 0.20, 0.11)$ respectively. It is not necessary to do statistical tests to demonstrate the disparity. On the other hand, it should not have been expected that these figures would 'fit' particularly well. First, the simulation treats time in a way entirely ignored by the analytical model. The model assumes that the system can move from one stage to another 'immediately,' and that the rates of moving from one stage to another are equal. The simulation, however, explicitly provides for 'waiting times' or finite amounts of time in which the system is, in effect, in transition from one stage to another. This is because action requires a response, but a delayed response – the amount of delay being dependent on the kind of action. Hence, non-co-operative acts usually have a shorter delay than other kinds, and neutral, or noise-making, acts have a long delay before their consequences are enacted (see Pelowski's table 3 for specifications of delay). This verbal description might indicate why the analytical model described above had the system spending more of its time in crisis than did the simulation or the referent system. Non-co-operative acts occur much more frequently in times of crisis than they do in other stages. Moreover, they have the shortest delay between action and system response, the effect of which, when the system is already in crisis, is to keep it in crisis. The effect is to 'clog up' the system during the crisis, with many non-co-operative acts taking place within a short period of time. This clogging up is not reflected at all in the analytical model, since the assumption of equal time intervals is in force. Hence, all the non-co-operative acts spawned by and in turn contributing to maintenance of crisis are 'spread out' in the analytical model, so it appears that the system spends most of its time in the crisis stage.

It is possible, however, to correct for these effects, and still remain within the assumptions of a Markov process (i.e., equal time intervals between the acts). The basic technique will be to call the actual transition a 'stage in itself.' For example, not only can the system be in non-crisis and pre-crisis, but it can also be in transition from non-crisis to pre-crisis, and vice versa. In order to build such stages into the model, we need associated probabilities of going from, say, crisis to 'transition to pre-crisis,' as well as probabilities of going from 'transition to pre-crisis' to pre-crisis itself. The needed stages are listed in table B.

TABLE B

Seventeen stages and pseudo-stages of expanded model

Stage number	Stage description
1	Non-crisis*
11	Transitional pseudo-stage from non-crisis to non-crisis
12	Transitional pseudo-stage from non-crisis to pre-crisis
2	Pre-crisis*
21	Transitional pseudo-stage from pre-crisis to non-crisis
22	Transitional pseudo-stage from pre-crisis to pre-crisis
23	Transitional pseudo-stage from pre-crisis to crisis
3	Crisis*
33	Transitional pseudo-stage from crisis to crisis
34	Transitional pseudo-stage from crisis to post-crisis
4	Post-crisis*
44	Transitional pseudo-stage from post-crisis to post-crisis
45	Transitional pseudo-stage from post-crisis to inter-crisis
5	Inter-crisis*
55	Transitional pseudo-stage from inter-crisis to inter-crisis
51	Transitional pseudo-stage from inter-crisis to non-crisis
52	Transitional pseudo-stage from inter-crisis to pre-crisis

* Indicates the same stage as in the previous model

Table B needs to be clarified. First, it should be noted that each transitional stage represents a non-zero element in table A. This is needed to bring the time element explicitly into the model and will be described below. Second, it should not be confusing that there are five pseudo-stages that lead to themselves. Note that stage 11 is a transition from non-crisis to non-crisis. Since a co-operative act during crisis means that the system will stay in non-crisis, and since there is 'waiting time' associated with co-operative acts, there will be some delay as the system moves 'from' non-crisis back 'to' non-crisis. The other five pseudo-stages which lead to themselves can be interpreted similarly.

The reason for creating such 'pseudo-stages' is as follows. The waiting times, as given by Pelowski in table 3, are deterministic, that is, after a certain amount of time the prescribed event will take place. It is possible, however, to interpret the waiting times as probabilistic, to make the assumption that if an event is scheduled to occur n units from now, then its probability of occurring in the next time unit is $1/n$. This is an admittedly simple assumption, but it provides the ability to bring time into the model. This is done first by assigning the previously found transition probabilities to the associated pseudo-stages. In other words, the probability (from table A) of staying in non-crisis was 0.556, and the probability of moving from non-crisis to pre-crisis was 0.444. We now say that the probability of going from non-crisis to pseudo-stage 11 is 0.556, and the probability of going from non-crisis to pseudo-stage 12 is 0.444. Second, the probability of moving out of the pseudo-stage to the appropriate 'real' stage is the reciprocal of the waiting time associated with the event that got the system into the pseudo-stage. (Since there is only one way of getting into any pseudo-stage, we maintain the validity of the Markov process which necessitates dependence on not more than one stage in the past.) The calculation of those waiting times is reasonably straightforward. First, we must calculate the effective average waiting time. This is different from that reported by Pelowski in that each pair of nations has a different probability of being the actors. The probability of the USA-USSR pair is 0.03, the probability of the TAI-PRC is 0.53, and the probability of either TAI-USSR or USA-PRC is 0.44. Thus, the effective average waiting time for two co-operative actions is 4.47; for two non-co-operative actions it is 2.95; for one co-operative and one noise-making it is 9.00; for one non–co-operative and one noise-making it is 11.03. These figures are consistently lower than those of table 3 because the least likely pair of nations (USA-USSR) consistently had the longest waiting time.

One problem of interpretation arises at this point. The model has been based on the idea that a single action creates the change in the state of the system, while the simulation was based on the idea that pairs of actions occurred, and jointly affected, the state of the system. Thus it becomes necessary to express a pair of actions as if it were a single one for the purposes of the model. If both actions are of the same type, there is no problem. But if, for example, one action is co-operative and the other in the pair is neutral, how is this to be interpreted? The model moves from one state to the next on the basis of a single action. While this can be handled in the simulation, the model needs the following kinds of assumptions: 1 / if both actions were the same, the action is directly interpretable; 2 / if one action was noise-making, the effective action is the other one (either non-co-operative or co-operative); 3 / if one action was co-operative and the other non-co-operative, the effect is noise-making (this point will be reconsidered below); 4 / the event (moving from one stage to a pseudo-stage) is considered to have occurred as a result of combinations of the a priori probabilities of all possible actions leading to the event. Those probabilities are multiplied by the reciprocals of the waiting times associated with the actions, and summed to form the effective probability of getting out of the pseudo-stage. For example, the only way a system could have arrived in stage 11 (pseudo-stage from non-crisis to non-crisis) is by a co-operative action occurring during a period of non-crisis. There are two possible co-operative action-pairs: a / both co-operative, or b / one co-operative and one noise-making. The probability of both sides being co-operative is 0.30 (since the probability of one side being co-operative is 0.6 and the other is 0.5); the probability of one side being co-operative and the other noise-making is 0.33 [(0.6 × 0.3) + (0.5 × 0.3)]. The probability of leaving a stage as a result of a joint co-operative action is the reciprocal of the waiting time of 4.47 or 0.224. The probability of leaving a stage as a result of one co-operative and one noise-making action is the reciprocal of that waiting time of 9.00 or 0.111. The weighted average, then, is:

Average probability of leaving stage 11 at next time interval

$$= \frac{0.3 \times 0.224 + 0.33 \times 0.111}{0.3 + 0.33}$$

$$= \frac{0.0674 + 0.0366}{0.063}$$

$$= 0.16$$

This then is the probability of leaving the pseudo-stage 11 in any given time period. Conversely, the probability of remaining in that pseudo-stage is 1.00 − 0.16, or 0.84.

To summarize the above, in the expanded model, the probabilities of going from a 'real' stage to a pseudo-stage are the same as the probabilities in the simple model, while the probabilities of leaving the pseudo-stage are functions of the waiting times associated with getting into the pseudo-stages. The transition matrix of the expanded model is presented in table C.

TABLE C

Transition probabilities associated with the seventeen-state model[a]

Sending states	Receiving states																
	1	11	12	2	21	22	23	3	33	34	4	44	45	5	55	51	52
1	0	55	45	0	0	0	0	0	0	0	0	0	0	0	0	0	0
11	16	84	0	0	0	0	0	0	0	0	0	0	0	0	0	0	0
12	0	0	88	12	0	0	0	0	0	0	0	0	0	0	0	0	0
2	0	0	0	0	20	55	25	0	0	0	0	0	0	0	0	0	0
21	12	0	0	0	88	0	0	0	0	0	0	0	0	0	0	0	0
22	0	0	0	9	0	91	0	0	0	0	0	0	0	0	0	0	0
23	0	0	0	0	0	0	83	17	0	0	0	0	0	0	0	0	0
3	0	0	0	0	0	0	0	0	90	10	0	0	0	0	0	0	0
33	0	0	0	0	0	0	0	25	75	0	0	0	0	0	0	0	0
34	0	0	0	0	0	0	0	0	0	86	14	0	0	0	0	0	0
4	0	0	0	0	0	0	0	0	0	0	0	50	50	0	0	0	0
44	0	0	0	0	0	0	0	0	0	0	.17	83	0	0	0	0	0
45	0	0	0	0	0	0	0	0	0	0	0	0	87	13	0	0	0
5	0	0	0	0	0	0	0	0	0	0	0	0	0	0	45	30	25
55	0	0	0	0	0	0	0	0	0	0	0	0	0	9	91	0	0
51	14	0	0	0	0	0	0	0	0	0	0	0	0	0	0	86	0
52	0	0	0	17	0	0	0	0	0	0	0	0	0	0	0	0	83
Fixed-point vector	2	7	7	3	5	17	4	7	21	5	1	4	5	1	6	3	2

[a] Numbers in cells are transition probabilities multiplied by 100 and rounded to the nearest integer. 'State' names are given in table B. Probabilities underlined are those of table A.

As is shown above, the transition probabilities of leaving the pseudo-stages are all below 0.5, and all but one below 0.25. This properly implies that the system spends a large portion of its time in the various pseudo-stages. An examination of the fixed-point vector associated with the 17 x 17 transition matrix bears this out. Only 14 per cent of the time is the system in the 'real' stages 1 through 5. On the other hand, the five 'self-directing pseudo-stages,' numbers 11, 22, 33, 44, 55, are the most popular states of the system, with a total of 54 per cent of the time.

The fixed-point vector can be interpreted from a comparison with the simple model. Since the pseudo-stages are merely constructs to enable the modeller explicitly to bring in the element of time, it would seem legitimate to say that when the system is in a pseudo-stage, it is really in the stage from which it came. Thus, stages 1, 11, and 12 can be combined; stages 2, 21, 22, and 23 can be combined, etc. The resulting vector is (0.16, 0.29, 0.33, 0.10, 0.12). When this is compared to the fixed-point vector of the simple model, one difference stands out: the system spends much more of its time in stages associated with pre-crisis and less with stages associated with crisis in the more complex model – the data are more like both the simulation and the referent system.

There is one difficulty with the above analysis. The main transition probabilities (table A) were calculated on the basis of an average probability: the action of either a member of the USA-TAI coalition, or the USSR-PRC coalition, would determine the next stage. In calculating transition probabilities associated with the pseudo-stages, however, joint probabilities were used. It would be somewhat more consistent if joint probabilities were used in both sets of transitions. Another analysis was performed using a different set of main transition probabilities: the joint probability of pairs of actions from each coalition. Five sets of joint probabilities were calculated (one for each stage) from Pelowski's table 2, and these are presented in table D.

Grouping the probabilities by action pairs is the next task, so that one of the three basic action types can determine the next transition. It

TABLE D

Joint probabilities of action at each crisis stage

| Action pair | Crisis stage | | | | |
	Non-crisis	Pre-crisis	Crisis	Post-crisis	Inter-crisis
Non-co-operative Non-co-operative	0.02	0.06	0.56	0.06	0.06
Non-co-operative Noise-making	0.09	0.27	0.23	0.13	0.23
Co-operative Co-operative	0.30	0.03	0.01	0.25	0.09
Co-operative Noise-making	0.33	0.23	0.03	0.25	0.27
Noise-making Noise-making	0.09	0.30	0.02	0.06	0.20
Co-operative Non-co-operative	0.17	0.11	0.15	0.25	0.15

is relatively straightforward to combine the categories of joint co-operation and co-operation-noise-making to form co-operation, and similarly for non-co-operation. Joint noise-making is also straightforward. The problem is how to interpret the last action pair: co-operation–non-co-operation. A first guess might be that the two would cancel each other out to create noise-making. An analysis was performed on this assumption. For the sake of common comparison, both the simple model and the model with waiting-times were calculated. The simple transition matrix is presented in table E, and the complex transition matrix is identical to that of table C, with the substitution of the new simple probabilities.

TABLE E

Simple transition probabilities for joint action with co-operative–non-co-operative pairs as noise-making

Sending stage	Receiving stage				
	Non-crisis	Pre-crisis	Crisis	Post-crisis	Inter-crisis
Non-crisis	0.63	0.37	0	0	0
Pre-crisis	0.26	0.41	0.33	0	0
Crisis	0	0	0.96	0.04	0
Post-crisis	0	0	0	0.50	0.50
Inter-crisis	0.36	0.29	0.35	0	0
Fixed-point vector	0.08	0.07	0.74	0.06	0.05

As can be seen, the fixed-point vector indicates that the system will spend three-quarters of its time in crisis, if the interpretation of co-operative–non-co-operative action pairs as noise-making is legitimate. This finding is reaffirmed upon examining the fixed-point vector of the seventeen-stage, complex model:

(0.02, 0.07, 0.05, 0.02, 0.03, 0.08, 0.03, 0.13, 0.39, 0.03, 0.01, 0.03, 0.04, 0.01, 0.03, 0.02, 0.01).

When grouped by 'sending stages' as in the previous example, the system spends 14 per cent of its time in non-crisis, 16 per cent in pre-crisis, 55 per cent in crisis, 8 per cent in post-crisis, and 7 per cent in inter-crisis. This again is more spread out than in the simple model but is substantially more crisis-prone than either the simulation or referent world would indicate.

It is, however, possible to reinterpret the co-operative–non-co-operative action pair. It is clear that if that pair were interpreted as a kind of non-co-operative act, the system would spend even more of its time in crisis. Similarly, if the action pair were interpreted as some kind of co-operative act, less of the time would be spent in crisis. The model was re-examined under the latter interpretation, and the simple transition probabilities are shown in table F.

TABLE F

Simple transition probabilities for joint action with co-operative–non-co-operative pairs as co-operative

Sending stage	Receiving stage				
	Non-crisis	Pre-crisis	Crisis	Post-crisis	Inter-crisis
Non-crisis	0.80	0.20	0	0	0
Pre-crisis	0.37	0.30	0.33	0	0
Crisis	0	0	0.81	0.19	0
Post-crisis	0	0	0	0.75	0.25
Inter-crisis	0.51	0.29	0	0	0.20
Fixed-point vector	0.38	0.13	0.25	0.20	0.06

A comparison of tables E and F show two major differences in the fixed-point vectors. First, the system spends substantially less of its time in crisis under the latter interpretation (down from three-quarters of its time to one-quarter). Second, the greatest increases were in the non-crisis and post-crisis stages. The fixed point vector for the seventeen-stage model

(0.06, 0.25, 0.09, 0.02, 0.06, 0.07, 0.04, 0.04, 0.09, 0.04, 0.03, 0.11, 0.05, 0.01, 0.02, 0.03, 0.01)

can also be combined by sending stage to the following

(0.40, 0.19, 0.17, 0.19, 0.07),

which is substantially different from either of the two models previously discussed. Again, no longer is 'crisis' the modal stage of the system. In fact, it is now less common than any stage except inter-crisis. It is clear that this model 'fits' the simulation and the referent data better than either of the two models previously considered.

SUMMARY

Based on insights gained from building and operating an event-based crisis simulation, it is possible to construct a related series of analytical models of the system under consideration. Three pairs of Markov chain models were created with transition probabilities based on the initial data for the simulation. Through a series of interpretations, a model which appears to 'fit' the simulation outputs and referent system data was created. The phenomenon under consideration was the percentage of time the system spends in each of the five stages of crisis, and by combining the likelihoods of three kinds of action – co-operative, non-co-operative, and neutral – with estimates of waiting time between stages, it is possible to find fixed-point vectors (final distributions of the five stages) which seem to match the simulation and referent system, at least with some face validity.

REFERENCES

KEMENY, JOHN G., J. LAURIE SNELL, and GERALD L. THOMPSON *Introduction to Finite Mathematics*. Englewood Cliffs, NJ: Prentice-Hall, 1957.
MC CLELLAND, CHARLES A., DANIEL P. HARRISON, WAYNE R. PHILLIPS, and ROBERT A. YOUNG 'The Communist Chinese Performance in Crisis and Non-crisis: Quantitative Studies of the Taiwan Straits Confrontations, 1950–1964,' Behavioral Sciences Group, Naval Ordinance Test Station, China Lake, California, 14 December 1965.
NAYLOR, THOMAS H., JOSEPH L. BALINTFY, DONALD S. BURDICK, and KONG CHU *Computer Simulation Techniques*. New York: Wiley, 1966.

PART FIVE

Man and man / computer simulations

Image and reality in simulated international systems*

It is always the image, not the truth, that immediately determines behavior.
KENNETH BOULDING

I   INTRODUCTION

The concept of 'image' has been discussed and used by numerous social scientists who are concerned with what might be called 'actor-oriented' analysis. It is a basic assumption in this field of reasoning that no individual is ever able to perceive objective reality. One always selects certain elements from the environment and then structures the elements into a

*   The project on which this report is based is a cross-cultural study of decision-making behaviour, initiated in 1966. Co-ordinating director was John Raser, Western Behavioral Sciences Institute, La Jolla, California. Central expenses of the project were in part covered by the US Office of Naval Research under contract number 00014-66-c0279. The local simulation runs in Oslo took place in January 1967. They were conducted and partly financed as a co-operative effort of the Institute of Peace and Conflict Research, Copenhagen, and the International Peace Research Institute, Oslo, with Anders Boserup and the author as co-directors. The US runs were conducted at the University of Oregon under the direction of John Raser.

I wish to thank the political science students who participated in the experiment with loyalty and enthusiasm and the PRIO staff members who in various ways assisted in the conducting of the Oslo runs.

A preliminary version of this report was presented to the Third Nordic Peace Research Conference, Orenäs, Sweden, 19–22 May 1968. It may be identified as PRIO publication 1–16.

coherent pattern of some kind. The organizing factor is what is usually called 'image.' A good definition of the image concept is the following: 'All the accumulated, organized knowledge that the organism has about itself and the world' (Holsti 1969, p. 544). Image thus emerges as a central concept in social behaviour on the personal level as well as on the organizational and the national level.

This paper is concerned with images held by decision-makers on the national level, using perceptual data generated during a simulation experiment. The analysis is to a large extent inspired by and partly based on Kenneth Boulding's stimulating discussion of the effects of images held at the national level on the relations and 'temperature' of the international system. In his article, Boulding concentrates on the role of images on the national level in particular. He identifies the nation as a complex, decision-making organization and argues that 'in a system in which decision-makers are an essential element, the study of the ways in which the image grows and changes, both of the field of choice and of the valuational ordering of this field, is of prime importance' (p. 423).

Boulding goes on to distinguish between 'the image of the small group of people who make the actual decision' (on behalf of their nation) and 'the image of the mass of ordinary people who are deeply affected by these decisions but who take little or no direct part in making them' (p. 423). He identifies the elite image as being of most direct importance to the understanding of a nation's major political decisions.

The problem of how to make the concept of image operational has been discussed by Sprout and Sprout who sum it up as follows:

> The first step in linking environmental factors to policy decisions is to find out how the given policy-maker, or policy-making group, conceives the milieu to be and how that unit interprets the opportunities and limitations implicit therein with respect to the ends to be accomplished. This task presents formidable difficulties. The task is to construct at second hand, from what the decision-maker says and does, a description of his image, or estimate, of the situation and his orientation to it (p. 49).

In the following an attempt will be made to discuss one way of empirical image analysis: by using data generated during a simulation experiment.

II PROJECT AND DATA

The project on which the present analysis is based represents an effort to gather data relevant to decision-making behaviour on a cross-national basis, through the use of InterNation Simulation. The data consist of records of behaviour and interpersonal perceptions gathered during two INS runs conducted in Norway and two in the US.[1] A 'standard' INS model with a simulated international system of eight nations was used.

The focus of this study, however, is not so much on the structure of the simulated world at various stages of the simulation as on how the players perceive and evaluate the structure, the events occurring during the course of a run, and their fellow players. We do not consider the worlds created by the simulation participants primarily as a more or less probable sample from a range of all possible international systems. Rather, our concern is with the simulated international system as a reflection of the participants' way of thinking and acting in politics in general – their political culture. Consequently problems of validity relating to the structure of the INS model are not essential for the present analysis. The most comprehensive discussion of validation problems in connection with simulation has been made by Harold Guetzkow (1968).

The test factor in this experiment is closely tied to the participants. Consequently, efforts were made to make the teams of players as comparable as possible concerning such factors as age, sex, and field of study (they were all students of political science).[2]

The data gathered during the four INS runs were endogenous as well as exogenous. Endogenous data are generated as a result of simulation activities, such as trade relations, investment and armaments, and patterns of communication. In a previous article (Ruge 1970) some of these data have been analysed to study the different perspectives on foreign

1 Originally researchers from five nations participated in the project: Japan, Mexico, Korea, Norway, and the US. However, because of a variety of difficulties only the data from two of the research teams were completed in time for inclusion in the present analysis. Further analysis, particularly on the Japanese data, is being planned. The planning conference was held in September 1966 and the runs completed in January/February 1967.

2 Norway: of the 48 participants (44 male and 4 female) 47 were political science students of an intermediary level (mellomfag), twenty to twenty-four years old. One was a sociology major with political science as a minor subject. In order to secure recruitment they had been told that participation in the simulation was compulsory. However, as these students in fact have no compulsory courses they did not believe this but seem to have registered mainly out of curiosity. They were allowed to choose the run which suited them best, but were assigned to nation and office on a random basis, immediately prior to the start of the first period. US: 48 political science majors at the third- and fourth-year university level, 45 men and 3 women. They were all students in a 'World Politics' course who signed up voluntarily, choosing the run in which they wanted to participate, but were assigned to nation and office at the end of orientation on a random basis. The present analysis is based on data from one-third of the participants: those performing as central decision-makers.

policy displayed by the participants from a small power (Norway) and a big power (US).

Exogenous data are attitude tests and other subjective data generated by having the participants fill in questionnaires before, during, or after the simulation. Such data are not directly related to activities in the simulation, but may perhaps be regarded as a kind of by-product. During the runs, at the end of each of the nine periods, the participants filled in an evaluation form. The purpose of this form was to record the players' reactions to and evaluation of internal and external developments in the simulated system during the last period. In addition they had to estimate the degree of friendly or hostile intentions on the part of each of the other nations towards their own during the previous period, as well as to state the intentions of their own nation towards each of the other seven. The data from the evaluation forms are the basis for the present discussion. Contrary to the previous analysis made on data from this cross-cultural simulation project (Ruge 1970), the nationality of participants is not used as an independent variable in this case – the perception data are pooled.

The purpose of setting up an experiment like the InterNation Simulation is, of course, to generate data on phenomena which are unobservable in the real world for one reason or another. In this case data on the images which the actors held of each other's intentions were simply produced by having the participants estimate the intentions towards them from each of the others. In this way the images can be studied directly, whereas in the real world, as mentioned above, image is an inferred construct. It is conceived of as an intervening factor between perception and decision. In this respect our experimental data represent an advantage over real data on perception, because they permit direct measurment of the images.

We shall make an attempt in this direction by reformulating some of the main arguments raised in Boulding's article into hypotheses. The hypotheses are then tested using perceptual data generated during the simulation runs.

The participants in the simulation are requested to evaluate their partners as well as to state their own intentions towards their partners. We have chosen to regard this as simple expressions of their image of the environment (evaluation of others) and of reality (their own stated intentions). By comparing these two measures we hope to be able to indicate which kinds of variables seem best suited as image determinants in the real world.

III HOSTILITY/FRIENDLINESS

In his discussion of effects of various kinds of images held by nations of themselves and of their environment, Boulding places a special emphasis on the hostility/friendliness dimension:

> At any one time a particular national image includes a rough scale of the friendliness or hostility of, or toward other nations. The relationship is not necessarily either consistent or reciprocal – in nation A the prevailing image may be that B is friendly, whereas in nation B itself the prevailing image may be one of hostility of B toward A; or again in both nations there may be an image of friendliness of A toward B but of hostility of B toward A (p. 426).

The above discussion of the hostility/friendliness of intentions among nations contains two different elements which in the following will be analysed separately: 1 / the intentions which nation A has towards B and vice versa, and 2 / the perception which A has of B's intentions and vice versa. If one wants to obtain some kind of 'measure of the overall friendliness or hostility of the system' (p. 427), one has to decide whether to look at stated intentions or at perceived intentions.

In his discussion Boulding does not explicitly distinguish between the self-images of A and B on the one hand and their images of the environment on the other. He suggests that the intentions which each of the members of an international system has towards the other system members may be placed on some kind of hostility/friendliness scale and inserted into a matrix of the following kind (figure 1).

He summed up the properties of this matrix as follows: 'The sum totals of the rows represent the overall friendliness or hostility of the nation at the head of the row; the sum totals of the columns represent the degree of hostility or friendliness *toward* the nation at the head of the column. The sum of either of these sums is a measure of the over-all friendliness or hostility of the system' (p. 427). However, this is the point at which the problem of perception arises. What the scores in the matrix indicate is the overall degree of friendliness or hostility of intentions from one nation in the system to another. The matrix contains no information on the degree to which the intentions are being adequately perceived and understood by the target nation.

The image which the matrix conveys is the image held by the actors (nations) about the other system members. This self-image, as it will be

Intentions to

	a	b	c
a	X		
b		X	
c			X

Intentions from

Figure 1 Type of matrix used to relate hostility/friendliness scales.

called in the following discussion, may or may not be transmitted and adequately received by the target nations. A different matrix would be needed in order to show how actors perceive intentions from other actors – in other words, their image of the environment.

This is not an attempt to discuss which of the two matrices is more 'realistic' – the one which shows scores of stated intentions or the one containing perceived intentions – but according to the reasoning referred to above, decisions and behaviour are closely related to one's perception or image of the environment. If the matrices are identical, then the intentions are being correctly perceived by the targets. If they differ, then it is probably more important to analyse the perception matrix than the intention one.

The problem of perception among actors in internation relations has been discussed by Robert Jervis, whose main concern is precisely misperception and the factors which contribute to it. His list of hypotheses of misperception contains a variety of possibilities for systematic empirical testing along the lines suggested here (Jervis 1968).

The following discussion is organized into three main parts: a / presentation and analysis of stated intentions of the simulation decision-makers in terms of their self-images; b / comparison of self-images with estimates of intentions (other images) and measure of the degree of misperception, if any; c / measure of the tendency to over- or underestimate degree of friendliness in terms of the direction of misperception.

IV STATED INTENTIONS AMONG SIMULATION DECISION-MAKERS

In order to establish a base-line for the analysis of image-related variables we shall first present 'reality' in the form of an expressed degree of friendliness of intentions towards other nations. The intentions were recorded on a seven-point Likert scale which runs from 'extremely hostile' (score 1) via 'neither hostile nor friendly' (score 4) to 'extremely friendly' (score 7). The scores presented in table 1 are mean scores for all nine periods of a run. The table does not distinguish between individual runs or between Norwegian and American respondents. An independent variable, alliance membership, distinguishes three categories: within alliances (six nation-pairs in each run); between alliances (nine nation-pairs + the pairs consisting of the two non-aligned nations); and the neutral nations versus the allied (twelve nation-pairs).

TABLE 1

Intention level and alliance membership among simulated nation-pairs

	1.0 – 3.0	3.1 – 4.0	4.1 – 5.0	5.1 – 6.0	6.1 – 7.0	Sum
Intrabloc	0	0	4	14	6	24
Interbloc	1	3	22	12	2	40
Bloc/Neutral	0	0	16	25	7	48
TOTAL	1	3	42	51	15	112

The distribution of intention scores on the H-F scale falls almost exclusively on the 'friendly' end, with a median score a little above 5 ('somewhat friendly'). Only four of the 112 scores fall below the neutral point of 4.[3]

Our scores support Boulding's assumption that there is a tendency for mutually friendly nations to form alliances (p. 427) insofar as they show a tendency for allied pairs to have friendly intentions towards each other when compared with interbloc pairs. However, such a finding does not reveal the causal direction of the relationship, because the nations are bloc members at the start of the simulation and presumably set their intention levels accordingly.[4]

3   However, the intention levels ranged from 'extreme hostility' to 'extreme friendliness' from period to period, reflecting quite well the type of events occurring during the simulation. Thus the whole scale of intention scores was used by the participants.
4   For a discussion of alliance-related behaviour in the simulate see 'Small-power versus Big-power Perspective of Foreign Policy' (Ruge 1971). The most

V   INTERNAL VERSUS EXTERNAL IMAGE
    COMPONENTS

Having stated the level of intended friendliness between actors in the
simulated system, the discussion now turns back to the problem of perception. The image which an actor has of any particular environment
consists of internal and external components. By internal components is
meant the collection of personality factors, internalized cultural and social
norms, and experience from previous similar situations which have been
accumulated in the mind of the actor. Internal image components could
also be termed self-based. By external image components is meant those
elements from the environment which are perceived and included in the
image. This section reports on an effort to find some empirical ways of
measuring the relative importance of external and internal components
of the image which the participants hold of one another.

   Experiments in social psychology have shown that persons who are
asked to evaluate others often make use of projective techniques. They
use their self-image as a frame of reference for interpreting their environment (Brown 1965). Presumably one knows oneself better than one
knows anything – or anyone – else. The function of a frame of reference
is precisely to bring new impressions into a familiar context, make them
consistent with the established image, and thus give them meaning to
oneself.

   At time 0, when a relationship is initiated, the actors have no accumulated experience in dealing with one another. At this point internal
factors will by definition play a decisive part in determining the actors'
perceptions of the others. To the extent that the actors are members of a
common group, be it a primary relationship, a nation, or a 'culture,' the
internal components of their mutual images will to a large extent be
identical. As the relationship develops, external factors should increasingly contribute to the image, thus making it more realistic, or accurate,
in an objective sense. If this were not the case no learning or socialization
would take place. However, with the lag and all the constant factors
which are inherent in an established image, it will never reach the level
of complete realism. A completely realistic image of the environment in
the sense that the total environment is reproduced with no distortions is
an impossibility. The function and purpose of an image is precisely to

significant thing in this connection was the difference between the Norwegian
and the US runs. A number of alliance changes were made by the Norwegians
and none by the US participants.

select, simplify and interpret the environment to the actor. Thus the tendency is for actors to prefer information which supports and strengthens their image and to reject or reinterpret information which might distort it. This tendency to cognitive and evaluative consonance contributes to the high level of stability over time which is an important characteristic of images.

We tried to construct a measure of the relative importance of internal and external determinants of images which the participants in the simulation held of their fellow players by comparing their answers to the questions recorded on an evaluation form where three different scales (labelled I, II, III in the appendix) gave us 1 / a measure of a given player's intentions towards another player, 2 / a measure of that player's perceptions of the other's intentions towards him, and 3 / a measure of the actual intentions of the other player. An image completely dominated by external factors is indicated by identical answers on scales II and III. On the contrary, the similarity of scores on scales I and II indicates that it is the image of the self which is projected on the environment.

To test the relative importance of these factors, the image scores (scale 2) were compared with the self-image (scale 1) and with reality (scale 3), respectively, for each of the eight simulated nations. The sum of scores for all nine periods was ranked for all three categories, and rank order correlations computed between the images on the one hand and self-image and reality on the other. By using rank correlations we are measuring not the players' ability to guess the correct intention scores from the others, but whether they could estimate correctly which of the others was most friendly, second most friendly etc.

The main reason for using rank correlations was that we wanted to be able to compare different sets of data. Amount of trade or communication, economic or military power, etc., cannot be compared with evaluation scores directly. By converting scores as well as behaviour and structural data into ranks, it became possible to run inter-correlations. The null hypothesis for this comparison of relative importance of image components is that there is no difference between self-based and environmental factors. Table 2 gives the distribution of rank correlation coefficients for self-intent/image and for image/reality respectively.

With $N = 7$, Spearman's *rho* has to be at least 0.71 in order to be significant at the 0.05 level, while the 0.01 level requires a correlation of at least 0.89. As correlations decrease below 0.70, the probability for accidental results increases. The distribution suggests that self-intent is more closely correlated with the way participants perceive their environ-

TABLE 2

Distribution of rank correlation coefficients for self-intent-image and image-reality for thirty-two simulation participants

magnitude of rho	Self-intent-image	Image-reality
−0.10 – 0	1	2
0.01 – 0.10	1	2
0.11 – 0.20	0	1
0.21 – 0.30	2	2
0.31 – 0.40	0	0
0.41 – 0.50	1	7
0.51 – 0.60	4	2
0.61 – 0.70	2	8
0.71 – 0.80	5	6
0.81 – 0.90	8	1
0.91 – 1.00	8	1
SUM	32	32

ment than reality. As many as twenty-one of the correlations for the first column are significantly higher than 0, while only eight of the second column are equally high.

In order to test whether the two distributions of correlation coefficients are significantly different, the Wilcoxon matched-pairs signed-ranks test was used (Siegel 1956, pp. 75–83).[5] The result was a value of $z = -3.3$, which has a probability of occurring of 0.0005. Thus the two sets of correlations are differently distributed. The participants have used themselves rather than external factors as a reference when asked to evaluate the others.

This of course will be the case the more similar the perceiver and his object. A young boy is unlikely to attribute elements from his own self-image to the object when asked to evaluate an old woman whom he does not know well as a person. Chances are that differences in background are seen as more important than they in fact are, and serve to blur the factors which any two human beings have in common. In our experimental situation, however, with actors all belonging to the same subgroup of students roughly the same age, etc., a transfer from self-image to other-image should be rather common.

Actors in real-life situations who face each other for the very first time, and who have no experience of what to expect and how to behave in that particular situation, will still have some kind of experience from similar occasions, perhaps with holders of the same status, which can

5   Seigel notes that such a test requires ordinal measurement of differences both within pairs and also between pairs. We have assumed that it is meaningful to consider rank correlation coefficients as ordinal data.

help them along. This cumulative experience in turn becomes a part of the internal component of their image, as noted above.

In the artificial simulation situation with the absence of a significant past, projective evaluation will obviously be more prominent than in real-life relationships. Consequently projection should be more easily identified than in the much more complex referent system. However, we assume that the difference between the experimental and the real-life situation is merely a matter of degree, not of substance. Further general social psychological research confirms the tendency among our simulation participants to use their self-image as a basis for judging others. In a discussion on 'contact with the object,' William A. Scott sums up the results of interpersonal perception studies as follows:

... interaction between two people leads to increasing correspondence between each person's image of himself and of the other's image of him. In fact, one would suppose that interpersonal interaction can be stable and mutually rewarding only insofar as this condition develops with respect to attributes relevant to the interaction. Such an increasing consensus is only in part due to changes in one person's impression of the other. It often happens that, in crucial respects, one's own self-image is molded by the reactions of those around him, which in turn are based on *their* view of him (p. 94).

Roger Brown discusses 'determinants of accuracy in response-predicting' and concludes that three factors increase the likelihood of realistic perception of others: projection, knowledge of (the perceived) group, and response sets. It seems that our findings result from projection rather than from group knowledge, although the participants had a great deal of information available about their fellow players. This response set factor will be discussed in connection with the tendency to consistent under- or overestimation.

The results in table 2 are based on the sums of scores over all the nine periods of a simulation run. They convey no information on whether duration and contact had any effect on the relative importance of internal and external image components. As the simulation develops, the contacts established and the communication between the nations should provide the participants with better clues to realistic perception of each other. Towards the end of a run's intensive activity, after the exchange of hundreds of written communications, one would expect the decision-makers to be quite well informed about the behaviour of their fellow players. They should be better equipped to make realistic estimates than at the start of the experiment. The hypothesis in this case is that the image scores at the end should be more closely correlated with reality than at the beginning.

To measure learning effects over time during the simulation we used the estimate scores from the two first and the two last periods of each run. The sum of scores for two periods were used to cancel accidental deviations in a single period. Table 3 shows the development from beginning to end for both sets of correlations.

TABLE 3

Distributions of rank correlation coefficients (*rho*) for self-intent-image and image-reality for thirty-two simulation participants in periods 1 and 2 and periods 8 and 9

magnitude of *rho*	self-intent-image		image-reality	
	1 and 2	8 and 9	1 and 2	8 and 9
−0.39 – 0.30	0	0	0	1
−0.29 – 0.20	0	0	1	0
−0.19 – 0.10	0	0	0	0
−0.09 – 0	0	1	0	2
0.01 – 0.10	1	0	2	0
0.11 – 0.20	0	0	1	1
0.21 – 0.30	1	1	2	3
0.31 – 0.40	1	1	3	2
0.41 – 0.50	0	3	4	7
0.51 – 0.60	3	4	2	1
0.61 – 0.70	5	2	5	4
0.71 – 0.80	7	8	7	8
0.81 – 0.90	4	3	4	3
0.91 – 1.00	10	9	1	0
SUM	32	32	32	32

Our primary concern in this table is with the two right-hand columns. Note that the number of correlations significantly different from 0 does not increase from the start of the experiment to the end. There are twelve correlations above 0.71 in periods 1 and 2 and eleven in the last two periods. There does not seem to be a change in the predicted direction. The Wilcoxon test used to test significance between the two distributions gave a value of $z = -0.4$, whose probability of occurring is 0.34. A hypothesis of a difference existing between the two distributions is not supported. There is no tendency for the participants in the simulation to make more realistic estimates of each other at the close of the experiment than at the beginning.

But what about the self-centred perspective? Does it change over time? As table 3 shows (in the two left columns) there is a high proportion of significant correlations at the beginning as well as at the end of the experiment. This indicates persistence of the established self-image as a yardstick. This time the hypothesis states that there should be no significant difference between the two distributions. The test yielded a z-value of -1.14, which has a probability of 0.13. The hypothesis of self-image stability cannot be rejected. There is no evidence of a decrease in self-image dominance as a result of time alone.

Does this self-image dominance hold up not only over time, but also during major changes in the actors or their environment? 'Actor' in this connection may mean 'self' as well as 'other.' Changes in the situation or position of either of the two partners in a relationship may produce changes in their image of each other, or of themselves. Our results so far suggest that only a change in the self-image will in turn lead to actors' perceiving their environment differently.

Structural characteristics of the simulation nations which might serve as indicators of the actor-based variables are military power, economic position, and alliance membership. Changes in the environment can be measured on communication and trade patterns, changes in alliance membership, etc. However, when tested against image stability none of these factors appeared to have any significant effect. The changes which took place in the actors or in the system around them have not been perceived as important enough to override the primacy of the self-image.

A study of interpersonal perception in international relations by Dina Zinnes, 'Expression and Perception of Hostility in Prewar Crisis, 1914,' relates to the theme discussed in this chapter. Using as data the documents circulating among top decision-makers in the major European powers involved in the outbreak of the first world war, she found positive correlations between perceptions of hostility (from others) and expressions of hostility in general. Perception of hostility from a specific actor was also positively correlated with expressions of hostility towards that actor. In other words, a decision-maker who perceives himself to be the object of hostility from another decision-maker will in turn express hostility towards the other party. However, Zinnes did not find empirical support for the related hypotheses that a / expressed hostility will be adequately perceived by the object, and that b / expressed hostility will lead to the object expressing hostility back. The findings of Zinnes seem to support our results on the importance of the internal components of an image.

If an actor x feels persecuted or threatened, he is likely to act on the basis of his perception. If his behaviour is not adequately perceived by his object y, then y's response may be very different from what x expected.

But it may also be that x, in his need for consonance, misperceived y's behaviour. Other studies based on the 1914 crisis have shown that self-based perceptions are more common the higher the amount of stress in the situation (Holsti, North, and Brody 1968).

Dina Zinnes has also compared her own analysis of the 1914 data and the data produced in Brody's simulation experiment. She concludes from the comparative analysis that 'a decision-maker's perception of a hostile environment is a function of ... the international alliance structure and the extent to which the decision-maker received hostile communications.' Further, 'there are at least three variables that can account for a state's hostile behavior: its perception of a hostile environment, its receipt of hostile messages, and the international alliance system' (Zinnes 1966, p. 495).

Brody's and Zinnes's results place more importance on expressed hostility as related to perception of hostility than our data do. It may be that in their analysis the focus is specifically on hostility, while our perspective has been on the influence of external events in general. Further analysis is needed to understand the amount of impact different kinds of external events will have on actors' images of others.

Our discussion of image components will be concluded with the following tentative hypothesis: self-based image components are more important in determining perception of the environment the more structurally similar the object is thought to be, and the more ambiguous the information from the environment.

VI   PARANOIDS AND BLUE-EYED OPTIMISTS:
     DIRECTION OF MISPERCEPTION

In the previous section it was shown that the estimates of intention tended to be more influenced by the participants' self-image than by external factors. We were able to observe this because the intention scores given by the participants differed. Had they all been on the same level, the correlation coefficients for self-image/other-image and for other-image/reality would also have been of the same magnitude. In other words, the matrices of intentions and perceptions would have been identical.

In this section the direction of misperceived intentions will be explored. In his article, Boulding places a particular emphasis on what he sees as a destructive tendency in international relations: 'Most nations seem to feel that their enemies are more hostile toward them than they are toward their enemies. This is a typical paranoid reaction: the nation visualizes itself as surrounded by hostile nations toward which it has only the nicest and friendliest of intentions' (p. 426). Boulding outlines the 'paranoid' reaction as an exception to a presumed general tendency to consistency and reciprocation between national images. He thinks, in particular, of the way in which enemies by definition perceive each other. Accordingly, we should expect that a nation which feels hostile towards other nations, will perceive the object of its hostility to be even more hostile towards itself.

To test this hypothesis in our simulated system, 'estimate-intention difference scores' for each nation were developed. The sum of intention scores, over all nine periods, of one nation towards each of the others was substracted from the sum of estimate scores recorded by each of the target nations towards the first nation. A negative E–I difference score means that the 'intending nation' is considered less friendly than it professes to be. Conversely, a nation which is considered more friendly than it actually is will get a positive difference score. Difference scores between +3 and −3 were classified as 'zero,' because within their limits the estimates were considered to be realistic. Table 4 presents the distribution of pessimistic, realistic, and optimistic estimates for different intention levels. 'Optimistic' stands for the number of times a simulated nation was seen as more friendly than it actually was (positive E–I differences score); 'pessimistic' records the number of negative E–I scores. The vertical variable shows the distribution of stated intentions on the different levels of the hostility-friendliness scale. There are fifty-six units for each run, since each of the eight participants estimated the seven others. The intentions are mean scores for all nine periods.

TABLE 4

Intention level and intention estimates recorded by thirty-two participants during four simulation runs

	Optimistic	Realistic	Pessimistic	SUM
1.0 – 4.0	7	8	3	18
4.1 – 5.0	22	33	27	82
5.1 – 6.0	3	38	56	97
6.1 – 7.0	1	4	22	27
TOTAL	33	83	108	224

Looking at the marginals first, the sum column shows that on the whole the participants have rather friendly intentions towards each other. The median score is 5 ('fairly friendly'). The 'total' row shows that the great majority of misperceived intentions are on the pessimistic side. Only 15 per cent of the estimates are too optimistic.

The immediate technical reason for the difference in the distribution pattern of estimates compared to intentions is that the participants have made use of a smaller part of the scale when estimating other nation's intentions than when recording their own intentions towards each other. They have hesitated to believe that their partners had less friendly intentions towards them, as well as to make extremely optimistic guesses. But, as noted above, there is a striking difference between the proportion of optimistic versus pessimistic estimates. The general direction of misperception is towards scepticism.[6]

The large group of pessimistic estimates contains the special cases of paranoia which are characterized by a tendency to perceive one's environment as being more hostile than oneself. A pessimistic estimate clearly involves a certain element of distrust, and hence it could be argued, as stated in Boulding's hypothesis, that this will particularly be the case between enemies. However, the distribution in table 4 suggests that the opposite is actually the case. The majority of pessimistic estimates are given to nations which feel very friendly towards their partners, while the optimistic estimates are located on the lower end of the friendliness scale. The realistic estimates are more evenly distributed between high- and low-intention friendliness.

Before discarding the hypothesis predicting a positive correlation between hostility and paranoia, however, we want to study the circumstances under which a negative discrepancy between actual and perceived intentions can occur, because not all such instances can be said to result from paranoid tendencies on behalf of certain actors.

VII SENDERS AND RECEIVERS OF DISTRUST:
     MISPERCEIVERS AND MISPERCEIVED

It seems fruitful to distinguish between actors who tend to distrust their environment in general and those who are the objects of general distrust from the environment. Only the first type could be called paranoid. This would be the actor who does not differentiate within his environment out of cautiousness and suspicion. In the simulation we have defined as 'paranoids' those participants who estimate pessimistically five or more of the seven others. There is a total of nine such cases out of the thirty-two

6   Preliminary analysis of a part of the Japanese data suggests that there may be
    a higher frequency of optimistic estimates among the participants in the
    Japanese runs. Of 56 nation-pairs in these two runs, 3 were optimistic. Previous
    pair analysis of the Norwegian and the US runs showed no optimistic pair
    relations. These figures were not directly comparable with the figures in table
    4, which are based on individual nations.

possible in our four runs. These nine simulated nations made fifty-one pessimistic estimates, or about half of the total. Of these fifty-one, thirty occurred with the estimating actor noting his own intention to be lower than score 5. According to table 4, there are exactly thirty cases of pessimistic estimates coupled with average intention scores below 5. The hypothesis based on Boulding's discussion cannot be rejected.

This result also ties in well with the self-based perception of the environment demonstrated in the previous section. The paranoia hypothesis sees the actor as expressing hostility because he perceives hostility. The self-image hypothesis assumes that an actor with hostile intentions will perceive his environment the same way in order to preserve his established image. However, there is no reason to assume a one-way causal relationship.

The misperceived

The objects of general distrust are different from the paranoids. They are the victims of low credibility, not being able to convince their environment of their friendly intentions. The reasons for lack of credibility may be of two kinds: active or passive. In the active case a nation is being distrusted because 'deeds speak louder than words.' The nation in this category may conduct a policy which leads its environment to estimate it as less friendly than it sees itself (and presumably would like others to see it as well). The relationship between a large number of powerful nations and their satellites (us–Latin America, ussr–Czechoslovakia) may illustrate this phenomenon.[7]

However, distrust has been defined in a relative manner as a difference between two sets of scores. Therefore a nation may experience low credibility not only because of hostile behaviour, but as a result of its own unrealistically high levels of intentions. For instance, in the simulated system there are actors who list almost uniformly maximum intention scores towards all the others but who through inactivity, fail to convince their partners of this intention.

We would expect passive rather than active low credibility to be more frequent in an interaction system, because active behaviour will be estimated differently by different members of the system. An act appearing friendly to one may look like (and of course actually be) a threat to another. Non-behaviour, or passivity, will probably be more consensually

---

7 The problem of deception in international relations is discussed in detail by Robert Jervis (1970).

estimated as either potentially friendly or hostile. Whether such an actor is estimated positively or negatively by others, may possibly be related to how much power he possesses – or how powerful the environment perceives him to be.

Another reason why active low credibility occurs rarely is precisely the fact that real intentions are communicated through activity. The environment thus gets cues on which to pin their estimates, and the result should be E–I difference scores closer to 0. The passive interaction partner provides the environment solely with his initial image. In the simulation, the initial information which the participants get of their own and the other nations comes from the 'World History,' a source of information which is almost solely concerned with struggle, conflict, and war as characteristics of the internation relations in the simulated system.

It should also be pointed out that this pattern occurs especially when maximum intention scores are used (6 and 7). It follows that extremely friendly behaviour would be needed to induce decision-makers to make sufficiently optimistic estimates to obtain a zero E–I difference score. The failure to make adequate guesses of intentions as high as 6 or 7 is one reason why low credibility is so frequent in friendly relationships. However, there is a total of eight actors in the simulated system who have received distrust from five or more of the others. Of these only two have listed such high intention scores throughout the run to all other partners. The rest differentiate between actors in addition to giving fluctuating scores from one period to another. However, they are unable to convey their self-image to the others.

The misperceivers

How do low-credibility actors estimate their partners' intentions? It has been postulated above that it is primarily a lack of contact with the environment which leads to unrealistic self-upgrading. According to the self-image hypothesis, lack of such contact will cause internal components of the image held of others to dominate. In other words, the low-credibility actors should be the ones who have a tendency to overestimate others. Table 4 shows that there are very few overestimates occurring in the simulated systems – an average of only 1.0 per actor. However, the eight low-credibility actors made an average of 2.3 overestimates. They see themselves as friendly and perceive the world in the same way. In Norwegian political jargon this pattern is called 'blue-eyed optimism.'

While the low-credibility actors overestimate the friendliness of others, the paranoids, who consistently distrust others, are often seen as more friendly than they actually feel. Overestimates cluster around them: the average number of overestimates given to the paranoid actors is 2.3 compared to the general level of 1.0.

The analysis so far indicates that wrong estimates or misperceptions are closely correlated with the self-image held by the actors. Those who have been defined as 'paranoids' and who see the other members of the system as more hostile than they are also have rather unfriendly intentions towards the others. On the other end of the intention scale are the 'low-credibility' actors. They picture themselves as more friendly than the environment is willing or able to accept and they tend to perceive their co-actors as more friendly than they profess to be. Thus the paranoia hypothesis becomes a special case of the self-image hypothesis. We can thus explain the misperceptions at the lower as well as at the upper end of the hostility-friendliness intention scale. However, when Boulding describes the paranoid nation as one which 'visualizes itself as surrounded by hostile nations toward which it has only the nicest and friendliest of intentions' (p. 426), he seems to contradict his former postulate of paranoia as a pattern of perception peculiar to relations between enemies. Our data do not support his interpretation.

The previous section concluded with a hypothesis on the conditions under which an actor's self-image will dominate his perception of the environment. Here two patterns of misperception have been analysed, and they have both been found to be related to the way the actors picture themselves. This apparent consonance between image components and paranoid/optimist estimates leads to another hypothesis: actors who record unrealistically pessimistic and/or optimistic estimates of other actors will also have a close correlation between their self-image and their perception of others. The hypothesis was tested by the Mann-Whitney U-test, which indicates whether two independent samples have been drawn from the same population (Siegel 1956, pp. 116–27). The result was a lower correlation between paranoids/optimists and self-based estimates than for the rest of the actors, but the difference is too small to be significant. Thus the hypothesis is not supported or clearly rejected by our data. More complex models are needed to understand the relationships between the structural factors in the environment, the actors' self-images, and the way the environment is perceived.

VIII IMAGES OF THE SIMULATED SYSTEM

The two previous sections concentrated on the perceptual relations between pairs of actors. In this section the focus is on the way participants

312   Mari Holmboe Ruge

perceived the entire simulated system, in particular the effect of events in
the system.

Again scores from the evaluation form make up the dependent variable. The answers to question IV which asked the participants to estimate
the 'degree of tension or co-operation in the world in general during the
last period' shows that the tension/co-operation dimension is closely
related to the hostility/friendliness dimension on which the participants
estimated their own and each of the others' intentions. Let us try to
compare the scores on the two dimensions, in order to show the way in
which self-image influences the participants' perception of events in the
system, even though we cannot this time measure the effect of self-image
on perception, as it was done in the two previous sections. The reason
for this impossibility is that we have no independent information on which
events may have influenced the actors in their estimates. We can, however,
infer from our general knowledge of the simulation and from the inspections of the changes in score levels, that the participants in the simulation
tend to interpret the state of the entire system in terms of their own
situation. Again the actors' self-image seems to be a major factor. Decision-makers whose simulated nations had great problems saw the environment as very conflict-filled. On the other hand the optimist who started
a disarmament on his own saw a world which was much more co-operative
than it appeared to any of the other participants at that time.

IX   CONCLUSION

Our simulation observations are supported by studies made in the real
world, especially our major finding on the predominance of subjective
actor-related over structural factors as determinants in decision-making.
The stability of the strategic image of John Foster Dulles has been demonstrated by Finlay, Holsti, and Fagen (1967). Philip Burgess (1967), who
analysed public policy statements in order to relate the 'strategic image'
held by the two Norwegian foreign ministers during the nine-year period
1940-9 to subsequent policy choices, found that the major changes in
Norway's foreign-policy orientation, from an essentially neutral position
at the outbreak of the second world war to the decision to join NATO in
1949 were the result not of modification in established images held by
particular politicians, but were the result of the 'substitution of decision-
makers'.

APPENDIX

Evaluation form

Hostility/friendliness scale

1 extremely hostile
2 very hostile
3 fairly hostile
4 neither hostile nor friendly

5 fairly friendly
6 very friendly
7 extremely friendly

Write zero in boxes corresponding to own nation

I   Other nations' present intentions towards this nation

LA	UA	ERGA	INGO	OMNE	UTRO	RENA	SORO

II   Estimate of how other nations see intentions of this nation towards them

LA	UA	ERGA	INGO	OMNE	UTRO	RENA	SORO

III   This nation's present intentions towards other nations

LA	UA	ERGA	INGO	OMNE	UTRO	RENA	SORO

IV   Degree of tension or co-operation in the world in general during the last period:

1   extreme tension
2   much tension
3   some tension
4   neither tension nor co-operation
5   some co-operation
6   much co-operation
7   extreme co-operation

REFERENCES

BOULDING, KENNETH 'National Images and International Systems,' in James Rosenau, ed. *International Politics and Foreign Policy*. New York: Free Press, 1969.
BROWN, ROGER 'Determinants of Accuracy in Response-predicting,' *Social Psychology*. New York: Free Press, 1965.

BURGESS, PHILIP M. *Elite Images and Foreign Policy Outcomes: A Study of Norway.* Columbus: Ohio State University Press, 1967.

FINLAY, DAVID J., OLE R. HOLSTI, and RICHARD R. FAGEN *Enemies in Politics.* Chicago: Rand McNally, 1967.

GUETZKOW, HAROLD 'Some Correspondences between Simulations and Realities,' in Morton Kaplan, ed. *New Approaches to International Relations.* New York: St. Martin's Press, 1968.

HOLSTI, OLE R. 'The Belief System and National Images: A Case Study,' in James Rosenau, ed. *International Politics and Foreign Policy.* New York: Free Press, 1969.

HOLSTI, OLE R., ROBERT C. NORTH, and RICHARD BRODY 'Perception and Action in the 1914 Crises,' in David Singer, ed. *Quantitative International Politics.* New York: Free Press, 1968.

JERVIS, ROBERT 'Hypotheses on Misperception' in James Rosenau, ed. *International Politics and Foreign Policy.* New York: Free Press, 1969.

– *The Logic of Images in International Relations.* Princeton: Princeton University Press, 1970.

KELMAN, HERBERT 'Social Psychological Approaches to the Study of International Behaviour' in Herbert Kelman, ed. *International Behaviour.* New York: Holt, Rinehart and Winston, 1965.

RUGE, MARI HOLMBOE *Decision-makers as Human Beings: An Analysis of Perception and Behaviour in a Cross-cultural Simulation Experiment.* University of Oslo, Institute of Political Science, 1970. (Mimeographed.)

– 'Small-power versus Big-power Perspective on Foreign Policy,' *Proceedings from the Third IPRA General Conference, Karlovy Vary 1969.* Van Gorcum, Assen. PRIO publication number 1–14, 1971.

SCOTT, WILLIAM A. 'Psychological and Social Correlates of International Images' in Herbert Kelman, ed. *International Behaviour.* New York: Holt, Rinehart and Winston, 1965.

SIEGEL, SIDNEY *Non-parametric Statistics for the Behavioral Sciences.* New York: McGraw-Hill, 1956.

SPROUT, HAROLD and MARGARET SPROUT 'Environmental Factors in the Study of International Politics,' in James Rosenau, ed. *International Politics and Foreign Policy.* New York: Free Press, 1969.

ZINNES, DINA 'The Expression and Perception of Hostility in Prewar Crisis: 1914,' in David Singer, ed. *Quantitative International Politics.* New York: Free Press, 1968.

– 'A Comparison of Hostile Behaviour of Decision-makers in Simulate and Historical Data,' *World Politics,* 18, 3 (April 1966), pp. 474–502.

PAUL SMOKER

International
processes simulation:
a description

I   INTRODUCTION

a   *Comparison of INS and IPS*

The International Processes Simulation (IPS), like the InterNation Simulation (INS), incorporates theoretical assumptions abstracted from literature relevant to inter and intranational relations. National characteristics such as the nature of the political system, are assumed to influence international characteristics, such as alliance structure. Similarly, international characteristics, such as 'balance of power,' are assumed to influence national characteristics, such as national security (Guetzkow *et al.* 1963, pp. 126). These theories used in INS have been retained in IPS, either in their original form as in the case of the programmed assumption concerning probability of a revolution being successful should one occur (Guetzkow *et al.*, 1963, pp. 131), or in a revised form as in the case of national security. A significant difference between INS and IPS concerns an additional theoretical model that is used to define the central focus of IPS. Major structural features such as an international cultural and economic system are included in IPS in such a way that the resulting simulation is consistent with modern theories about global society.

The fact that this metatheory adopts a Parsonian viewpoint is secondary to the general correspondence of the resulting simulation model with modern theoretical positions concerning international relations (Alger 1968, Galtung 1967). These adopt a multilevel, systemic, multientity position far removed from traditional balance of power theories. They operate through time on many levels, including international, national, and transnational, and incorporate individuals, nations, international corporations, international governmental and non-governmental organizations.

b   A Parsonian model

The model used (Smoker 1967) takes as its starting point an interpretation of national political systems by Karl Deutsch (Deutsch 1964), who used a theoretical framework developed by Talcott Parsons for the analysis of social systems (Parsons 1951). He argues that to a first approximation the four basic requirements of a social system suggested by Parsons – namely, pattern maintenance, adaptation, goal attainment, and integration – can, at the national level, be equated with specific subsystems. At the national level the nation can be viewed as individuals and groups who are mainly responsible for pattern maintenance through activities such as practising cultural values and providing labour, a governmental subsystem mainly responsible for goal attainment of the nation, an economy mainly responsible for adaptation, and a cultural subsystem responsible for social integration.

While Deutsch was not concerned with international relations in his interpretation, it is possible to extend this theoretical position in the following way. A nation-state system is for our purposes defined as a system where interaction between nations is primarily an interaction between goal attainment subsystems; a classical interpretation of this is power politics (Schwartzenberger 1964, Morgenthau 1960). There is, by definition, no integrative subsystem between nations in such a situation. The situation resembles a zero-sum game where might is right. A nation-state system for a three-nation world is illustrated in figure 1. Interaction between subsystems, represented by squares, is shown by arrows. This system defines nation-state interaction as motivated purely by goal attainment subsystems.

Much of the recent international relations literature speaks of perceived worlds made up primarily of nations.[1] But it is possible to construct models of the world containing other behavioural entities (Haas 1964).

---

1   It is easy to confuse models of the world with reality. It can be argued that science will never know what reality is, but will just produce models of reality which are scientists' perceptions. There are many possible perceptions of a reality which can all be behaviourally consistent.

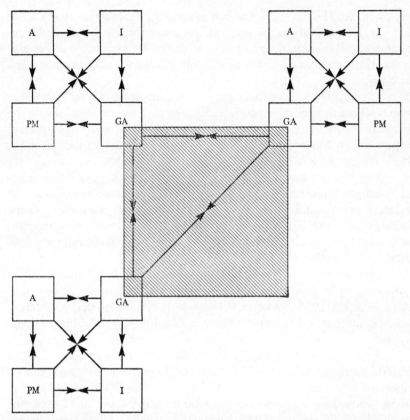

Figure 1 A nation-state system. A – adaptive subsystem; I – integration subsystem; PM – pattern maintenance subsystem; GA – goal attainment subsystem. The shaded area represents a nation-state system.

In addition to nations, a model might include international governmental organizations, international non-governmental organizations, international corporations, and various subnational entities. Against this background, it is possible to extend Parson's framework still further to define a model international system so that:

1   The pattern maintenance function may be characterized by individuals and families throughout a model international system. The individuals might be referred to as 'international man' and may represent, at present, a tiny minority in the actual world system. While the number is irrelevant for the theoretical purpose of constructing an international system's model as defined, international man is increasingly making his

presence felt. He may work for international governmental organizations like the United Nations, for any of the more than two thousand non-governmental organizations,[2] or as an executive for international corporations. He is even to be found in the entertainment and communications business.[3]

2   The adaptive subsystem might be represented roughly by an international economic system, which includes international corporations. In the world of the future these corporations may play an increasingly important role. General Motors' sales exceeded the gross national product of the Netherlands and one hundred other countries in 1965.[4]

3   The goal attainment subsystem might be represented by an international government. While some organs of the UN are concerned with cultural, educational, or social matters – for example, UNESCO – others, such as the General Assembly and the Security Council, are concerned with world politics and might be seen as performing an international goal attainment function.[5]

4   The international integrative subsystem may be characterized in world affairs by cultural activities of some non-governmental organizations (Smoker 1965, Brogden 1966, Angell 1965) and certain international conferences. The same position is taken in the model international system.

An international system is represented pictorially in figure 2. At a general level the defined nation-state and international systems can be regarded as extreme cases of a world system. This is shown in figure 3. Here, when the international component is insignificant, there exists the extreme case of a nation-state system and, when the nation-state system is insignificant, the extreme case of a defined international system. Figure 3

2   Details of international governmental and non-governmental activities are given in *The Yearbook of International Associations*, and the monthly publication, *International Associations*, both published by the Union of International Associations, Brussels.

3   Apart from individual globetrotters, such as international journalists, holidayers and students, there have been entertainers with mass international following giving them the status of international man, for example, the Beatles, Bob Dylan, Joan Baez, and Judy Collins.

4   It has been estimated that by the year 1975, through international mergers, overseas investment and assorted practices, three hundred corporations will control 75 per cent of all industrial assets. For details of international businesses, see *Fortune Magazine, World Businesses*. Recently international business has received increasing attention from international relations theorists.

5   Every international organization has some international aspects, some are goal attainment and others not. International organizations can be placed on a political (goal attainment) non-political (integrative) scale. This has been done elsewhere using empirical data (Smoker 1965ii).

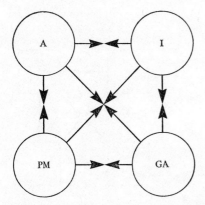

Figure 2 An international system. A – adaptive subsystem; I – intergrative subsystem; PM – pattern maintenance subsystem; GA – goal attainment subsystem.

illustrates a theoretical framework for the overall design of IPS and also provides a basis for constructing important substructures within IPS. The shifting mix of international and nation state in this model[6] world system are likely to be critical. The nation state and international components may be equal in size, but behaviour of a model world system in which both are small is likely to differ from that in which both are large.

Two interpretations of figure 3 have been used in experiments conducted with IPS. One interpretation is nearer to nation state as defined and is called international processes simulation (Nation State). The other includes a significant international component and is called international processes simulation (International). Figure 4 illustrates major structural requirements of nation state and international versions of IPS.

In fact many other alternative worlds could be constructed by researchers or educators by adjusting parameters in the programmed part of IPS and creating an appropriate data base. Other experiments with IPS could use alternative interpretations of this general model. In order to satisfy these structural requirements some other innovations have been introduced, for example, private citizens, independent corporations, a new economic system, and full-time international organization delegates. These and other structural additions to INS are described below.

6   The term, model, can be used as a noun meaning representation, as an adjective implying perfection, and as a verb meaning to demonstrate. It is used in the text to imply all of these meanings. It tries to represent states, objects, and events, is idealized and simplified to include only those propositions considered relevant to perceived reality, and attempts to show what the perceived reality is like.

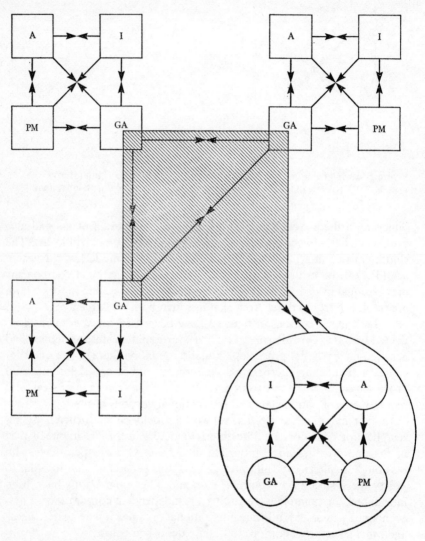

Figure 3 A world system. A – adaptive subsystem; I – integrative subsystem; PM – pattern maintenance subsystem; GA – goal attainment subsystem.

FUNCTIONAL SUBSYSTEM	VARIABLE	INTERNATIONAL PROCESSES SIMULATION	
		Nation State	*International*
Nation state goal attainment	Nation size (six nations)	Relatively small	Relatively large
Nation state goal attainment	Military power	Just conventional forces. No nuclear nations	Four large nuclear nations. One potential nuclear nation
International and national adaptation	Corporation size and structure (five corporations)	Relatively small. All but one national to begin with (factories all in one nation)	Relatively large. Four international, one national to begin with
International adaptation	International trade	Relatively little to begin with	Relatively much to begin with
International goal attainment	International governmental organization	None at start of simulation	Full time international governmental organization at start of simulation
International Integrative	International non-governmental activity	None scheduled at start of simulation	Regularly scheduled non-governmental meetings at start of simulation

Figure 4 Major structural differences between two model world types.

II STRUCTURAL CHANGES IN IPS

a Introduction

The structural changes in IPS relative to INS have been determined by the theoretical perspectives described above. INS represents a world system using nations and an international governmental organization (Guetzkow *et al.* 1963, p. 107). It consists of components at three levels, that is, individuals (decision-makers), groups (nations), and supragroups (government alliances and international organizations). IPS incorporates the same three levels, each level undergoing expansion and greater differentiation.

At the international level a differentiation is introduced between public and private and governmental and non-governmental. International governmental organizations, international non-governmental organizations, and international corporations are included in IPS. At the national level a similar distinction between public and private and a greater role differentiation within national political systems are found. Public and private economic systems exist within IPS, while decision-making roles within each national political structure are head of state, domestic adviser, foreign affairs diplomat, international organization delegate, citizen, and executive director of a corporation. At the individual level each role requires at least one person and as a result a six nation, five corporation, one international organization IPS requires upwards of forty participants to act as decision-makers.

As in INS three types of communications exist. Written communication between participants is possible either using message forms or decision forms. Verbal communication is possible through scheduled or unscheduled conferences, and in addition a World Press is read by all participants.

In both nation-state and international versions, nations are prototypes and are named Algo, Bingo, Somne, Utro, Yora, and Zena. The three largest nations represent three distinct types of political structures. Algo has a decision latitude (Guetzkow et al. 1963, p. 115) of nine, complete government control over all national industry, and relatively little trade with other nations when the simulation starts. Yora also has a high decision latitude – eight on the decision latitude scale – and much control over national industry. Industry in Yora exports significant amounts to groups in other nations. Bingo has a relatively low decision latitude – four – and a government that does not exercise direct control over industry. Bingo is the largest nation at the start and includes industries with high export potential and consumers with high import potential.

The three smaller nations, Somne, Utro, and Zena, also differ significantly from each other. Somne is allied to Bingo, has industries that sell much to groups in Yora, and even a little to the citizens in Algo. Somne has a decision latitude of four, exercises no control over industrial enterprises in the country, and is the largest small nation. Utro and Zena are less involved in general political disputes of the tripolar simulation world, and both have a decision latitude of five. Groups in Zena do most of their trade with groups in Bingo and Somne, while groups in Utro trade mostly with groups in Yora. The trading structure is illustrated in figure 5, using the conventional notion that nations trade with each other. Of course, trade in IPS and international relations is between companies and customers in non-socialist economies. Most nations do not trade with each other in fact.

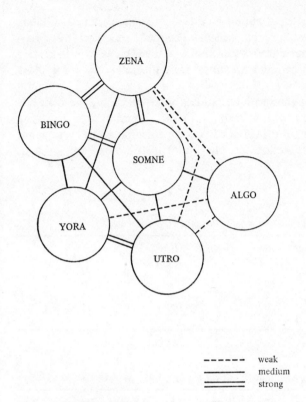

- - - - -	weak
———————	medium
═══════	strong

Figure 5 Trade structure.

b National and international corporations: description

In section 1b emphasis was placed on national and international adaptive subsystems. National and international corporations in IPS represent these subsystems. In the nation-state interpretation, Algo Manufacturing, Somne Merchandise, Utro Development, and Yora Industrial are completely national at the start of the simulation, all their factories and plants being in one country. The fifth and largest corporation, Bingo Enterprises, is international. It has 80 per cent of its plant in Bingo, the largest nation, and 20 per cent in Zena, the smallest. National identity is thus incorporated into nation-state corporations both by integrating the economic structure of each corporation with a particular nation and by naming the corporation after that nation.

In the international interpretation, Algo Manufacturing is the only corporation that is entirely nation based and nation identified. Globus Products, International Supplies, Magnus Products, and Worldwide Products are the other four corporations, none of them being identified with just one nation. Non-national identities are deliberately used for these corporations.

In both nation-state and international interpretations, the distribution of each industry within each period is communicated to every participant using computer printout from the research and development program described in section III. The initial distributions are given in tables 1 and 2.

TABLE I

Percentage distribution of each industry at start of IPS (Nation state)

	Algo	Bingo	Somne	Utro	Yora	Zena
Algo manufacturing	100	0	0	0	0	0
Bingo enterprises	0	90	0	0	0	0
Somne merchandise	0	0	100	0	0	0
Utro development	0	0	0	100	0	10
Yora industrial	0	0	0	0	100	0

TABLE 2

Percentage distribution of each industry at start of IPS (International)

	Algo	Bingo	Somne	Utro	Yora	Zena
Algo manufacturing	100	0	0	0	0	0
Globus products	0	40	30	10	0	20
International supplies	0	70	10	0	10	10
Magnus products	0	0	0	10	90	0
Worldwide products	0	40	30	10	0	20

c   *National and international corporations: operation*

Each corporation is able to sell three products – basic resources, consumer goods, and force capability – to governments and citizens. To make this possible, a monetary unit, the Ipscript, has been introduced. Trading is carried out using a trade agreement form and a trade termination form.

A trade agreement is concluded when both the seller, a corporation, and the buyer, a government or citizen or international organization, have signed a trade agreement form giving details of the agreement. Simulation control checks that the corporation has sufficient spare productive capacity and the buyer has sufficient funds before the agreement is considered ratified. This is done using computer program agreement described in section IIIh. When ratified, simulation control informs the parties to the agreement using a courier.

The trading operations are simplified by two procedures. The first procedure concerns duration of existing trade agreements, which remain in effect until explicitly broken using a trade termination form. The second procedure concerns the trade termination form. A trade termination form delivered to simulation control in period n before the trade termination deadline, comes into effect the next period, period $n + 1$. This is implemented by computer program termination described in section IIIh.

If the period in IPS is eighty minutes long, the trade termination deadline comes at thirty minutes. The trade agreement deadline then comes after forty-five minutes. Trade agreements concluded after this time do not count for the current period and are held over until the following period. Obviously other experimenters may lengthen an IPS period. Experience suggests an eighty-minute period is the lower time limit for effective operation of IPS.

Because of the distribution given in tables 1 and 2, and the relative size of both nations and corporations in IPS (Nation State) compared to IPS (International), correspondingly different trading structures characterize the starting positions in each case. The starting data are included in program load, which is described in section IIIb.

The major decisions of corporations concerning capital investment and research and development are recorded on a corporation plan for the period. During each period each corporation is given its part of computer printout from the research and development program. This tells it current unit costs on each product to each nation and its production ceilings for the next period. Costs are set to begin with such that costs in countries where corporations lack plant are higher than for those where plant exists. They include production and distribution costs to each country. Research and development in IPS brings down unit costs so that a company selling heavily to one country can invest research and development funds in that country, using a corporation plan for the period to achieve this goal.

Unit costs are given to each company on the printout of the research and development program. They do not include reductions in costs achieved for mass production. Unit costs decrease by fixed amounts as the size of a particular agreement increases, the bigger the agreement the greater the cut in unit costs. The mass production effect tapers off: above a certain level no extra decrease in costs can be gained by large orders. Company directors are told the size of their mass production effect. They are able to use mass production savings to improve bargaining power in negotiations with prospective customers.

Capital investment by a corporation in a country increases plant and equipment in that country and in proportion increases total production potential of factories in that country. Capital investment, like research and development, can be directed at any nation or combination of nations using corporation plan for the period. In this way a company can change its geographical distribution and influence the international trade structure. Similarly a government or citizens invest in a corporation using the national investment form. Research and development investment will decrease costs to purchasers in that country. The executive director may or may not pass along these reductions to customers.

d   National and international corporations: structure

Perlmutter (1966) has suggested three structural forms for international corporations. 1 / The ethnocentric organization is a nation-based corporation dominated by one set of nationals but having factories abroad. 2 / The polycentric organization is made up of autonomous national branches with poor communications. 3 / The geocentric organization is worldwide but ethnocentric within its cosmopolitan and international headquarters. Communication is good and so is understanding of local conditions. In the international interpretation of IPS, four out of five corporations are international and tend to be polycentric. The fifth is ethnocentric and based in the nation with highest decision latitude. It is possible to represent all three types in IPS.

With ethnocentric corporations, more than half the factories can be placed in one country and all the profit boost goes to one national economy. Cost prices for an ethnocentric corporation can be reduced by research and development. Only the corporation or nation base can provide funds to do this. Any reduction in cost prices for an item would apply to corresponding prices in every country for that corporation. This simulates the spread of innovations found by research.

Cost prices for polycentric corporations can also be decreased by research and development. Government and citizenry can make available research and development funds for subsidiaries in their own nation. But research payoffs in cutting cost prices would apply only to prices for that nation. This simulates bad communications in a polycentric organization and the destructive competition described by Perlmutter. A gradual diffusion of payoff is possible, the speed of diffusion being proportional to the degree to which an organization is moving towards geocentricity. Polycentric organization profits return to the nation base of the subsidiary.

For geocentric corporations any nation as well as the corporation itself, can make funds available for research, and research is measured by the sum of all research funds as outlined by Perlmutter. Any payoffs apply to the particular product in all nations, while the profit boost is distributed similarly to a polycentric corporation.

Future experiments with IPS might include national and international banking systems as well as national currencies which would make possible a number of new economic acts, for example, devaluation of a national monetary unit, credits, and stocks and shares in corporations. This would mean more complexity. The option to start new companies is not included in the simulation at present, but there is no structural reason for this. Streamlining some technical feature, such as computer usage, should make it possible at a future date.

Because no banking system exists within the simulation at the present time, funds allocated for purchasing a particular product – basic resources, say – but not all used for this purpose are converted to that product at the unfavourable rate of 25 Ipscripts per unit. This is a weakness in the economic system of IPS.

e   Trading and economic structure

Introducing corporations as distinct entities has made possible a new economic and trading structure. While in INS consumer goods, basic resources, and force capability are produced by governments using generation rates, in IPS citizens can improve their standard of living by buying as many consumer goods as their income allows, and governments can get as much as possible with available income. The trade matrix for IPS is calculated each period by the economic program described in section IIIe. Unlike in INS, trade is not under the direct control of governments.

Governments are able to tax citizens and industrial enterprises to raise necessary monies for implementing government policies. Thus in each period governments are given a computer printout that tells taxable profits on corporations or subsidiaries operating in the country and the total amount of other monies expected in the national economic system. Governments then decide how much tax they require and tax citizens and corporations accordingly. This is done using the budget allocation form.

Funds raised by governments in this way are allocated on a budget allocation form for expenditures on basic resources, capital investment,

research and development, and force capability. A citizen's income remaining after taxation is reported on his income form. Similarly the profits
after tax are reported on a profits after tax form. These funds are then
used by corporations during the following period. When deciding on taxation levels governments take into account dividends to shareholders. These
payments have no direct programmed consequences in IPS.

Profit and loss accounts for each corporation are calculated each
period by the economic program. The computer printout provides a
balance sheet for each corporation and gives a complete breakdown of
profits by product and nation as well as current inventory. A research and
development program uses the total profit figure to calculate profits of
each corporation in each nation.

f   Other non-governmental activity

The introduction of a citizen role in IPS met some requirements of the
economic or adaptive subsystem and the cultural or integrative subsystem.
In the international interpretation of IPS international non-governmental
conferences, each lasting five minutes, are scheduled during each period
to promote further activity at this level. An invitation is circulated by
simulation control, and citizens attend voluntarily. Further non-governmental activities sometimes evolve from these conferences. The programmed influence of these activities on international opinion is explained
later. No such programmed structure is present in the nation-state interpretation.

A new range of political conflicts have become possible in IPS. The
role differentiation involved in citizen, foreign affairs diplomat, head of
state, and corporation executive has made possible twenty-four types of
conflict not previously possible in INS. Citizens now have a demonstration
form which may be used any time for antigovernment or antiforeign
demonstrations and riots. Details of this form are reported to World Press
when it is submitted to simulation control. Governments concerned are
also informed. While such acts have no immediate influence on the programmed structure of IPS, under certain conditions they can seriously
inconvenience governments by influencing evaluations of others.

While demonstrations and riots enable citizens to make demands on
governments in a stronger way than written or verbal communication,
strikes provide a method for making strong demands on industry. In IPS
a citizen may strike at any time against any corporation with a plant in his
country by using a strike form. When a strike takes place citizens lose
income for the period of the strike, while corporations lose production in

that country. Simulation control adjusts the citizen's income form and corporation balance sheet accordingly. Three strike-breaking methods are available to a government through the internal control form:

1   The government issues a court order to strikers requesting them to return to work. Citizens are not obliged to accept this order.
2   The government mans the factory with military forces. Forces used in this way are not available for national defence at the same time. The force required equals loss in citizen's income divided by twenty-five.
3   The government uses military force to get citizens back to work, but forced labour pushes up production costs by 5 per cent.

Citizens can purchase force capability from corporations in IPS. This can be used through the subversion form for two purposes. 1 / to undertake assassination attempts against members of their government; 2 / to wage guerrilla warfare. The success of an assassination attempt depends upon the amount of force used for internal control by a government. This is recorded under item 3 of the force utilization form. The outcome of guerrilla warfare is calculated using a war program. If guerrilla warfare is successful, a citizen becomes the new head of state. In both cases the citizens must have previously purchased force and distributed it in the nine national zones using a subversion form.

Force capability purchased by citizens from home industry can represent a purely indigenous subversive uprising. Citizens may be offered arms, subsidized by a foreign power or by a foreign corporation. This represents activities of international and revolutionary movements.

A government may protect itself from subversion by inspecting for illegal forces in its nine zones using the internal control form. Such inspections are considered purges of dissenting elements in which all materials are appropriated and subversives are assumed to be imprisoned. Simulation control is then able to erase any subversive forces operating in the country.

g   *Governmental activity*

Zinnes (1966), in her comparison of communication in INS and the 1914 crisis, suggests that a lack of indirect governmental channels as alternatives to top level communication causes severe distortion in INS. While INS includes an external decision-maker with secondary diplomatic functions, Zinnes suggests a decision-making role explicitly responsible for such activities. This has been done in IPS by creating a diplomatic position. Larger nations in IPS have two diplomats when possible. One of these operates in a dual role as a diplomat and second international organization delegate. The sole function of an IPS diplomat is to carry out negotiations on behalf of his government.

In the international interpretation of IPS there is a full-time international organization and for each nation an international organization delegate. For ten minutes in each period the international organization recesses and delegates attend a national council meeting in their nations. At all other times they are in the international organization chamber. In keeping with Alger's findings (Alger 1966), an international organization delegates' lounge is provided which can be used by them at any time for informal interaction.

Governments can impose a variety of negative sanctions in IPS. They can place tariffs on imports or exports of any or all types of products. They can place a complete embargo on imports or exports of any or all products. They can place limitations on travel by their citizens to another country (to attend a non-governmental meeting) or on foreign citizens attending a meeting in their country. All of these acts are implemented using a negative sanction form. Troop movements, mobilization, and war are made possible through the force utilization form. If war is declared a computer program war calculates outcomes.

On the diplomatic front three types of conflict behaviour are now possible. 1 / Diplomatic relations can be broken, established, or re-established. When broken, direct conferences between diplomats of the two governments are not allowed. 2 / An ambassador can be expelled or recalled. 3 / A diplomat of less than ambassador status can be expelled or recalled. In diplomatic conflict a continuum of acts from mild to strong is thus available and a diplomatic form is used for this purpose.

III   PROGRAM CHANGES IN IPS

a   *Introduction*

In INS 'relations among nations are embodied in the simulation by the postulation of programs of operation with respect to the internal functioning of the several nations constituting the over-all inter-nation system. Using these programs the decision-makers of each nation then freely develop relations between their states as they deem appropriate, given their unfolding circumstances.' The simulation is based on 'explicit specification of a basic set of variables and programmed relations among them,' as well as the variety of additional factors introduced by using human beings as decision-makers within the system (Guetzkow *et al.* 1963, p. 104). In a similar way IPS is based on both explicit programmed relationships and unprogrammed activity of human decision-makers. The programmed activities in IPS are incorporated in eight Fortran computer programs. These programs are listed in the appendix and described below.

b   Program load

1   Description
Program load is used to place starting data in nineteen data files. Starting data are stored with the program in the first instance. Depending on the particular version of IPS being used by the experimenter, the appropriate data base is stored after the DATA statement, line 1040, in the program. The program itself simply places data in the computer's memory.

While all programs listed in the appendix are written in GE Fortran and use the file conventions of a particular commercial on-line system, it should be possible to modify them to run on other systems without too much difficulty. The bulk of the program is written in relatively simple Fortran which could be modified to suit particular machines.

Since program load is simply a bookkeeping program, definitions and assumptions will not be discussed. All programs involving assumptions about international relations theory are described in greater detail.

c   Program facts

Program facts can be used at any time during the simulation to provide a comprehensive listing of the state of the simulation environment. It is also of value to run program facts after program load before the simulation starts. This enables the experimenter to check up on any system malfunction that might have occurred while loading the data with program load. In addition a printout of the state of the world at the start of the simulation is then available for the World Press and for simulation records.

Program facts simply reads data currently in store in each of nineteen data files within the computer's memory. When printing information out at the computer terminal, facts adds labels to the information so that the experimenter can check that information is correct. As for program load, program facts is a bookkeeping routine and no important assumptions are included.

d   Research and development program

1   Description

The introduction of independent corporations into IPS requires programming of corporations' capital investment and research and development.
Both nations and corporations can invest in corporations, the source of
investment in part determining geographical distribution of corporations'
assets and factories. Capital investment in a nation by a corporation
simulates construction of plants in that country and subsequently im-
proves that nation's trading position. Not all investment is used to create
new plants. As 5 per cent depreciation on existing plants occurs each
period, investment is used in part to offset this loss.

Research and development by nations and corporations has the
effect of lowering production costs where these include both production
and delivery costs. Research and development is directional. A company
can invest research and development funds in any particular nation or
combination of nations to lower costs, but not necessarily prices, to these
countries.

The research and development program converts research and development and capital investment appropriations into research and development payoffs, increases basic capabilities for industries, and creates a
continually changing geographical distribution of industrial plants. This,
in turn, increases export capability.

2   Definitions

This program represents a completely new set of programmed assumptions. The programmed variables used are defined in the following way.

1   BCBR the basic capability of a corporation to produce basic re-
      sources
2   BCCG the basic capability of a corporation to produce consumer
      goods
3   BCFC the basic capability of a corporation to produce force cap-
      ability
4   BCTOT the total basic capability of a corporation
5   BCPROD the total production of a corporation
6   BRPROD the total basic resources production of a company
7   CI the capital investment in a company in a nation
8   CITOT the total capital investment in a company
9   COSTS the unit costs of production for each product to each nation
10 CFPROD the production of conventional force

11 CGPROD the production of consumer goods
12 IND the name of the industry
13 PERC the percentage of a company in a nation
14 PROF the total corporation profits in a nation
15 PROFBT the profits before tax of each corporation in each nation
16 PROFCS the total profit of a corporation
17 RANDD funds invested in research and development
18 WHO the nation names

3 Assumptions

The first part of the program implements a research and development routine.

Research and development: Unit costs The assumption used is that up to a saturation ceiling, the greater the investment in research and development, the greater the payoff in terms of reduction in unit costs. Beyond this maximum an increased investment does not bring any further reduction in unit costs. Thus for RANDD < RANDDmax

$$\text{COSTSold} - \text{COSTSnew} = \text{DELTA1.RANDDlevel.} \qquad 1$$

While for RANDD = RANDDmax

$$A[\text{COSTS}(BC)\text{old} - \text{COSTS}(BC)\text{new}] + \beta[\text{COSTS}(CG)\text{old} - \text{COSTS}(CG)\text{new}] + C[\text{COSTS}(FC)\text{old} - \text{COSTS}(FC)\text{new}] \qquad 2$$
$$= \text{DELTA1.RANDDlevel,}$$

where RANDDmax is the saturation ceiling for investment, DELTA1 is the incremental drop associated with each increase in level of RANDD, and RANDDlevel is the level of RANDD in terms of an interval scale. *A*, *B*, and *C* are constants.

In initial runs with IPS RANDDmax was made equal to 600 Ipscripts, DELTA1 was set at 0.1, the RANDD level was defined on a seven-point scale such that 0 to 99.9 Ipscripts invested became zero RANDDlevel, 100 to 199.9 became 1, 200 to 299.9 two, and so on in a linear fashion up to RANDDmax. *A*, *B*, and *C* were all set at 1, thus giving equal research and development payoffs in all three sectors for RANDDmax. By adjusting *A*, *B*, and *C* the orientation of a corporation might be influenced by giving a bigger research and development payoff in one sector relative to others.

Capital investment: Basic capability The total basic capability for each corporation is then calculated by assuming that this production potential depends upon how much production potential was utilized during the current period and how much capital investment there is in the corporation. The nearer to maximum production in the current period, the greater the production potential next period. This simulates the fact that if men and machines are not being used to the maximum, then maximum production in the next period is lower because of training and retooling problems. Similarly the greater the capital investment, the greater the production potential next period because new equipment and personnel are acquired. The same assumptions are taken for each particular product as well as for total production. A company that has been producing to its maximum in consumer goods and not in force capability will find its basic capability for producing consumer goods will tend to increase relative to its capability for producing force.

Imposed on these two assumptions is a standard depreciation per period. This simulates natural wastage that occurs in both men and machines in every industrial enterprise. The equation representing these three interacting assumptions is

$$\text{BCTOTnew} = [(100 - C)/100].(\text{BCTOTold} + \text{BCPROD})/(\text{BCTOTold.2}) + \text{CI/ZETA}, \qquad 3$$

where D is the depreciation rate, expressed as a percentage, and ZETA is a multiplier associated with returns on capital investment; the higher ZETA, the lower the returns.

Geographical distribution: Profits The geographical distribution is then estimated by calculating how much of each corporation is in each nation, depreciation and new plant introduced by capital investment having been taken into account.

$$\text{PERC}(K,L) = \text{PERC}(K,L).\text{BCTOT}(L)/100. \qquad 4$$

The percentage of industry L in nation K in absolute figures, depreciation having been taken into account as well as the increase from capital investment, is then used in the equation

$$\text{PERC}(K,L) = \text{PERC}(K,L) + \text{CI}(K,L)/\text{ZETA}. \qquad 5$$

This absolute figure is then reconverted to a percentage by dividing by total size of company and multiplying by 100.

This new geographical distribution of factories is then used to determine national distribution of profits for each company. Thus profits of each corporation L in each nation K are given by the equation

$$\text{PROFBT}(K,L) = \text{PERC}(K,L).\text{PROFCS}(L)/100. \qquad 6$$

The program then calculates total profits of each corporation and prints out new unit costs, new total and particular basic capabilities, profits by nation and corporation, and new geographical distribution of each corporation.

e   Economic program

1   Description

Because of the changed economic structure a special program is required
to calculate simulated world trade patterns and profit and loss accounts
of corporations. Trade between nations in IPS is not directly controlled
by government except under special circumstances. Import and export
patterns in the simulation depend on the amount of industrial plant in each
nation, needs of government and citizenry, and available foreign markets.
The economic program calculates an import / export matrix by taking into
account geographical distribution of industry and company sales.

The balance sheet of each corporation gives statements of profit
and loss on each product (consumer goods, basic resources, force capability) to each nation for each corporation. This is calculated knowing
cost price, which changes through research and development, and sale
price, which changes through bargaining between corporations and customers. A mass production effect is incorporated into the computer
program to simulate effects of decreasing unit costs on increasing quanti-
ties of a product. Inventory is also updated by the program.

2   Definitions

Like IPS research and development, this program represents a new set of
assumptions in IPS. These assumptions relate to the economic system in
operation in IPS and programmed variables used are defined in the following way.

1   CORP the name of the industry
2   DSTOCK the change in inventory, or stock, for the corporation
3   INST the period number
4   PERCEN the percentage of a company in a nation
5   PRODCT the production of each corporation of each product
6   PROFIT the profit of each corporation on sales of each product to
    each nation
7   PROFPN profit by product and industry
8   SALES the sales of each product to each nation by each corporation
9   STOCK the stock of each product by corporation
10 SALEPR the sales price of each product to each nation for each
    corporation expressed as the deviation from the unit cost
11 TOT the total trade of a nation
12 TRADE the total trade of a nation with each other nation
13 TOTEXP the total exports of a nation
14 TOTIMP the total imports of a nation

15 TPROFC the total profits of a corporation
16 TPROFN the total profits of each corporation in each nation
17 TSALES the total sales of each corporation in each nation
18 WHO the nation names
19 XMPORT the imports and exports of each nation to each other nation

3   Assumptions

Mass production: Unit costs The first part of the program adjusts
unit costs to allow for mass production effects. It is assumed that up to a
saturation ceiling, the larger the trade agreement for a particular product
to a particular nation, the greater the reduction in unit costs. Thus for
SALES and SALESmax the general expression is

$$\text{SALEPRnew} = \text{SALEPRold} - \text{DELTA2.SALESlevel} \qquad 7$$

and for all other values of SALES

$$\text{SALEPRnew} = \text{SALEPRold} - \text{DELTA2.SALESmax}, \qquad 8$$

where SALESmax is a saturation ceiling for the mass production effect,
DELTA2 is the incremental drop associated with each increase in level of
SALES, and SALESlevel is the level of SALES in terms of an interval scale.
For each corporation the particular interpretations of these equations
for basic resources, BR, say, are

$$\text{SALEPR(BR)new} = \text{SALEPR(BR)old}$$
$$- \text{DELTA2(BR).SALES(BR)level} \qquad 9$$

and

$$\text{SALEPR(BR)new} = \text{SALEPR(BR)old}$$
$$- \text{DELTA2(BR).SALES(BR)max.} \qquad 10$$

Trade Matrix The total sales of each corporation to each nation are
first calculated using the formula

$$\text{TSALES} = \sum_{J=1}^{J=3} \text{SALES}(J), \qquad 11$$

where SALES(J) is sales of product J.

The import/export matrix is then calculated using the formula

$$\text{XMPORT} = \text{TSALES.PERCEN}/100. \qquad 12$$

This assumes that production of national subsidiaries relative to total
production of a company is a linear function of the percentage of the
company within that nation. Having calculated the import/export mat-

rix XMPORT, it is possible to calculate TOTEXP, TOTIMP, TRADE, and TOT by simple additions. The complete trade structure is calculated in this way and subsequently printed out.

The program then calculates a profit and loss account for each corporation. Thus

PROFIT = SALES.SALEPR,   13

that is,

PROFIT = SALES.(unit sale price–unit cost price),

since for each product SALEPR is the mass production corrected excess of unit sale price minues unit cost price.

Using this simple formula the complete profit matrix is calculated and printed out. In addition the program calculates current stock by using the formula

STOCKnew = STOCKold + PRODCT – SALES.   14

The corporation balance sheet includes STOCKnew and DSTOCK as well as the complete PROFIT matrix for each company.

f   Political program

1   Description
This program has been developed from the programmed relations in INS (Guetzkow *et al.* 1963, pp. 103–49) and is best understood in terms of INS assumptions. In each period the program updates current political and economic conditions in each nation. It calculates the probability of holding office, probability of a revolution and other indicators of office-holding (Guetzkow *et al.* 1963, p. 110), and orderly and disorderly transference of power (Guetzkow *et al.* 1963, p. 117). It calculates various national attributes and capabilities, such as national security and consumer satisfaction (Guetzkow *et al.* 1963, pp. 122–217) and it esti-mates national economic variables such as the level of basic resources.

2   Definitions
The programmed political variables used in IPS are:

1   AF nuclear force level
2   AFBEG nuclear force level at start of period
3   AFINC nuclear forces acquired by nation during period
4   BP exports minus imports

5 BR basic resources of a nation
6 BRDL cost in basic resources for forced change in decision latitude
7 BRINC increase in basic resources
8 CF conventional force level
9 CS consumer satisfaction
10 CSO starvation level of consumer goods
11 CFDL conventional force cost for forced change in decision latitude
12 CFIC forces used for internal control
13 CFBEG conventional force at start of period
14 CFDEP depreciated conventional force
15 CFINC increase in conventional force
16 CSMAX maximum possible level of consumer goods
17 CSMIN the minimum level of consumer goods acceptable to a nation's people
18 DL decision latitude
19 DDL government instigated change in decision latitude
20 DDLV programmed pressure to change decision latitude
21 F sum of nuclear and conventional force
22 F2 sum of nuclear and conventional forces for two nations
23 OPI world opinion index
24 OVS political effectiveness
25 OPIN opinion of one nation about another
26 PO public opinion
27 PR probability of a revolution
28 PHO probability of holding office in the event of an election
29 PSR probability of a successful revolution in the event of a revolution taking place
30 PSS probability of system stability
31 SEC national security
32 TOT total trade of a nation
33 TRADE trade of each nation with each other nation
34 WHO names of nations.

3   Assumptions

Consequences of pressured changes in decision latitude are calculated using the same formula as INS (Guetzkow *et al.* 1963, pp 128–30). Conventional force levels are also updated in a similar manner to INS by assuming that

$$CFnew = CFDEP + CFINC - CFDL, \qquad 15$$

where

$$CFDEP = CFold.depc \qquad 16$$

where depc is the depreciation rate. Similarly, nuclear force is updated using the equation

AFnew = AFBEG.depa + AFINC,   17

where depa is the depreciation rate of nuclear force.

National Security In INS, Validator Satisfaction with respect to National Security is directly related, within limits, to the ratio of force strength of a nation and its allies to the strongest nation or group of nations not allied with it (Guetzkow *et al.* 1963, pp. 125–7). IPS replaces Validator Satisfaction with Respect to National Security with a redefined index called national security. National security is defined using the following considerations.

Richardson (1960) in his study of arms races, developed the concept of directed intentions to extend his model of a two-nation situation to an *n*-nation situation. Galtung (1964) in another context put forward a sociological model of polarization which appears to apply to various situations ranging from relatively completely polarized (Jenkins and MacRae 1967) to relatively complex situations in which differential polarization is present (Smoker 1965ii). In the latter type of situation, polarization ceases to be a bipolar concept, and with nations, relations gain an intensive aspect, for example, the degree to which a government is involved with another government. The power political definition of national security used in INS has, therefore, been modified to include degrees of involvement of a nation in behavioural groups. These are defined using Smoker's interpretation of Galtung's polarization model (Smoker 1965ii).

This can be summarized in the following way. Galtung defines a completely polarized situation as one in which all positive relations are within blocks and all negative relations are between blocks. Conversely, in a completely unpolarized situation, it would be impossible to define blocks between which there was a significant difference in distribution of positive and negative relations. Between completely polarized and non-polarized, the degree of polarization can be defined. Polarization as defined is not necessarily bipolarization. A tri- or *n*-polarization would also satisfy the criteria of all positive relations within, and all negative relations between blocks.

If trade is assumed to index a positive relation between nations, then it is possible to define a relative index F_{mn} where,

$$F_{mn} = t_{mn}\left(\frac{1}{T_m} + \frac{1}{T_n}\right) \qquad 18$$

to measure the positive bonds between nations. In this definition t_{mn} is the intertrade between the two nations, and T_m, T_n are total trade of the mth and nth nations. This index, which averages relative importance of trade between two nations, has been used in an empirical study of the present arms race (Smoker 1965ii). The adopted model when applied to seven nations, US, USSR, UK, China, Federal Republic of Germany, Poland, and France, for the ten years 1952 to 1962 gives a strong correlation with actual behaviour. If the same model with no allowance for differential polarization is used the agreement is weaker. On the basis of this study the national security index in IPS takes differentiated polarization, as defined, into account. For each nation F_{mn} is defined as above, and a polarization weighting is calculated according to the deviation of F_{mn} from the mean value of all F_{mn}s.

The assumption is that the greater the positive deviation of F_{mn} from the mean, the better the relations between the two nations; the greater the negative deviations from the mean, the more the two nations are opposed to each other. These measures are then used to define behavioural groups and to weight power terms in the national security index.

The program implements this definition of national security by calculating positive deviations RHO of F_{mn} from the mean F and the negative deviations SIGMA. For each nation it is then possible to define a weighted positive strength,

$$\text{GOOD} = \Sigma \text{ F2.RHO,} \qquad 19$$

and a weighted negative strength,

$$\text{BAD} = \Sigma \text{ F2.SIGMA.} \qquad 20$$

National security is then defined in terms of the relative magnitude of GOOD and BAD.

$$\text{SEC} = \text{COEFF.GOOD/BAD,} \qquad 21$$

where COEFF is a weighting parameter.

World Opinion A Vietnam simulation developed by the Peace Research Centre, England, and the Canadian Peace Research Institute (MacRae and Smoker 1967) introduced world opinion as an explicit determinant of the political effectiveness of governments. The underlying assumption was that opinions of foreign political elites, as recorded on the so-called world opinion form, are important to a nation's political decision-makers, the importance of foreign opinion being proportional to the behavioural groupings as defined by Galtung's polarization model. The opinions of political decision-makers of nations which are positively linked carry more weight than those of hostile nations. In fact the index is constructed so that negative evaluations of foreign political decision-makers of hostile nations cause a positive score on the international opinion scale. In the international interpretation of IPS the citizen can influence world opinion. If he attends an international non-governmental conference the index for his nation is boosted. This means that two complementary effects are incorporated into the index: relationships between governments are dependent upon current behavioural groupings, while good will generated by citizens is not. This is expressed in the program using the equation

$$\text{OPI} = \text{OPIN.} (\text{RHO} - \text{SIGMA}) + \text{GWS}, \qquad 22$$

RHO and SIGMA being such that for a particular pair of nations one is always zero, and GWS being the good will score generated by citizens. GWS was set at 2 for IPS and was added to OPI by hand.

Consumer satisfaction The Elder/Pendley studies of consumer satisfaction (1966) suggest that programmed equations for VSCS (validator satisfaction for consumption standards) (Guetzkow *et al.* 1963, pp. 123–6) be altered to

$$\text{VScs} = \text{constant.} \text{Log}_e (\text{CG/CSmin}) + \text{constant} \qquad 23$$

and

$$\text{CSmin} = \text{constant.} \text{Log}_e (\text{CSmax/CS}_o) + \text{CS},$$

where CG is consumer goods purchased, CSMIN is consumer minimum, CSMAX is maximum producer goods which could be purchased, and CS_o is the starvation level.

Basic Resources Basic resources, like force capability, are calculated using the equation

$$\text{BRnew} = \text{depbBRold} + \text{BRINC} - \text{BRDL}, \qquad 26$$

but the value of BRNEW is then modified to allow for balance of trade. It is assumed that, since balance of payments cannot at the present time be incorporated into IPS without the addition of a banking system, the balance of trade influences a nation's economy. Deviations from the balance boost or hold back growth. Thus a booster is defined in terms of the difference between exports and imports. This booster RO is defined as

$$\text{RO} = \text{BP/TOT}, \qquad 27$$

and BRNEW is then modified by multiplying by $(1 + \text{RO})$; the complete equation for BRNEW then becomes

$$\text{BRnew} = (\text{depbBRold} + \text{BRINC} - \text{BRDL}) (1 + \text{RO}). \qquad 28$$

Public opinion Another innovation from the Vietnam simulation is a public opinion index. It uses current evaluations of political decision-makers concerning performance of national governments. These are recorded on the world opinion form. Only opinions of nationals are used in evaluating performance of their own government. In practice this means that public opinion is taken as an average of opinions of head of state, domestic adviser, foreign affairs diplomat, international organization delegate, citizen, and business executive. Public opinion is on a one to ten scale as are national security, international opinion, and consumer satisfaction.

Probability of holding office The INS probability of holding office index (Guetzkow *et al.* 1963, p. 111) was reconsidered by Pendley and Elder (1966) in terms of contemporary political theory about stability of regimes and government. They assert that programmed relations in INS tend to express relationships between system stability and its determinants, rather than regime stability. Thus they argue that the INS equation

$$pOH = a(b - DL)VSm + c(DL - d) \qquad 29$$

should be retained, but that it should be interpreted as the probability of system stability, pss. This has been done in IPS.

The new probability of holding office at elections is redefined in terms of public opinion and changes in public opinion. The probability of holding office, pOH, is defined by the equation

$$pOH = 1 - pLO, \text{ where } pLO = M \times DPO + N/PO, \qquad 30$$

where pLO is the probability of losing office, DPO is the drop in public opinion during the period PO is current public opinion, and M and N are constants. This equation assumes that the probability of holding office depends both on current levels and current trends in public opinion.

Political Effectiveness In INS Overall Validator Satisfaction (VSm) is defined in terms of two component parts corresponding to national security and consumers satisfaction (Guetzkow *et al.* 1963, p. 114). IPS adopts a corresponding strategy, the difference being an increased number of component parts, four as against two. Thus political effectiveness OVS is defined as

$$OVS = eCS + gNS + hIO + iPO \qquad 31$$

where e, g, h, and i are weighting parameters.

g War program

1 Description
The war program calculates outcomes in the event of war. It assumed

each nation can deploy forces in four ways: attack, active defence, passive defence, and reserve.

Attack forces are directed against a particular nation or combination of nations. Forces may be transferred to the attack status at any time but are only used when a statement is made to that effect in writing by the head of state. Active defence forces have the capability of destroying incoming attack forces. They simulate defences of the antiaircraft gun and antimissile missile type. Passive defence forces cannot destroy incoming attack forces but can protect civilian and or military installations. They simulate hardened missile sites or fallout shelters. Reserve forces are held to replenish forces of the other three types.

The war program provides governments with a variety of strategies ranging from all-out military conquest (100 per cent attack) to complete non-violent resistance (100 per cent passive defence). In addition attack and defence forces may be deployed against or in protection of all civilian, all military, or any civilian/military mix to provide again a range of strategies.

2   Definitions
The programmed variables used in IPS war are:

1   ATTACK force used by one nation to attack another
2   SHIELD passive defence forces of a nation
3   REATAK active defence forces of a nation
4   DAMAGE effectiveness coefficient for ATTACK
5   PROTEK effectiveness coefficient for SHIELD
6   REPULS effectiveness coefficient for REATAK
7   DATTAC losses in ATTACK
8   DSHIEL losses in SHIELD
9   DREATA losses in REATAK
10   RATIOS military/non-military mix of attack and defence forces
11   RATIO mean military/non-military mix of all ATTACK forces
12   BCLOSS non-military loss from an attack
13   SUMDAT sum of DATTAC
14   WHO nation names.

3   Assumptions
The program calculates loss of attacking forces by assuming attacking forces suffer losses before defending forces, the losses being

$$DATTAC = REATAK.REPULS. \qquad 32$$

The value of RATIO is then calculated by averaging across all RATIOS, and the total loss in attacking forces SUMDAT is calculated by summing all DATTAC for each nation. Passive defence losses are then calculated using the expression

$$\text{DSHIEL} = \text{DAMAGE.ATTACK,} \qquad 33$$

where ATTACK has been modified to allow for losses DATTAC. A correction is then made to allow for protective effectiveness using the equation

$$\text{DSHIELnew} = \text{DSHIELold} - \text{SHIELD.PROTEX,} \qquad 34$$

and civilian and protective losses are calculated using the equations

$$\text{SHIELDnew} = \text{SHIELDold} - \text{DSHIEL.RATIO} \qquad 35$$

and

$$\text{BCLOSS} = \text{DSHIEL}(1 - \text{RATIO}). \qquad 36$$

Active defence losses are then calculated by assuming the greater the other losses, the greater these losses. Thus

$$\text{REATAKnew} = \text{REATAKold} - \text{CONST.(BCLOSS} + \text{DSHIEL),} \qquad 37$$

where CONST is a constant. The program then reports total attack forces destroyed, passive defence forces left and destroyed, active defence force left and destroyed, and total civilian losses. The data base is modified by the computer.

h   Trade agreement program and trade termination program

1   Description

These two programs operate together on a second computer terminal. They are both bookkeeping programs and the results of their operations are automatically transmitted to the programs on the other terminals via the data base. In each period the trade agreement program is put into operation each time a trade agreement is sent to simulation control. The program checks if the agreement is possible and records it if it is in the computer's memory. As a rule the program is running all the time up to the trade agreement deadline. After all agreements have been processed the trade termination program is run. This program implements trade terminations and adjusts the data base for the next period's operation. It also prints out existing agreements for the start of the next period, providing a hard copy for every participant of their own trading situation.

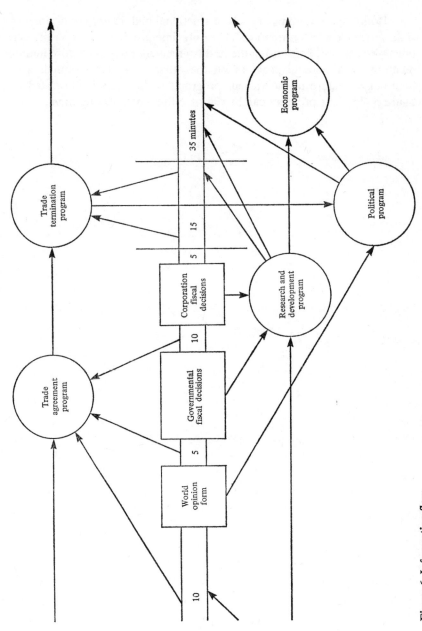

Figure 6 Information flow.

Both these programs are self-instructional and do not permit impossible agreements or terminations. The only time problem the experimenter must observe is to finish using the trade agreement program before implementing the economic program on the other computer terminal. The interlocking nature of the various programs or modules is illustrated in figure 6. The war program can be run on either computer terminal.

APPENDIX

```
X
 100.PROGRAM LOAD
 110       DIMENSION DUM(6,3,6), DOB(6,6,2,2)
 120 $FILE A1,A2,A3,A4,A5,A6,A7,A8,A9,A10,A12,A13,A14,A15,A16,A17,A18,A19$
 130      READ,NI
 140      READ 1,(DUM(J,1,1),J=1,NI)
 150      WRITE(1) NI
 160      WRITE(1,1)(DUM(J,1,1),J=1,NI)
 170    1 FORMAT(4X,6A6)
 180      REWIND 1
 190 PRINT,"FILE 1 LOADED"
 200      READ,NN
 210      READ 1,(DUM(J,1,1),J = 1,NN)
 220      WRITE (2) NN
 230      WRITE(2,1)(DUM(J,1,1),J=1,NN)
 240      REWIND 2
 250 PRINT,"FILE 2 LOADED"
 260      READ,(((DUM(J,K,L),J=1,NN),K=1,3),L=1,NI)
 270      WRITE(3)(((DUM(J,K,L),J=1,NN),K=1,3),L=1,NI)
 280      REWIND 3
 290 PRINT,"FILE 3 LOADED"
 300      READ,((DUM(J,1,L),J=1,4),L=1,NI)
 310      WRITE(4)((DUM(J,1,L),J=1,4),L=1,NI)
 320      REWIND 4
 330 PRINT,"FILE 4 LOADED"
 340      READ,((DUM(J,1,K),J=1,NN),K=1,NI)
 350      WRITE(5)((DUM(J,1,K),J=1,NN),K=1,NI)
 360      REWIND 5
 370 PRINT,"FILE 5 LOADED"
 380      READ,(DUM(J,1,1),J=1,NI)
 390      WRITE (6)(DUM(J,1,1),J=1,NI)
 400      REWIND 6
 410 PRINT,"FILE 6 LOADED"
 420      READ,((DUM(J,K,1),K=1,3),J=1,NI)
 430      WRITE(7)((DUM(J,K,1),K=1,3),J=1,NI)
 440      REWIND 7
 450 PRINT,"FILE 7 LOADED"
 460      READ,((DUM(J,1,K),J=1,NN),K=1,NN),((DUM(M,N,1),M=1,NN),N=2,3)
 470      WRITE (8)((DUM(J,1,K),J=1,NN),K=1,NN),((DUM(M,N,1),M=1,NN),
 480 +    N=2,3)
 490      REWIND 8
 500 PRINT,"FILE 8 LOADED"
 510      I = 1
 520      WRITE(9) I
 530      REWIND 9
 540 PRINT,"FILE 9 LOADED"
 550      READ,((DUM(J,1,K),J=1,6),K=1,NN)
 560      MG = 6
 570      MP = 8
 580      WRITE(10)((DUM(J,1,K),J=1,6),MG,MP,K=1,NN)
 590      REWIND 10
 600 PRINT,"FILE 10 LOADED"
 610      READ,(DUM(J,1,1),J=1,NN)
 620      WRITE(19)(DUM(J,1,1),J=1,NN)
```

```
630        REWIND 19
640 PRINT,"FILE 11 LOADED"
650        READ,(DUM(J,1,1),J=1,NN)
660        WRITE(11)(DUM(J,1,1),J=1,NN)
670        REWIND 11
680 PRINT"FILE 12 LOADED"
690        READ,(((((DOB(I,J,K,L),I=1,NI),J=1,NN),K=1,2),L=1,2)
700        WRITE(12)(((((DOB(I,J,K,L),I=1,NI),J=1,NN),K=1,2),L=1,2)
710        REWIND 12
720 PRINT"FILE 13 LOADED"
730        READ,(((((DOB(I,J,K,L),I=1,NI),J=1,NN),K=1,2),L=1,2)
740        WRITE(13)(((((DOB(I,J,K,L),I=1,NI),J=1,NN),K=1,2),L=1,2)
750        REWIND 13
760 PRINT"FILE 14 LOADED"
770        READ,(DUM(J,1,1),J=1,NN)
780        WRITE (14)(DUM(J,1,1),J=1,NN)
790        REWIND 14
800 PRINT"FILE 15 LOADED"
810        READ,(((DUM(J,K,L),K=1,3),J=1,NI),L=1,NN)
820        WRITE(15)(((DUM(J,K,L),K=1,3),J=1,NI),L=1,NN)
830        REWIND 15
840 PRINT"FILE 16 LOADED"
850        READ,(((DUM(J,K,L),K=1,3),J=1,NI),L=1,NN)
860        WRITE(16)(((DUM(J,K,L),K=1,3),J=1,NI),L=1,NN)
870        REWIND 16
880 PRINT"FILE 17 LOADED"
890        READ,((DUM(J,K,1),K=1,3),J=1,NN)
900        WRITE(17)((DUM(J,K,1),K=1,3),J=1,NN)
910        REWIND 17
920 PRINT"FILE 18 LOADED"
930        READ,((DUM(J,K,1),K=1,3),J=1,NI)
940        WRITE(18)((DUM(J,K,1),K=1,3),J=1,NI)
950        REWIND 18
960 PRINT"FILE 19 LOADED"
970        PRINT,^^"ALL FILES ARE NOW LOADED.  TO GET A PRINTOUT OF"
980        PRINT,"STARTING DATA FOR INFORMATION OR CHECKING"
990        PRINT,"CALL AND RUN PROGRAM FACTS."
1000 PRINT, "THIS SHOULD BE DONE WELL BEFORE STARTING SIMULATION"
1010 PRINT,"AS DISPLACEMENT OF A SINGLE ENTRY CANNOT BE FOUND EASIL
1020        STOP
1030C    THE FOLLOWING  ARE THE DATA FOR THE SIMULATION.
1040 $DATA
1050 5,
1060    AM   BE   SM   UD   YI,
1070 6,
1080   ALGO BINGO SOMNE  UTRO  YORA  ZENA,
1090 15.5,16.1,16.0,16.0,15.8,15.8,18.0,18.6,18.5,
1100 18.5,18.2,18.3,16.0,16.6,16.5,16.5,16.3,16.3,
1110 16.1,15.6,15.6,15.7,15.7,15.8,18.4,18.0,18.0,
1120 18.1,18.1,18.2,16.6,16.0,16.0,16.1,16.1,16.2,
1130 16.1,15.6,15.6,15.7,15.7,15.8,18.4,18.0,18.0,
1140 18.1,18.1,18.2,16.6,16.0,16.1,16.1,16.1,16.2,
1150 15.5,15.5,15.3,15.3,15.2,15.4,17.8,17.8,17.6,
1160 17.6,17.5,17.7,16.0,16.8,15.8,15.8,15.7,15.9,
1170 16.1,15.6,15.6,15.7,15.8,15.5,18.4,18.0,18.0,
1180 18.1,18.2,18.0,16.6,16.0,16.1,16.1,16.2,16.0,
1200 14700.0,500.0,14000.0,1000.0,19300.0,1500.0,18000.0,1000.0,413
1210 4500.0,38000.0,2000.0,24700.0,3000.0,19000.0,3500.0,27000.0,90
1220 12000.0,6500.0,
1240 100,0,0,0,0,0,0,40,30,10,0,20,0,70,10,0,10,10,0,0,0,10,90,0,0,
1250 10,0,20,
```

```
1270  1032,37800,88466,38154,52800,
1290  25,1347,75,137,1721,32,393,3581,143,256,1873,310,850,1185,580,
1310  26992.0,352.0,894.0,333.0,95.0,226.0,352.0,51218.0,18225.6,5050.8,
1320  4771.0,8587.0,894.0,18225.6,8893.6,3788.6,5715.8,5699.8,333.0,
1330  5050.8,3788.6,1776.4,3735.9,2720.4,95.0,4771.0,5715.8,3735.9,
1340  27376.2,4142.0,226.0,8587.0,5699.8,2720.4,4142.0,3200.0,1900.0,
1350  36986.4,34323.8,15628.7,18459.7,21375.2,
1370  40.0,4664.4,-8558.6,-3718.9,6297.9,1275.2,
1390  3500,9,0,24500,80,11900,7500,4,0,79100,470,25800,1800,5,0,23500,50,
1400  19500,1200,5,0,19000,0,7500,4100,8,0,38200,320,15510,1600,5,0,22900,
1410  0,10000,
1430  10,10,20,10,10,
1450  203000,520000,400000,160000,300000,204000,
1470  12500,0,0,0,0,0,28240,0,0,630,4000,6130,3730,5870,240,1300,1440,
1480  400,4972,50,2910,0,12700,1000,50,8000,0,1900,0,
1500  0,0,0,0,0,0,0,0,0,0,0,0,0,0,0,0,0,0,0,0,0,0,0,0,0,0,0,0,0,0,
1520  200000,0,0,0,0,0,508320,0,0,11470,72800,116470,72035,105660,4560,
1530  24700,2781607200,20410,950,53835,0,222250,19200,950,166500,0,34200,0
1550  0,0,0,0,0,0,0,0,0,0,0,0,0,0,0,0,0,0,0,0,0,0,0,0,
1570  246,880,0,50,0,0,0,0,0,7900,0,0,3928,0,0,0,490,0,1000,0,0,0,0,509,
1580  600,0,0,0,1000,0,
1600  750,0,0,0,0,0,0,1430,0,4200,0,0,0,0,1600,0,320,0,400,0,0,0,0,2000,0,
1610  0,0,0,700,0,
1630  3764,15224,0,800,0,0,0,0,0,123240,0,0,62062,0,0,0,8477,0,14600,0,0,
1640  0,0,7737,9300,0,0,0,15300,0,
1660  11475,0,0,0,0,0,25740,0,63040,0,0,0,0,27040,0,5696,0,6600,0,0,0,0,
1670  31400,0,0,0,0,11200,0,
1690  33000,230000,94000,37000,51000,28000,
1770  3764,200000,11475,15224,0,0,0,0,0,800,0,0,0,0,0,
```

INTERNATIONAL DATA BASE FOR LOAD

```
1040  $DATA
1050  5,
1060    AM    GP    IS    MP    WP  ,
1070  6,
1080    ALGO BINGO SOMNE  UTRO  YORA  ZENA,
1090  15.5,16.1,16.0,16.0,15.8,15.3,18.0,18.6,18.5,
1100  18.5,18.2,18.3,16.0,16.3,16.5,16.5,16.3,16.3,
1110  16.1,15.6,15.6,15.7,15.7,15.8,18.4,18.0,18.0,
1120  18.1,18.1,18.2,16.6,16.1,16.0,16.1,16.1,16.2,
1130  16.1,15.6,15.6,15.7,15.7,15.8,18.4,18.0,18.0,
1140  18.1,18.1,18.2,16.6,16.1,16.1,16.1,16.1,16.2,
1150  15.5,15.5,15.3,15.3,15.2,15.4,17.8,17.8,17.6,
1160  17.6,17.5,17.7,16.0,16.3,15.3,15.8,15.7,15.9,
1170  16.1,15.6,15.6,15.7,15.3,15.5,18.4,18.0,18.0,
1180  18.1,18.2,18.0,16.6,16.3,16.1,16.1,16.2,16.2,
1200  14700.0,500.0,14000.0,1300.0,19300.0,1500.0,18000.0,1000.0,41800.0,
1210  4500.0,38000.0,2000.0,24700.0,3000.0,19000.0,3500.0,27000.0,9000.0,
1220  12000.0,6500.0,
1240  100,0,0,0,0,0,0,40,30,17,0,20,0,70,10,0,10,10,0,0,0,10,90,0,0,40,30,
1250  10,0,20,
1270  1032,37800,88466,38154,52800,
1290  25,1347,75,137,1721,32,393,3581,143,256,1873,310,850,1185,580,
1310  26992.0,352.0,894.0,333.0,95.0,226.0,352.0,51218.0,18225.6,5050.8,
1320  4771.0,8587.0,894.0,18225.6,8893.6,3788.6,5715.8,5699.8,333.0,
1330  5050.8,3788.6,1776.4,3735.9,2720.4,95.0,4771.0,5715.8,3735.9,
1340  27376.2,4142.0,226.0,8587.0,5699.8,2720.4,4142.0,3200.0,1900.0,
1350  36986.4,34323.8,15628.7,18459.7,21375.2,
1370  40.0,4664.4,-8558.6,-3718.9,6297.9,1275.2,
1390  3500,9,0,24500,80,11900,7500,4,0,79100,470,25800,1800,5,0,23500,50,
```

```
1400 19500,1200,5,0,19000,0,7500,4100,8,0,38200,320,15510,1600,5,0,2
1410 0,10000,
1430 10,10,20,10,10,10,
1450 200000,508320,378935,154186,296235,201650,
1470 12500,0,0,0,0,0,28240,0,0,630,4000,6130,3730,5870,240,1300,14
1480 400,4972,50,2910,0,12700,1000,50,8000,0,1900,0,
1500 0,0,0,0,0,0,0,0,0,0,0,0,0,0,0,0,0,0,0,0,0,0,0,0,0,0,0,
1520 200000,0,0,0,0,0,0,508320,0,0,11470,72300,115470,72035,105660,4
1530 24700,27816,7200,89500,950,53835,0,222250,19200,950,166500,0,
1531 34200,0,
1550 1,0,0,0,0,0,0,0,0,0,0,0,0,0,0,0,0,0,0,0,0,0,0,0,0,0,0,0,0,0,
1570 246,880,0,50,0,0,0,0,0,7900,0,0,3928,0,0,0,490,0,1300,0,0,0,0,5
1580 600,0,0,0,1000,0,
1600 750,0,0,0,0,0,1433,0,4200,0,0,0,0,1600,0,320,0,400,0,0,0,0,20
1610 0,0,0,700,0,
1630 3764,15224,0,300,0,0,0,0,0,123240,0,0,62062,0,0,0,8477,0,14600,
1640 0,0,7737,9300,0,0,0,15300,0,
1660 11475,0,0,0,0,0,25740,0,63040,0,0,0,27240,0,5696,0,6600,0,0
1670 31400,0,0,0,0,11200,0,
1690 33000,230000,94000,37300,51700,28000,
1710 246,12500,750,880,0,0,0,0,0,50,0,0,0,0,0,0,0,0,0,0,0,28240,14
1720 0,0,0,7900,0,4200,0,630,0,0,4000,0,3928,6130,0,0,3730,0,0,5870,
1730 0,240,0,490,1300,320,0,1440,0,1000,400,400,0,4972,0,0,50,0,0,29
1740 0,0,0,509,12700,2000,600,1000,0,0,50,0,0,8000,0,0,0,0,1000,1900
1750 0,0,0,
1770 3764,200000,11475,15224,0,0,  0,0,800,0,0,0,0,0,
1780 0,0,0,0;0,0,0,508320,25740,0,0,0,123240,0,58340
1790 0,11470,0,0,72300,0,62062,115470,0,0,72035,0,0,105660,27840,
1800 0,4560,0,8477,24700,5696,0,27816,0,14600,7200,6600,0,89500,0,
1810 0,950,0,0,53835,0,0,0,0,7737,222250,31400,9300,19200,0,
1820 0,950,0,0,166500,0,0,0,0,15300,34200,11200,0,0,0,
1840 1176,12500,750,7900,28240,5630,3928,20360,1600,1490,8352,720,
1850 1109,16660,2000,1000,950,700,
1870 246,13470,750,1370,16210,320,3928,35810,1430,2559,18730,3100,85
1880 11842,5800,


100.PROGRAM FACTS
110 REAL DIMENSION WHO(6),IND(6),DUM1(6,3,6),PO(6)
120 $FILE A1,A2,A3,A4,A5,A6,A7,A8,A10,A12,A13,A14,A15,A16,A17,A18
130 READ(1)NI
140 READ(1,1)(IND(J),J=1,NI)
150 PRINT^^"CORPORATION NAMES ARE",
160 PRINT 1,(IND(J),J=1,NI)
170 1 FORMAT(4X,6A5)
180 READ(2)NN
190 READ(2,1)(WHO(J),J=1,NN)
200 PRINT^^"NATION NAMES ARE",
210 PRINT 1,(WHO(J),J=1,NN)
220 READ(3)(((DUM1(J,K,L),J=1,NN),K=1,3),L=1,NI)
230 REWIND 1
240 REWIND 2
250 REWIND 3
260 2 FORMAT(A6,4X,3(F4.1,2X))
270 DO 100 L=1,NI
280 PRINT^^^"UNIT COSTS FOR",
290 PRINT 1,IND(L)
300 PRINT^            BR      CG      FC "
310 DO 101 J=1,NN
320 101 PRINT 2,WHO(J),(DUM1(J,K,L),K=1,3)
330 100
```

```
340 READ(4)((DUM1(M,1,L),M=1,4),L=1,NI)
350 3 FORMAT(I8)
360 DO 102L=1,NI
370 PRINT^"FOR INDUSTRY"
380 PRINT 1,IND(L)
390 PRINT^^"BCTOT=",
400 PRINT 3,DUM1(1,1,L)
410 PRINT"BCBR =",
420 PRINT 3,DUM1(2,1,L)
430 PRINT"BCCG =",
440 PRINT 3,DUM1(3,1,L)
450 PRINT"BCFC =",
460 PRINT 3,DUM1(4,1,L)
470 102
480 REWIND 4
490 READ(5)((DUM1(J,1,L),J=1,NN),L=1,NI)
500 REWIND 5
510 PRINT^^^"PERCENTAGE DISTRIBUTION OF EACH INDUSTRY"
520 PRINT^
530 PRINT 5,(WHO(J),J=1,NN)
540 5 FORMAT(10X,6(4X,A6))
550 DO 105 L=1,NI
560 105 PRINT 6,IND(L),(DUM1(J,1,L),J=1,NN)
570 6 FORMAT(2X,A6,2X,6F10.1)
580 READ(6)(DUM1(1,1,L),L=1,NI)
590 REWIND 6
600 PRINT^^^"PROFIT FOR CORPORATIONS"
610 PRINT^
620 DO 108L=1,NI
630 108 PRINT 6,IND(L),DUM1(1,1,L)
640 READ(7)((DUM1(1,K,L),K=1,3),L=1,NI)
650 REWIND 7
660 PRINT^^^
670 PRINT"STOCK (INVENTORY) OF EACH CORPORATION"
680 PRINT^"          BR      CG      FC"
690 10 FORMAT(A6,3I8)
700 DO 110 L=1,NI
710 110 PRINT 10,IND(L),(DUM1(1,K,L),K=1,3)
720 PRINT^^^"TOTAL TRADE"
730 READ(8)((DUM1(J,1,L),J=1,NN),L=1,NN),(DUM1(J,2,1),J=1,NN)
740 +,(DUM1(J,3,1),J=1,NN)
750 PRINT 5,(WHO(J),J=1,NN)
760 DO 15 L=1,NN
770 15 PRINT 6,WHO(L),(DUM1(J,1,L),J=1,NN)
780 PRINT^"    TOTAL",
790 PRINT 16,(DUM1(J,2,1),J=1,NN)
800 16 FORMAT(6I10)
810 PRINT^"EXP - IMP ",
820 PRINT 16,(DUM1(J,3,1),J=1,NN)
830 REWIND 8
840 READ(9)((DUM1(J,1,K),J=1,6),X,PO(K),K=1,NN)
850 PRINT^^^"FOR THE NATIONS"
860 PRINT 5,(WHO(J),J=1,NN)
870 PRINT^"CFBEG =",
880 PRINT 16,(DUM1(1,1,L),L=1,NN)
890 PRINT"DL    =",
900 PRINT 16,(DUM1(2,1,L),L=1,NN)
910 PRINT"DDI.V =",
920 PRINT 16,(DUM1(3,1,L),L=1,NN)
930 PRINT"BR    =",
940 PRINT 16,(DUM1(4,1,L),L=1,NN)
```

```
950 PRINT"NFBEG =    ",
960 PRINT 16,(DUM1(5,1,L),L=1,NN)
970 PRINT"CS0   =
980 PRINT 16,(DUM1(6,1,L),L=1,NN)
990 REWIND 9
1000 READ(10)(DUM1(J,1,1),J=1,NN)
1010 PRINT^^"CITIZENS"
1020 PRINT"INCOME
1030 PRINT 16,(DUM1(J,1,1),J=1,NN)
1040 REWIND 10
1050 READ(13)(DUM1(J,1,1),J=1,NN)
1060 PRINT^^"GOVERNMENT"
1070 PRINT"INCOME
1080 PRINT 16,(DUM1(J,1,1),J=1,NN)
1090 REWIND 13
1100 READ(16)((DUM1(J,K,1),K=1,3),J=1,NN)
1110 REWIND 16
1120 PRINT^^"BRINC =    "
1130 PRINT 16,(DUM1(J,1,1),J=1,NN)
1140 PRINT"CG =
1150 PRINT 16,(DUM1(J,2,1),J=1,NN)
1160 PRINT"CFINC =
1170 PRINT 16,(DUM1(J,3,1),J=1,NN)
1180 PRINT"PUB OPIN =",
1190 PRINT 16,(PO(K),K=1,NN)
1200 PRINT^^"^" TO GET BREAK DOWN OF AGREEMENTS CALL PROGRAM TERM
1210 + AND ENTER NO TRADE TERMINATIONS"
1220 PRINT^^"TO GET BREAK DOWN OF PROFITS(CORPORATION BALANCE SHEET
1230 +) AND TRADE MATRIX CALL PROGRAM ECON."
1240 STOP
1250 END


100C..............PROGRAM FOR R AND D........I.P.S.
110 REAL DIMENSION COSTS(3,6,5),CI(6,6),RANDD(6,6),PERC(6,5),BCTOT(
120 +,BCBR(6),BCCG(6),BCFC(6),PROFCS(6),PROFBT(6,6),CITOT(6),
130 +PROF(6),IND(6),WHO(6),BCPROD(6),CGPROD(6),CFPROD(6),BRPROD(6),
140 +SUM(6)
150 $FILE A1,A2,A3,A4,A5,A6,A19
160 READ(1)NI
170 READ(1,1)(IND(J),J=1,NI)
180 1 FORMAT(4X,6A5)
190 READ(2)NN
200 READ(2,1)(WHO(J),J=1,NN)
210 REWIND 1; REWIND 2
220 READ(3)(((COSTS(J,K,L),K=1,NN),J=1,3),L=1,NI); REWIND 3
230 READ(4)(BCTOT(L),BCBR(L),BCCG(L),BCFC(L),L=1,NI)
240 READ(5)((PERC(K,L),K=1,NN),L=1,NI);REWIND 4; REWIND 5
250 INT=1;PRINT^^"TO BEGIN WITH SPECIFY INVESTMENT IN RESEARCH
260 + AND DEVELOPMENT FOR THE   CORPORATIONS.        FOR EACH
270 + CORPORATION GIVE THE INVESTMENT FIGURES IN THE ORDER"
280 PRINT^
290 PRINT 1,(WHO(J),J=1,NN)
300 PRINT^"BE SURE TO PUT COMMAS BETWEEN EACH ITEM"
310 PRINT^^"WHAT ARE",NN," R AND D INVESTMENTS FOR"
320 PRINT^
330 2 PRINT 1,IND(INT),
340 INPUT,(RANDD(K,INT),K=1,NN)
350 INT=INT+1; IF(INT-NI-1)2; PRINT^^"THANKS. NOW WE NEED THE
360 + SAME INFORMATION FOR CAPITAL INVESTMENT"
370 INT=1
```

```
380 PRINT^^"WHAT ARE",NN," CAPITAL INVESTMENTS FOR "
390 3 PRINT 1,IND(INT),
400 INPUT,(CI(K,INT),K=1,NN)
410 INT=INT+1
420 IF(INT-NI-1)3; PRINT^^"THANKS. AND FINALLY FOR EACH CORPORATION
430 + GIVE THE TOTAL PRODUCTION,  BR PRODUCTION,CG PRODUCTION, AND
440 + FORCE PRODUCTION"; INT=1; PRINT^^"CORPORATION"
450 PRINT^
460 4 PRINT 1,IND(INT),;L=INT
470 INPUT,(BCPROD(L),BRPROD(L),CGPROD(L),CFPROD(L))
480 INT=INT+1;IF(INT-NI-1)4; PRINT^^ THANKS. DATA INPUT COMPLETE"
490 WRITE(7)(BRPROD(J),CGPROD(J),CFPROD(J),J=1,NI)
500 REWIND 7
510 READ(6)(PROFCS(L),L=1,NI)
520 L=J=1; 49 DO 30 K=1,NN; IF(RANDD(K,L)-1000)31; RANDD(K,L)=1000
530 31 IF(X=.75*RANDD(K,L)-RND(P)*1000)41; IF(X-100)41
540 IF(200-X)34:COSTS(J,K,L)=COSTS(J,K,L)-.1;GOTO41
550 34 IF(300-X)36; 38 COSTS(J,K,L)=COSTS(J,K,L)-.1
560 IF(J-3)37,37; J=1 ;37 COSTS(J,K,L)=COSTS(J,K,L)-.1
570 GOTO41; 36 DO 51 I=1,3; 51 COSTS(I,K,L)=COSTS(I,K,L)-.1
580 IF(400-X)52,41,41; 52 IF(X-520)37 ;IF(X-600)38
590 DO 56 I=1,3; 56 COSTS(I,K,L)=COSTS(I,K,L)-.1
600 41 J=J+1; IF(J-3)30,30; J=1; 30
610 L=L+1; IF(L-NI-1)49; L=1
620 62 BCTOT(L)=BCTOT(L)*.95*(BCTOT(L)+BCPROD(L))/(BCTOT(L)*2)
630 BCBR(L)=BCBR(L)*.95*(BCBR(L)+BRPROD(L))/(BCBR(L)*2)
640 BCCG(L)=BCCG(L)*.95*(BCCG(L)+CGPROD(L))/(BCCG(L)*2)
650 BCFC(L)=BCFC(L)*.95*(BCFC(L)+CFPROD(L))/(BCFC(L)*2)
660 DO51K=1,NN; PERC(K,L)=PERC(K,L)*BCTOT(L)/100
670 BCTOT(L)=BCTOT(L)+CI(K,L)/20;BCBR(L)=BCBR(L)+CI(K,L)/30
680 BCCG(L)=BCCG(L)+CI(K,L)/30;51 BCFC(L)=BCFC(L)+CI(K,L)/30
690 L=L+1; IF(L-NI-1)62; DO65 K=1,NN; DO65 L=1,NI
700 PERC(K,L)=PERC(K,L)+CI(K,L)/20;65 CITOT(L)=CITOT(L)+PERC(K,L)
710 DO56 K=1,NN; DO66 L=1,NI; 66 PERC(K,L)=100*PERC(K,L)/CITOT(L)
720 DO 70 K=1,NN; DO70 L=1,NI;70 PROFBT(K,L)=PERC(K,L)*PROFCS(L)/100
730 DO72 K=1,NN; DO72 L=1,NI; 72 PROF(K)=PROF(K)+PROFBT(K,L)
740 L=1
750 100 PRINT^^^^^^"UNIT COSTS FOR",
760 PRINT 1,IND(L)
770 PRINT^         BR   CG    FC"
780 DO777 K=1,NN; 777 PRINT101,WHO(K),(COSTS(J,K,L),J=1,3)
790 101 FORMAT(A6,X,F3.1,3X,F3.1,2X,F3.1)
800 PRINT^"BCTOT=
810 PRINT 372,BCTOT(L)
820 PRINT"BCBR=
830 PRINT 372,BCBR(L)
840 PRINT"BCCG=
850 PRINT 372,BCCG(L)
860 PRINT"BCFORCE=
870 PRINT 372,BCFC(L)
880 372 FORMAT(I10)
890 L=L+1
900 IF(L-NI-1)100
910 PRINT^^^^^^
920 PRINT"PROFIT OF EACH CORPORATION IN EACH NATION"
930 PRINT^
940 PRINT 96,(IND(K),K=1,NI),
950 96 FORMAT(5X,6(3X,A6))
960 PRINT" TOTAL";DO900K=1,NN;DO900L=1,NI;900 SUM(K)=SUM(K)+PROFBT
970 +(K,L)
980 DO778 K=1,NN;778 PRINT97,WHO(K),(PROFBT(K,L),L=1,NI)
```

```
 990 +,SUM(K)
1000 97 FORMAT(A6,7I9)
1010 PRINT^^^^^^"DISTRIBUTION OF EACH INDUSTRY"
1020 PRINT"EXPRESSED AS A PERCENTAGE OF INDUSTRY"
1030 PRINT^
1040 PRINT 323,(WHO(J),J=1,NN)
1050 323 FORMAT(6X,6(4X,A6))
1060 DO779 L=1,NI;779 PRINT99,IND(L),(PERC(K,L),K=1,NN)
1070 99 FORMAT(A6,8F10.1)
1080 PRINT^^^^^" R AND D CALCULATIONS COMPLETE"
1090 WRITE(3)(((COSTS(J,K,L),K=1,NN),J=1,3),L=1,NI)
1100 WRITE(4)(BCTOT(L),BCBR(L),BCCG(L),BCFC(L),L=1,NI)
1110 WRITE(5)((PERC(K,L),K=1,NN),L=1,NI); STOP; END


X
 100.PROGRAM POLITICAL
 110 DIMENSION RHO(6,6),TAW(6,6),CFDEP(6),CFDL(6),BRDL(6),AF(6),CF(6
 120 + F(6),SIGMA(6,6),F2(6,6),BAD(6),GOOD(6),SEC(6),OPI(6),CSMIN(6)
 130 + CSMAX(6),PR(6),PSR(6),RO(6),OVS(6),CFBEG(6),CFINC(6),DL(6),BP
 140 + PSS(6),DDL(6),DDLV(6),BR(6),AFBEG(6),AFINC(6),TRADE(6,6),TOT(
 150 + WHO(6),OPIN(6,6),CS(6),CS0(6),GAMMA(6),BRINC(6),PO(6),POLT(6)
 160 + PHO(6),CFIC(6),IPS(6)
 170 $FILE A2,A10,A8,A18,A11
 180 READ(1) NN
 190 READ(1,1)(WHO(J),J=1,NN)
 200 1 FORMAT(4X,6A6)
 210 READ(2)(CFBEG(J),DL(J),DDLV(J),BR(J),AFBEG(J),CS0(J),GAMMA(J),
 220 +POLT(J),J=1,NN);REWIND 2
 230 READ(3)((TRADE(J,K),J=1,NN),K=1,NN),(TOT(J),J=1,NN),
 240 + (BP(J),J=1,NN)
 250 READ(4)(BRINC(J),CS(J),CFINC(J),J=1,NN); REWIND 4
 260 PRINT^^"FOR EACH OF THE",NN," NATIONS";PRINT2,(WHO(J),J=1,NN)
 270 2 FORMAT(6(A6,2X)); PRINT"GIVE THE FOLLOWING DATA IN NATION ORD
 280 PRINT^"PERCENTAGE CONVENTIONAL FORCE ",;INPUT,(AFINC(J),J=1,NN)
 290 DO999 J=1,NN; DUM=CFINC(J)
 300 CFINC(J)=CFINC(J)*AFINC(J)/100
 310 999 AFINC(J)=(DUM-CFINC(J))*.1
 320 PRINT"FORCES USED FOR INTERNAL CONTROL",;INPUT,(CFIC(J),J=1,NN)
 330 PRINT"CHANGE IN DECISION LATITUDE IMPOSED BY GOVERNMENT",
 340 INPUT,(DDL(J),J=1,NN)
 350 PRINT"PUBLIC OPINION",;INPUT,(PO(J),J=1,NN);PRINT^"THANKS"
 360 NAT=1;PRINT^^"FOR EACH NATION GIVE INTERNATIONAL
 370 + OPINION SCORES IN NATION ORDER"; PRINT,NN," SCORES IN ALL GIV
 380 + OPINION OF EACH NATION ABOUT ALL NATIONS"
 390 NEXT: PRINT1,WHO(NAT),;PRINT" OPINIONS",;INPUT,(OPIN(J,NAT),J=1
 400 NAT=NAT+1; IF(NAT-NN-1)NEXT; PRINT^^"THANKS. INPUT DATA COMPLET
 410 DO7J=1,NN; IF(DDL(J)-DDLV(J))183,184,183; 183 IF(8-DL(J))S
 420 CFDL(J)=CFBEG(J)*.1; BRDL(J)=BR(J)*.1; GOTO184; S CFDL(J)=CFBEG
 430 +2; BRDL(J)=BR(J)*.2; 184 CFDEP(J)=CFBEG(J)*.7
 440 CF(J)=CFDEP(J)+CFINC(J)-CFDL(J); DL(J)=DL(J)+DDL(J)
 450 AF(J)=(AFBEG(J)*.65)+AFINC(J); F(J)=AF(J)+CF(J)+(.5*BR(J))-CFIC
 460 DO7L=1,NN; 7 TAW(J,L)=TRADE(J,L)/TOT(J); RBAR=0
 470 DO11L=1,NN; DO11J=1,NN; RHO(J,L)=.5*(TAW(J,L)+TAW(L,J))
 480 11 RBAR=RBAR+RHO(J,L); RBAR=RBAR/(NN*(NN-1))
 490 DO16L=1,NN; DO16J=1,NN;SIGMA(J,L)=0;IF(X=(RBAR-RHO(J,L)))15
 500 SIGMA(J,L)=X/RBAR; RHO(J,L)=0; GOTO16;15 RHO(J,L)=-X/(1-RBAR)
 510 16 F2(J,L)=F(J)+F(L); DO19J=1,NN; DO19 L=1,NN
 520 BAD(J)=BAD(J)+F2(J,L)*SIGMA(J,L)
 530 GOOD(J)=GOOD(J)+F2(J,L)*RHO(J,L)
 540 19 OPI(J)=OPI(J)+OPIN(J,L)*(RHO(J,L)-SIGMA(J,L))
```

```
550 DO28 J=1,NN; SEC(J)=10*GOOD(J)/BAD(J)
560 IF(SEC(J)-10)24;SEC(J)=10;24 IF(1-SEC(J))23;SEC(J)=1
570 23 IF(OPI(J)-10)29;OPI(J)=10;29 IF(1-OPI(J))28;OPI(J)=1
580 28 ALHPA=2; BETA=80
590 DO34L=1,NN;CSMAX(L)=BR(L)*ALPHA;IF(CS0(L)-CSMAX(L))3
600 CSMAX(L)=CS0(L)+1;3 CSMIN(L)=BETA*ALOG(CSMAX(L)/CS0(L))+CS0(L)
610 GAMMA(L)=30
620 IF(CSMIN(L)-CS(L))34; CS(L)=CSMIN(L)+1
630 34 CS(L)=GAMMA(L)*ALOG(CS(L)/CSMIN(L));DO35L=1,NN
640 PR(L)=.9-.055*CS(L)-.035*SEC(L)+.01*CFIC(L)/(CF(L)+AF(L))
650 35 PSR(L)=1-CFIC(L)/CF(L)
660 DO36L=1,NN; RO(L)=BP(L)/TOT(L);A=-1;IF(RO(L))752; A=1
670 752 IF((A*RO(L)*100)-5)751;RO(L)=.05*A;751 BR(L)=(.9*BR(L)+BRINC(L)
680 +-BRDL(L))*(1+RO(L)); 36
690 DO38L=1,NN;OVS(L)=SEC(L)+OPI(L)+CS(L)+PO(L); OVS(L)=OVS(L)/4
700 IF(OVS(L)-2.5)199
710 PR(L)=0
720 PSR(L)=0
730 199 PSS(L)=.01*(11-
740 +DL(L))*OVS(L)+.1*(DL(L)-1)*10
750 CSMAX(L)=BR(L)*ALPHA;IF(CS0(L)-CSMAX(L))YES
760 CSMAX(L)=CS0(L)+1;YES: CSMIN(L)=BETA*ALOG(CSMAX(L)/CS0(L))+CS0(L)
770 IF(PR(L)-RND(0))760;PRINT^^"REVOLUTION FOR ",;PRINT1,WHO(L)
780 IF(PSR(L)-RND(0))761; PRINT^"REVOLUTION SUCCESFULL";GOTO760
790 761 PRINT"REVOLUTION UNSUCCESFULL";760 PRINT^^^;38 ;PRINT^^^"
800 + CALCULATIONS COMPLETE"
810 PRINT^^^^"STATE OF NATIONS";PRINT40,(WHO(L),L=1,NN)
820 40 FORMAT(12X,6(4X,A6))
830 PRINT"P HOLD OFF",
840 DO51 J=1,NN; PHO(J)=1-.1*(POLT(J)-PO(J))-2/PO(J)
850 IF(-PHO(J))TUT; PHO(J)=0 ;TUT: IF(PHO(J)-1)51
860 PHO(J)=1 ; 51
870 PRINT 234,(PHO(J),J=1,NN)
880 52 FORMAT(6F10.0)
890 PRINT"PROB REVOL",;PRINT234,(PR(J),J=1,NN)
900 PRINT"STABILITY ",;PRINT52,(PSS(J),J=1,NN)
910 234 FORMAT(6F10.1)
920 READ(5)(IPS(J),J=1,NN)
930 REWIND 5
940 PRINT^^ "IPSCRIPTS "
950 PRINT 52,(IPS(J)*BR(J),J=1,NN)
960 PRINT ^^
970 PRINT"POLITICAL";PRINT"EFFECTIVE ",;PRINT52,(OVS(J),J=1,NN)
980 PRINT"PUBLIC OPI",;PRINT52,(PO(J),J=1,NN)
990 PRINT"CON SATISF",;PRINT52,(CS(J),J=1,NN)
1000 PRINT"DECISION L",;PRINT52,(DL(J),J=1,NN)
1010 PRINT"BASIC RES ",;PRINT52,(BR(J),J=1,NN)
1020 PRINT"CON MIMIM ",;PRINT52,(CSMIN(J),J=1,NN)
1030 PRINT"INT OPIN ",;PRINT52,(OPI(J),J=1,NN)
1040 PRINT"NAT SECUR ",;PRINT52,(SEC(J),J=1,NN)
1050 PRINT"CONV FORCE",;PRINT52,(CF(J),J=1,NN)
1060 PRINT"NUCL FORCE",;PRINT52,(AF(J),J=1,NN)
1070 PRINT"P SUC REV ",;PRINT234,(PSR(J),J=1,NN)
1080 DO55J=1,NN; IF(RND(0)-.6)56; DDLV(J)=-1;GOTO55
1090 56 DDLV(J)=0;55
1100 PRINT"RANDOM CHANGE";PRINT"DECISION L",;PRINT52,(DDLV(J),J=1,NN)
1110 WRITE(2)(CF(J),DL(J),DDLV(J),BR(J),AF(J),CS0(J),GAMMA(J),
1120 +PO(J),J=1,NN)
1130 STOP; END
```

```
100. PROGRAM ECONOMIC
110 DIMENSION SALES(3,6,6),PROFIT(3,6,6),SALEPR(3,6,6),PRODCT(3,6),
120 +STOCK(3,6),DSTOCK(3,6),WHO(6),CORP(6),XMPORT(6,6),TSALES(6,6),
130 +TOTEXP(6),TOTIMP(6),PERCEN(6,6),SALEPN(3,6),PROFPN(3,6),
140 +TPROFN(6,6),TPROFC(6),TOT(6),TRADE(6,6),TAW(6,6)
150 $FILE A1,A2,A3,A5,A6,A7,A8,A9,A16,A17,A19
160 READ(1)NI; READ(1,1)(CORP(J),J=1,NI);  1 FORMAT(4X,6A6)
170 READ(2)NN; READ(2,1)(WHO(J),J=1,NN)
180 READ(6)((STOCK(J,K),J=1,3),K=1,NI);NUM=1;2 NAT=1
190 REWIND 1; REWIND 2; REWIND 6
200 READ(11)((PRODCT(J,K),J=1,3),K=1,NI)
210 REWIND 11
220 PRINT^^"NO DATA INPUT IS REQUIRED FROM THE TERMINAL"
230 PRINT^"THE DATA IS ENTERED INTO THE PROGRAM VIA SAVED FILES"
240 READ(9)(((SALES(J,K,L),J=1,3),K=1,NI),L=1,NN);REWIND 9
250 READ(10)(((SALEPR(J,K,L),J=1,3),K=1,NI),L=1,NN);REWIND 10
260 READ(4)((PERCEN(K,L),K=1,NN),L=1,NI)
270 REWIND 4
280 DO5 K=1,NI; DO6 J=1,3;DO7 L=1,NN
290 READ(3)X
300 IF(SALES(J,K,L))7,7
310 SALEPR(J,K,L)=(SALEPR(J,K,L)/SALES(J,K,L))-X
320 7
330 6
340 5
350 DO 50 J=1,3; DO 50 K=1,NI; DO 50 L=1,NN
360 IF(999-SALES(J,K,L))POP; SALEPR(J,K,L)=SALEPR(J,K,L)+SALES(J,K,L)
370 +1000;GOTO50 ;POP: IF(1199-SALES(J,K,L))9;SALEPR(J,K,L)=
380 +SALEPR(J,K,L)+1; GOTO50
390 9 IF(1399-SALES(J,K,L))11; SALEPR(J,K,L)=SALEPR(J,K,L)+1.1
400 GOTO50 ;11 IF(1699-SALES(J,K,L))13; SALEPR(J,K,L)=SALEPR(J,K,L)+1
410 GOTO50 ;13 IF(1999-SALES(J,K,L))15; SALEPR(J,K,L)=SALEPR(J,K,L)+1
420 GOTO50 ;15 IF(2299-SALES(J,K,L))17; SALEPR(J,K,L)=SALEPR(J,K,L)+1
430 GOTO50 ;17 IF(2699-SALES(J,K,L))19; SALEPR(J,K,L)=SALEPR(J,K,L)+1
440 GOTO50 ;19 IF(3099-SALES(J,K,L))21; SALEPR(J,K,L)=SALEPR(J,K,L)+1
450 GOTO50 ;21 IF(3699-SALES(J,K,L))23; SALEPR(J,K,L)=SALEPR(J,K,L)+1
460 GOTO50 ;23 IF(4399-SALES(J,K,L))25; SALEPR(J,K,L)=SALEPR(J,K,L)+1
470 GOTO50 ;25 IF(5199-SALES(J,K,L))27; SALEPR(J,K,L)=SALEPR(J,K,L)+1
480 GOTO50 ;27 SALEPR(J,K,L)=SALEPR(J,K,L)+2; 50
490 DO110 K=1,NI; DO110 L=1,NN; DO110 J=1,3
500 110 TSALES(K,L)=TSALES(K,L)+SALES(J,K,L)
510 DO115 K=1,NI; DO115 L=1,NN; DO115 M=1,NN
520 115 XMPORT(L,M)=XMPORT(L,M)+TSALES(K,L)*PERCEN(M,K)/100
530 DO118 M=1,NN; DO118 L=1,NN; IF(L-M)119,118,119
540 119 TOTIMP(L)=TOTIMP(L)+XMPORT(L,M);TOTEXP(L)=TOTEXP(L)+XMPORT(M,
550 118 ;DO136 L=1,NN;DO136 M=1,NN;136 TSALES(L,M)=0
560 DO 133 L=1,NN; DO133 M=1,NN;133 TRADE(L,M)=TRADE(L,M)+XMPORT(L,M)
570 ++XMPORT(M,L); READ(8)INST; REWIND 8;L=1
580 PRINT^^^^"TRADE MATRIX FOR PERIOD ",INST; NAT=1
590 PRINT 120,(WHO(J),J=1,NN),; PRINT" TOTAL"
600 120 FORMAT(15X,6(2X,A6))
610 131 PRINT 121,WHO(NAT),(XMPORT(NAT,M),M=1,NN),TOTIMP(NAT)
620 121 FORMAT(A6,9H IMPORTS ,7I8)
630 PRINT 123,WHO(NAT),(XMPORT(L,NAT),L=1,NN),TOTEXP(NAT)
640 123 FORMAT(A6,9H EXPORTS ,7I8)
650 TOT(NAT)=TOTIMP(NAT)+TOTEXP(NAT)
660 PRINT 124,WHO(NAT),(TRADE(L,NAT),L=1,NN),TOT(NAT)
670 124 FORMAT(A6,9H TOTAL ,7I8)
680 NAT=NAT+1; IF(NAT-NN-1)131; DO145 J=1,6; DO145 K=1,6
690 145 TSALES(J,K)=0
700 DO 876 J=1,NN;876 TOTEXP(J)=TOTEXP(J)-TOTIMP(J)
```

```
710 WRITE(7)((TRADE(J,K),J=1,NN),K=1,NN),(TOT(J),J=1,NN),
720 +(TOTEXP(J),J=1,NN)
730 DO146L=1,NN; DO146J=1,3; DO146K=1,NI;146 TSALES(J,K)=TSALES(J,K)
740 ++SALES(J,K,L);  DO147 J=1,3;DO147K=1,NI; STOCK(J,K)=STOCK(J,K)
750 ++PRODCT(J,K)-TSALES(J,K); DSTOCK(J,K)=PRODCT(J,K)-TSALES(J,K)
760 IF(-STOCK(J,K))108; DO109L=1,NN;109 PROFIT(J,K,L)=(PRODCT(J,K)
770 ++STOCK(J,K))*SALEPR(J,K,L)*SALES(J,K,L)/TSALES(J,K); GOTO147
780 108 DO 107 L=1,NN; 107 PROFIT(J,K,L)=SALES(J,K,L)*SALEPR(J,K,L)
790 147 ; DO200 L=1,NN; DO200J=1,3; DO200K=1,NI;200 PROFPN(J,K)=
800 +PROFPN(J,K)+PROFIT(J,K,L); DO201 J=1,3;DO201K=1,NI;DO201L=1,NN
810 201 TPROFN(K,L)=TPROFN(K,L)+PROFIT(J,K,L)
820 DO202 L=1,NN; DO202 K=1,NI;202 TPROFC(K)=TPROFC(K)+TPROFN(K,L)
830 IND=1;NEXT: PRINT^^^^CORPORATION BALANCE SHEET,PERIOD",INST,
840 +" FOR",;PRINT1,CORP(IND);PRINT^"              BR      CG
850 +        FC    TOTAL"
860 X=STOCK(1,IND)+STOCK(2,IND)+STOCK(3,IND)
870 PRINT400,(STOCK(J,IND),J=1,3),X
880 401 FORMAT(10H CHANGE =     ,4I8)
890 Y=DSTOCK(1,IND)+DSTOCK(2,IND)+DSTOCK(3,IND)
900 PRINT401,(DSTOCK(J,IND),J=1,3),Y
910 400 FORMAT(10H STOCK  =     ,4I8)
920 PRINT^^"PROFITS ON";PRINT"SALES TO"
930 PRINT 172,(WHO(L),(PROFIT(J,IND,L),J=1,3),TPROFN(IND,L),L=1,NN)
940 172 FORMAT(2X,A6,2X,4I8)
950 PRINT185,(PROFPN(J,IND),J=1,3),TPROFC(IND)
960 185 FORMAT(10H TOTAL       ,4I8)
970 IND=IND+1; IF(IND-NI-1)NEXT
980 WRITE(5)(TPROFC(L),L=1,NI)
990 WRITE(6)((STOCK(J,K),J=1,3),K=1,NI)
1000 INST=INST+1; WRITE(8)INST
1010 REWIND 8
1020 STOP; END


100.PROGRAM WAR
110 DIMENSION ATTACK(7,7),SHIELD(7),REATAK(7),DAMAGE(7),PROTEK(7),
120 +REPULS(7),DSHIEL(7),DRFATA(7),RATIO(7),BCLOSS(7),SUMDAT(7),
130 +SUMATT(7),RATIOS(7,7),DATTAC(7,7),WHO(7)
140 +,NUM(7),BR(7),CFBEG(6),AFBEG(6)
150 $FILE A2,410
160 READ(1)NN
170 READ(1,1)(WHO(J),J=1,NN)
180 REWIND 1
190 1 FORMAT(4X,7A6)
200 PRINT^^"ALL INFORMATION FOR RUNNING THIS PROGRAM COMES FROM
210 + THE FORCE           UTILIZATION PLAN"
220 PRINT^^^"TO BEGIN WITH WE NEED TO KNOW WHICH NATIONS ARE AT WAR"
230 PRINT^"IF A NATION IS AT WAR ENTER 1, IF NOT 0 (ZERO)"
240 PRINT^^
250 DO 900 J=1,NN
260 PRINT 901,WHO(J),
270 900 INPUT,NUM(J)
280 PRINT^^"THANKS. IS THE INTERNATIONAL ORGANIZATION (IF ANY)
290 + OR SOME OTHER         POLITICAL ENTITY INVOLVED"
300 PRINT^"TYPE 1 IF YES AND 0 (ZERO) IF NOT",
310 INPUT,NUM(7)
320 IF (NUM(7))804,804
330 PRINT^"WHAT IS NAME OF POLITICAL ENTITY(6 CHARACTERS MAXIMUM)"
340 INPUT 901,WHO(7)
350 901 FORMAT(A6)
360 804
```

```
370 PRINT^^"ARE NUCLEAR FORCES INVOLVED",;INPUT,NNN
330 IF(NNN-"NO")800,801,800; 800 IF(NNN-"YES")802,803
390 802 PRINT^^"PLEASE ANSWER YES OR NO";GOTO804;801 INDEX=1;GOTO805
400 803 INDEX=1000; PRINT^^"FOR NUCLEAR FORCES";GOTONEXT
410 805 PRINT^^"FOR CONVENTIONAL FORCES"
420 NEXT: PRINT"WE REQUIRE THE MILITARY CIVILIAN MIX OF ATTACK FORCES
430 + AND ACTIVE DEFENCE FORCES. THESE ARE GIVEN ON THE FORCE
440 + UTILIZATION FORM,ITEM2 AND ITEM 6 OF FORCE DECISIONS"
450 PRINT^"FOR EACH NATION GIVE THE RATIOS IN THE ORDER"
450 I=0
470 DO724 J=1,7
430 IF(NUM(J))724,724
490 PRINT 901,WHO(J)
500 I=I+1
510 724
520 II-1
530 PRINT^^"A NATIONS RATIO WITH ITSELF IS ITEM 6. THE OTHER",I,
540 +" RATIOS ARE IN ITEM 2"
550 I=I+1
560 PRINT^"WHAT ARE RATIOS FOR"
570 DO 721 J=1,7
530 IF(NUM(J))721,721
590 DO573 N=1,7
600 IF(NUM(N))573,573
610 PRINT^
620 PRINT 735,WHO(J),WHO(N),
630 INPUT,RATIOS(N,J)
640 573
650 721
660 PRINT^^
670 PRINT"THANKS- AND NOW WE NEED ATTACK
630 + FORCES USED BY EACH NATION AGAINST OTHERS IN ORDER, AND
690 + TOTAL FORCE(FORCE INFORMATION ITEM1 FOR CONVENTIONAL AND ITEM 2
700 + FOR NUCLEAR). TOTAL FORCE IS ENTERED FOR A NATION WITH ITSELF
710 + WHILE ATTACK FORCES FROM ITEM 1 FILL OTHER",I-1," PLACES"
720 PRINT^^"ATTACK/TOTAL FORCE FOR"
730 736 FORMAT(A6," AGAINST    ,A5)
740 DO 719 J=1,7
750 IF(NUM(J))719,719
760 DO737 N=1,7
770 IF(NUM(N))737,737
780 PRINT^
790 PRINT 736,WHO(J),WHO(N),
800 INPUT,ATTACK(N,J)
810 737
820 719
830 PRINT^^^"THANKS-AND FINALLY FOR EACH NATION GIVE DEFENCE FORCES
840 + ACTIVE ON ALERT, ITEM 3 FORCE DECISIONS,AND DEFENCE FORCES
850 + PASSIVE, ITEM FOUR"
860 DO 917 J=1,7
870 IF(NUM(J))917,917
880 PRINT 901,WHO(J),
890 INPUT,REATAK(J),SHIELD(J)
900 917
910 IF(INDEX-2)825; PRINT^^"DATA INPUT COMPLETE FOR NUCLEAR FORCE"
920 GOTOSTART; 825 PRINT^^"DATA INPUT COMPLETE"
930 START: DO 11 K=1,7
940 IF(NUM(K))11,11
950 DO 10 J=1,7
960 IF(NUM(J))12,12
970 IF(J-K)6,10
```

```
980 S RATIO(K)=RATIO(K)+RATIOS(K,J);10 DSHIEL(J)=0
990 12
1000
1010 RATIO(K)=(RATIO(K)/(I-1)) + RATIOS(K,K)* .5
1020 11
1030
1040 DO 30 J=1,7
1050 IF(NUM(J))30,30
1060 DO 20 K=1,7
1070 IF(NUM(K))20,20
1080 SUMDAT(K)=SUMATT(K)=0
1090 IF(J-K)19,20
1100 19 DSHIEL(J)=DSHIEL(J)+INDEX*ATTACK(K,J)
1110 20
1120 DSHIEL(J)=DSHIEL(J) - SHIELD(J)
1130 IF(-DSHIEL(J))22;DSHIEL(J)=0;22 DSHIEL(J)=MIN1F(DSHIEL(J),SHIELD(J))
1140 IF(DSHIEL(J)-SHIELD(J))24; SHIELD(J)=0;GOTO25
1150 24 SHIELD(J)=SHIELD(J)-DSHIEL(J)*RATIO(J)
1160 25 BCLOSS(J)=DSHIEL(J)*(1-RATIO(J));DREATA(J)=.1*(BCLOSS(J)+
1170 +DSHIEL(J)); DREATA(J)=MIN1F(DREATA(J),REATAK(J))
1180 REATAK(J)=REATAK(J)-DREATA(J);29 PRINT 60,WHO(J)
1190 DO 750 K=1,7
1200 IF(NUM(K))750,750
1210 DATTAC(K,J)=REATAK(K)
1220 DATTAC(K,J)=MIN1F(DATTAC(K,J),ATTACK(K,J))
1230 ATTACK(K,J)=ATTACK(K,J)-DATTAC(K,J)
1240 SUMATT(J)=SUMATT(J)+ATTACK(K,J)
1250 750 SUMDAT(J)=SUMDAT(J)+DATTAC(K,J)
1260 60 FORMAT(///"FOR COUNTRY",A6," : /)
1270 PRINT" AGAINST COUNTRIES
1280 DO 927 K=1,7
1290 IF(NUM(K))927,927
1300 PRINT 61,WHO(K),
1310 927
1320 61 FORMAT(A7)
1330 PRINT "
1340 PRINT" ATTACK FORCES LEFT
1350 DO971 K=1,7
1360 IF(NUM(K))971,971
1370 PRINT 62, ATTACK(K,J),
1380 971
1390 62 FORMAT(F7.1)
1400 PRINT"
1410 PRINT" ATTACK FORCES DESTROYED
1420 DO 837K=1,7
1430 IF(NUM(K))837,837
1440 PRINT62,DATTAC(K,J),
1450 837
1460 PRINT64,SUMATT(J),SUMDAT(J),SHIELD(J),DSHIEL(J),REATAK(J),DREATA(J)
1470 +,BCLOSS(J)
1480 64 FORMAT(/3X,"TOTAL ATTACK FORCES LEFT",8X,F7.1/3X,"TOTAL ATTACK
1490 + FORCES DESTROYED",3X,F7.1/3X,"PASSIVE DEFENSE LEFT",
1500 +12X,F7.1/3X,"PASSIVE DEFENSE DESTROYED",7X,F7.1/3X,
1510 +"ACTIVE DEFENSE LEFT",13X,F7.1/3X,"ACTIVE DEFENSE DESTROYED",
1520 +8X,F7.1/3X,"TOTAL CIVILIAN LOSSES",11X,F7.1/)
1530 30
1540 READ(2)(CFBEG(J),A,B,BR(J),AFBEG(J),C,J=1,NN)
1550 REWIND 2
1560 IF(INDEX-2)847
1570 DO 537 J=1,7
1580 IF(NUM(J))537,537
```

```
1590 AFBEG(J)=AFBEG(J)-SUMDAT(J)-DSHIEL(J)-DREATA(J)
1600 BR(J)=BR(J)-BCLOSS(J)
1610 537
1620 INDEX=1
1630 GOTO805
1640 847 PRINT^^
1650 DO 538 J=1,7
1660 IF(NUM(J))538,538
1670 CFBEG(J)=CFBEG(J)-SUMDAT(J)-DSHIEL(J)-DREATA(J)
1680 BR(J)=BR(J)-BCLOSS(J)
1690 IF(BR(J))540,541,541
1700 540 BR(J)=0
1710 541 IF(CFBEG(J))542,543,543
1720 542 CFBEG(J)=0
1730 543 IF(AFBEG(J))544,545,545
1740 544 AFBEG(J)=0
1750 545
1760 538
1770 READ(2)(SUMATT(J),SUMDAT(J),SHIELD(J),DSHIEL(J),
1780 + REATAK(J),DREATA(J),J=1,NN)
1790 REWIND 2
1800 WRITE(2)(CFBEG(J),SUMDAT(J),SHIELD(J),BR(J),AFBEG(J),
1810 + DREATA(J),J=1,NN)
1820 DO 437 J=1,7
1830 IF(NUM(J))437,437
1840 PRINT^^
1850 PRINT 438,WHO(J),BR(J),CFBEG(J),AFBEG(J)
1860 437
1870 438 FORMAT(3X,A5,3X,"BR=",I8/12X,"CF=",I8/12X,"NF=",I8)
1880 PRINT^^^" END OF PROGRAM"
1890 STOP
1900 END


100.PROGRAM AGREEMENT
110 REAL DIMENSION GEXP(6),CEXP(5), CIT(6,6,2,2),GOV(6,5,2,2)
120 + IND(5),WHO(5),BR(6),CS(6),ARMS(5)
130 $FILE A1,A2,A12,A13,A14,A15,A16,A17,A18
140 READ(1)NI;READ(1,1)(IND(J),J=1,NI);1 FORMAT(4X,5A5);REWIND 1
150 READ(2)NN;READ(2,1)(WHO(J),J=1,NN;REWIND 2
160 READ(4)((((CIT(I,J,K,L),I=1,NI),J=1,NN),K=1,2),L=1,2)
170 READ(5)((((GOV(I,J,K,L),I=1,NI),J=1,NN),K=1,2),L=1,2)
180 REWIND 4;REWIND 5
190 INPUT,NSTRUCT
200 IF(NSTRUCT)NEXT,NEXT
210 PRINT^^^"NUMBER CODES FOR NATIONS AND CORPORATIONS ARE"
220 DO2J=1,NN;PRINT1,WHO(J),;2 PRINT,J; PRINT^
230 DO3J=1,NI;PRINT 1,IND(J),;3 PRINT,J
240 PRINT^"CODE FOR CITIZEN=CIT.  CODE FOR GOVERNMENT=GOV"
250 PRINT^"CODE FOR BASIC RESOURCES=1. FOR CONSUMER GOODS=1"
260 PRINT"CODE FOR FORCE =2"
270 NEXT:
280 PRINT^^^"HAVE YOU ENTERED CITIZENS INCOME FOR PERIOD",;
290 INPUT,NNN
300 IF(NNN-"YES")4,5;4 IF(NNN-"NO")6,7;6 PRINT^"YES OR NO";
310 GOTONEXT
320 7 PRINT^"FOR NATIONS IN ORDER GIVE";PRINT"CITIZENS INCOME",
330 INPUT,(CEXP(J),J=1,NN);PRINT^"THANKS";WRITE(3)(CEXP(J),J=1,NN)
340 GO TO8;5 READ(3)(CEXP(J),J=1,NN);8 REWIND 3
350 31 PRINT^^^"TYPE 1 IF MORE AGREEMENTS,2 IF NOT",;INPUT,IT
360 GOTO(9,32)IT
```

```
370 9 PRINT^^"IS NEXT TRADE AGREEMENT MADE WITH A CITIZEN(CIT)
380 + OR A GOVERNMENT(GOV)";14 INPUT,NNN
390 IF(NNN-"CIT")10,11;10 IF(NNN-"GOV")12,13;12 PRINT^"CIT OR
400 + GOV"
410 GOTO14;11 PRINT^^"NATION NUMBER CODE=",;INPUT,JJ
420 PRINT"CORPORATION NUMBER CODE=",;INPUT,II
430 PRINT"PRODUCT(CG=1,FORCE=2)=",;INPUT,KK
440 Q=CIT(II JJ,KK,1); P=CIT(II,JJ,KK,2)
450 PRINT"QUANTITY =",;INPUT,CIT(II,JJ,KK,1)
460 PRINT"PRICE=",;INPUT,CIT(II,JJ,KK,2);A=CIT(II,JJ,KK,2)/
470 +CIT(II,JJ,KK,1);PRINT^"THIS GIVES UNIT PRICE =",;PRINT,A
480 EXP=0;DO15I=1,NI;DO15K=1,2;15 EXP=EXP+CIT(I,JJ,K,2)
490 IF(CEXP(JJ)-EXP)20
500 PRINT^^^"AGREEMENT RATIFIED"
510 PRINT"AVAILABLE INCOME=",;PRINT, CEXP(JJ)
520 PRINT"EXPENDITURE TO DATE INCLUDING THIS AGREEMENT",EXP
530 GO TO31
540 20 PRINT^^^"AGREEMENT IMPOSSIBLE-OVERSPENDING"
550 PRINT^"AVAILABLE INCOME = ", CEXP(JJ)
560 PRINT"THIS AGREEMENT WOULD MADE EXPENDITURE ", EXP
570 CIT(II,JJ,KK,1)=Q; CIT(II,JJ,KK,2)=P;GOTO31
580 13 PRINT^^^"HAS GOVERNMENT INCOME BEEN ENTERED",;INPUT,NNN
590 IF(NNN-"YES")21,22;21 IF(NNN-"NO")23,24; 23 PRINT^"YES OR NO"
600 GOTO13;24 PRINT^"IS IT AVAILABLE",;INPUT,NNN
610 IF(NNN-"YES")25,26; 25 IF(NNN-"NO")27,28; 27 PRINT"YES OR NO"
620 GOTO24
630 28 PRINT"WELL JUST ENTER CITIZENS AGREEMENTS UNTIL IT IS"
640 GO TO 31
650 26 PRINT^"THE",NN," GOVERNMENT INCOMES ARE";INPUT,(GEXP(J)
660 +,J=1,NN)
670 WRITE(6)(GEXP(J),J=1,NN);GOTO30;22 READ(6)(GEXP(J),J=1,NN)
680 30 REWIND 6;PRINT^"NATION NUMBER CODE =",;INPUT,JJ
690 PRINT"CORPORATION NUMBER CODE=",;INPUT,II
700 PRINT"PRODUCT(BR=1,FORCE=2)=",;INPUT,KK
710 Q=GOV(II,JJ,KK,1); P=GOV(II,JJ,KK,2)
720 PRINT"QUANTITY =",; INPUT,GOV(II,JJ,KK,1)
730 PRINT"PRICE=",;INPUT,GOV(II,JJ,KK,2)
740 A=GOV(II,JJ,KK,2)/GOV(II,JJ,KK,1)
750 PRINT"THIS GIVES A UNIT PRICE OF",A
760 EXP=0; DO40I=1,NI; DO40K=1,2; 40 EXP=EXP+GOV(I,JJ,K,2)
770 IF(EXP-GEXP(JJ))41,41;PRINT^"AGREEMENT IMPOSSIBLE-GOVERSPENDING"
780 PRINT"AVAILABLE INCOME=",GEXP(JJ)
790 PRINT"THIS AGREEMENT WOULD MAKE EXPENDITURE",EXP
800 GOV(II,JJ,KK,1)=Q ; GOV(II,JJ,KK,2)=P;GOTO31
810 41 PRINT^^"AGREEMENT RATIFIED"
820 PRINT"AVAILABLE INCOME =",GEXP(JJ)
830 PRINT"EXPENDITURE TO DATE INCLUDING THIS AGREEMENT=",EXP
840 GOTO31
850 32 DO DANCE,J=1,NN; DANCE: BR(J)=CS(J)=ARMS(J)=0
860 DO SING,J=1,NN
870 DO SING,I=1,NI
880 BR(J)=BR(J)+GOV(I,J,1,1)
890 CS(J) = CS(J) + CIT(I,J,1,1)
900 SING: ARMS(J)=ARMS(J) + GOV(I,J,1,1)
910 WRITE (9)(BR(J),CS(J),ARMS(J),J=1,NN); REWIND 9
920 DO 61 J=1,NN; DO 60 I = 1,NI
930 SUM=GOV(I,J,2,1)+CIT(I,J,2,1)
940 60 WRITE(7)(GOV(I,J,1,1),CIT(I,J,1,1),SUM);61    ;REWIND 7
950 REWIND 8
960 DO62J=1,NN;DO63 I=1,NI
970 SUM=GOV(I,J,2,2)+CIT(I,J,2,2)
```

```
980 63 WRITE(8)(GOV(I,J,1,2),CIT(I,J,1,2),SUM);62      ;REWIND 8
990 WRITE(4)((((CIT(I,J,K,L),I=1,NI),J=1,NN),K=1,2),L=1,2)
1000 WRITE(5)((((GOV(I,J,K,L),I=1,NI),J=1,NN),K=1,2),L=1,2)
1010 STOP    ;   END


090 PROGRAM TERMINATION
100 REAL DIMENSION IND(6),WHO(6),CIT(6,6,2,2),GOV(6,6,2,2),TOT(6)
110 $FILE A1,A2,A13,A14
120 READ(1),NI;READ(1,1)(IND(J),J=1,NI);1 FORMAT(4X,SA6);REWIND 1
130 READ(2),NN;READ(2,1)(WHO(J),J=1,NN);REWIND 2
140 READ(3)((((CIT(I,J,K,L),I=1,NI),J=1,NN),K=1,2),L=1,2);REWIND 3
150 READ(4)((((GOV(I,J,K,L),I=1,NI),J=1,NN),K=1,2),L=1,2);REWIND 4
160 INPUT,NSTRUCT
170 IF(NSTRUCT)50,50
180 PRINT^^"NUMBER CODES FOR NATIONS AND CORPORATIONS ARE"
190 DO2J=1,NN;PRINT1,WHO(J),;2 PRINT,J;PRINT^^
200 DO3J=1,NI;PRINT1,IND(J),;3 PRINT,J
210 PRINT^^"CODE FOR CITIZEN IS CIT, FOR GOVERNMENT IS GOV"
220 PRINT"CODE FOR BASIC RESOURCES IS 1, FOR CONSUMER GOODS ALSO 1"
230 PRINT"CODE FOR FORCE IS 2"
240 50 PRINT^^^"ANY MORE TRADE TERMINATIONS ",;!4 INPUT,NNN
250 IF(NNN-"YES")10,11;10 IF(NNN-"NO")12,13;12 PRINT"YES OR NO";GOTO
260 11 PRINT^"CITIZEN(CIT)OR GOVERNMENT(GOV) ",;19 INPUT,NNN
270 IF(NNN-"CIT")15,16;15 IF(NNN-"GOV")17,18;17 PRINT"CIT OR GOV";
280 GO TO19;16 PRINT^"NATION NUMBER",;INPUT,JJ
290 PRINT"CORPORATION NUMBER",;INPUT,II
300 PRINT"PRODUCT NUMBER",;INPUT,KK
310 PRINT^"THIS IS AN AGREEMENT TO SUPPLY A QUANTITY",
320 PRINT,CIT(II,JJ,KK,1)
330 PRINT"AT A PRICE OF",;PRINT,CIT(II,JJ,KK,2)
340 PRINT^"IS THAT CORRECT",;
350 34 INPUT,NNN;IF(NNN-"YES")30,31;30 IF(NNN-"NO")32,33
360 32 PRINT"YES OR NO";GOTO34
370 33 PRINT^"WELL CHECK BACK WITH TERMINATOR AND TRY AGAIN";GOTO50
380 31 CIT(II,JJ,KK,1)=CIT(II,JJ,KK,2)=0;PRINT"AGREEMENT TERMINATED"
390 GOTO50
400 18 PRINT^^"NATION NUMBER",;INPUT,JJ
410 PRINT"CORPORATION NUMBER",;INPUT,II
420 PRINT"PRODUCT",;INPUT,KK
430 PRINT^^"THIS IS AN AGREEMENT TO SUPPLY A QUANTITY",;
440 PRINT,GOV(II,JJ,KK,1)
450 PRINT"AT A PRICE OF",;PRINT,GOV(II,JJ,KK,2)
460 PRINT"IS THAT CORRECT",;50 INPUT,NNN; IF(NNN-"YES")51,62
470 51 IF(NNN-"NO")53,64;63 PRINT"YES OR NO";GOTO60
480 54 PRINT"WELL CHECK BACK WITH THE TERMINATOR AND TRY AGAIN"
490 GOTO50;62 GOV(II,JJ,KK,1)=GOV(II,JJ,KK,2)=0
500 GOTO50
510 13 WRITE(3)(((((CIT(I,J,K,L),I=1,NI),J=1,NN),K=1,2),L=1,2);REWIND
520 WRITE(4)((((GOV(I,J,K,L),I=1,NI),J=1,NN),K=1,2),L=1,2);REWIND 4
530 PRINT^^^"DO YOU WANT PRINT OUT OF EXISTING AGREEMENTS FOR
540 + INDUSTRIES",;70 INPUT,NNN;IF(NNN-"YES")71,72;71 IF(NNN-"NO")73
550 73 PRINT"YES OR NO";GOTO70; 72 I=1
560 80 PRINT^^^"EXISTING AGREEMENTS FOR",;PRINT 1,IND(I)
570 PRINT^"QUANTITY",;PRINT 81,(WHO(J),J=1,NN),;PRINT"   TOTAL "
580 81 FORMAT(6(3X,A6));L=1
590 90 SUM1=SUM2=SUM3=SUM4=SUM5=0
600 DO 83 J=1,NN;83 TOT(J)=0
610 DO 82 J=1,NN;SUM1=SUM1+GOV(I,J,1,L);SUM2=SUM2+CIT(I,J,1,L)
620 SUM3=SUM3+GOV(I,J,2,L);SUM4=SUM4+CIT(I,J,2,L)
```

```
630 D082K=1,2;SUM5=SUM5+GOV(I,J,K,L)+CIT(I,J,K,L)
640 82 TOT(J)=TOT(J)+GOV(I,J,K,L)+CIT(I,J,K,L)
650 PRINT"BR(GOV)" ,;PRINT84,(GOV(I,J,1,L),J=1,NN),SUM1
660 PRINT"CG(CIT)" ,;PRINT84,(CIT(I,J,1,L),J=1,NN),SUM2
670 PRINT"FC(GOV)" ,;PRINT84,(GOV(I,J,2,L),J=1,NN),SUM3
680 PRINT"FC(CIT)" ,;PRINT84,(CIT(I,J,2,L),J=1,NN),SUM4
690 PRINT"TOTAL   " ,;PRINT84,(TOT(J),J=1,NN),SUM5
700 84 FORMAT(X,7F9.0)
710 L=L+1;IF(2-L)91
720 PRINT^"PRICE    " ,;PRINT81,(WHO(J),J=1,NN),;PRINT"   TOTAL ";GOTO90
730 91 I=I+1;IF(I-NI-1)80;74 PRINT^^^"DO YOU WANT EXISTING AGREEMENTS
740 + FOR CITIZENS" ,;95 INPUT,NNN;IF(NNN-"YES")96,97
750 96 IF(NNN-"NO")98,99;98 PRINT"YES OR NO";GOTO95
760 97 J=L=IX=1
770 111 PRINT^^^"EXISTING AGREEMENTS FOR",;PRINT1,WHO(J)
780 PRINT^^^"QUANTITY",;PRINT81,(IND(I),I=1,NI),;PRINT"    TOTAL"
790 100 SUM1=SUM2=SUM3=0;DO 101 I=1,NI;101 TOT(I)=0
800 DO 102I=1,NI;SUM1=SUM1+CIT(I,J,1,L);SUM2=SUM2+CIT(I,J,2,L)
810 DO102K=1,2;SUM3=SUM3+CIT(I,J,K,L);102 TOT(I)=TOT(I)+CIT(I,J,K,L)..
820 IF(IX)200
830 PRINT"CG    " ,;PRINT84,(CIT(I,J,1,L),I=1,NI),SUM1;GOTO201;200
840 PRINT"BC    " ,;PRINT84,(CIT(I,J,1,L),I=1,NI),SUM1;201
850 PRINT"FC    " ,;PRINT84,(CIT(I,J,2,L),I=1,NI),SUM2
860 PRINT"TOTAL " ,;PRINT84,(TOT(I),I=1,NI),SUM3
870 L=L+1;IF(2-L)110
880 PRINT^^"PRICE   " ,;PRINT81,(IND(I),I=1,NI),;PRINT"   TOTAL";GOTO100
890 110 L=1;J=J+1;IF(J-NN-1)111;99 IF(IX)LAST
900 PRINT^^^"DO YOU WANT EXISTING AGREEMENTS FOR GOVERNMENTS"
910 124 INPUT,NNN;IF(NNN-"YES")120,121;120 IF(NNN-"NO")122,123
920 122 PRINT"YES OR NO";GOTO124
930 121 IX=-1;L=1;300 DO301I=1,NI;DO301J=1,NN;DO301K=1,2
940 301 CIT(I,J,K,L)=GOV(I,J,K,L); L=L+1; IF(L-3)300
950 L=J=1;GOTO111
960 123
970 LAST: STOP ; END
```

REFERENCES

ALGER, CHADWICK A. 'Interaction and Negotiation in a Committee of the United Nations General Assembly,' *Peace Research Society (International) Papers*, v (1966), pp. 141–59.

— 'International Relations. I. The Field' in *International Encyclopedia of the Social Sciences*. New York: Macmillan and Free Press, 1968.

ANGELL, ROBERT C. 'An Analysis of Trends in International Organizations,' *Peace Research Society (International) Papers*, III (1965), pp. 185–95.

BROGDEN, MICHAEL *INGOs in Perspective*. Peace Research Centre, England, Publication no 11–2 (December 1966).

CHADWICK, RICHARD *Theory Development through Simulation: A Comparison and Analysis of Associations among Variables in an International*

364 Paul Smoker

System and an Inter-nation Simulation. Evanston: Northwestern University, 1966. (Mimeographed.)

– *Extending Internation Simulation Theory: An Analysis of Intra and International Behavior.* Evanston: Northwestern University, 1966. (Mimeographed.)

– *Developments in a Partial Theory of Internationl Behavior: A Test and Extension of Inter-Nation Simulation Theory.* PH D thesis. Evanston: Northwestern University, 1966.

DEUTSCH, KARL W. 'Integration and the Social System: Implications of Functional Analysis,' in Philip Jacob and James Toscano, eds., *The Integration of Political Communities.* Philadelphia and New York: J.B. Lippincott, 1964, pp. 179–208.

ELDER, CHARLES and ROBERT PENDLEY *An Analysis of Consumption Standards and Validation Satisfactions in the Inter-Nation Simulation in Terms of Contemporary Economic Theory and Data.* Evanston: Northwestern University, 1966. (Mimeographed.)

GALTUNG, JOHAN 'Summit Meetings and International Relations,' *Journal of Peace Research,* no 1 (1964), pp. 36–54.

– 'Entropy and the General Theory of Peace,' International Peace Research Association Conference, 1967.

GUETZKOW, HAROLD, C. ALGER, R. BRODY, R. NOEL, and R. SNYDER *Simulation in International Relations: Developments for Research and Teaching.* Englewood Cliffs, New Jersey: Prentice-Hall, 1963.

HAAS, ERNST B. *Beyond the Nation-State: Functionalism and International Organization.* Stanford: Stanford University Press, 1964.

JENKINS, ROBIN and JOHN MACCRAE *Religion, Conflict and Polarization in Northern Ireland.* Peace Research Centre, England, Publication no v-4 (June 1967). (Mimeographed.)

MACCRAE, JOHN and PAUL SMOKER 'A Vietnam Simulation: A Report on the Canadian/English Joint Project,' *Journal of Peace Research,* no 1 (1967), pp. 1–25

MORGENTHAU, HANS *Politics among Nations.* New York: Knopf, 1960.

PARSONS, TALCOTT *The Social System.* New York: Free Press of Glencoe, 1951.

PENDLEY, ROBERT and CHARLES ELDER *An Analysis of Office-Holding in the Inter-Nation Simulation in terms of Contemporary Political Theory and Data on the Stability of Regimes and Governments.* Evanston: Northwestern University, 1966. (Mimeographed.)

PERLMUTTER, HOWARD *Social Architectural Problems of the Multi-national Firm.* Evanston: Northwestern University, 1966. (Mimeographed.)

RICHARDSON, LEWIS *Arms and Insecurity.* Pittsburg: Boxwood Press, 1960.

SCHARTZENBERGER, GEORGE *Power Politics.* London: Stevens, 1964.

SMOKER, PAUL 'Trade, Defense and the Richardson Theory of Arms Races: A Seven Nation Study,' *Journal of Peace Research,* no. 2 (1965i), pp. 161–76.

- 'A Preliminary Empirical Study of an International Integrative Sub-system,' *International Associations*, no 11 (1965ii), pp. 638–46.
- 'Nation State Escalation and International Integration,' *Journal of Peace Research*, no 1 (1967), pp. 61–75.

ZINNES, DINA 'A Comparison of Hostile State Behavior of Decision-makers in Simulate and Historical Data,' *World Politics*, XVIII (1966), pp. 474–502.

PART SIX

Experimentation, simulation, and social change

A planned change in organizational style: underlying theory and some results*

This research is a hybrid. Basically, it derives from a concern with the broad analytical issues being dealt with in today's political science. However, its specific thrust is towards understanding and controlling basic organizational phenomena. This pilot study uses as an experimental population a small number of managers from a business organization, although its results do not differ significantly from on-going research in public agencies that is less far along.[1]

Specifically, this study reports on the design and results of an effort to change an organization's climate, and to modify the quality of the interpersonal and intergroup relations in a small population of managers. The learning design was derived from the laboratory approach to organization development and sought to create a specific kind of social order as well as to provide for the managers some experience with appropriate attitudes, skills, and behaviours. In sum, the goal was to approach a specific model of the good administrative life as a conscious pilot study for larger scale efforts presently underway. Two basic requirements were a learning design capable of inducing the changes considered desirable, and a research design which permitted estimates of the changes.

*   Technical reports of the design and results have appeared in the *Administrative Science Quarterly* (March and September 1970). Those sources can be consulted for details lacking here.
1   For a preliminary statement of the conditions in public agencies that tend to complicate the attainment of organization development objectives in public agencies, see Robert T. Golembiewski, 'Organization Development In Public Agencies: Perspectives On Theory and Practice,' *Public Administration Review*, 29 (July–August 1969), pp. 367–77.

TWO EXTREME WORLD VIEWS FOR
POLITICAL SCIENCE:
A CHANGE IN THE PREVAILING WELTANSCHAUUNG?

This research is self-consciously related to major analytical concerns at
the frontiers of today's political science. These concerns centre around an
apparent change in disciplinary focus which may imply a new weltanschauung. It certainly implies a shift in the analytical centre of gravity of
the old weltanschauung, or world view, that has defined the leading edge
of political science over the last decades.[2] Van Dyke distinguishes the two
analytic world views at the level of first approximation.[3] The first is concerned with the form, or processes, of public policy and shares much conceptual ground with the behavioural persuasion. The second analytic
world-view stresses the content of public policy. Table 1 attempts to add
substance to the basic distinction, at the risk of overdrawing the differing
emphases.

Any weltanschauung is a tether, and that is its strength and its
weakness. At different times the balance of benefits over costs will vary.
At its best a world view can provide researchers with a valuable map to
significant analytic territory, and at its worst, a weltanschauung may
enmesh researchers in a set of sentiments which subscribers to the theory
sense only dimly or not at all, a 'metaphysical pathos of ideas.' As
Gouldner developed the point:

> ... commitment to a theory often occurs by a process other than the
> one which its proponents believe and it is usually more consequential
> than they realize. A commitment to a theory may be made because
> the theory is congruent with the mood or deep-lying sentiments of
> its adherents, rather than merely because it has been cerebrally in-
> spected and found valid. This is as true for the rigorous prose of social
> science as it is for the more lucid metaphor of creative literature,
> for each has its own silent appeal and its own metaphysical pathos.[4]

This report is consistent with the new weltanschauung of political
science in major particulars; at the same time it seeks to restrain it in

2   Albert Somit and Joseph Tanenhaus, *The Development of Political Science*
    (Boston: Allyn and Bacon, 1967), esp. pp. 173–94.
3   Vernon Van Dyke, 'Process and Policy as Focal Concepts in Political Re-
    search,' pp. 23–39, in Austin Ranney, ed., *Political Science and Public Policy*
    (Chicago: Markham, 1968).
4   Alvin W. Gouldner, 'Metaphysical Pathos and the Theory of Bureaucracy,'
    American Political Science Review, 44 (December 1955), p. 498.

TABLE 1

Two alternative world views for political science

Old weltanschauung: form or processes	New weltanschauung: content
1 emphasis on developing general knowledge, theory, and science	1 emphasis on promoting human welfare
2 emphasis on value-free findings	2 emphasis on values, goals, moral judgments
3 emphasis on overall patterns of activity and behaviour, on general and enduring features of governmental processes	3 emphasis on specific even if transient features of the content of public policies or issues
4 emphasis on those processes considered presently susceptible to scientific analysis	4 emphasis on structure, dynamics, or policies that are considered relevant to public welfare, their susceptibility to scientific analysis being a lesser concern
5 emphasis on large groups, institutions, aggregates	5 emphasis on feelings, attitudes, and motivations of individuals
6 emphasis on the individual as a type, an aggregate statistic, a role-player subject to massive determinative forces that are (largely) uncontrollable by him	6 emphasis on the individual as a valuing, deciding, and choosing organism who can and should define his environment in significant ways
7 emphasis on non-rational and irrational behaviour and upon the situational factors inducing them	7 emphasis on purposive behaviour by individuals who reason or act in support/opposition to specific policies
8 tendency to be action-distant, not of direct relevance to the policy-maker	8 desire to be action-proximate, of direct relevance to the policy-maker

others. Basically, the emphases of the new world view are necessary reactions against extreme extensions of its predecessor. However, history urges caution in such cases. At an extreme, for example, the new world view might encourage a neglect of man's collective experiences and needs and it might even curtail the development of an expanding science. At the very least, lack of caution might exacerbate the inherent potential for conflict. If nothing else, for example, win-lose competition concerning world views can engage powerful forces, including the bittersweet succession of one scholarly generation by another, the related testing of concepts of self-worth and of professional standing, and so on. Such competition would be regrettable since, at least in today's political science, the two world views contain notions of complementary value that should not be sacrificed.

So caution it is, even though we can hope for greater equanimity than characterized the recent unpleasantness about world views for political science reflected in the debate over the 'new science of politics.' The metaphysical pathos associated with the new world view fortunately does not today seem to generate extensions in extremis, although it is still early. Even if it did, the old weltanschauung may have been accepted so essentially that its useful features will persist.

The theory and results below, in any case, seek to forge one kind of *media via* between the two world views in table 1, as should become clearer in the discussion below. Here note only that, while limiting the new world view, this research also seeks to expand the old by emphasizing a research vehicle that directs attention to empirical methodology, permits tests of prevailing assumptions about man and his behaviour, and highlights values defining the good life. That is to say that the metaphysical pathos of the old world view of political science was such as to undercut much of its overt thrust.[5] This research reflects another effort to overcome this self-defeating strategy of the old world view, while recognizing its substantial contributions to political science.

TWO TRADITIONS IN ORGANIZATIONAL ANALYSIS: A CONFLUENCE OF POLITICAL AND ADMINISTRATIVE THEORY

These broad considerations about world views are reflected in miniature in two traditions of organizational analysis, the specific point of departure for this pilot study. What may be called the classical approach to the possibility of the good life in organizations reflects a basic fatalism in its guiding metaphysical pathos. In this concept, Gouldner concluded, 'there is a Hegelian dialectic in which "good" and "bad" are viewed as inseparably connected opposites; bureaucracy, "the bad thing," is represented as the inescapable price that has to be paid for the good things, the efficiency and abundance of modern life.'[6] The overriding, but typically unexamined, concept is that there is a 'one-best way' to organize work. Conceptually there is no escape from its determinative logic, except by reversion to small-scale organization.[7] Increasing size, 'technological advance,' 'organic necessity,' and even the second law of thermodynamics

5   For an extended effort to demonstrate the point, see Robert T. Golembiewski, William Welsh, and William Crotty, *A Methodological Primer for Political Scientists* (Chicago: Rand McNally, 1969).
6   Gouldner, 'Metaphysical Pathos,' p. 500.
7   Robert T. Golembiewski, *Men, Management, and Morality* (New York: McGraw-Hill, 1965), pp. 11–21.

all inexorably and fatalistically are seen as tending towards the bureaucratic form in which man is the pawn of increasingly overwhelming situational forces.[8]

The classical approach has profound implications for political theory. Consider only that political theory and administrative theory share substantial areas of concern, such as emphasis on ways of 1 / generating the obedience and purposefulness required for organizational survival; 2 / developing structures for achieving co-ordination; and 3 / reconciling collective objectives with those of individuals.[9] The classical approach to the administrative good life prescribes asymptotic approximations of the bureaucratic ethos, a greater emphasis on conditioning if not coercion of individuals, a greater recourse to central direction, plus a massive and growing bias in favour of the formal collectivity. Specifically, the 'bureaucratic ethos' consists of some explicit propositions as well as a reinforcing set of more or less implicit assumptions or beliefs.[10] Exhibit 2 provides detail on both components of the bureaucratic ethos. Without straining the comparison, the view of human nature in table 2 shares much common ground with the old weltanschauung of political science.

Much political theory generates no more sanguine outcomes. Consider the tradition of Roberto Michels. His work is seminal in the old world view of political science and is also half-way echoed in many versions of 'the new politics.' Michels' 'iron law of oligarchy' maintains the universal proposition that a 'system of leadership is incompatible with the most essential postulates of democracy.' Unfailingly, oligarchy is seen as deriving 'from the tactical and technical necessities which result from the consolidation of every disciplined political aggregate ...' Oligarchy 'is the outcome of organic necessity, and consequently affects every organization, be it socialist or even anarchist,' Michels also observes. 'It is probable that this cruel game will continue without end.'[11]

Similar conclusions influence issues great and small in political theory, with the general effect of making apparently trivial what seem issues of moment. Consider the issue of capitalism versus socialism, whose resolution becomes less momentous given the universality of bureaucracy. 'If it is correct that ... bureaucracy saps the fervor of the socialist offensive,'

8   The point is made in Roderick Seidenberg, *Post-historic Man* (Boston: Beacon Press, 1957).
9   Herbert Kaufman, 'Organization Theory and Political Theory,' *American Political Science Review*, 58 (March 1964), pp. 5–14.
10 The underlying assumptions and beliefs here are based on Douglas McGregor, *The Human Side of Enterprise* (New York: McGraw-Hill, 1960), esp. pp. 33–58.
11 Roberto Michels, *Political Parties* (Glencoe, Ill.: Free Press, 1949), pp. 405, 408.

TABLE 2

Two components of the 'bureaucratic ethos'

Explicit propositions of the bureaucratic model	Assumptions or beliefs underlying the bureaucratic model
1 a well-defined chain of command that vertically channels formal interaction	1 work is inherently distasteful to most people
2 a system of procedures and rules for dealing with all contingencies at work, which reinforces the reporting insularity of each bureau and functionary	2 most people prefer to be directed and have little desire for responsibility in developing and maintaining a social system
3 a division of labour based upon specialization by major function or process that vertically fragments a flow of work	3 most people have little capacity for creativity in work or in developing values or norms to guide behaviour
4 promotion and selection based on technical competence defined consistently with 1–3 above	4 motivation occurs only (or mostly) at an elemental stimulus-response level
5 impersonality in relations between organization members and between them and their clients	5 therefore, people in organizations must be closely controlled and directed, and often coerced

Gouldner concludes, 'it also undermines the stamina of the capitalist bastions. If socialism and capitalism are similar in being bureaucratic, then not only is there little *profit* in substituting one for the other, but there is also little *loss*.'[12]

A second tradition in administrative theory has developed of late which reflects a more optimistic metaphysical pathos. This tradition does not deny that reality often has been consistent with the pessimistic tradition. Rather, the optimistic tradition argues basically that real alternatives are available which allow more scope for individual choice and behaviour than does the bureaucratic ethos. In addition, these alternatives are seen as increasingly useful if not necessary for organizational well-being and survival.

This optimistic tradition, although in its relatively early developmental stages, is a composite of goals and learning designs for achieving them. At least two distinct subtraditions can be isolated. The first stresses changes in structure and tasks so as to increase the congruence between their demands and high-preference behaviours and attitudes of organization members.[13] The second subtradition stresses changes in organization

12   Gouldner, 'Metaphysical Pathos,' p. 498. His emphases.
13   Robert N. Ford, *Motivation through Work Itself* (New York: American Management Association, 1969).

climate or atmosphere, that is, changes in the social values that guide interpersonal and intergroup relations in an organization so as to legitimate high-preference behaviours and attitudes typically held by most organization members. Both subtraditions attempt to respond to Gouldner's challenge of some fifteen years ago, when he criticized the way in which 'some social scientists have approached the study of organizational pathology' in these terms:

> Instead of telling men how bureaucracy might be mitigated, they insist that it is inevitable. Instead of explaining how democratic patterns may, to some extent, be fortified and extended, they warn us that democracy cannot be perfect. Instead of controlling the disease, they suggest that we are deluded, or more politely, incurably romantic, for hoping to control it. Instead of assuming responsibilities as responsible clinicians, striving to further democratic potentialities wherever they can, many social scientists have become morticians, all too eager to bury men's hopes.[14]

A THEORETICAL FRAMEWORK:
TOWARDS INTEGRATING INDIVIDUAL AND
COLLECTIVE NEEDS

The present response to Gouldner's challenge rests upon a complicated theoretical orientation outlined in table 3. The basic premise of that orientation is that individual and organization needs not only can be, but increasingly must be, integrated. Table 3 also suggests how the laboratory

TABLE 3
A simplified model of findings/hypotheses underlying an organization development program based on the laboratory approach

Basic premise   When individuals can meet their own needs while meeting organizational needs, output will be qualitatively and quantitatively best.

An individual's basic needs centre around self-realization and self-actualization. The former involves a person seeing himself as he is in interaction with others, with the goal of increasing the congruence between his intentions and his impact on others. Self-actualization refers to the processes of growth by which an individual realizes his potential.	An efficient organization will develop an appropriately shifting balance between institutionalization and risk-taking. The former refers to infusing with value the activities of the organization, so as to elicit member support, identification, and collaboration. Risk-taking is necessary in innovating more effective ways to deal with existing activities, and in adapting to environmental changes in society, markets technology, and so on.

14   Gouldner, 'Metaphysical Pathos,' p. 507.

TABLE 3 *(continued)*

An individual whose basic needs are being met experiences corresponding psychological growth, the prime conditions for, and consequences of, are
– a growing awareness of the needs and motivations of self and others
– a lessening of the degree to which his relations and actions are distorted, as by more actively inducing feedback from others and by more effectively interpreting it
– an increasing ability to modify behaviour in response to feedback about its impact on others, to respond appropriately rather than stereotypically
– a growing tendency to seek or develop conditions that promote psychological growth for self and others
– an expanding capacity to determine goals and internal motivation for self

An individual who experiences psychological growth will be correspondingly motivated to search for work, challenge, and responsibility.

An organization's successful balancing of institutionalization and risk-taking will depend upon
– the increasingly complete use of people as well as non-human resources
– the development and maintenance of a viable balance between central control and local initiative
– fluid lines of communication, vertically, horizontally, and diagonally
– decision-making processes that solve problems that stay solved without creating other problems
– infusing the organization with values that support both its existence as a stable institution and that also motivate its developmental change as an adaptive structure

Satisfaction of both individual and organization needs will be facilitated by, if such satisfaction does not in fact crucially depend upon, skill and competence in interpersonal and intergroup situations.

An individual's growth and self-realization are facilitated by interpersonal relations that are honest, caring, and non-manipulative. Individuals can gain convenient experience with these personal needs and with ways of satisfying them in 'sensitivity training,' which is a managed process of gaining experience with attitudes and skills for inducing greater openness about positive and negative feelings, attitudes, or beliefs. Such openness leads to greater trust and reduced risk in communicating and is intended to suggest possible transfers into other environments.

Organizational 'family' teams can be exposed to sensitivity training, with the intention of increasing confidence, trust, and responsibility that can be applied directly to solving organizational issues. Skill and competence in interpersonal and intergroup situations can be increased in sensitivity training groups composed of strangers, but the real test is the application of such learning in life-relevant situations. Such application will require that substantial numbers of organization members learn appropriate interpersonal skills, as well as that they internalize a set of values which support and reinforce such learning.

Persons in groups which develop greater openness tend to identify strongly with other members and with the goals of the group.

Groups characterized by strong identification with members and goals become increasingly capable of dealing with issues facing their members, and hence increasingly capable of influencing their environment in desired ways.

Groups whose members identify strongly and who can influence their environment are likely to be effective reinforcers of decisions about change. Such groups also can provide emotional support necessary to sustain required changes in the values, attitudes, or behaviours of their members.

approach provides a vehicle for beginning the integration of individual and collective needs in programs of organization development. Overall, table 3 contrasts sharply with the dark diagnosis and prognosis in the pessimistic tradition of organization analysis.

As is the case with all theories, table 3 reflects an amalgam of empirically verified regularities as well as of its own special metaphysical pathos. Enough research had been accumulated by 1964 that a substantial volume could summarize hundreds of studies concerning the value of integrating individual and organization needs, and that literature continues to expand.[15] With all that research, table 3 basically rests upon belief systems which stress how organizations can be and should be. The most influential of these belief systems provides that, if conditions permit or provide encouragement,

1   most people can find work as natural as play;
2   most people prefer to be self-controlling in the pursuit of organization objectives, and can develop and maintain appropriate social systems;
3   most people can exercise significant creativity in organizational problem-solving and in developing values or norms to guide behaviour;
4   motivation often occurs in response to opportunities for personal and group development, as well as in response to opportunities to control the work environment; and
5   therefore, most people can be allowed substantial initiative for self-control, self-direction, and self-motivation.[16]

The concept of man underlying table 3 is both dynamic and optimistic, to highlight one major feature of the theoretical framework of this effort. This view of man is rooted in 'growth psychology,' managerially relevant versions of which are associated with such names as Maslow, McGregor, Argyris, and Herzberg. Their common concept provides that when the conditions are appropriate men are characterized by a positive thrust towards growth, development, and change. In common, also, frustration of that positive thrust is conceived as having negative effects on a person's motivation and, more broadly, on his psychological health. Phrased positively, a person who is allowed to grow, develop, and change will be highly motivated and psychologically healthy. Specifically, in this view the major costs of the bureaucratic ethos are a definite failure to engage the massive motivational forces implied in man's thrust towards

15   Chris Argyris, *Integrating the Individual and the Organization* (New York: Wiley, 1965).
16   See McGregor, *The Human Side of Enterprise.*

growth, development, and change, as well as the probable creation of individuals who are psychologically and emotionally deprived in various degrees by the organizational experiences induced by the bureaucratic ethos.

The concept of organization in table 3 also deserves brief discussion. Broadly, the basic underlying notion is that organizations can be located along such continua as those in table 4. As organizations approach the conditions in the right column, it becomes increasingly costly to 'fit the man to the organization' built on the model of the bureaucratic ethos. Today's organizations are, on balance, moving rightward on the dimensions in table 4, although some technologies resist that trend and probably will continue to do so.[17] Consequently, on balance, as I explained elsewhere,

> Today's organizations reflect a growing need for an organic and evolving integration, as opposed to a mechanical structuring. Adherence to a mechanical system can be enforced; but commitment to an organic integration can only be elicited and encouraged. Put another way, the integrity of a stable and simple technology may be safeguarded by culling deviants. But changing and complex technologies require the careful husbanding of selected kinds of innovation or adaptability in a widening range of employees. Hence the growing importance of ... freedom to act ... [of] learning how and when individuals can more often meet their own needs while contributing more effectively to a total flow of work with which they identify their interests.[18]

Table 3 must be limited in two ways. First, of course, simultaneously meeting individual and organization needs is a goal to be approached in various degrees under various conditions. The laboratory approach to organizational development seeks to institutionalize processes, underlying attitudes, and behavioural skills that will facilitate working towards that goal. Second, no unanimity exists about the optimistic rationale in table 3. But no matter. The present purpose is to begin testing the credibility of the theoretical framework in table 3, not to defend it. Hence subsequent sections will describe a learning design consistent with that framework and will begin to test the consequences of that design.

17 Paul R. Lawrence and Jay W. Lorsch, *Organization and Environment* (Boston: Graduate School of Business Administration, Harvard University, 1967).
18 Robert T. Golembiewski, 'Organization Patterns of the Future,' *Personnel Administration*, 32 (November–December, 1969), p. 11.

TABLE 4

Some continua for distinguishing stages of organizational development

From basic emphasis upon	To growing emphasis upon
regularity in operations	creativity in concept; adaptability in execution
programmed decisions	novel decisions
stable and simple competencies, technologies, and market	volatile and complex competencies, technologies, and markets
stop-and-go processing	continuous processing
stable product lines, programs	volatile product lines, programs
monolithic product lines, programs	variegated product lines, programs
demands of hierarchy	demands of task, technology, profession
bureau or departmental orientation	system orientation
expanding volume at central site	developing national and international field units

VALUES, GOALS, AND MAJOR FEATURES OF THE
LEARNING DESIGN:
TOWARDS THE GOOD ADMINISTRATIVE LIFE

The present learning design is based on the 'laboratory approach.'[19] Basically, the laboratory approach to organization development seeks to create a specific kind of social order; it also provides experience with appropriate skills and attitudes. The values underlying that social order can guide interpersonal and intergroup relations while helping meet important personal as well as organizational needs.

How this application of the laboratory approach went about seeking to create a specific kind of social order can be suggested briefly by five emphases. First, the values underlying the learning design will be sketched. Second, the approach to gaining experience with the values and behavioural skills appropriate for the laboratory approach in small, temporary learning environments will be described. Third, the transfer of learning into large organizations will be discussed. Fourth, the operating goals of this effort at planned organizational change will be sketched. Fifth, several major features of the learning design will be outlined.

A Values underlying the learning design

Programs of organization development based on the laboratory approach are explicitly value-loaded, to begin, in complex ways that can only be sketched here. In brief, three classes of laboratory values and their characteristics guide the development of interpersonal and intergroup relations.

19   Leland P. Bradford, Jack R. Gibb, and Kenneth D. Benne, eds., *T-Group Theory and Laboratory Method* (New York: Wiley, 1964).

Meta-Values of Laboratory training

1   An attitude of inquiry reflecting (among others) a willingness to analyze and to experiment with behavior.
2   An expanded consciousness about the effects of behavior and a sense of increased alternatives available to the individual.
3   A value system stressing a spirit of collaboration and open resolution of conflict through a problem-solving orientation.
4   An emphasis on mutual helping relationships as the best way to express the interdependency of people.

Proximate goals of laboratory training

1   Increased insight and self-knowledge.
2   Sharpened diagnostic skills at all levels, that is, on the levels of the individual, group, organization, and society.
3   Awareness of, and practice of skills in creating, conditions of effective functioning at all levels.
4   Testing of self-concepts and skills in interpersonal situations.
5   Increased capacity to be open, to accept feelings of self and others, and to risk interpersonally in rewarding ways.

Desirable means for laboratory training

1   Emphasis on 'here-and-now' occurrences.
2   Emphasis on the individual act rather than on the total person acting.
3   Emphasis on feedback that is nonevaluative in that it reports the impact on the self of others' behavior, rather than feedback that is judgmental or interpretive.
4   Emphasis on 'unfreezing' behaviors the trainee feels are undesirable, on practice of replacement behaviors, and on reinforcement of new behaviors.
5   Emphasis on 'trust in leveling,' on psychological safety of the trainee.
6   Emphasis on creating and maintaining an organic community of mutual helpers.[20]

These values were the normative backbone for the learning design. For example, exercises for giving and receiving feedback were designed to highlight the prescriptions sketched above under the heading 'Desirable

20   Edgar H. Schein and Warren G. Bennis, *Personal Growth and Organizational Change through Group Methods* (New York: Wiley, 1965), pp. 30–8.

means for laboratory training,' and these exercises encouraged the development of attitudes and behavioural skills appropriate to those values. Specifically, the flow of the learning design successively emphasized the three classes of values.[21]

B   Gaining experience with laboratory values

Initial experience with the values above, and with their associated attitudes and behavioural skills, may be gained in a variety of temporary learning environments. The T-group, or sensitivity training group – a small number of people with the goal of learning about one another from one another, usually operating in the presence of a professional 'trainer' and seeking to develop a social order consistent with the values above for guiding interpersonal and intergroup relations – is a particularly useful learning environment.[22] Experience with appropriate values and skills can also be gained in other learning contexts, however, such as managerial grid training or the confrontation design.[23] The key notion is that the learning is basically 'experiential,' which here means that the individual comes to know the satisfaction and demands implicit for him in the values and behaviours consistent with the laboratory approach, as a direct consequence of his on-going relations with other people.

The various temporary learning environments derived from the laboratory approach commonly attempt to provide a model for interpersonal and intergroup relations that emphasizes increasing trust and decreasing risk among the participants. The specific goal is to permit the individual to relax his attachment to his 'old' values, attitudes, and behavioural skills at least enough to experiment with and evaluate 'new' ones. Such relaxation is possible and usually exhilarating for most people, although a few find it unpleasant and fewer still react even more negatively.[24] As Mill has argued, 'regression' is an important part of the dynamics of such relaxation.[25] If the regression is severe enough, ego

21   The training design is elaborated in Robert T. Golembiewski and Arthur Blumberg, 'Sensitivity Training In Cousin Groups: A Confrontation Design,' *Training and Development Journal*, 23 (August 1969), pp. 18–23.

22   For details, see such sources as Schein and Bennis, *Personal Growth*; Robert T. Golembiewski and Arthur Blumberg, *Sensitivity Training and the Laboratory Approach* (Itasca, Ill.: F.E. Peacock, 1970).

23   Robert T. Blake and Jane S. Mouton, *The Managerial Grid* (Houston, Texas: Gulf Publishing, 1964).

24   Bernard Lubin and Marvin Zuckerman, 'Level of Emotional Arousal in Laboratory Training,' *Journal of Applied Behavioral Science*, 5 (December 1969), pp. 483–90.

25   Cyril R. Mill, 'A Theory for the Group Dynamics Laboratory,' *Adult Leadership*, II (1962), pp. 133–4 and 159–60.

disintegration can occur. In this sense, the present design is a very safe one, for the focus is narrowly on managerially relevant dynamics, as opposed to a total life style; participants are not strangers on a cultural island; totally new relations need not be developed among participants; and so on.

C   Transfer of the initial learning experience

The crucial issue in the laboratory approach to organizational development is the transfer into large organizations of the initial experiences with laboratory norms, attitudes, and behavioural skills that typically have been gained in small groups.[26] The present 'bridging sequence' includes these progressive steps:

1   A learning design based on the laboratory approach provides managers with an off-site experience with a value-loaded set of behaviours, attitudes, and skills.
2   The learning design suggests how laboratory values and dynamics can be built into more complex organizations, as by improving feedback processes in large units.
3   This experience encourages managers to build analogs of laboratory values and dynamics into their work setting, by
a   adopting 'new' patterns of behaviour highlighted by their off-site experience, or
b   reordering the frequencies of performing 'old' behaviours already in the repertoires of managers, increasing those behaviours that are consistent with the laboratory approach, as well as decreasing the incidence of inconsistent behaviours.
4   The resulting behavioural changes by managers help to change
a   the 'old' organization climate of interpersonal and intergroup relations, as well as
b   the norms supporting the 'old' climate.
5   The changes in 'old' climate norms reinforce changes in managerial behaviour which, in turn, encourages further changes in the 'old' climate and its norms.

The basic goal of the transfer was to provide individuals with more of the satisfaction and psychological growth at work they had experienced

26   Alexander Winn, 'The Laboratory Approach to Organization Development: A Tentative Model of Planned Change,' *Journal of Management Studies*, 6 (1969), pp. 155–66.

in their temporary learning environment. The following organization values were advanced as necessary to approach that goal:

1   Full and free communication within and between hierarchical levels.
2   Reliance on open consensus in managing conflict, as opposed to use of coercion or compromise.
3   Basing influence on competence rather than on formal power or on personal whim.
4   Development of norms that permit expression of emotional as well as task-oriented behaviour.
5   Acceptance of conflict as a phenomenon to be coped with willingly and openly.

D   Goals of the planned change

The program of planned change reviewed here had three short-run and three long-run goals. They were a combination of operating needs, as well as of consultant strategies intended to meet these needs.[27]

Short-run goals
First, the paramount short-run goal of the planned change was to integrate a new management team at the top three levels of a national field sales organization (figure 1). Within the year preceding the program, there had been personnel changes at all three management levels, including a new national sales manager, a divisional sales manager, and three regional sales managers. The goal was to develop effective and adaptive top-to-bottom and bottom-to-top relations among all three managerial levels of the experimental unit.

Second, horizontal linkages were to be developed between divisional managers and especially between the regional managers. Changes in managerial roles and in product required complex and unparallelled cooperative and innovative effort. The underlying concept of the planned change was the creation of three interlocking teams.[28] This concept required building a sense of team identification within hierarchical levels, as well as between them, and implied rejection of the common strategy of building cohesiveness in each of the divisional units by inducing win-lose competition between them.

27   For details, see Robert T. Golembiewski and Stokes B. Carrigan, 'Planned Change in Organization Style based on the Laboratory Approach,' *Administrative Science Quarterly* (in press).
28   Rensis Likert, *New Patterns of Management* (New York: McGraw-Hill, 1961).

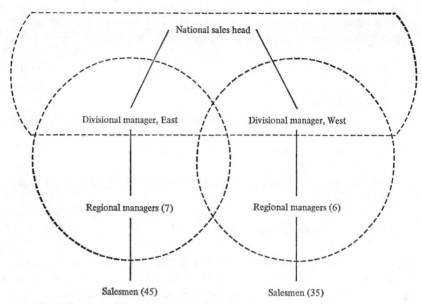

Figure 1 Interrelationships within experimental unit.

Third, the planned change was intended to help confront and resolve some nagging problems of personal style and organization history. It suffices here to note that upward communication was inhibited at the very time it was most vital and that relations between peers were stressful just when goodwill and trust were needed most.

Long-run goals

The first long-run goal of the organization development program was to increase the congruence between the behaviours that the prevailing organization style elicited from the managers and the behaviours that the men preferred. For example, all of the managers feared that the existing relations of the experimental unit called for substantial mistrust and secrecy, while the managers themselves preferred to be more trusting and open.

A second long-run goal was a change in organizational style seen as necessary to permit a greater congruence of individual needs and organization demands. Roughly, the goal was movement towards an open adaptive and problem-solving system such as Shepard describes,[29] in contrast to a closed, coercive, and hierarchy serving system. The experimental

---

29   Herbert A. Shepard, 'Changing Interpersonal and Intergroup Relations in
     Organizations,' pp. 1122–35, in James G. March, ed., *Handbook of Organizations* (Chicago: Rand McNally, 1965).

unit initially was perceived as somewhere between these polar extremes, but under the new managers it was widely seen by their subordinates as threatening to move significantly in the closed direction.

The third long-run goal of the organization development program was to permit a 'psychological success-experience' for all managers. They were encouraged to consider a change in the style of their interpersonal and intergroup relations, for example, but they also were urged to assess the constraints on what they and their immediate superiors could reasonably do. Similarly, the learning design featured a number of decision points explicitly intended to test commitment by various levels of management to the unfolding program of organization development. The consequence to be avoided was a feeling by any of the managers that they had had a program imposed on them or that they had been manipulated into a position they found uncomfortable but from which they could not gracefully escape. In positive terms, the overall objective was a feeling of psychological success among the managers: a sense of personal owning of the program of planned change in organization style, of commitment to and collaboration in the program.

E   Four major features of the learning design

This application of the laboratory approach in a program of planned organization development also had four other major features. First, the initial phase of the learning design was a T-group experience for the regional managers, which lasted four-and-a-half days and at which the consultants served as trainers. The overall goal was to improve interpersonal and intergroup relations in the organization, not necessarily to enhance personal growth or to provide an emotionally moving experience. Specifically, the regional managers were told that the T-group experience was designed as a preparation for the day-and-a-half following their T-group experience when they could confront the two divisional managers with their concerns about interpersonal and intergroup relations at work. The words 'could confront' were emphasized. Consultants[30] had arranged with the two division managers that they be available on short notice should their presence seem appropriate. This arrangement was shared with the regional managers, who correctly perceived it as an 'escape hatch' should a confrontation with superiors seem too risky to them or inappropriate to the consultants.

During the initial phase of the learning design, the regional managers were encouraged to explore their feelings and reactions both about the

30   The author and Stokes B. Carrigan.

organization and the T-group experience. The discussion shifted between emphasis on 'here-and-now' socio-emotional dynamics triggered in the T-group and on 'there-and-then' organizational issues. Consultants used that discussion to help the regional managers become more aware of their feelings and reactions, to attach them more precisely to the stimuli that induced them, and to test how widely their concerns and reactions were shared. This was crucial preparation for the possible confrontation with the divisional managers, when a premium would be put on how and why the regional managers were reacting and feeling. Moreover, the regional managers tested how rewarding for them openness was in their T-group, consciously weighed the openness they were willing to risk in the confrontation with the two divisional managers that might follow, and also gained experience with attitudes and skills that would facilitate the confrontation between superior and subordinate.

Second, the regional managers proved eager for the confrontation. During that phase, they met either as two divisions, each with their superior, or as a joint group with both divisional managers present. Only minimal structuring cues were provided for the regional managers. They were given a half-day to make a decision about whether to hold the confrontation and to plan it, following a specific model. The confrontation was described by consultants as an opportunity for the regional managers to test the degree to which the national sales head and the two divisional managers really wanted an open, problem-solving system. From the start, the learning design stressed the risks implied in the confrontation. Indeed, our motto was drawn from the experience of the Crusaders: 'More went than came back.' Instructions to the regional managers also underscored the need to concentrate on issues that were within the competence of superiors or could be influenced by them. For their part, the divisional managers were instructed only to try to understand any feedback that the regional managers offered, to explore both ideas and feelings with as little defensiveness as possible, and to try to do so without projecting an attitude of 'catharsis is good for them.' The consultants were available during the confrontation to provide support and to reinforce adherence to the norms of the laboratory approach.

Third, following the confrontation, the divisional managers met individually with the national sales head to clarify their own relations, in part in response to the confrontation with the regional managers. This phase was preplanned and announced to the regional managers as a possibility in the introductory session on the training design.

Fourth, 'process observers' who were trained company employees attended subsequent meetings at work sites of managers at all three levels.

Their position as observers symbolized the transfer of the guardianship of the laboratory values from outside consultants to agents of the organization. Process observation was intended to reinforce laboratory values in action settings, both by the very presence of the observer and through his interventions, which encouraged looking at the socio-emotional process of the meeting as well as its content.[31] The goal was to preclude the initial off-site training experience being seen as a 'magic mountain' phenomenon, unique and perhaps precious, but remote from the workaday world.

In sum, the learning design sought both to initiate attitudinal and behavioural change in a temporary learning environment, as well as to transfer that change into the organization. The T-group experiences were meant to relax old attitudes about interpersonal and intergroup relations. The confrontation provided a kind of half-way house to practise new attitudes and behaviours, as well as to test the risk involved for all. And process observers at subsequent work meetings of the regional managers helped to reinforce the new behavioural skills and attitudes in organizational settings.

MEASURING PROGRESS TOWARDS PLANNED CHANGE:
LIKERT'S PROFILE AS AN OPERATIONAL MEASURE

Progress towards planned change in organization style was measured by self-reported changes in the forty-eight items of Likert's profile of organizational characteristics. Six features highlight the use here of the profile as an operational measure of planned change. First, each item is represented by a twenty-point scale anchored by four descriptions. A typical item is illustrated in figure 2.

Second, Likert distinguishes the four major intervals as different 'systems of organization,' with the participative group system being most consistent with the laboratory approach. Therefore, scores on the forty-eight profile items can provide estimates of the degree to which the style of an organization approaches the norms of the laboratory approach.[32]

Third, each profile item is rated twice on each administration: once as *ideal*, that is, as respondents feel their organization unit should be; and also as *now*, that is, as respondents actually see their organization unit. Responses from individuals were identifiable, which made possible matched comparisons of the self-reports of all respondents for all administrations.

31 Edgar H. Schein, *Process Consultation* (Reading, Mass.: Addison-Wesley, 1969).
32 Rensis Likert, *The Human Organization* (New York: McGraw-Hill, 1967).

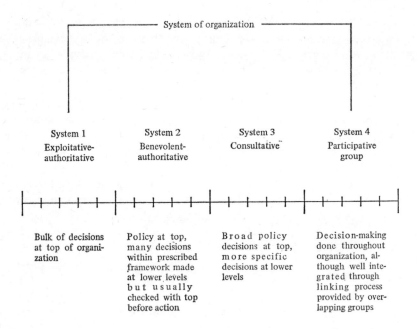

Item 33: At what level in the organization are decisions formally made?

Figure 2 A representative item from the Likert profile of organizational characteristics.

Fourth, responses to the profile items were uniformly coded so that scores run from 1 for the extreme exploitative-authoritative rating to 20 for the extreme participative-group rating. The Likert scales vary in direction, so as to inhibit a response set; however, all discussion below is based on the uniform coding of all responses, irrespective of the direction of the scale of an item.

Fifth, the Likert profile taps a broad range of processes that determine an organization's style. They are: 1 / leadership, 2 / character of motivational forces, 3 / character of communication, 4 / character of interaction-influence, 5 / character of decision-making, 6 / character of goal setting or ordering, and 7 / character of control. Table 5 provides detail on the items intended to tap each of these processes.

Sixth, respondents were instructed to think of the experimental unit as a whole in making their ratings. The data treated in this paper are the self-reports on the Likert profile by the regional managers.

A   Expectations about planned change

The present research design called for four observations of change in organization climate as measured by managerial self-ratings on the Likert profile, over a period of some eighteen months. Following the approximate schedule below, the managerial population was exposed to the learning design about one week after observation I. Observation II (O_2) was intended to determine whether the learning design influenced the climate in the experimental unit over the short-run. Observations III and IV sought to establish the persistence of any changes over an extended period.

Observation I	Experimental treatment	Observation II	Observation III	Observation IV
Day 1	Days 8–15	Day 135	Day 345	Day 525

The schedule of administrations reflects a blend of convenience, realism, and necessity. The last two administrations were simply convenient, given the managers' other obligations. The four-month interval between O_1 and O_2 attempted to be realistic. The managers involved were part of a headquarters/field complex, and researchers felt considerable elapsed time was necessary to test whether various aspects of the organization's climate really had changed. Observations necessarily ceased after day 525 because a major reorganization was impending.

The general expectation about the learning design, to provide some overall perspective, was that it would increase the congruence between the existing organizational climate and the climate preferred by the regional managers. Observation I provides a benchmark for the incongruence which initially existed. Thus Ideal I scores are greater than Now I in all 48 cases, 43 of which reach the 0.05 level of statistical significance. In other terms, managers concentrated over 90 per cent of their Ideal I scores in the participative group system of the Likert profile, while nearly 90 per cent of their Now I scores were in the consultative or benevolent-authoritative systems. These differences suggest that the experimental population of managers initially functioned in an organizational climate that fell significantly short of meeting their expressed needs concerning interpersonal and intergroup relations at the work site.

Somewhat more specifically, it was expected that the experimental treatment would have two effects on this initial incongruence. Thus significant shifts were expected in scores on the Likert items towards the ideals of the laboratory approach, comparing observations I and II. A successful experimental treatment, in addition, was defined in terms of the essential persistence over an extended period of these changes in self-reports about organizational climate.

The second general criterion of a successful experimental treatment was a strict one. That is, any marked persistence of the changes in climate beyond O_2 would be noteworthy because the experimental unit's broad work environment had probably worsened so as to stress interpersonal and intergroup relations. For example, the organization unit and especially its parent company were beset by a variety of serious issues, which worsened during the period of observation. These broad systemic issues were counter-balanced to some unknown but probably uncomplete extent. For example, the experimental unit between observations II and III had successfully introduced a new product line whose prospects looked favourable despite manifold problems, and a reclassification study raised the first-level manager's job to the next higher class between observations III and IV in response to the escalating complexities associated with marketing the new product line. Given this mixed bag of systemic trends, any persistence beyond O_2 of the changes in climate implies the power of the basic learning design.

Any persistence of changes in organization climate also would be noteworthy because the original learning experience was not specifically reinforced. Consultants had recommended a 'booster' learning experience of two or three days, to be held approximately one year after the experimental treatment, but the recommendation could not be acted upon in the interval of day 325–350. Beyond that time, no further interventions were recommended because a reorganization was taking shape that would later increase the size of the target organization by some 20 per cent. It seemed unwise to reinforce existing ties only to rupture them shortly hereafter. A variety of concomitant personnel changes also were in the works. Literally, then, too much uncertainty existed after day 325–50 about who the players were, what the teams would be, and who would be playing on which team. The gathering of data terminated at approximately day 525 for much the same reason, just after two personnel switches had been made but still some time before more basic changes would occur. Note, however, that a half-day data-feedback session was held shortly after O_3, at which time summary data from the first two administrations were shared and discussed. Consultants considered this feedback session a mild reinforcer.

Specifically, the success of the learning design was defined in terms of four pairs of expectations concerning the design's short-run and long-range effects. These expectations are:

1A   A successful planned intervention should significantly change the organization style in the directions that participants prefer (i.e., Now II scores will be significantly greater than Now I scores); and

1B   these changes in interpersonal and intergroup climate will persist throughout the full observational period (i.e., Now III and IV scores will tend to remain significantly greater than Now I scores).

2A   A successful planned intervention should significantly raise participants' expectations about how need gratifying their organization should be (i.e., Ideal II scores will be significantly greater than Ideal I); and

2B   these increased expectations will persist throughout the full observation period (i.e., Ideal III and IV scores will tend to remain significantly greater than Ideal I scores).

3A   A successful planned intervention need not eliminate the differences between expectations of organization members and the existing interpersonal and intergroup climate (i.e., Ideal II scores may still differ significantly from Now II); and

3B   the differences between ideal and existing organizational climate may persist throughout the full period of observation (i.e., Ideal III and IV scores may still differ significantly from Now III and IV scores).

4A   Although a successful planned intervention need not eliminate Ideal versus Now gaps, in the aggregate the differences should at least remain constant if they do not actually decrease, so as to avoid gaps that are so large as to be demotivating (i.e., at a minimum, in the aggregate differences in [Ideal II–Now II] scores will be no larger than [Ideal I–Now I scores]); and

4B   these differences in Ideal versus Now gaps should remain constant, in the aggregate, if they do not actually decrease, over the full observation period.

B   Some results of the planned intervention

Data gathered over an eighteen-month period imply that the learning design induced significant changes in the climate of the experimental unit and that these changes persisted over time. In general, these changes in managerial self-reports about interpersonal and intergroup relations implied that managers were more free to behave at work in ways they preferred. Put another way, managers reported that their immediate work climate became more what they wished it to be.

Table 5 reflects the magnitude of the changes in managerial self-reports.[33] These changes can be viewed in terms of the four pairs of expectations above. Note that system IV of the Likert profile – the participative group system – is taken to define the behaviours, attitudes, and skills consistent with the values of the laboratory approach. Consequently, observed changes often will be conveniently described as 'towards the laboratory model,' or 'away from the laboratory model.'

1 Managers reported that the interpersonal and intergroup relations existing in their organization unit changed in expected ways, and also that these changes were substantially preserved over the full observation period. This fulfills expectations 1A and 1B above. As table 6 shows, Now II scores were greater than Now I in 46 of 48 cases, with 27 of these changes reaching the 0.05 level of statistical significance. Some regression did occur on observation III, but Now IV scores are still greater than Now I scores in 38 cases, nearly half of which reach the 0.05 level.

The data in table 6 support a direct conclusion. Following exposure to a learning design based on the laboratory approach, managers' Now scores changed in the expected direction and remained basically stable throughout the period of observation. This pattern implies the potency of the learning design.

2 Self-reports on the Likert profile clearly revealed that managers expected more of their organizational relations immediately after experiencing the learning design and also that these expectations increased even more by the end of the eighteen-month period of observation. Specifically, table 7 shows that Ideal II scores were greater than Ideal I scores in 43 of 48 cases, with nearly half of the differences reaching the 0.05 level. At observation IV, the level of change had been maintained and somewhat increased, despite a substantial regression that appeared in the comparisons of Ideal III with Ideal I scores.

In sum, the data seem consistent with expectations 2A and 2B. The two sets of comparisons above imply that the training design was able to change both managerial expectations as well as actual organization climate in the direction of the values of the laboratory approach.

3 Managers initially perceived a significant difference, or 'gap,' between their own ideals about organization climate and their perceptions of the climate in which they worked. These significant differences persisted through observations III and IV. Specifically, table 8 shows that Ideal scores are greater than Now scores in all 192 cases on the four administra-

33 The self-reports are provided by the regional managers. Two regional managers were reassigned after observation III, and data from them are not utilized below, so as to permit consistent comparisons of observations I–IV. Data trends differ only minutely in observations I–III when these men are included and when they are excluded.

TABLE 5

Summary results of changes in four administrations of the Likert profile: A three-month period

Means of the differences between selected combinations of 'ideal' and 'now' ratings on four administrations of the Likert profile

	$N_2 - N_1$	$N_3 - N_1$	$N_4 - N_1$	$I_2 - I_1$	$I_3 - I_1$	$I_4 - I_1$	$I_1 - N_1$	$I_2 - N_2$	$I_3 - N_3$	$I_4 - N_4$
LEADERSHIP PROCESSES										
1 Extent to which superiors have confidence and trust in subordinates	3.10***	3.00**	1.70**	0.30	1.00**	−0.10	5.70***	2.90***	3.70***	3.90***
2 Extent to which subordinates, in turn, have confidence and trust in superiors	3.90***	3.20***	1.70*	0.80	0.60	0.90*	6.10***	3.00***	3.50***	5.30***
3 Extent to which superiors display supportive behaviour towards others	3.70***	2.40	3.20***	3.50***	2.80***	3.30***	4.10***	3.90***	4.50***	4.20***
4 Extent to which superiors behave so that subordinates feel free to discuss important things about their jobs with their immediate superior	2.80*	2.44*	3.00	1.30*	1.67**	2.00***	5.60***	4.10***	5.00***	4.60***
5 Extent to which immediate superior in solving job problems generally tries to get subordinates' ideas and opinions and make constructive use of them	3.30***	4.33***	4.50***	0.40	1.00	2.80*	5.90***	3.00***	3.56***	4.20***
CHARACTER OF MOTIVATIONAL FORCES										
6 Underlying motives tapped	3.60***	2.30	3.00**	0.60	−1.00	2.20**	6.40***	3.40***	3.10**	5.89***
7 Manner in which motives are used	2.10**	2.30**	1.11	0.30	1.10	0.67	3.40***	1.60*	2.20**	2.89***
8 Kinds of attitudes developed towards organization and its goals	3.00***	2.80**	0.90	2.30***	2.20***	2.10***	3.50***	2.80***	2.90**	4.70***
9 Extent to which motivational forces conflict with or reinforce one another	5.30**	2.50	2.20	1.90*	1.30	0.80	6.40***	3.00***	5.20***	5.00***

10	Amount of responsibility felt by each member of organization for achieving organization's goals	2.00*	1.80	0.0	2.80**	3.00***	2.60**	2.80*	3.60***	4.00***	5.40***
11	Attitudes towards other members of the organization	0.60	1.20	−0.40	1.90*	2.10**	2.50***	3.00***	4.30***	3.90***	5.90***
12	Satisfaction derived	2.80*	2.30**	1.00	1.20	1.50	1.90*	3.70**	2.10**	2.90***	4.60***
	CHARACTER OF COMMUNICATION PROCESSES										
13	Amount of interaction and communication aimed at achieving organization's objectives	2.50	1.30	2.20*	1.30*	1.20	1.10*	4.60***	3.40***	4.50***	3.50***
14	Direction of information flow	2.50	2.40*	1.40	0.90	1.10	1.70	5.30***	3.70***	4.00**	5.60***
15	Where downward communication is initiated	3.90**	1.80	2.50*	2.60*	1.70	2.40	3.80***	2.50***	3.70**	3.70***
16	Extent to which superiors willingly share information with subordinates	2.90*	1.90***	2.60*	1.70*	1.70*	2.60***	3.40***	2.20***	3.20***	3.40**
17	Extent to which communications are accepted by subordinates	1.60	0.90	0.0	3.00*	2.90*	3.00*	1.50	2.90**	3.50***	4.50***
18	Adequacy of upward communication via line organization	3.10*	1.80	2.80**	1.80***	0.80	1.10	4.90***	3.60***	3.90***	3.20***
19	Subordinates' feeling of responsibility for initiating accurate upward communication	0.60	0.60	0.10	1.20*	0.70	1.20*	3.90***	4.50***	4.00***	5.20***
20	Forces leasing to accurate or distorted upward information	0.70	1.10*	0.40	1.20	0.90	1.30*	2.20***	2.70***	2.00***	3.10**
21	Accuracy of upward communication via line	2.10**	2.50**	1.50	0.70	1.20	1.20*	4.50***	3.10***	3.20***	4.20***
22	Need for supplementary upward communication system	3.90**	2.20	4.22**	3.60	3.20	3.67	1.20	0.90	2.20	0.89*
23	Sideward communication, its adequacy and accuracy	3.60*	2.30*	2.50*	0.80	0.90	1.00	5.80***	3.00***	4.40***	4.30***

Means of the differences between selected combinations of 'ideal' and 'now' ratings on four administrations of the Likert profile

24	Psychological closeness of superiors to subordinates (i.e., friendliness between superiors and subordinates)	2.40*	1.50	2.70	4.30**	3.10	4.90**	1.80	3.70***	3.40***	4.00***
25	How well does superior know and understand problems faced by subordinates?	1.20	1.40	2.80	1.00	1.60*	2.10**	3.70**	3.50***	3.90**	3.00***
26	How accurate are the perceptions by superiors and subordinates of each other?	3.30***	2.40*	0.0	1.20*	0.80*	0.0	5.70***	3.60***	4.10***	5.70***
	CHARACTER OF INTERACTION-INFLUENCE PROCESSES										
27	Amount of character of interaction	1.90*	1.10	0.60	1.70	1.60	1.30	5.00***	4.80***	5.50***	5.70***
28	Amount of co-operative teamwork present	0.89	0.22	−0.78	2.00*	1.11	1.78**	2.00	3.20***	3.10***	4.50***
29	Extent to which subordinates can influence the goals, methods, and activity of their units and departments, as seen by superiors	3.50**	3.30*	4.00***	1.50*	1.50	1.50*	4.50***	2.50***	2.70***	2.00***
30	Extent to which subordinates can influence the goals, methods, and activity of their units and departments, as seen by subordinates	1.40	1.80	1.20	0.50	1.00	1.00	4.90***	4.00***	4.10***	4.70***
31	Amount of actual influence which superiors can exercise over the goals, activity, and methods of their units and departments	2.20	1.11	1.50	−0.60	−0.11	0.30	4.40***	1.60	3.22**	3.20**
32	Extent to which an effective structure exists enabling one part of organization to exert influence upon other parts	1.10	0.80	0.20	2.50*	1.20	2.20*	4.80***	6.20***	5.20***	6.80***

Means of the differences between selected combinations of 'ideal' and 'now' ratings on four administrations of the Likert profile

CHARACTER OF DECISION-MAKING PROCESSES

33 At what level in organization are decisions formally made?	4.40**	3.00	2.90*	2.00	4.60**	5.90**	3.50***	5.90**	7.60***
34 How adequate and accurate is the information available for decision making at the place where decisions are made?	0.60	−0.10	2.30*	−1.30*	0.0	5.30***	3.40***	3.90**	3.00***
35 To what extent are decision-makers aware of problems, particularly those at lower levels in the organization?	1.90	0.50	0.90	0.40	0.80	3.90*	2.40**	3.50**	3.80***
36 Extent to which technical and professional knowledge is used in decision-making	3.80*	0.22	3.30*	1.80	2.10	5.70***	3.70***	4.11*	4.50**
37 Are decisions made at the best level in the organization as far as availability of the most adequate information bearing on the decision?	−1.60	−0.30	−1.70	−1.50	1.80	1.90	2.00*	3.20*	5.40***
38 Does the decision-making process help to create the necessary motivations in those persons who have to carry out the decisions?	3.90**	1.30	0.50	0.60	0.50	5.20***	1.90*	3.70**	5.20***
39 To what extent are subordinates involved in decisions related to their work?	2.67*	2.67*	1.11	−0.44	−0.33	6.78***	4.00***	3.90***	5.10***
40 Is decision making based on man-to-man or group pattern of operation? Does it encourage teamwork?	0.11	0.11	−1.78	1.33*	0.56	2.67*	3.70***	3.50***	4.90***

CHARACTER OF GOAL SETTING OR ORDERING

41 Manner in which goal setting or ordering is usually done	3.78**	2.22	3.37*	3.11**	2.33	4.33**	3.50***	4.50***	5.11***

Means of the differences between selected combinations of 'ideal' and 'now' ratings on four administrations of the Likert profile

#											
42	To what extent do the different hierarchical levels tend to strive for high performance goals?	1.56	0.67	−0.11	2.00*	1.44	2.78**	1.44	1.90**	2.40***	4.00***
43	Are there forces to accept, resist, or reject goals?	3.00*	1.00	1.22	2.56*	1.67	2.11	3.67***	3.10***	3.90***	4.50***
	CHARACTER OF CONTROL PROCESSES										
44	At what hierarchical levels in organization does major or primary concern exist with regard to the performance of the control function?	1.00	−0.78	2.25*	−0.22	−0.89	0.50	4.56**	3.70***	4.20***	3.22***
45	How accurate are the measurements and information used to guide and perform the control function, and to what extent do forces exist in the organization to distort and falsify this information?	−0.11	0.0	−1.00	0.89	1.56	1.67*	1.78	2.70***	3.40***	4.00***
46	Extent to which the review and control functions are concentrated	1.22	−0.11	−1.33	0.44	0.0	1.11	3.33***	3.00***	3.10***	5.20**
47	Extent to which there is an informal organization present and supporting or opposing goals of formal organization	1.56	−0.75	1.22	0.44	0.25	0.0	3.89***	2.70***	3.78***	2.40*
48	Extent to which control data (e.g., accounting, productivity, cost, etc.) are used for self-guidance or group problem solving by managers and non-supervisory employees, or used by superiors in a punitive, policing manner	2.33	1.44	1.00	0.44	1.00	0.33	3.89**	2.50***	3.60***	2.90**

*** indicates a difference statistically significant at the 0.001 level, one-tailed test
** indicates a difference statistically significant at the 0.01 level, one-tailed test
* indicates a difference statistically significant at the 0.05 level, one-tailed test

TABLE 6

Summary of changes in now scores over four administrations of the Likert profile

	Statistically significant changes towards laboratory model	Changes towards laboratory model	No changes	Changes away from laboratory model	Statistically significant changes away from laboratory model
Now II – Now I	27	19	0	2	0
Now III – Now I	15	27	1	5	0
Now IV – Now I	17	21	3	7	0
Now III – Now II	0	11	1	32	4
Now IV – Now II	0	8	0	35	5
Now IV – Now III	2	17	1	22	6

TABLE 7

Summary of changes in ideal scores over four administrations of the Likert profile

	Statistically significant changes towards laboratory model	Changes towards laboratory model	No changes	Changes away from laboratory model	Statistically significant changes towards laboratory model
Ideal II – Ideal I	21	22	0	5	0
Ideal III – Ideal I	12	29	1	6	0
Ideal IV – Ideal I	24	19	3	2	0
Ideal III – Ideal II	1	17	3	24	3
Ideal IV – Ideal II	4	21	3	17	3
Ideal IV – Ideal III	6	24	6	10	2

TABLE 8

Summary of differences between Ideal and Now scores on four administrations of the Likert profile

	Ideal scores significantly greater than Now scores	Ideal scores greater than Now scores	No difference	Now scores greater than Ideal scores	Now scores significantly greater than Ideal scores
Ideal I – Now I	41	7	0	0	0
Ideal II – Now II	46	2	0	0	0
Ideal III – Now III	47	1	0	0	0
Ideal IV – Now IV	48	0	0	0	0

tions of the Likert profile. To the same point, all 48 of the differences on observation IV reach the 0.05 level. On test I, only 41 of the 48 Ideal versus Now comparisons reached usually accepted levels of statistical significance.

These results are consistent with Expectations 3A and 3B about the effects of the training design. These expectations are permissive criteria of a successful planned intervention, providing only that I–N might persist throughout the full period of observation. The rationale for these expectations is uncomplicated. A gap is defined as the difference between Ideal and Now scores, the distance between what is preferred and what exists. Normally, scores on the Likert profile indicate that aspirations exceed achievement. Consequently, the I–N gap typically is positive, although the differences between Ideal and Now scores may be slight.[34] The I–N gap is assumed to have motivating properties, moreover, up to some undetermined point at which the difference grows so large as to encourage despair. Hence expectations 3A and 3B provide only that I–N gaps might persist.

4   More strictly, expectations 4A and 4B conceive changes in I–N gaps as a boundary condition for the training design. That is, any marked increase in the gaps would be taken to indicate a significant problem with the training design, even though that design did successfully increase both Ideal and Now scores. Directly, the point of this boundary condition is a conservative one: to avoid gaps so large as to pass that unknown point at which they become demotivating. The initial expectation was that the Ideal versus Now gaps probably would be reduced somewhat as a result of the learning design, but 'no change' would have been acceptable. The minimum goal was to balance roughly increases/decreases in the sizes of the gaps, comparing observations I and II. In addition, the minimum goal was to maintain that balance throughout the observation period.

The data in table 5 meet the stricter criterion for a successful planned intervention proposed by expectations 4A and 4B. Table 9 shows that managerial self-reports indicate a major trend towards smaller gaps between Ideal and Now scores, although some decay occurred towards the end of the 525-day period of observation. Specifically, because of the way the comparisons are defined, negative entries in exhibit 11 reflect a closer fit between perceived climate and managerial ideals, comparing later administrations of the Likert profile with earlier ones. Thirty-six of the 48 Ideal–Now gaps are smaller for observation II than observation I. This implies a closer approach of existing organizational relations to the ideal

34   Arthur Blumberg and W. Wiener, 'One From two: A Behavioral Science Design for Merging Organizations,' unpublished manuscript (1970).

conditions defined by the managers. The third and fourth administrations reflect some decay of this data trend. But at their worst, on observation IV, 27 of the 48 gaps still are smaller or no different than the gaps on test I.

These data meet the strict requirement of expectations 4A and 4B and suggest that the learning design did not generate a kind of unfulfilled revolution of rising expectations.

The data in table 9 provide a strict test of the learning design's capacity to help induce persisting changes in an organization's climate. The test is severe in at least the sense that both Ideal and Now scores could have changed massively, with an increase in the size of the Ideal–Now gaps, and this might even be a desirable outcome in that increases in Ideal–Now gaps probably have motivating properties, up to a point. One could not easily deny the change-inducing properties of the underlying learning design in such a case, that is clear. But such a case would violate our conservative limiting condition that derives from ignorance about when differences between the ideal and the existing organization climate become so great as to inspire pessimism that anything constructive can be done to realize the ideal. At this unknown point, Ideal–Now gaps become so great as to be demotivating.

SOME CONCERNS ABOUT RESEARCH DESIGN: THE TYRANNY OF SERENDIPITY

To the author, the most credible hypothesis explaining these results attributes multiple effects to the training design. That design helped induce major changes in both Ideal and Now self-reports that more closely approached the values of the laboratory approach. And the design also reduced the absolute and relative differences between Ideal and Now scores.

However, one cannot attribute the reported effects to the training experience without some qualification. The basic reservation inheres in the methodology underlying the reported data. Or, perhaps more accurately, the reservation is inherent in the very nature of field experimentation. That is, available research opportunities do not often permit methodological elegance. Research opportunities in the field tend to be serendipitous and to require various methodological concessions.

The methodological inelegancies of this pilot study are several. First, it was not possible to use the most powerful research designs, those using control groups of one kind or another. The entire managerial population was exposed to the experimental treatment, since various features of the learning design contraindicated exposing only some of the managers to

TABLE 9

One approach to estimating the approach of existing interpersonal and intergroup relations to managerially defined ideals, by paired comparisons of four administrations of the Likert profile

	Significantly greater gaps in later administration	Greater gaps in later administration	No difference	Smaller gaps in later administration	Significantly smaller gaps in later administration
(Ideal II – Now II) – (Ideal I – Now I)	0	12	0	27	9
(Ideal III – Now III) – (Ideal I – Now I)	0	19	0	25	4
(Ideal IV – Now IV) – (Ideal I – Now I)	2	19	3	22	2
(Ideal III – Now III) – (Ideal II – Now II)	0	40	0	8	0
(Ideal IV – Now IV) – (Ideal II – Now II)	10	32	1	5	0
(Ideal IV – Now IV) – (Ideal III – Now III)	8	26	2	12	0

the experimental treatment.[35] Relatedly, the use as a control of a 'matched group' of managers at similar levels from throughout the organization was considered inappropriate. The experimental unit was unique in many senses: it was adding a radically different product line, it had experienced a major managerial succession, and its history had a strong and distinctive flavor.

The use of control groups in behavioural research has its mixed consequences,[36] but their absence here encourages a tentativeness in attributing all effects to the training design. At the same time, it does not seem likely that the effects reported here were due to the passage of time or to the three new managers alone. Basically, the changes in self-reports in the experiment are contrary to the history of the experimental unit as well as to the previous styles of the national sales head and the divisional managers. Furthermore, the changes in self-reports were marked and consistent with the broad theory underlying the laboratory method. These factors are only suggestive of the potency of the training design, of course.

Second, the research design employed in this case does have its advantages but less so than a 'time series' design, which in turn implies more interpretive ambiguity than various control group designs.[37] A time series design may be generalized as $O_B X O_A$, where O_B represents more than one observation with the test instrument before the experimental treatment X, and O_A represents more than one observation after the X. Specifically, the time series design reduces the likelihood that observed effects are due to such alternatives to the X as:

1   increases in the dependent variable which are due to practice effects in responding to the measuring instrument,[38] or which are due to the incomplete correlation of several administrations of the same instrument,[39] difficulties that especially plague a $O_1 X O_2$ design which has only one 'before' and one 'after' measurement;
2   common historical events affecting the experimental population but independent of the experimental treatment; and
3   already ongoing maturational effects in the experimental population that are independent of the experimental treatment.

35 See Golembiewski and Blumberg, 'Sensitivity Training in Cousin Groups.'
36 Chris Argyris, 'Issues in Evaluating Laboratory Education,' *Industrial Relations*, 8 (October 1968), pp. 28–40.
37 Donald T. Campbell, 'From Description to Experimentation: Interpreting Trends as Quasi-experiments,' pp. 214–23, in Chester W. Harris, ed., *Problems in Measuring Change* (Madison: University of Wisconsin Press, 1963).
38 V.R. Cane and A.W. Heim, 'The Effects of Repeated Testing, III,' *Quarterly Journal of Experimental Psychology*, 2 (1950), pp. 182–95.
39 The incomplete correlation may inhere in both the validity and the reliability of the measuring instrument.

Campbell evaluated the time series design in careful terms which reflect its advantages but which also imply that there are more useful research designs in behavioural research. The time-series experiment, he concludes, 'is one of the frequent research designs of the biological and physical sciences. While to date appropriate and successful applications may be lacking in the social sciences, the design should probably, nonetheless, be granted a position of semirespectability.'[40]

Specifically, the present research design may be described as O_1X-$O_2O_3O_4$. It has some but not all the advantages of the time-series design, since it has only a single pre-treatment observation. The point can be established in terms of figure 3, in which the line segments $ABCD$ represent the data trends summarized above. Specifically, the dependent variable showed significant and expected O_1 versus O_2 changes after the experimental treatment X, which changes essentially persisted over the extended period O_2 through O_4.

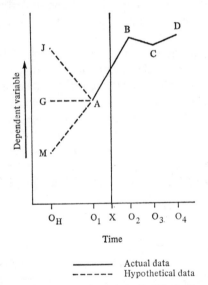

Figure 3 Representation of an $O_1XO_2O_3O_4$ research design compared to a true time series.

Results like $ABCD$ in figure 3 can be explained in terms of various hypotheses, given an $O_1XO_2O_3O_4$ research design. Maturational processes in the population of managers, for example, might be said to cause the observed effects, independent of the experimental treatment. That is, one can argue that some hypothetical observation O_H in figure 3 might

40   Campbell, 'From Description to Experimentation,' p. 230.

yield a dependent variable score M, and maturational effects are implied in the line segments $MABCD$. Similarly, an O_H might generate a score at J, in which case $JABCD$ might be said to reflect some common historical event between J and B, as opposed to the X. Or positively, if O_H generated a score G in a time-series design, the case would be very strong for considering $ABCD$ as an effect of the experimental treatment.

While inferior to the time series, and certainly to the 'control group' design, the present design does have significant advantages over O_1XO_2. For example, test/retest effects are minimized in $O_1XO_2O_3O_4$. Moreover, a maturational hypothesis is less credible, if only because the analyst must then explain the peaking of the maturational processes coincident with the post-treatment observations. Common historical events still remain an alternative hypothesis explaining any observed effects, whose plausibility only some form of control-group design can really destroy.

A mixed conclusion seems appropriate. The data imply the potency of a learning design based on the laboratory approach. The underlying research design, however, does not rule out the possibility that alternative hypotheses can explain the observed effects.

Third, other methodological issues also must temper interpretation of any observed changes in self-reports about organization style until replicatory studies are made. For example, the data above may not reflect changes in behaviour. Trainees may have learned the kinds of behaviours that consultants valued; they may have dutifully reported appropriate changes in their self-reports as co-operative subjects in an experiment often do; yet behaviour in their organization might not have changed at all. Similarly, changes in self-reports may be due in some part to the practice gained in responding to the Likert form, or to reliability problems with the instrument.

The possibility that the changes reported below do not reflect actual behavioural changes must be taken seriously, even though a plausible counter-case can be built. Substantial anecdotal evidence suggests that extensive behavioural change did take place. In addition, rating each Likert dimension as Ideal and Now was an attempt to force respondents to distinguish between wish fulfilment and reality. Various technical details – such as spacing the four administrations of the Likert items over an eighteen-month period and varying the direction of scales for individual Likert items to prevent a response set – also encouraged respondents to base their reports on actual behaviour. However, the present research design does not deal directly with behavioural change, and the possibility that the data reflect a subtle kind of wish-fulfillment therefore cannot be rejected.

CONCLUSION

The learning design to change an organization's style in planned ways seems, in general, to have had the intended effects. The design appeared to induce or reinforce appropriate values in the experimental unit. These values governing interpersonal and intergroup relations, in turn, were reported by managers to have changed attitudes as well as behaviours over the full period of observation.

This pilot study generates at least two levels of conclusions. First, and for me of greater importance, this study should indicate one way of potentially having the best of two analytic traditions. Epigrammatically, one can help promote human welfare (as in the emerging new world view of political science) as well as help develop general knowledge, theory, and science (as in the old weltanschauung). In the present approach one can emphasize the individual as a valuing, deciding, and choosing organism who consciously selects among alternative climates that influence the quality of his life, while not neglecting the truism that norms often will, once established, continue to induce even behaviours which individuals do not prefer. As was said before, this pilot study seeks a *media via*.

Second, this pilot study implies many intriguing research questions that elude the available data. Five special lacunae will be highlighted as 'shoulds' for subsequent research. Thus subsequent research should deal with larger populations in more complex combinations, since the organization unit involved in this case was small, had few levels, and was not organizationally complex. Such work is already well underway.

Moreover, subsequent testing of the basic training design should give greater attention to observations of behavioural change, especially non-obtrusive measures.[41] In contrast, present measures have relied on self-reports that are probably reactive and which are consequently open to the charge that they act as confounding variables in explaining any observed change, that is to say, the very processes of measuring may change what is being measured. Or respondents may become 'questionnaire-bright,' returning to the experimenter what he seems to want. The effect has been commonly observed, even when what the experimenter wanted intentionally placed subjects in conflict situations. For example, acquiescence is common even when the experimenter tells subjects to

41 The present measure of change may interact with the training design, as might the weigh-in before a reducing regimen interact with the regimen. See Eugene J. Webb, Donald T. Campbell, Richard D. Schwartz, and Lee Sechrest, *Unobtrusive Measures* (Chicago: Rand McNally, 1966).

administer apparently powerful electrical shocks to a person who is actually a stooge of the experimenter.[42]

In addition, subsequent research should increasingly specify those conditions under which the learning design can be expected to generate desired effects. Questions come easily. When is an organization 'culturally prepared' for the laboratory approach? Do organizations differ enough so that the laboratory approach is tailor-made for one organization, but not for another? And so on. Research answers will come only grudgingly. The provisional suspicion is that the laboratory approach is unlikely to have effects like those reported above under at least two conditions: 1 / when the gaps between Ideal and Now scores on the Likert profile are initially so great as to inspire pessimism that any change is possible; and 2 / when the Now scores on the Likert profile are widely discrepant from laboratory models, that is, when Now scores cluster in system 1 or perhaps 2.

Future research should more explicitly assess the value of the Likert profile for estimating changes in organization climate. One approach involves an item analysis to variously check for any clusterings of items. One preliminary study, for example, usefully distinguished two batches of items in the Likert profile, 'process' items and those concerned with 'outcomes.'[43] More basically, future research should address the clasic empirical issue. That is, to what extent do the Likert items isolate dimensions of organizational reality, as opposed to being mere variables?[44] A factor analysis of the data now being gathered from a large managerial population, for example, may provide insights into this classic issue of empirical science.

Finally, subsequent research should emphasize changes in the effectiveness and efficiency of experimental units. The present case provides no help in this regard, largely because the mission and roles of the experimental unit have changed rapidly. Participants report more involvement and satisfaction at work, and they generally agree that the style changes cannot help but enhance their performance in the long-run. In addition, sound theoretical reasons urge that high output will co-exist with high satisfaction of the interpersonal and intergroup needs of organization members. But such considerations stop far short of supplying the necessary demonstration that the present change in organization style has

42   Milgram, S. 'Some Conditions of Obedience and Disobedience to Authority,' *Human Relations*, 18, 1 (1965), pp. 57–76.
43   Robert T. Golembiewski, 'Organizational Properties and Managerial Learning: Testing Alternative Models of Attitudinal Change,' *Journal of Academy of Management* (in press).
44   The Likert profile lacks the kind of effort devoted to such descriptive scales as that of Andrew W. Halpin and Don B. Croft, *The Organizational Climate of Schools* (Chicago: Midwest Administration Center, 1963).

favourable consequences on output.[45] Man after all lives by bread as well as by the quality of his relationships.

REFERENCES

ARGYRIS, CHRIS *Integrating the Individual and the Organization.* New York: Wiley, 1964.
– 'Issues In Evaluating Laboratory Education,' *Industrial Relations,* 8 (October 1968), pp. 28–40.
BARNES, LOUIS B. and LARRY E. GREINER 'Breakthrough in Organization Development,' *Harvard Business Review,* 42 (November-December 1964), pp. 139–65.
BLAKE, ROBERT T. and JANE S. MOUTON *The Managerial Grid.* Houston, Texas: Gulf Publishing, 1964.
BLUMBERG, ARTHUR and C. WIENER 'One From Two: A Behavioral Science Design for Merging Organizations,' unpublished MS (1970).
BRADFORD, LELAND P., JACK R. GIBB, and KENNETH D. BENNE, eds. *T-Group Theory and Laboratory Method.* New York: Wiley, 1964.
CAMPBELL, DONALD T. 'From Description to Experimentation: Interpreting Trends as Quasi Experiments' in Chester W. Harris, ed. *Problems in Measuring Change.* Madison: University of Wisconsin Press, 1963.
CANE, V.R. and A.W. HEIM 'The Effects of Repeating Testing, III,' *Quarterly Journal of Experimental Psychology* 2, 4 (1950), pp. 182–95.
FORD, ROBERT N. *Motivation through Work Itself.* New York: American Management Association, 1969.
GOLEMBIEWSKI, ROBERT T. *Men, Management, and Morality.* New York: McGraw-Hill, 1965.
– 'Organization Development in Public Agencies: Perspectives on Theory and Practice,' *Public Administration Review,* 29, 4 (July/August 1969), pp. 367–77.
– 'Organization Patterns of the Future,' *Personnel Administration,* 32, 6 (November–December 1969), p. 9–26.
– 'Organizational Properties and Managerial Learning: Testing Alternative Models of Attitudinal Change,' *Academy of Management Journal,* 13, 1 (March 1970), pp. 13–24.
GOLEMBIEWSKI, ROBERT T., WILLIAM WELSH, and WILLIAM CROTTY *A Methodological Primer for Political Scientists.* Chicago: Rand McNally, 1969.
GOLEMBIEWSKI, ROBERT T. and ARTHUR BLUMBERG 'Sensitivity Training in Cousin Groups: A Confrontation Design,' *Training and Development Journal,* 23 (August 1969), pp. 18–23.
– *Sensitivity Training and the Laboratory Approach.* Itasca, Ill.: F.E. Peacock, 1970.

45 For such an effort see Louis B. Barnes and Larry E. Greiner, 'Breakthrough in Organization Development,' *Harvard Business Review,* 42 (November–December 1964), pp. 139–65.

GOLEMBIEWSKI, ROBERT T. and STOKES B. CARRIGAN 'Planned Change in Organization Style Based on the Laboratory Approach,' *Administrative Science Quarterly*, 15, 1 (March 1970), pp. 79–93.

GOULDNER, ALVIN W. 'Metaphysical Pathos and the Theory of Bureaucracy,' *American Political Science Review*, 49, 2 (June 1955), pp. 496–507.

HALPIN, ANDREW W. and DON B. CROFT *The Organizational Climate of Schools*. Chicago: Midwest Administration Center, 1963.

HERZBERG, FREDERICK, *et al. The Motivation to Work*. New York: Wiley, 1959.

KAUFMAN, HERBERT 'Organization Theory and Political Theory,' *American Political Science Review*, 58, 1 (March 1964), pp. 5–14.

LAWRENCE, PAUL R. and JAY W. LORSCH *Organization and Environment*. Boston: Graduate School of Business Administration, Harvard University, 1967.

LIKERT, RENSIS *New Patterns of Management*. New York: McGraw-Hill, 1961.

–   *The Human Organization*. New York: McGraw-Hill, 1967.

LUBIN, BERNARD and MARVIN ZUCKERMAN 'Level of Emotional Arousal in Laboratory Training,' *Journal of Applied Behavioral Science*, 5 (December 1969), pp. 483–90.

MASLOW, ABRAHAM *Eupsychian Management*. Homewood, Ill.: Irwin-Dorsey, 1965.

MCGREGOR, DOUGLAS *The Human Side of Enterprise*. New York: McGraw-Hill, 1960.

MICHELS, ROBERTO *Political Parties*. Glencoe, Ill.: Free Press, 1949.

MILGRAM, STANLEY 'Some Conditions of Obedience and Disobedience to Authority,' *Human Relations*, 18, 1 (1965), pp. 57–76.

MILL, CYRIL R. 'A Theory for the Group Dynamics Laboratory,' *Adult Leadership*, II (1962), pp. 133–4 and 159–60.

SCHEIN, EDGAR H. *Process Consultation*. Reading, Mass.: Addison-Wesley, 1969.

SCHEIN, EDGAR R.H. and WARREN G. BENNIS *Personal Growth and Organizational Change through Group Methods*. New York: Wiley, 1965.

SEIDENBERG, RODERICK *Post-historic Man*. Boston: Beacon Press, 1957.

SHEPARD, HERBERT A. 'Changing Interpersonal and Intergroup Relations in Organizations' in James G. March, ed. *Handbook of Organizations*. Chicago: Rand-McNally, 1965.

SOMIT, ALBERT and JOSEPH TANENHAUS *The Development of Political Science*. Boston: Allyn and Bacon, 1967.

VAN DYKE, VERNON 'Process and Policy as Focal Concepts in Political Research,' in Austin Ranney, ed. *Political Science and Public Policy*. Chicago: Markham, 1968.

WEBB, EUGENE J., DONALD T. CAMPBELL, RICHARD D. SCHWARTZ, and LEE SECHREST *Unobtrusive Measures*. Chicago: Rand McNally, 1966.

WINN, ALEXANDER 'The Laboratory Approach to Organization Development: A Tentative Model of Planned Change,' *Journal of Management Studies*, 6, 2 (1969), pp. 155–66.

ILAN VERTINSKY

Methodology for social planning: simulation and experimentation processes for participatory social development*

A INTRODUCTION

Social development methodology is one of the important challenges confronting the social scientist today. Neither comprehensive planning nor political process seem to provide a satisfactory framework for decision-making which could lead to socio-economic development. Comprehensive planning techniques often introduce a systematic bias in the choice of value premises, minimizing the importance of those elements of the social system which are either controversial, intangible, or problematic. In addition, vital implementational aspects are often discounted in plans which are derived under conditions of uncertainty. Centralization and the relative isolation of armchair planning make mobilization of the system without measures of extreme coercion an improbable event, yet in many social systems the process of development is radically impaired unless total mobilization takes place.

The democratic political process frequently provides workable solutions, but these are not necessarily satisfactory or effective. The competition of forces which do not aim at a common interest may lead to the exploration of latent societal goals in a society facing uncertain environ-

*   This study was supported by a grant from the Ford Foundation administered by the Council of Intersocietal Studies at Northwestern University. The opinions reflected in this paper are the author's. The author is indebted to H. Guetzkow, R. Schwartz, and P. Smoker and the members of CIMS at the Universidad del Valle for stimulating comments. Dr Prieto and Mrs E. Rincon assisted in organizing the research.

ments, but only under certain conditions. These conditions include the free flow of information and the interaction (rather than confrontation) of conflicting points of view.

The methodology developed in this paper attempts to provide an apparatus whereby the benefits of comprehensive planning are inter-twined with a semipolitical process to define goals for the system as a whole and subgoals for subsystems. The procedure is iterative and dynamic and concerns not only present and past states of the social system, but also possible future environments.

B   DESIRED METHODOLOGICAL CHARACTERISTICS

Scientific research methods have traditionally been aimed at knowledge inventory-building, which is rarely of direct use to the decision-maker. Integration and processing of accumulated knowledge have been assigned to the decision-making level. However, the decision-maker is often faced with an enormous set of relevant but unstructured information which does not provide a meaningful scenario of the problem at hand. In addition to the probable saturation of these streams of information, the format through which they are related to him constrains their usefulness. An evaluation of basic or implied assumptions is often impossible, for the decision-maker can hardly ascertain the value of the information for the solution of the problem at hand.

While disciplinary standpoints often try to limit the reactive char-acteristics of the research environment, applied social system develop-ment research should magnify these characteristics. The interaction of research and environment is considered an essential educational process for both. This concept of the research process places emphasis on mean-ingful participation and interaction. For the scientist, this educational process generates a standpoint derived from the developmental process, rather than particularized disciplinary standpoints; for the social system the process is a stimulant which increases the flow of information and ideas.

This paper emphasizes the need for a flexible research apparatus which is adaptable to a broad spectrum of research conditions (limited research resources, lack of hard data, etc.). The concept is founded on the premise of 'informational efficiency of the research project' as the main criterion of relevance.[1] To illustrate the meaning of this concept,

1   I. Vertinsky, 'Measurement: *Some Aspects of Culture and Culture Change*' (unpublished PHD thesis; University of California, Berkeley, 1968).

let us use the analogy of the accounting system in an industrial enterprise which dictates information processing satisfying a basic set of axioms (e.g., objectivity). However, from an informational efficiency point of view, that is, the actual contribution of the information to managerial decisions, the accounting system is nearly obsolete. 'Objectivity,' for example, often leads to a larger bias in the information processed than the one created by the personal bias of subjective opinions.

1 Total system approach in planning

The need for total system approach is widely recognized by theoreticians and practitioners alike, yet planning is usually based on an unsystematic process of merging holistic considerations and unitary consideration on an ad hoc basis.

It is agreed that in developing countries the social forces generated in the process of change channel this process into a particular path. Any program, economic or social, is doomed to failure without the creation of social forces to back it. Hence, planning which lacks the understanding of a present and future network of these social processes and institutions is often sterile, reinforcing its own defeat. Traditional prescriptions, such as capital generation through taxation, stabilizing monetary policies, etc., have hardly been implemented, and where piecemeal implementation was attempted, unexpected, contradictory results were often manifested.[2]

Comprehensive planning presumes available knowledge of the social system. However, the state of the behavioural sciences is far from encouraging. The main efforts of research in the social sciences (excluding economics and political science) were channelled to microstudies. Traditional preoccupation with the so-called hard data or objectively derived measurements and the traditional scientific method of verification made a macrosocial study, if not a methodological impossibility, at least a financial one. Ironically, a macrostudy under traditional methodological requirements is completely ruled out for the systems that need it most – developing countries for which the sources of hard data are scarce and often of shaky credibility. Another, and maybe graver, constraint that the traditional methodology of the social sciences imposes upon the building up of a comprehensive model of the social system is its inadequacy to deal with future states of the social system.

---

2 Counter-intuitive results. See, for example, J.W. Forester's *Urban Dynamics* (Cambridge: MIT Press, 1969).

These two basic shortcomings of the prevailing methodologies in the social sciences are a cause of much frustration for social scientists in developing countries. The aesthetic requirements of the scientific method proved to be too expensive and luxurious for these countries, where resources for research, both human and monetary, are limited and the time deadline is pressing. This frustration may lead to the abandonment of the scientific method in the social sciences altogether in these countries for the politicization of the social sciences. A new type of pragmatic methodology is needed to cope with these basic frustrations caused by incompatibilities of methodologies that proved (more or less) useful in developed countries with the specific needs of developing countries. The following are the elements required for a new methodology to be useful in developing a social system:

1   Basic flexibility of the mathematical (logical) structures to be adapted to the particular social realities, that is, the models built should be homomorphic to the particular social system and not merely a replication of logical structures that proved useful in inquiries of other social systems.

2   Efficient use of any kind of information available on the social system, that is, the ability to integrate data from various sources such as microstudies, insights, experiences in the system, available hard data, etc. This requirement implies that the best or most reliable knowledge should be used in each area of inquiry, without any a priori exclusion of a particular source of data.

3   The methodology should provide for iterative stages of the research. The research strategy should be structured so that a built-in control would direct the research efforts for continuous improvement and allocate in each stage, the research resources to the area which may provide the highest marginal benefits.

4   The methodology has to provide new ways for verification and validation to cope with the new type of data used, as well as provide for validation techniques for models for future states of the social system.

5   The methodology has to recognize ideological conflicts in the evaluation of the social state and contribute to a resolution of those conflicts that stem from ambiguous research environments. The process should encourage productive conflicts of evaluation to generate more information about the social system.

In conformity with these prerequisites this paper proposes a new type of research strategy. The principle on which this strategy is formed is an efficient, flexible use of available information with an emphasis on adaptability to the particular needs and realities of a given system.

2 Judgment techniques and subjective data sources

The use of subjective judgment processes is a common phenomenon in government, industry, and business.[3] Attempts to formalize and structure these procedures of subjective information processes helped to improve the relevance and credibility of the derived information. Business, faced with immediate problems to be solved, successfully adapted some of these pragmatic methodologies. For example, after four years of applying one of those structures (PATTERNS) in a variety of fields such as R & D and development planning, an independent appraisal of this technique concluded:

> The judgments, though subjective in nature, are representative of the type of managerial decisions required in resource allocation, program planning, etc., where the manager must weigh all factors influencing a decision. Hence, the techniques used closely parallel and contribute to the managerial function of decision making.
> ... When qualified personnel (personnel of the type which line managers usually seek for advice and opinions) are used in the judgment process, the results achieve a high degree of value to managers, are quite specific, and provide data far more useful to the ultimate decision.
> ... Repeated tests of the data have shown that with similar information and discussion the results of these judgments are highly repeatable when averaged for a group of at least five experts in the field, and that they accurately reflect the consensus of the consulted community.[4]

The subjective process of evaluation integrates the benefits of the human expert, a pattern-recognizing information processor, and measured parameters and technological coefficients.

An alternative process of judgment was attempted in one of the largest industries in the US,[5] where an experiment with a dialectic decision

3 It is sufficient just to mention the existence of a voluminous literature on business applications of subjective probabilities. For example, H. Raiffa, *Decision Analysis* (New York: Addison-Wesley, 1968).
4 Aaron L. Jestice, *Pattern: Long Range Corporate Planning* (Arlington, Va.: Honeywell, 1967) (AM–97), p. 30.
5 The dialectic judgment model designed by Dr C.W. Churchman in SDC was applied to production decisions by Dr R. Mason; according to management evaluation, the results were extremely encouraging. R.O. Mason, 'Dialectics in Decision-Making: A Study in the Use of Counter Planning and Structured

process resulted in the improvement of managerial outlooks and decisions. A structured debate was planned and the management sat in on the case as a jury of experts. This dialectic process brought out the underlying and unverified assumptions of plans.

These two industrial experiments manifest the great potential of two important features of our proposed methodology: 1 / obtaining subjective evaluations through a structured teleological process of questioning and information retrieval; and 2 / the application of structured debate and the use of expert juries.

3   The resolution of conflict in judgment procedures

One of the principal problems of utilizing judgment and debate was how to handle the differences of logic expressed by the deviation in evaluations. Deviation in evaluation – disagreement – is not a homogenous phenomenon. Solutions, such as the averaging of opinions, if applied without qualifications may intensify biases rather than decrease them. Averaging implies convexity of the domain of evaluation,[6] an assumption which rarely applies in evaluation of social processes. Averaging can be applied only within limited neighbourhoods of opinions. This implies that disagreement has to be categorized as too much disagreement – an alternative opinion which cannot be averaged[7] – and neighbourhood disagreement which is subject to resolution through averaging. We are referring here to legitimate disagreement. It should be noted that some opinions which consist of self-contradictory premises, or opinions which are logical consequences of information proved to be in error, are ruled out as illegitimate opinions.

In defining 'too much' disagreement of opinions one can apply the statistical concept of significance. From the distribution of opinions one can identify those which are representative of alternative populations. Instead of eliminating insignificant opinions and reaveraging, the insignificant opinions are treated as alternative opinions. This procedure calls for the development of a technique whereby the conflict would be structured to produce more knowledge about the system.

Debate,' in *Management Information Systems. Dissertation Abstracts* (July 1969), p. 15.
6   Convexity implies that an average measure derived from observations is of the same defined set.
7   Professor Singer has pointed out the significance of 'too much' and 'too little' agreement in a research process. While 'too much' agreement implies tautology, 'too little' agreement implies the existence of an alternative hypothesis E.P. Singer, *Experience and Reflection* (Philadelphia: University of Pennsylvania Press, 1959).

At this stage an additional typology of disagreement is needed, so the concept of efficiency is introduced. Alternative hypotheses which lead to the same logical consequences – isomorphism from the system's point of view – are defined as inefficient or irrelevant conflicts. The sensitivity of the system to differences in evaluations will dictate whether the alternative opinions should be kept in the memory of the system or one of the opinions arbitrarily ruled out as an irrelevant alternative to the system.

To summarize, the following are the basic requirements of the judgmental process of the proposed methodology: 1 / a technique to validate opinions as legitimate; 2 / a distinction between convex and non-convex conflicts; and 3 / the elimination of inefficient conflict from the system. Hence, judgment becomes a sequential process of validation, a restructuring of information (the role of conflict management in the system), and guidance to the direction of future research.

4 *Interinstitutional interdisciplinary participation*

The myth of objectivity is often confused with indifference. It can be noted that Max Weber, the master of objectivity, long ago accepted this premise, implying that objectivity in this sense was equivalent to compromise with the status quo. The separation of social agents, social processes, and the scientists studying them is artificial and a prime cause for failure of many plans. Developmental research should be based on the continuous interaction of implementing agents, the groups affected, the planners, and the social scientists. The role of scientists and planners does not end in the implementation stage, just as the role of implementors and participants does not start at this point.

While the weight of participation changes during the process of planning and implementation, constant interaction between groups is necessary to keep the macromodel adapted to new functions and new knowledge generated in the process. In addition to making the model more applicable to the environmental requirements, the interaction should improve the social agents' perception of the system, as well as operate as a co-optative mechanism. Experience with implementation or, to be exact, unimplemented OR projects in industry has proved the importance of these functions.[8]

'Participation' and 'interaction' imply a structure which stimulates

8 At the IFORS Conference in Venice in 1969, a significant number of unimplemented OR projects was reported. At present, research efforts are directed towards solving the problem of implementation. Most noted in this respect are the experiments conducted by Dr C.W. Churchman and P. Ratoosh in a management science laboratory at the University of California, Berkeley.

flows of communications and change. Without specification of the apparatus of flows, participation and interaction remain at best stimulating slogans. Though methodological papers often avoid dealing with the organization of research, this variable is decisive in research methodology for system development. It is sufficient to explore the fate of interdisciplinary teamwork to realize how important the organizational design is in methodology.

The need for interdisciplinary research is frequently emphasized. Occasionally, some attempts are made in this direction, but more often interdisciplinary research projects become multidisciplinary projects. The prevailing view of an OECD discussion group on social change and economic growth, expressed by Just Faaland, was that 'efforts to develop a super theory ... enveloping all social sciences, would be fruitless.'[9] For example, interdisciplinary teams in OR were the style in the fifties, but their fast emergence was surpassed by their untimely demise.[10] Some so-called interdisciplinary teams developed undesirable features for coping with conflicts such as authoritarian structures. (For example, the idea of the roof of science, or alternatively stated, choosing a leading discipline, while viewing other disciplines as peripheral, service disciplines.) It is clear that the magic directive to co-operate is a vague directive to action – all the mal-characteristics of teamwork mentioned above are co-operation in some form. The question remains how is co-operation possible?

C   MODEL FOR ORGANIZING RESEARCH AND
     PLANNING ACTIVITIES

The problem of developing a social system is more complicated and inclusive than merely developing effective interdisciplinary teamwork and creating meaningful knowledge about the system. The research process has to lead to necessary changes in the existing conflicting value systems to facilitate implementation of the plan. In a world of conflicting value systems intertwined with complex technical relationships and consequences, the research apparatus has to provide a stimulus and a structure to a change of value systems as well as guarantee some degree of control of the system by the members of the social system. Control often implies a static situation of imposed constraints and restrictions. However, a static concept of control is incompatible with the dynamic characteristics of the

9   *Social Change and Economic Growth* (Paris: OECD Development Center, 1967), p. 75.
10 M. Radnor *et al.*, 'Integration and Utilization of Management Science Activities in Organizations,' *Operational Research Quarterly*, 19 (1968), p. 117.

system. Planning constrained by a static system of checks may be more harmful than no planning at all. A dynamic concept of control has to be embedded in the research organization.

Dynamic control may be achieved through a feedback system whereby the researcher and the decision-maker undergo a continuous process of resocialization through research work, as well as through long-run restructuring of the educational and training programs. To illustrate the meaning of these processes, let us entertain an outstanding example: the medical school at the University of Valle. The example is only an indicator of the type of processes of resocialization and re-education that the research apparatus should provide. The historical account given here of the development of the 'multi-disciplinary team of health sciences' – CIMS – is concise and only the features of interest to this paper are described.[11] The medical school in Valle was originally designed to provide professional training similar to that provided in the schools of Spain and the US. Medicine was basically viewed as an art. The exception was emphasized rather than the normal, treatment rather than prevention, and illness rather than health. Being service-oriented, the school soon realized that the services did not reach a substantial segment of potential clients. Thus it was decided to add field-service extensions to the main research hospital facilities. This territorial diffusion proved to be an important stepping stone in the school's development. Through client-doctor interaction the inadequacy and incompatibility of the professional standpoint and the needs of the system were realized.

First, it became obvious that prevention rather than treatment should be emphasized in a mass society. Second, the necessity was perceived of utilizing local social infrastructures to bring about some changes of attitudes and values concerning problems of health. Third, it was necessary to change and broaden the concept of health – from the disciplinary standpoint, that of pathology – to a positive concept derived from the system: social 'well-being.' This in turn led to the realization that a comprehensive total approach should be developed where a tradeoff between medical, engineering, psychological, and sociological technologies could be recognized in the process of health production and definition.

Through territorial diffusion the research community realized some of the needs of the social system and consequently some changes in the curriculum took place. However, territorial diffusion and ad hoc problem-oriented interdisciplinary work did not provide a permanent structure for

11   CIMS (Comite de Investigacion Multidisciplinaria en Salud) was formed with the co-operation of WHO to develop regional health and social planning for the State of Valle, Colombia.

a concerted process of interaction. The doctor in the field and his associates went through a process of value change, but this process was unstructured and uncontrolled and at times was manifested by a fragmented emotional change rather than a systematic value change. Reshaping the curriculum induced a broadening of perspective but failed to provide an overview of the system and its processes of interaction. As a result the school of health sciences is attempting to create an organ for concerted research and interaction.[12]

1   *Territorial diffusion*

Given the experience gained in CIMS operations, the following basic structure for a research organization is suggested. This structure can be generalized to deal with other social systems, such as big industrial complexes, cities, etc. Figure 1 schematically describes the organizational structure – institutions and links of interaction.

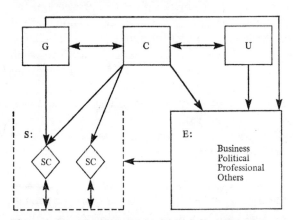

Figure 1 Suggested structure of interaction links for a research organization.
C – the interdisciplinary research and planning centre; U – the university;
G – government; S – the social system; E – leadership (including business, political, professional, and community leadership; SC – field research and service stations.

The links (from the research apparatus point of view):

U→G   university producing government bureaucracy and political leadership at various levels
U→E   university educating the elite

---

12   The original concept of CIMS as a university centre was broadened to include governmental and community representatives in addition to the scientific staff: an interdisciplinary, interinstitutional project was created.

G→S government social and economic resources affecting the social system

E→S elite providing leadership and exercising control over the social system

E→G elite controlling government

C→U centre providing information to university and suggestions for curriculum change

U→C university using the centre for research and as a laboratory for apprenticeship

C→SC the centre provides the field research and the service teams with total system orientation through experimentation (the following chapters will discuss in detail the content and structure of this type of orientation)

S→SC microresearch and processed feedback from the social system (problems, needs, etc.)

SC→C field data transmitted to centre (experiments in realities)

SC→S contact with grass-root leadership and its mobilization, providing services and initiation of projects

C→G providing government with advisory services on planning. Plans will be developed with the various planning bureaus. The centre will also provide retraining for planners and politicians through the process of experimentation

G→C through participation in the experiment the particular experiences and problems of government will lead to modifications of the total model

C→E through the process of experimentation elite representatives will be oriented to the problems and relationships in the systems and provide information derived from their particular experiences and views

In fact, through experimentation (scenario evaluation) and the jural process, it is hoped that co-optation of values will result.

This particular organizational structure provides for a gradual change of values. Through a closed loop of interactions, the knowledge of the system shared by the social agents and the planners can thus be improved. The centre would become the agent of information processing, integration, and diffusion in the system.

2 The human input in the proposed organization

The original concept of an interdisciplinary think tank is not sufficient to carry out the proposed role of the centre. Support for the integrative function is needed, or for the position of a 'generalist.'[13] In traditional management literature, this was described as an integrative function in a complex, highly specialized organization. In confronting developmental problems, the need for a functional training of a generalist is pertinent. In most of the research and planning institutes surveyed, the leadership underwent a process of 'untraining' to fulfil this integrative role. The untraining was a process of socialization where the leadership co-opted a broader system of values than that commonly shared by their professional reference group. (In most of the institutions the leadership consisted of economists for whom the process of untraining was more difficult than for social scientists coming from the so-called softer fields.) Yet untraining and partial co-optation of values are not a satisfactory basis for creative, comprehensive, interdisciplinary problem-solving. These remedies often lead to a unidimensional approach where the dimensions are varied sequentially, or to a specialized approach with modifications, which are usually a token recognition for the larger, deeper aspects of the problem. The result is that real integration is nearly impossible.

The training of planners failed to produce the necessary characteristics needed for this integrative role, because training programs are composed of the presentation of research methods in different fields which at best succeed in creating an awareness of progress made in these fields. The synthesis of knowledge is expected to be achieved at the personal level, but results are not encouraging. The confusion of conflicting scientific paradigms usually leads the trainee to adopt the more attractive value system presented to him, given his initial background, abilities, and inclinations. Thus a type of program which has as its primary purpose the creation of this integrative function through the process of training is needed. The purpose of the training is to create the scientist of the system, the one who can direct the research of the specialist and integrate it into a larger comprehensive system of knowledge. The generalist need not possess the insight and creativity that specialization provides, for the specialist will remain the researcher in the frontier of his specific area. Yet the generalist will be able to incorporate the diversified segmented bits of knowledge into a system which will enrich and generate holistic knowledge, and in turn enrich and direct the specialized research. The generalist, in a sense, is the one who asks the questions rather than the one who provides answers; he is an information processor, rather than an information source. The basic premise of training for a generalist is recognition of alternative logical structures and understanding of the

13   I. Vertinsky, *The Generalist: A New Concept for Training the Planner* (unpublished paper; Evanston: Northwestern University, 1968).

characteristics of the particular system defined as the problem area. To use an analogy, the programs in existence today in planning produce bi- or trilingual scientists, while the training should produce a linguist. In developing a strategy for research it is essential to take into account the supply of proper role players (especially when large research organizations are designed).

D   CHOICE OF A COMMON LANGUAGE: A FLOW AND
NETWORK PRESENTATION

To facilitate communication and economize in processing efforts, a common flexible and logical framework is suggested in the form of a network representation of the system, because 1 / it is amenable to an analysis of static as well as dynamic processes; 2 / it is highly decomposable, allowing introduction of changes with minimum costs; and 3 / it is highly compatible with existing computer simulation languages and facilities (efficient 'real time' mode utilization).

In this framework, behavioural units (institutions, organizations, social agents, etc.) are the nodes of the system and are connected by channels. Channels represent structured flows of social inputs and outputs (economic resources, decisions, information, strategic resources – possible threats and bribes – etc.). Each node is characterized by transformation rules, which describe the conditional transformations of inputs into outputs. They also describe which of the channels or configurations of channels may be used. The transformation rules can be divided into:

A   Technological (e.g., technological coefficients in industry).
B   Decision transformation rules. The transformations are subject to the constraints imposed on a particular node. For example, in allocating economic resources, the budget constraint will indicate the feasible region of allocations. In case of social decisions cultural constraints may indicate the region of feasibility.

Channels are characterized by capacities, efficiency, costs, and other constraints such as cultural or institutional constraints. They may also be characterized by 'noise,' for example, an economic decision of the government implemented by an inefficient or incompetent bureaucracy. In addition to the decomposed constraints on the network (nodes and channels), the system is characterized by holistic properties: constraints on the pattern evolution of channel utilization given a specific basic value structure.

The network can be meaningfully decomposed through the identification of closed and quasi-closed loops in the system (e.g., community political structure is such a quasi-closed loop in some areas of Columbia. It was identified as a closed loop by a micro in-depth community study carried out by Adams and Havens at the Land Tenure Center of the University of Wisconsin).

Where interaction – channel utilization – is low, the scientists may choose a subsystem as a manageable unit for research at a given stage of the model building. The basic framework also provides for the formation of alternative networks (future possible state of the system) under defined switching rules (e.g., basic reform in the formal governmental structure).

The transformation rules for each node can be replaced by alternative rules to identify the impact on the system of a basic change in a behavioural unit. For example, if a linear programming computer program is used to allocate resources in education in a particular department, the LP model will replace some of the decision units of the agency responsible for these decisions.

E   MODEL BUILDING PROCEDURES

1   *Formal systems as a stepping stone*

Building the model of the total system necessitates a mix of research strategies. While an identification of components can be made on the basis of the subjective evaluations of a group of experts (the think-tank idea), utilization of the institutional structure of the system, whenever possible, as a stepping stone leading to the behavioral model of the system is recommended. As an exploratory experiment the 'legal structure' is used as a base for developing the political behavioural model. The example illustrates the steps and the conceptual problems involved in building the model, and generalizations and conclusions are reached for other systems for which a formal structure is not readily available.

The first step was to prepare a scenario of the formal network of legal institutions and present the channels of communication. Fortunately, the presentation of the formal legal system is easier than that of most of the other systems because the institutions and channels are defined by the law, as well as the rules (or at least the boundaries to the rules) of transformation of inputs into outputs. The outputs are decisions to be executed, information structuring (e.g., where a court of first instance is entrusted with fact-finding duties and appeal is always limited to questions of law – the court serves as information-filtering processor), threats (powers of impeachment, or implied power of renomination at the end of tenure), etc. The channels are characterized by 1 / legal standing – the power to initiate a flow in the system; 2 / legal and administrative procedures and formal customs; and 3 / costs and parameters of birth and service processes. Two types of channels were identified: functional and control.

The inputs and outputs of functional channels are well defined by the law; channels of control were divided into two types: flows of review, and control through nomination and impeachment powers. While flows of review are visible and well defined, flows of control through review are largely invisible. An essential part of control is not exercised through actual flows in the system (they exist but are relatively rare), but through anticipated consequences. As Kelsen observed, the sanctions are efficient if the need to apply them is rare.

An additional complicating feature of the Colombian control system was the cyclical system of checks and the parallel cross-structures. Figure 2 is an illustration of a typical cross-structure. A submits a list of candidates for C, and B selects from the list. B initiates impeachment of A, subject to approval of C. In reality these cross-structures are much more complex.

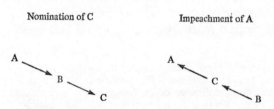

Figure 2 Typical parallel cross-structure.

Hence, to define the flows of control, the following possibilities were available:
1   Quantification of the structural component of control was done through a definition of Shapley-Values for the variety of institutions, and by deriving flows of control as functions of the 'balances' (i.e., taking into account the complexity of procedures and the alliance of institutions needed to initiate such flows).
2   Whenever possible, the behavioural record of the institution was utilized, especially if quasi-experimental legal situations existed. For example, to evaluate the implied control of the Council of State (which originates with article 189 of the *Co. Cont. Adm.* giving the council

'original and exclusive jurisdiction of cases regarding presidential, senatorial and representatives' elections') versus the control by nomination of the president, one may consider, in addition to evaluation of structural components, such as length of tenure, the behaviour of the council in a 'semi-experimental situation,' such as the Rojas Pinilla era.

In addition to the definition of the institutions, the flows of outputs and inputs and the transformation of inputs into outputs are to be defined: a / channel characteristics, which include service rates, costs, etc.; b / the rates of 'birth' of initial inputs to the system (types of cases initiated and their rates of arrival to the system at various 'nodes'). To evaluate channel characteristics and rates of 'birth' in the system, procedures of service had to be evaluated to choose the proper shape of the stochastic process. This was done on the basis of a priori axioms homomorphic to the procedures. Where such a set of a priori axioms could not be evaluated, an analysis of the moments of the sampling population through partial a priorism led to selection of the relatively most appropriate stochastic process. The next stage of the analysis was to estimate tradeoff of budget and service time to characterize the economic dimension of the legal structure.[14] An institutional standpoint in preliminary model-building is not limited only to highly structured systems.

A modification of the technique is required to include macro- and microdata sources, and thus the problem of data integration arises. Assimilation of knowledge derived from a wide range of sources neces-

14 The pilot study is reported in 'A legal game: A study of legal structure' (Northwestern University, 1970). It was noted that while our pioneering efforts were limited to the conceptualization of the model of the formal legal system, the analysis at this stage led to some interesting results, manifesting the continuous fruits that the suggested research strategy may bear, even at the initial stages of model building. A review of the structural scenario led to a recognition of the following deformities of the formal legal system in conflict management in Colombia:
1 Localization of conflict The system is decentralized functionally and territorially. The separate systems compose closed loops. This decentralization added to the vertical localization of conflict achieved by restrictive procedures of appeals (often the appeal is limited to one level and in some cases decisions are final) guarantees to localize conflict at non-cataclysmic levels.
2 A system of checks without balances Parallel cross-structures of review, nomination, and control systems indicate that separation of power is a fiction. The system is identified by tight circuits of control where often the regulated nominate the regulators. Without balance of power, a system of checks guarantees preservation of the status quo. Recent political developments verified our theoretical observations. President Carlos Lleras Restrepo was engaged in trial by ordeal at the hands of a senate which refused him a constitutional amendment to enable the executive to alleviate some of the structural hurdles involved in implementing development.

sitates careful examination of the information contents of each source. For example, if one attempts to build the submodel of markets in Colombia, the question is raised as to how the information generated by available studies can be processed. Most of these studies are derived from a limited, neoclassical point of view, based on the assumption of perfectly competitive markets. The model-builder may observe that the neoclassical economic model is not homomorphic with the basic characteristics of the Colombian economy and choose a more appropriate model. If he remodels phenomena as a stochastic process, how is the available information based on neoclassical models to be used? A careful examination of available studies of the market structures in Colombia suggests that the neoclassical static point of view can be projected onto a new framework through the following dimensions: 1 / inventory of problem area; 2 / inventory of governmental policies; 3 / inventory of variables and initial statistical identification of elasticities; 4 / identification of the survival space (if the neoclassical theory is interpreted as a long-run behavioural theory or a 'steady-state' description); 5 / provide inventory of homomorphic partial systems to explain particular phenomena.

While a direct projection in purely formal systems (e.g., projection from Euclidean to non-Euclidean systems) is available, in semiformal systems the information has to be projected indirectly through interpretation. In this case these models provided the static long-run components of the system as well as a guidance to the statistical efficiency of variables in explaining the phenomena. Looking for a natural structure of institutional network in systems for which the structures are not visible will necessitate the incorporation of some of the techniques discussed in the next section dealing with behavioural aspects.

2   *Extending the formal model*

The additional information required to form the behavioural system can be classified into the following broad categories: the informal network (informal channels, institutions, rules of transformation, and holistic characteristics); membership and potential membership (typology of people filling the roles or potential roles performers); characterization of possible flows in the system; and possible structural changes in the system.

The following are the sources of data to be generated for the model:

1   Inventory of past behavioural histories of the system (legal records, published research data, etc.).
2   Analysis of the formal structure; discovering deformities in the

structure. These areas of deformities indicate the most probable areas for extensive development of informal structures.

3   The experiences of agents in the system (here, lawyers, judges, politicians, etc.). The insights and information held by participants are the most valuable source of data available.

4   Experts out of the system (researchers).

To generate an inventory of future states of the system, the analysis has to concentrate on the following:

5   The possible evolutionary processes of the system.

6   Analysis of potential flows in the system (legislative programs, legal problems, etc.).

Categories 1, 2, and 5 do not pose any particular methodological problems. The guidelines for these steps are outlined.

a   Identify operational definitions for the system (variables, flows, etc.).

b   Analyse the inventory of propositions on the behaviour of the system to produce possible generalizations. This can be done by identifying clusters of values of the independent variables leading to a particular state of the system or cluster of states.

c   Use comparative data (e.g., intersocietal comparisons) to create an inventory of future states of the system. This sometimes implies resorting to a fiction widely accepted among development scientists who assume that the characteristics of the intersocietal systems are a function of the evolutionary cycle, an assumption which may be useful only under restrictive qualifications.

Because categories 3 and 4 pose some methodological problems, two complementary methods are suggested: 1 / unstructured reaction to scenario and free scenario creation; 2 / teleological (tree-format based) questionnaires.

An unstructured reaction to the scenario (in this case the model of the formal legal system) will stimulate the experts to reveal the informal system. Reactions should be directed at those areas of 'deformities' identified by the structural analysis. The interviewed specialists present their own perception of the structure and flows (utilizing their abilities of 'pattern recognition').

The purpose of the tree-format-based interview is to assist the individual questioned in remembering information from which he can make rational judgments. This type of teleological analysis is based on a comprehensive prognostication of the social state. The objectives, policies, and probabilities are weighted by the resources possessed by their initiators as well as by a willingness to resort to these resources. The specialist is asked to estimate resources, define additional resources, identify potential resources and technological relationships which constrain the flows, and identify the domain of actions. He makes his final evaluation after he is made aware of the relevant data already accumulated. The tree structure of the interview allows for a reversible process of evaluation. Conclusions can be traced to the original assumptions. This is an important check in repeat interviews, as well as an important characteristic for due review by the juries at the compiling stage. This particular structure stimulates consistency in judgment.

To illustrate the structural design of a possible interview with an expert, let us entertain an incomplete example of interview structure to evaluate political flows in the system. The first step is to identify the sources of these flows, that is, the political groups competing in the system. For each group, the following may be the basic categories of information required to estimate flow probabilities and intensities: 1 / desired objectives; 2 / ranges and ranking of objectives; 3 / resource constraints; 4 / intensity of resource utilization; 5 / vocabulary of strategies. The basic teleological structure implies that the questionnaire will first specify observations and hard data before evaluations and interpretations take place so that the logical consequences are kept clear. For example, the economic scarcity of resources possessed by a political group and their survival capabilities (wealth, distribution of wealth, etc.) will limit the strategy space of the group (determine time limits on the capability to strike, military capability, etc.).

The structure of the questionnaire has to utilize the inventory of hypotheses related to a subject to identify the branches of the tree. If 'organizational resources' are evaluated, the body of knowledge in organization theory indicates some of the relevant variables explaining organizational effectiveness. We may start branching the tree into organizational effectiveness. The next level in the hierarchy of research will then be to specify the variables explaining effectiveness. Organization theory suggests cohesiveness as one of the factors leading to effectiveness. In turn, geographic concentration may explain cohesiveness using Homans' small-group interaction hypothesis. In such fashion, the scientist may develop the logical sequence of the model. Accordingly, the questionnaire will produce the reverse sequence to derive maximum reliability in estimating

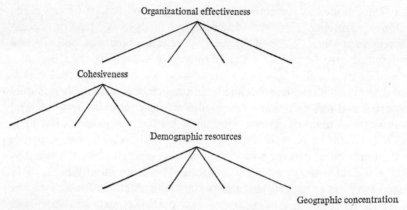

Figure 3 Typical flow chart for a tree-format-based interview.

the initial variable. The degree of branching will be determined by criteria of manageability (figures 3 and 4).

The first stage of processing the questionnaires is done on the basis of accuracy of information and consistency. Some of the questionnaires will call for a repeat interview to identify implied assumptions. This process can be done by a technique often utilized in the estimation of costs in operation research projects – reversible analysis. For example, to evaluate the implied value of individual life, one can evaluate the measures (in economic resources) taken to decrease the risk of fatal accidents. An experiment of this sort was made in an evaluation of a pilot's life during the second world war. Reversible analysis may increase the awareness of the expert about the unverified assumptions that he made in evaluating the phenomena. Once the technical jury eliminates illegitimate answers, the process of compiling opinions begins. Opinions with too much disagreement are recognized and formulated as counter-hypotheses.

The next stage in the teleological model-building is an evaluation of balance equations. Political flows through a given channel may flow in contradicting directions. The evaluation of flow intensities and the direction of a given channel are derived from the balance equations which are basically referee decisions in the system. The evaluation of these balance equations may be made through the same method of teleological questionnaires.

Once the exogenous parameters, status variables, endogenous variables, parameters, identities and operating characteristics of the model are identified, the model is ready for the initial stage of experimentation, which is the tuning stage.

The overview of the total questionnaire for an *Estimation of Potential Political Flows Originating Within a Group* is outlined below.

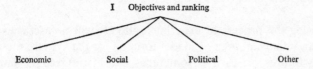

I   Objectives and ranking

Economic   Social   Political   Other

Desired levels and satisfactory ranges. (Satisfactory ranges would be those ranges of achieve – ment that do not lead to further employment of resources.)

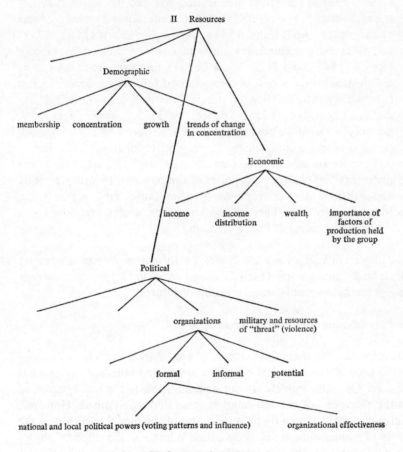

II   Resources

Demographic

membership   concentration   growth   trends of change in concentration

Economic

income   income distribution   wealth   importance of factors of production held by the group

Political

organizations   military and resources of "threat" (violence)

formal   informal   potential

national and local political powers (voting patterns and influence)   organizational effectiveness

III   Inventory of strategies

Eg. general strike, mobilization for violent action, lobbying, etc.

IV   Patterns of strategies and resource utilization

Probabilistic structure of stimuli-response patterns for the group-probabilistic matching of 'states', 'strategies' and resources.

Figure 4 Flow chart in the tree format for estimating political flows.

F   METHODOLOGY TO STUDY THE FUTURE

Before exploring the process of experimentation it will be useful to pay
attention to an important area of model-forming for the system, the area
of generating futures or, as it is sometimes called, futurology. Smoker
has observed that

> Social research for social anticipation has become an increasingly
> popular activity. The urgent future confronts city and global planners
> alike (Mayer, 1967; Kahn, 1968). Verbal predictions (Marx, 1959)
> and what once seemed the fantastic visions imagined by George
> Orwell (1949) and H.G. Wells (1964) are now supplemented by
> the electronic crystal ball of computerized futurology. Technological
> forecasting, extrapolation of trends (TEMPO), and statistical pre-
> diction (Boguslaw, 1956; Tocher, 1963) are increasingly used,
> not only to anticipate but to attempt control. Social research for social
> creation adopts a complementary perspective for future's research ...
> Alternative futures become 'experiments now' (Kariel, 1968), ex-
> periments that change perceptions of the possible; (Waskow, 1968)
> and generate new conceptions of what things may someday be.
> Model and 'reality,' interact and intertwine, evolve and adapt in a
> continuous process of image creation.[15]

Three classes of inquiry are available: 1 / formal inquiry of alternative
structures; 2 / non-formal (verbal) image creation; 3 / the mix-strategy
of image creation – semi-formal creation of futures.

1   *Formal inquiry of alternative structures*

In the preceding sections the example of free market models to discount
the relevance of a neoclassical economic approach to the 'real' system has
been used. Often the models are not homomorphic to the real system and
thus the relevance of the information generated was limited. However,
criticism was limited to a direct application of the models and not to the
process of model-building in economics. While specific applications of
the model are irrelevant, the contribution of this line of inquiry is relevant
to the system. The process serves as an excellent example of structural
inquiry, where interaction and intertwining of reality and image creation
in generating futures are clearly manifested.

15   P. Smoker, 'Social Research for Social Anticipation,' *American Behavioral
Scientist* (July–August 1968), p. 7.

The neoclassical model of free markets evolved as an attempt to create a homomorphic system for real markets. Analyses of the model have identified some structural properties (general equilibrium properties of efficiency and stability). The structural components (signals, reaction functions, and informational functions) and the properties were the basis for the creation of alternative allocation mechanisms. While initial attempts to create alternatives were closely tied to the mechanism of allocation (e.g., a centralized model of allocation with 'resource managers' announcing prices, substituting for the mystical 'invisible hand,' i.e. simulating mechanically the 'free market process'), research at present is aimed at a choice in the space of possible organizational designs.

Adopting alternative mathematical structures (such as mathematical programming and game theory) led to a diversification of the structural research, and the properties were emancipated from the mechanism. Hopefully, this line of model-building will produce an inventory of allocation mechanisms with their structural properties. It is a sequential process whereby image creation leads through analysis to a knowledge of structural properties, and a larger domain of properties leads to the creation of a new class of images. This example illustrates the formal process of image creation. The approach is based on Polya's 'plausibile assumptions' methodology.

2 Non-formal (verbal) creation of structures

A formal inquiry into the design of new structures is limited by both pragmatic constraints, such as the highly complicated technical abilities necessary to develop new images, and fundamental, inherent limitations of axiomatic systems. Russell's optimistic view that mathematics take us into the region of absolute necessity, to which the actual world and every possible world must conform, was challenged by Godël.[16] In his criticism of *Principia Mathematica*, he pointed out that the axiomatic system had certain inherent limitations which ruled out the possibility of full axiomatization of even simple mathematical systems. He proved that it was impossible to establish the internal, logical consistency of a very large class of deductive systems, unless one adopted principles of reasoning so complex that their internal consistency was as open to doubt as that of the systems' themselves.

Verbal predictions and visions of the future were in the past and are

16 A. Mostowski, *Sentences Undecidable in Formalized Arithmetic* (Amsterdam 1952), and E. Nagel and J.R. Newmann, *Gödel Proof* (New York: New York University Press, 1960).

in the present a rich source and probably the main source of image creation. However, we are often warned that 'the surface of our language is well trodden with paths tempting us in directions away from where we are trying to go.' Verbal expression is not only limited by the present and past experiences of the sender of a verbal message, but also by the experiences of the receiver.

3   *The mix strategy of image creation:*
    semi-formal creation of futures

The brief discussion of two ideal types, formal and non-formal, has illustrated the limitations of both. However, a semiformal system may improve upon a pure system: a system in which consequences and definitions are kept clear, yet partially structured insights can be admitted to the system. The research apparatus should accommodate a mechanism which efficiently generates 'experiences' in the system (i.e., provide experimental settings wherein the scientist and social agents can experience, either through participation ('gaming') or through observation ('scenario evaluation'), a variety of systems in a limited time). The method of experimentation through simulation provides this mechanism.

    For example, one could ask what are the properties of a society living in Utopia? The verbal image creation of Thomas More cannot be efficiently manipulated to provide the behavioural consequences of the system. Essential questions, such as properties of stability, feasibility, etc., cannot be answered through verbal manipulation. Varsavsky and Domingo formulated the social system of Utopia in a partially formal system where they introduced some plausible behavioural assumptions (relying, for example, on the theory of small-group interactions) and generated 'time series' for the system through machine simulation.[17] Through experimentation the long-run properties of the system were analysed. This semi-formal model could not have been solved mathematically and the dynamic paths could only be provided through a generation of time series. While machine simulation provides a basis for observing a system (and the variety of statistical methods for pattern recognition is richer than in 'real' experiments), the system could have also provided a participatory experience through gaming (man/machine simulation) where social agents perform roles in a new social system. Such participation serves two func-

17   Varsavsky and Domingo developed the model of Utopia at CENDES, Universidad Central de Venezuela, Caracas, and analysed its stability through simulation.

tions: 1 / it broadens the perception of the participants of futures and deepens their perception of the existing system (by providing alternative experiences to contrast with 'real' experiences); and 2 / gaming provides the scientists with 'creative' experiments where the social agent's participation is only partially structured. While the machine simulation provides efficient methods to test consequences of assumptions, the man/machine experiments may suggest alternative new assumptions.

4   Image creation and social change

Social scientists have departed from the strictly deterministic assumption that social reality obeys laws that are constant and have adopted the assumption that 'alternative futures in the social space might be represented by a complex, multi-dimensional statistical distribution. The complexity of the alternative future increases as greater granularity is sought and less generality is required.'[18] However, this limits the system to a status quo point of view and imprisons alternative futures in perceived pasts. In fact, this assumption may be a valuable strategy for a control of social change and short-run social planning. Yet without adopting a counter-non-deterministic point of view where man and society create the future, this point of view is dangerously limited. The two standpoints are not mutually exclusive; moreover, they may be complementary (through a dialectic constrast of a steady-state theory and the creation of new images). The steady-state assumption provides a workable apparatus to analyse and define the characteristics and properties of past, present, and extrapolated futures; properties which provide standards and the stimulus for the creation of new structures and a realization of new properties.

Feed-back and feed-forward mechanisms are complementary processes of interaction over time. As long as the systems are recognized as emancipated, based upon separated validity criteria, projections from one system to another will improve the knowledge generated by both (e.g., viewing the past through the standpoint of the future may lead to identification of implied, unverified assumptions made in observing the past).

The intertwining of both processes may lead to a partial emancipation of future creations from a limited point of view of time and space. Recent developments in the field of decision-making lent support to the opinion which stresses the necessity of incorporating contrasting points of view in

18   H. Guetzkow, 'Simulation in International Relations,' *Proceedings of the IBM Scientific Computing Symposium on Simulation Models and Gaming* Yorktown Heights, NY, Thomas J. Watson Research Center, 1964), pp. 249–78.

order to generate a knowledge of the system (e.g., Churchman's counter-planning strategy):[19]

> To make the most desirable the most probable, it may be necessary to integrate the two approaches into one methodology. Using multiple experiments in both laboratories and realities, and adopting validity criteria to correspond to the experimental environment, may progressively enable people to participate directly in the definition and creation of their own futures. Using models validated to correspond with realities, and realities validated to correspond with models, man might experience the way it is and create the ways it could be. By continually updating models and realities, a public dialogue, or more appropriately, a public multilogue, between realities and multiple alternative futures could be established.[20]

G   EXPERIMENTATION THROUGH SIMULATION:
THE INTERACTIVE MODE OF RESEARCH

The process of model-building described in the preceding sections was intertwined with simulation and experimentation. Pilot tests of the crude legal model reflected the potential of gaming and simple, man-simulation for theory-building. The flow-network presentation proved to be flexible and adaptable to both available hardware facilities and the degree of formalism of the models built. These characteristics allow for an economical research process. In the following sections attention is concentrated on the interactive simulation process. It is clear, however, that many of the research processes described are intertwined. The sequential separation of stages is primarily for clarity of presentation.

1   *Why simulate?*

Experimentation through simulation allows for the full use of prior knowledge through a choice of parameters, variables, interrelationships, and histories of the system. Simulation efficiently generates long-term data of the processes in the system and reflects the long-term or indirect consequences that might be expected to occur. The structure of the language chosen for the simulation provides a conceptual guidance for the team of researchers, and the efficiency (in terms of computing costs and methodological flexibility) may be constantly evaluated and lead to improvements in the mode of inquiry. The structure chosen provides for

19   See note 4.
20   Smoker, 'Social Research for Social Anticipation,' p. 13.

standardization of the Weltanschauung in the presentation (without restricting the individual variations of point of view of the world) to facilitate
inter- and intrasystem comparisons.

The simulation allows for immediate testing and contrasting of
conjectures which arise from the process of research and planning by
partially substituting subsystems of the simulation. The output of simulation is especially amenable to the application of statistical methods
(e.g., the researcher may use a variety of techniques to reduce the
variance of sampling populations, using quasi-random numbers, special
factorial designs, etc.). In addition to the information derived from statistical methods, experimentation provides, either through direct participation (man/machine simulation) or through review and evaluation of
behavioural histories (machine/man simulation), experiences for social
agents, researchers, etc., who can broaden their perspective of their role
in the system (e.g., reorientation of the specialists in terms of the total
system).

Simulation enables the researchers and planners to carry out a wide
variety of controlled experiments (and change the degrees of control)
which cannot be achieved by any other means.

To summarize, experimentation through simulation envelops analysis, synthesis, a theory, and a process of interaction (past – present –
future, social agents – planners – scientists, etc.).

2   Steps in the simulation process

The following sections discuss briefly the various stages of the experimentation process. The reader should note that some of these stages are
presented as a sequence, whereas in reality they may be a simultaneous
process. The recurrence of the stages is not necessarily constant but is
dictated by needs as determined by the research and planning process.
The following are the steps of experimentation: 1 / tuning, 2 / scenario
creation, evaluation, and gaming, and 3 / feedback to fieldwork. In each
step the process of validation, verification, and analysis of relevance is
embedded. However, for convenience of presentation, we will discuss
these processes separately.

3   The process of tuning

This initial stage of experimentation provides the experimenter with the
opportunity to identify gross errors of conceptualization and provides
guidance to essential structural improvements of the model. The 'histories'
produced may indicate internal inconsistencies in the decentralized model-

forming and will call for reconceptualization of some of the subsystems. Analysis through partial a priorism may indicate illegitimate relationships. For example, in analysing Cyert and March's behavioural model of the firm, experiments indicated that in eighty runs of the model internal inconsistencies resulted (the model 'exploded'): inventory levels assumed negative values which were inconsistent with the model.[21]

The stage of tuning also calls for a simplification of the model. Sensitivity of the behavioural path to variables will be examined as well as the sensitivity of the model to the inclusion or exclusion of certain variables. A re-examination of the complexity of the model through alternative homomorphic systems will call for a simplification of the model to a manageable size with a minimal loss of information and flexibility. Statistical methods of pattern recognition and statistical efficiency of explanations will provide the experimenters with the information necessary to redesign the model (e.g., using alternative factorial designs). The stage of tuning will also call for empirical research in those subsystems to which the behavioural path is sensitive (highly elastic).

4   Scenario evaluation, creation, and gaming

Once the initial process of redesigning and modifying the prior model is terminated, the runs of the simulation provide histories of the system for evaluation. Two complementary methods are available: 1 / statistical analysis of the generated 'time series'; 2 / participant evaluation of 'histories' of the system. In this paper statistical methods are not discussed, and the reader is referred to the voluminous literature discussing the relevant techniques (spectric analysis, correlation analysis, parametric modelling, etc.).[22]

Through the statistical methods, patterns of behaviour and clusters of states are identified. While these statistical methods may directly generate an inventory of hypotheses on the behaviour of the macrosystem, it also creates guidelines for directing the second phase of evaluation – participant evaluation of 'histories' of the system.

Participant evaluation of histories is a multipurpose process. It can be constructed in ways alternating from free reaction (i.e., the social agent, confronting the story of the behavioural path of the system, spon-

21   At the University of California, Berkeley, we experimented with the behavioural model of Cyert and March and observed negative inventories resulting after eighty runs of the model.
22   For bibliographies, see T.H. Naylor, ed. *The Design of Computer Simulation Experiments* (Durham: Duke University Press, 1969), pp. 200–3, 230–5.

taneously reacts to this story, indicating alternative paths or pointing out constraints of feasibility or discovering missing relationships, such as undiscovered informal processes) to highly structured evaluations by juries of experts reacting to particular substructures using the criteria of partial a priorism and comparison of correspondence to historical, real processes. Reaction of scenario corresponds to observation. To create a higher degree of involvement, man/machine simulation should be used where some of the components of the subsystems are replaced by actual social agents. Again, the scientist can alter the structure of the experiment and the possible space of outcomes by enlarging the unprogrammed components of the experiment. Deductions from man/machine simulation enlarge the space of possible consequences, a fact which argues for the use of this type of simulation.

The alternative techniques of participation and review are multipurpose processes.

1   *Educational process for both social agents and scientists* Participation (through actual involvement as a role performer, evaluator, or observer leads to a reorientation of the specialized outlook of the participant towards a comprehension of the system as a whole (past, present, and future) and the particular role or roles he performs and may perform in the system by enlarging the domain of his experiences. An experiment reflecting the importance of this function to facilitate social interactions in negotiation processes was described by Vertinsky.[23]

2   *Knowledge creation and model improvement* The varying degrees of structures in an evaluation of the model magnify the potential of knowledge derivation from the process. In fact, the wide range of structures utilizes the abilities of man as a pattern-recognizer, a source of knowledge, and a subject for experiment.

3   *The processes of review and gaming as a tool for interaction* The process structures interaction between social agents, scientists, and planners participating either as members of boards of review (juries) or as role performers. Interaction also occurs between the participant and the social system of the past, present, and future. Interaction is further facilitated by the possibility of testing conjectures in a relatively short time (e.g., discovering the consequences of alternative hypotheses or consequences of alternative planning techniques). Conflict is structured in well-defined channels where consequences of alternative opinions can be contrasted. The conflict through man/machine/man interaction becomes a knowledge-producing mechanism rather than a source of personal anta-

23   I. Vertinsky, *Negotiation, Co-optation and Participation*, paper presented at ORSA – IORS meetings, Tel-Aviv, Israel, June 1969.

gonism (often produced by man/man interaction where a conflict of ideas tends to become a conflict of egos). Conflict expression rather than suppression resides as a vital force in the research apparatus in expanding dimensions and perspectives.

5   Feedback to fieldwork

The research apparatus should provide guidance to the selection of empirical research projects. A rational process of selection of projects has long been desired; this is the process which philosophers of science called S-squared (i.e., the science of science) applying scientific method to decision making in sciences. One of the contributions of the suggested apparatus is the construction of iterative processes of project selection based on the criterion of informational efficiency.

Through sensitivity analysis and the application of statistical techniques to identify the variables and interrelationships which most efficiently explain the behavioural path of the system, research projects are selected. The time series provided by the process of experimentation provide the data necessary to plan efficiently future research projects.

Experimentation and 'feedback' to the field and 'feed-forward' of image creation provide a recursive process by which, through iteration, the models and the social system are modified.

No terminal point for the research is identified. The research will be terminated when the objective function of the research becomes insensitive to remaining disagreements in the system (e.g., in the case of planning a system, the terminal point would be at the stage at which alternative resolutions of disagreement would not change plans meaningfully).

H   VALIDITY, VERIFICATION, AND RELEVANCE

The variety of data sources and research paradigms involved in this study necessitated the development of a new approach to questions of validity and relevance. Historically, philosophers of science dealing with this problem area of scientific methodology can be crudely categorized into four positions: the synthetic a priorists, the ultra-empiricists, the positivists, and the proponents of what is called multistage verification, which is an eclectic position based on the former methodological positions applying them in different stages of the research. In fact, the methodology suggested in this paper could be classified as a variation of the multistage method.

Reconceptualization through statistical methods of the model manifests the ultra-empirical method. By applying judgment techniques, which we have termed partial a priorism, both empirical verification and a priorism are incorporated. Structural analysis dealing with properties of stability, especially in investigating futures is a prioristic. Feedback to the field, i.e., testing correspondences of homomorphic structures (the real historical data and the behavioural path produced by the model), is a positive method of validation.

The process of validation suggested here is dynamic and continuous in nature. In each stage of the research a variety of procedures for verifying the model is employed. The sequential processes of model building decrease the probability of tautology, a phenomenon often suspected when the system is derived from the same data used to test it. Our process satisfies the 'multiple validity criteria' requirement proposed by Hermann and supported by Guetzkow.[24]

1   Why verify?

It is our opinion that the processes of verification are intended to provide guidelines to research for improving its informational efficiency, i.e., improve the correspondence between past, present and future real and realizable systems and the models. Models are built as homomorphic systems to reality. It was suggested that the degree of homomorphism can be selected by a criteria of informational relevance.[25] Correspondences are not between histories of the real system and the model, but between a homomorphism of the real system and the model. (In fact, measurements in the real system are actually homomorphic models of the system.) Let us explore this idea through figure 5.

The real system includes a set of points. The measurement is defined as the convex hull of the points. The model corresponds to the model of measurement through a spheric mapping of the boundaries of the convex hull. If theorems produced by the model of measurement can be mapped directly to the model, then correspondence exists (in fact, translation of Euclidian geometry to spheric geometry exists). If only part of the theorems can be projected from one system to the other, correspondence exists if, and only if, from an informational point of view, these theorems are irrelevant. To summarize, validation should be a process of information improvement, rather than a process of control and suppression,

24   H. Guetzkow, 'Some Correspondences between Simulations and "Realities" in International Relations,' in Mortan A. Kaplan, ed., *New Approaches to International Relations* (New York: St Martin's Press, 1968), pp. 202–69.
25   Vertinsky, 'Measurement.'

which thus necessitates the adoption of alternative methods adapted to the sources of information and the means of manipulation.

2   *Relevance*

Validity and relevance are closely associated: the degree of homomorphism chosen is a function of the criteria of relevance, and this criteria is controversial today. Three approaches can be identified. The first two are a prioristic concepts and the third is a process concept: 1 / the traditional concept of elasticity; 2 / a decision-making concept of relevance; 3 / an interaction concept of relevance. The traditional concept of elasticity is geared to a status quo point of view. The sensitivity of variables and interrelationships, and their relative statistical efficiency in explaining phenomena determine their relevance. This approach is positivistic.

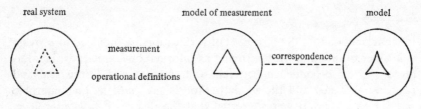

Figure 5 Correspondence between real systems and models.

From a decision-making standpoint, relevance is determined by the sensitivity of the available inventory of decision functions to the variables and interrelationships. Recent literature in the field of economics of information and accounting have developed this conceptual framework.[26] In fact, the first class is a special case of this class, where the decision functions are the implied decision, and objective functions are the implicit objective and decision functions of scientists.

The third concept is based on the assumption that, in the face of uncertainty and ignorance, an a priori determination of relevance dangerously limits the scientific process to a status quo point of view and eliminates many of the possibilities for creative decision-making. A concept of process is substituting for a priori axioms. Relevance is determined through the interaction of the various social agents, and is a product of conflict and interaction.

26   For bibliography, see *ibid*.

In considering the question of relevance, it is possible to emphasize the scientific concept of truth as the only constraining criteria for social science. Such a detached outlook is hard to defend, however, in a world where poverty, violence, and starvation remain pervasive facts of everyday life. It seems reasonable to demand that truth be relevant to solutions of the major problems and issues of society as a whole. Whether the problems be concrete, such as war or starvation, or abstract, such as the implementation of values of freedom and reason, it is possible to suggest important social problems and significant personal issues that deeply affect the human condition as a whole ...[27]

Our methodology has structured an interactive process of research where a prioristic and positivistic components in relevance determination are intertwined with a participatory process of interaction of social agents and scientists.

I   COUNTER-RESEARCH CENTRES

Schwartz[28] has pointed out the danger that the centralized process of reactive mechanism proposed here could produce in the long run in a society where the balance between ideas and powers of social agents does not exist. The standpoint of the privileged, those who possess the power, influence, and qualities of articulation of ideas, may dominate the standpoint of the underprivileged. Schwartz has suggested a mechanism similar to the democratic mechanism of loyal opposition which would provide the necessary balance and control for the process of planning. This idea is similar to Churchman's counter-planning strategy.

   To resolve a future threat of enlightened totalitarianism, the organization of research should explicitly provide this balancing factor. We suggest that, in view of these arguments, a 'counter' centre should be installed which could fulfil the role of loyal opposition. This should accommodate a built-in bias to magnify the opinions which otherwise may be subdued through the processes of co-optation and resocialization. A similar idea, termed 'advocacy planning,' has been applied in the urban social scene in the US. Institutes to protect and articulate the interests of the indigent were formed as counter-planning centres.

27   Smoker, 'Social Research for Social Anticipation,' p. 12.
28   Dr R. Schwartz of the State University of New York (Buffalo) in a private communication.

J   CONCLUSION

To face the challenge of 'action research'[29] in social planning, this paper proposed an interactive methodology. The important component of this methodology is the use of simulation as a framework for experimentation and interaction. The paper described the particular characteristics desirable in the organization of research and planning, the necessary human input, and the various possible methods of data collection and processing.

REFERENCES

CYERT, R and J. MARCH *A Behavioral Theory of the Firm.* Englewood, NJ: Prentice-Hall, 1963.
FORESTER, W.G. *Urban Dynamics.* Cambridge: MIT Press, 1969.
GUETZKOW, H. 'Simulation in International Relations,' *Proceedings of the IBM Scientific Computing Symposium on Simulation Models and Gaming.* Yorktown Heights, NY: Thomas J. Watson Research Center, 1964.
–   'Some Correspondences between Simulations and "Realities" in International Relations,' in Mortan A. Kaplan, ed. *New Approaches to International Relations.* New York: St Martin's Press, 1968.
JESTICE, AARON L. *Pattern: Long Range Corporate Planning.* Arlington, Va.: Honeywell, 1967.
KELSEN, HANS *The Theory of Law and State.* Cambridge: Harvard University Press, 1945.
MASON, RICHARD OWSLEY *'Dialectics in Decision-making: A Study in the Use of Counter Planning and Structured Debate'* in *Management Information Systems* (Berkeley 1968). *Dissertation Abstracts International* 30A (July 1969), p. 15.
MOSTOWSKI, ANDRZEJ, S. *Sentences Undecidable in Formalized Arithmetic: An Exposition of the Theory of Kurt Gödel.* Amsterdam: North-Holland Publishing, 1957.
NAGEL, E. and J.R. NEWMANN *Gödel Proof.* New York: New York University Press, 1960.
NAYLOR, T.H., ed. *The Design of Computer Simulation Experiments.* Durham, NC: Duke University Press, 1969.
RADNOR, MICHAEL, ALBERT H. RUBENSTEIN, and ALDEN S. BEAN 'Integration and Utilization of Management Science Activities in Organizations,' *Operational Research Quarterly,* 19, 2 (June 1968), p. 117.
RAIFFA, H. *Decision Analysis.* New York: Addison-Wesley, 1968.

29 The term 'action research' was suggested in the research program of 1970–5, the Council for Intersocietal Studies, Northwestern University.

SINGER, E.P. *Experience and Reflection*. Philadelphia: University of Pennsylvania Press, 1959.

SMOKER, PAUL 'Social Research for Social Anticipation,' *American Behavioral Scientist*, 12 (1969), pp. 7–13.

SOCIAL CHANGE AND ECONOMIC GROWTH. Paris: OECD Development Centre, 1967.

VERTINSKY, ILAN 'The Generalist: A New Concept for Training the Planner.' Unpublished. Evanston: Northwestern University, 1968.

– 'Some Aspects of Culture and Cultural Change' (University of California 1968). *Dissertation Abstracts*, 29A (1968), p.3684.

PART SEVEN

Subjects and researchers: rights and duties

C.MICHAEL LANPHIER

Ethical considerations
and research procedures

Political scientists and sociologists who, traditionally, have simply reacted
to rather than anticipated the disturbances created by their queries have
lately been forced to consider in the gravest terms the ethical implications
of their various research procedures. Some professional associations, not-
ably the American Psychological Association and the American Association for Public Opinion Research, were foresighted enough to establish
codes of professional standards. But even the disciplines which have made
such advances discover ambiguities and unmet challenges as the process
of behavioural research continues.

I   SECURING SUBJECTS: THE PROBLEM OF CONSENT

While the ideal would be that all subjects involved in a research endeavour
should provide informed consent prior to their participation in the project, departures from this ideal are numerous and important enough to
warrant exploration. Furthermore, there is a question as to which person,
group, or organization is empowered to grant consent.

Frequently research procedures will choose as units of analysis
either schools, classrooms, or other institutions which contain a population which is resident. A wide variety of types of consent may pertain
in such an instance: consent of parents, consent of principal or person
in charge, consent of governing body. Moreover, it is an open question
as to whether all such units must award consent or whether that of one
unit alone is sufficient. If the latter, which unit would be the appropriate
consenting agent?

It has frequently occurred, for example, that various community authorities grant a kind of implicit consent to researchers to conduct a research project. Typically, such permission provides an entrée to community leaders and to documents that might not otherwise be available. In such a case community leaders may be granting consent on behalf of the community as a whole.

Governments also grant consent for research, in that they may provide lists or other kinds of information which may direct the researcher to certain persons or, at least, known addresses or locations where the researcher might obtain the appropriate information. The guidelines governing the conditions under which such lists and other information may be made available are the subject of great dispute in Canada and the United States as well.

The question of consent becomes further complicated in cases where a certain research procedure requires observation of a group without the prior knowledge of the group or its leaders. If the question of 'naturalistic behaviour' is an issue, observation must occur in such a way as not to intrude on the ongoing group activities. In such a case, the investigator may become a member of the group or at least a peripheral observer and may often disguise his name and function.

The above instances reflect a certain ambiguity in the question of the meaning of consent or, indeed, the locus of consent. Clearly the individual person is neither the sole locus nor the only appropriate locus. Furthermore, informed consent or consent without specific information, is often gained in an informal and sometimes verbal procedure, so that the researcher may be proceeding on an assumption which cannot be fully substantiated. Or the question of consent may be granted a certain legitimacy in the light of great publicity. Such publicity demonstrates a certain community approbation of the research endeavour. Individual community members may feel coerced into co-operation in the research endeavour because of the publicity awarded the procedure.

II   MANIPULATION OF VARIABLES:
     THE PROBLEM OF DECEPTION

While the research endeavour may have variables which are extremely visible and whose content is manifest, certain other procedures cannot reveal the types of variables employed. They may either be too complex on the one hand or, on the other, a knowledge of the variables employed may prejudice the types of results obtained. Researchers have usually been advised to employ deception or the withholding of information only in those cases where no other research procedure will suffice to produce the effects necessary. Clearly this type of judgment involves a great deal of uncertainty about how much knowledge must be withheld from the subject in order not to prejudice results.

Often problems remain unresolved: How long a period of deception may elapse until the subject is informed of the intent of the investigation? Will any physical or mental harm result from the participation of the subject in the investigation long after the investigation process has been completed?

There has been much discussion to date about the question of the relationship between deception and the scientific merit of the experiment in question. In some intuitive sense, the more important the experiment for the expansion of scientific knowledge, the more risk may obtain in the procedures governing the research. By extension, deception may be justified in an extremely important experiment, where the same amount of deception may be forbidden if the experiment is adjudged to be of secondary significance. The complex interweaving of issues concerning the scientific merit of a given research endeavour and the type of discomfort experienced by research subjects remains an area which deserves increasingly close examination by researchers and other interested persons who will render judgment in such cases.

It has been argued in another context that the forms of access to respondents which are conventionally employed in the interviewing process, for example, in which the respondent consents to an interview at the doorstep, can in a certain sense constitute an invasion of privacy. In this argument, the respondent is seen as a person who may unwittingly reveal highly personal aspects of life which he may regret having revealed after the interview has been completed. Respondents are not always aware of their rights to refuse to participate; they may also be swayed by the prestige of the research organization or the official appearance of the interviewing process. While this type of instance rarely prompts a direct confrontation of principle, the questions of responsibility of the researcher to the respondents are raised in an indirect fashion (Carlson 1967).

III   REVELATION OF RESULTS:
THE PROBLEM OF DISCLOSURE

Researchers characteristically promise the subjects or agents that the results will be kept confidential and released only in aggregate form. In the case of community or group studies, the research team endeavours to protect the anonymity of the persons as well as the community. Such assurances are often improperly awarded. It may be possible to disguise personalities in research involving a large number of cases. More often than not, however, studies of communities or certain agencies may easily be identifiable because of the unique combination of a certain number of variables which made the community or agency a fitting locus for investigation in the first place. As a result, efforts to disguise the identities will result only in frustration or futility. I currently know of no community studies in which the identity of the community in question was not known within days after the appearance of the report.

IV   ANALYSIS OF DATA

While the researcher may have the purest of intentions, the types of analysis employed may have untoward consequences for the subjects in question. If analysis indicates that subjects have engaged in community behaviour which is somehow inappropriate, or that their status is either a threat to the community as a whole or is one which thrives on the repression of other sectors in a very impersonal sense, there may be serious repercussions on the researcher as a result of the types of analysis that he has produced. It is insufficient for the researcher to have obtained the permission of the agents in question prior to the gathering of data, for no amount of such protestation on the researcher's part will assuage the discontent so aroused.

Frequently it is necessary not to disguise roles or personages too greatly, for the very point the researcher may wish to make may otherwise be lost. While the scientific community may agree that the results do not amount to 'disclosure,' the public perception of the results ensuing from the research constitutes an entirely independent evaluation, which often cannot be anticipated in advance. The researcher then is left to justify his publication before an audience which is quite hostile. Furthermore, the chances for re-entry into that research setting a second time are doubtless foreclosed.

The researcher is also required to protect identity of respondents from indirect disclosure, resulting from the juxtaposition of two classifications of the same data. For example, if two aggregate statistical presentations differ in number of cases by only one, it is often possible to single out, through a process of simple subtraction, the characteristics of that one case. This eventuality is especially likely in research where social organizations or institutions form the units of analysis. Since the number of cases is usually small, it is possible to identify the features of any single case. There is little protection against such indirect disclosure other than the assurance on the part of the researcher that tabular presentation will never be so arranged. Such a promise is empty if other researchers do not bind themselves to the same stricture when analysing the same data.

V   PROTECTION OF RESEARCHERS

The points raised above refer primarily to the protection of the subjects, groups, or agencies serving as the units employed in research. It must be acknowledged simultaneously, however, that research in social science is itself a dialogue between the subjects on the one hand and the researcher on the other. While the researcher has responsibilities towards his subject, he also has rights, and frequently these rights are left unconsidered or implicit. It could be argued that the consent of a person or agency in granting the researcher the opportunity to research in that setting involves an obligation on the part of all members to protect the rights of the researcher in the research process. While the researcher is usually his own best defender of rights, there are times when he requires assistance. For example, it is usually assumed that a scholarly publication should follow after an academic research endeavour. Thus the researcher expects that the publication rights should be preserved even in the face of opposition of persons or communities, so that the research process may be taken to its final point. The fact that certain findings may be uncomplimentary to certain persons or groups is a question which should be of secondary significance in the publication of findings. Yet copyright arrangements are often not arranged well in advance. Even before the research is commenced, there can occur serious impediments to publication of findings, so that the report may either never appear or appear quite tardily in severely altered form.

In the laboratory-experimental context, certain experiments often require that the researcher obtain a waiver of responsibility from the subjects. This waiver is the only legal means under which a researcher may be protected should any untoward developments occur, even well after the conclusion of the experiment.

VI   THE PROBLEM OF JUDGMENT

Universities have been concerned in recent years about the question of how disputes involving ethical considerations may be judged. Ordinarily, scholars have considered that the types of questions involved in the behavioural research process are inappropriate for legal or quasi-legal processes. They prefer to install a body of peers, constituted as a research committee within a university or organization, which serves as a board of judgment in the case of disputes. Such an arrangement is usually efficacious, but it relies more on the prestige of the university or organization in question than it does upon legal due process. Furthermore, any correctives or punishments imposed on a researcher in such an event are usually private and clandestine.

It does not follow, however, that the questions cannot be brought forward as a civil matter. Most research organizations have been assured that their data may fall under subpoena at any time by constituted authorities. In such an event, the researcher is powerless to control the disposition of such data both physically, since the data are removed from the researcher's premises, and scientifically, since different canons of judgment will be applied to the research. Although universities have now devised certain procedures for the protection of research documents and the assurance of anonymity of the participant-subjects, the safeguards are anything but complete. Furthermore, it may be impossible to provide safeguards for certain data which can easily be identified within the set of protocols.

VII SAMPLING AND PRIVACY

It has been argued by governmental authorities that the provision of lists which contain names and addresses or other matter which will identify subjects completely cannot be furnished under most circumstances pertinent to the research process. As well, the question of record linkage, in which several different files of data are merged in such a way as to constitute a rather complete longitudinal history of various subjects or agencies, is a matter of great debate and uncertainty in North America at the present time.

A point has been raised by social scientists which deserves fairly careful consideration in this regard. If a sample of the population is chosen, so that each case may represent several thousand others not so chosen, the complete identities of the sample persons involved are simply matters of record rather than of the invasion of personal privacy. If only a small fraction of the given population is so sampled, the question of 'invasion of privacy' changes character because the cases are only exemplars of the population; in themselves, they are unimportant from an individual standpoint. As a matter of fact, all government agencies employ this principle in their use of data pertinent to census matters, where detailed information is obtained from the small sample of respondents involved. If such privilege is granted government agencies who are subject to certain acts regarding the disclosure of official statistics, it would seem possible that similar arrangements could be made for social scientists if the social scientists in question could bind themselves to similar principles of inhibition of disclosure.

Such longitudinal data may become more and more necessary when dealing with research populations. It was noted over a decade ago (Hovland 1959) that most experimental studies involve only short-run changes. A great amount of information is needed concerning the longer run effects of various experimental procedures. Clearly, the question of privacy becomes paramount, in that the action or attitudes of the persons or agencies originally in the experimental samples will be monitored for months and years to come. Whether or not the monitoring is unobtrusive is a side issue. The fact remains that piles of data can and will be maintained for long periods of time. It follows that a wide variety of persons will have access to the information simply because it is retained in the file which will be the responsibility of a succession of personnel in the normal maintenance process.

VIII SUMMARY

The questions involving the ethical rights and responsibilities of behavioural researchers to the subjects and agencies serving as units of data constitute a manifold of perplexing problems. It is insufficient, however, for these problems to receive token significance before a research procedure is contemplated and then only casual recognition after the publication of results. Furthermore, we are becoming aware of the fact that researchers are not passive recipients of data. They are active and sometimes manipulating in their approach. Thus the question of rights and responsibilities always involves the notion of reciprocity. As a result certain arrangements which may be convenient in one research procedure may be not as convenient or congenial in another because the disposition of one of the two parties may be different. Furthermore, the triad of questions which has concerned persons who have treated the ethical problems in behavioural research – informed consent, deception, disclosure – are now inadequate both in their definition and their coverage. They neither exhaust the domain of questions nor do they sufficiently differentiate the kinds of problems which may arise in this connection.

Behavioural researchers have been lax, if not sometimes indifferent, to the questions of the rights and responsibilities of researchers to their human subjects. Such attitudes are neither appropriate nor, in any moral system, justifiable. The question of the experimenter's role in the research process is one which merits the undivided attention of social science scholarship. It is integral to the dissemination of ideas in science.

APPENDIX

Selected articles of the code of ethics of the American Psychological Association relevant to experimentation on humans (see full text in APA, 'Ethical Standards of Psychologists').

Principle 3 *Moral and Legal Standards*
The psychologist in the practice of his profession shows sensible regard for the social codes and moral expectations of the community in which he works, recognizing that violations of accepted moral and legal standards on his part may involve his clients, students, or colleagues in damaging personal conflicts, and impugne his own name and the reputation of his profession ...

Principle 4 *Misrepresentation*
The psychologist avoids misrepresentation of his own professional qualifications, affiliations, and purposes, and those of the institutions and organizations with which he is associated ...

Principle 6 *Confidentiality*
Safeguarding information about an individual that has been obtained by the psychologist in the course of his teaching, practice, or investigation is a primary obligation of the psychologist. Such information is not communicated to others unless certain important conditions are met.

a   Information received in confidence is revealed only after most careful deliberation and when there is clear and imminent danger to an individual or to society, and then only to appropriate professional workers or public authorities.
b   Information obtained in clinical or consulting relationships, or evaluative data concerning children, students, employees, and others are discussed only for professional purposes and only with persons clearly concerned with the case. Written and oral reports should present only data germane to the purposes of the evaluation; every effort should be made to avoid undue invasion of privacy.
c   Clinical and other case materials are used in classroom teaching and writing only when the identity of the persons involved is adequately disguised.
d   The confidentiality of professional communications about individuals is maintained. Only when the originator and other persons involved give their express permission is a confidential professional communication

shown to the individual concerned. The psychologist is responsible for informing the client of the limits of the confidentiality.

e   Only after explicit permission has been granted is the identity of research subjects published. When data have been published without permission for identification, the psychologist assumes responsibility for adequately disguising their sources.

f   The psychologist makes provision for the maintenance of confidentiality in the preservation and ultimate disposition of confidential records.

Principle 7 *Client Welfare*
The psychologist respects the integrity and protects the welfare of the person or group with whom he is working.

a   The psychologist in industry, education, and other situations in which conflicts of interest may arise among various parties, as between management and labour, or between the client and employer of the psychologist, defines for himself the nature and direction of his loyalties and responsibilities and keeps all parties concerned informed of these commitments.

b   When there is a conflict among professional workers, the psychologist is concerned primarily with the welfare of any client involved and only secondarily with the interest of his own professional group.

c   The psychologist attempts to terminate a clinical or consulting relationship when it is reasonably clear to the psychologist that the client is not benefiting from it.

d   The psychologist who asks that an individual reveal personal information in the course of interviewing, testing, or evaluation, or who allows such information to be divulged to him, does so only after making certain that the responsible person is fully aware of the purposes of the interview, testing, or evaluation and of the ways in which the information may be used. ...

f   The psychologist who requires the taking of psychological tests for didactic, classification, or research purposes protects the examinees by insuring that the tests and test results are used in a professional manner.

g   When potentially disturbing subject matter is presented to students, it is discussed objectively, and efforts are made to handle constructively any difficulties that arise.

h   Care must be taken to insure an appropriate setting for clinical work to protect both client and psychologist from actual or imputed harm and the profession from censure ...

Principle 13 *Test Security*
Psychological tests and other assessment devices, the value of which depends in part on the naivete of the subject, are not reproduced or described in popular publications in ways that might invalidate the techniques. Access to such

devices is limited to persons with professional interests who will safeguard their use.

a   Sample items made up to resemble those of tests being discussed may be reproduced in popular articles and elsewhere, but scorable tests and actual test items are not reproduced except in professional publications.
b   The psychologist is responsible for the control of psychological tests and other devices and procedures used for instruction when their value might be damaged by revealing to the general public their specific contents or underlying principles ...

Principle 14 *Test Interpretation*
Test scores, like test materials, are released only to persons who are qualified to interpret and use them properly.

a   Materials for reporting test scores to parents, or which are designed for self-appraisal purposes in schools, social agencies, or industry are closely supervised by qualified psychologists or counselors with provisions for referring and counselling individuals when needed.
b   Test results or other assessment data used for evaluation or classification are communicated to employers, relatives, or other appropriate persons in such a manner as to guard against misinterpretation or misuse. In the usual case, an interpretation of the test result rather than the score is communicated.
c   When test results are communicated directly to parents and students, they are accompanied by adequate interpretive aids or advice ...

Principle 15 *Test Publication*
Psychological tests are offered for commercial publication only to publishers who present their tests in a professional way and distribute them only to qualified users ...

Principle 16 *Research Precautions*
The psychologist assumes obligations for the welfare of his research subjects, both animal and human.

a   Only when a problem is of scientific significance and it is not practicable to investigate it in any other way is the psychologist justified in exposing research subjects, whether children or adults, to physical or emotional stress as part of an investigation.
b   When a reasonable possibility of injurious aftereffects exists, research is conducted only when the subjects or their responsible agents are fully informed of this possibility and agree to participate nevertheless.
c   The psychologist seriously considers the possibility of harmful aftereffects

and avoids them, or removes them as soon as permitted by the design of the experiment.

REFERENCES

AMERICAN ACADEMY OF POLITICAL & SOCIAL SCIENCE *Ethical Standards & Professional Conduct*, by B.Y. Landis, vol. 297 (1955).

AMERICAN PSYCHOLOGICAL ASSOCIATION 'Ethical Standards of Psychologists,' *American Psychologist*, 18 (1963), pp. 56–60.

BARNES, JAMES A. 'Some Ethical Problems in Modern Field Work,' *British Journal of Sociology*, 14 (1963), pp. 118–34.

BAUMRIND, DIANA 'Some Thoughts on Ethics of Research: After Reading Milgram's Behavioral Study of Obedience,' *American Psychologist*, 19 (1964), pp. 421–3.

CARLSON, R.O. 'The Issue of Privacy in Public Opinion Research,' *Public Opinion Quarterly*, 31 (1967), pp. 1–8.

CASTANEDA, A. 'Behavioral Research: Ethics and Practice,' paper delivered to the Canadian Psychological Association (Calgary 1968).

COMMISSION DE DÉONTOLOGIE DE LA SOCIÉTÉ FRANÇAISE DE PSYCHOLOGIE 'Projet de code déontologique à l'usage des psychologues,' *Psychologie française*, 5 (1960), pp. 1–27.

HOBBS, N. 'Science and Ethical Behavior,' *American Psychologist*, 14 (1959), pp. 217–25.

– 'Ethical Issues in the Social Sciences,' in David L. Sills, ed., *International Encyclopedia of the Social Sciences*, 5 (1968), pp. 160–67.

HOVLAND, C.I. 'Reconciling Conflicting Results Derived from Experimental and Survey Studies of Attitude Change,' *American Psychologist*, 14 (1959), pp. 8–17.

KELMAN, H.C. 'Manipulation of Human Behavior: An Ethical Dilemma for the Social Scientist,' *Journal of Social Issues*, 21 (1965), pp. 31–46.

KING, A.J. and A.J. SPECTOR 'Ethical and Legal Aspects of Survey Research,' *American Psychologist*, 18 (1963), pp. 204–8.

LANGER, ELINOR 'Human Experimentation: New York Verdict Affirms Patient's Rights,' *Science*, 151 (1966), pp. 663–6.

MILGRAM, S. 'Issues in the Study of Obedience: A Reply to Baumrind,' *American Psychologist*, 19 (1964), pp. 848–52.

OFFICE OF SCIENCE AND TECHNOLOGY *Privacy and Behavioral Research.* Washington: US Government Printing Office, 1967.

RUEBHAUSEN, O.M. and ORVILLE G. BRIM 'Privacy and Behavioral Research,' *Columbia Law Review*, 65 (1965), pp. 1184–297.

SNOW, C.P. 'The Moral Un-neutrality of Science,' *Science*, 133 (1961), pp. 255–62.

'Statement on Ethics of the Society for Applied Anthropology,' *Human Organization*, 22 (1964), p. 237.

Index